NO BARRIERS

REACH

Erik Weihenmayer

Also by Erik Weihenmayer

Touch the Top of the World
The Adversity Advantage

Erik Weihenmayer and Buddy Levy

NO BARRIERS

A Blind Man's Journey to Kayak

the Grand Canyon

THOMAS DUNNE BOOKS

St. Martin's Griffin

New York

THOMAS DUNNE BOOKS.
An imprint of St. Martin's Press.

SMILE
Music by Charles Chaplin
Words by John Turner and Geoffrey Parsons
© Copyright 1954 by Bourne Co.
Copyright Renewed
All Rights Reserved
International Copyright Secured
ASCAP

www.thomasdunnebooks.com
www.stmartins.com

Designed by Kathryn Parise
Frontispiece courtesy of Shutterstock.com

The Library of Congress has cataloged the hardcover edition as follows:

Names: Weihenmayer, Erik, author. | Levy, Buddy, 1960– author.
Title: No barriers : a blind man's journey to kayak the Grand Canyon /
Erik Weihenmayer and Buddy Levy.
Description: First edition. | New York : Thomas Dunne Books/St. Martin's Press, 2017.
Identifiers: LCCN 2016037629 | ISBN 9781250088789 (hardcover) |
ISBN 9781250088802 (ebook)
Subjects: LCSH: Weihenmayer, Erik. | Weihenmayer, Erik—Travel—Arizona—Grand
Canyon. | Kayaking—Arizona—Lava Falls Rapids. | Blind athletes—United
States—Biography. | BISAC: BIOGRAPHY & AUTOBIOGRAPHY / Personal
Memoirs. | BIOGRAPHY & AUTOBIOGRAPHY / Adventurers & Explorers. |
BUSINESS & ECONOMICS / Leadership.
Classification: LCC GV782.42.W45 A3 2017 | DDC 797.122/409791—dc23
LC record available at https://lccn.loc.gov/2016037629

ISBN 978-1-250-08879-6 (trade paperback)

First St. Martin's Griffin Edition: February 2018

10 9 8 7 6 5 4 3 2 1

To my father, Ed, who embodied No Barriers before it had a name

—Erik

CONTENTS

This is a true story,
though some names and details have been changed.

FOREWORD

By Bob Woodruff, ABC News

Chances are that at some point in our lives, we will all be tested. The possibilities are endless, and they read like a litany of what-ifs. Which is why the interesting part of any story is not necessarily the exact nature of the obstacles we meet, but in how we choose to respond.

It was an honor to be asked to write the foreword for *No Barriers: A Blind Man's Journey to Kayak the Grand Canyon* because this story and its author embody what it means to meet adversity and not let "the bad thing" define us. In short, to quote my wife, you make a choice to get "bitter or better."

My own challenging moment came in January 29, 2006, when I was covering the Iraq war outside of Baghdad for ABC News. While standing halfway out of a tank with my cameraman, a 125-mm roadside bomb exploded, leaving me with a traumatic brain injury (TBI) and vastly changing the direction of my life.

The blast shattered my skull, embedding rocks and other debris in my body and shattering my scapula. But none of the other injuries mattered. They would heal. It was the TBI, the signature wound of these wars, that would prove to be my greatest obstacle. I would spend the next few years struggling to put my cognitive abilities back together, returning to my job as a journalist and working harder than I ever had in my life.

Immediately following the blast, my cameraman, Doug Vogt, and I were flown from Iraq to Germany, then on to National Naval Medical Center in Bethesda where I spent thirty-six days in a coma. When I finally woke up and began to understand the enormity of what I had lost, it was my family and friends who surrounded me, along with the other military families, all on the same journey, experiencing firsthand the devastation and legacy of war up close and at home.

I am a journalist, and although I understood the probability that I could be killed, I had spent very little time thinking about severe injury. My injury catapulted me into a world I had never seriously considered or contemplated. And from that tragedy, many positive things have resulted. I have been proud to use my story to help others traveling along the same road.

There is nothing courageous about my story. Hundreds of thousands of our troops who have volunteered to go to Iraq and Afghanistan when their country asked have returned home with both physical and invisible injuries. Unlike me, working for a news organization who cared for me and my family with unlimited rehabilitation and resources, many of our military families may not have access to the same level of resources all the way through. Not all of them have friends and family at home like I did to root for me and pick me up on the days when I felt low.

Erik Weihenmayer is simply one of the most remarkable men I have ever met. When Erik was in ninth grade, he lost his ability to see.

For many of us, navigating without vision would have circumscribed our world in a million different ways, but he came to a place where he decided to take "pain into purpose, darkness into light."

I first heard about Erik through my brother, Woody, who travels with an elite pack of mountain climbers and extreme adventurers. In 2013, Erik invited me to speak at his No Barriers annual event in Telluride, Colorado. I joined an amazing roster of speakers and guests, including some injured veterans, and it was clear when Erik spoke that he had a gift.

Erik spoke then, as he writes in this book, about the decision he made that nothing would stop him from achieving his goals. He was determined that his lack of vision not be viewed as a disability, but rather as a different ability. And that is where Erik's story becomes both interesting and inspiring.

Erik is the only blind climber to reach the top of Mount Everest, and this book details his journey by kayak through the Grand Canyon. But Erik didn't stop there. He kept setting goals for himself, moving ever forward, because in his words, he "would rather be punched and knocked flat than to be doomed to a life of quiet acquiescence."

The mark of true heroes is that they would never use that word to describe themselves. And Erik is no different. His many accomplishments have made him famous, but none of that matters to him. "You hang your pictures up on the walls," he wrote. "You set up your trophies, and it becomes a museum, even worse, a mausoleum."

Erik doesn't climb mountains or break records merely to receive medals and accolades. Instead, he operates from a need to prove to himself what he can accomplish and to use his story to help others.

In 2004, Erik cofounded the nonprofit No Barriers. His goal was to help those who have suffered from mental and physical injuries understand that although there exist plenty of barriers in our lives, there is also a map, a way to navigate these barriers and even obliterate them.

No Barriers USA has grown to include an annual summit, a four-day event that showcases cutting-edge adaptive technologies and provides interactive clinics in an outdoor setting. The summit also offers No Barriers University, featuring inspiring speakers telling life-changing stories. No Barriers Warriors improves the lives of veterans with disabilities through curriculum-based experiences in challenging environments. And No Barriers Youth challenges young people to contribute their absolute best to the world through transformative experiences, classroom tools, and real-world inspiration.

All of the No Barriers USA programs open up new paths, new gates where those who feel defined by life changes can feel no boundaries to accomplishment, and a supportive community of people with shared experiences, visions, and dreams.

One of the incredible attributes of humanity is resilience. We hear a great deal about that term these days, and when you read this book you understand what a critical component it is for life, not just to survive, but also to thrive, as Erik has done.

And while most anyone who has gone through trauma or put his or her family through a traumatic experience would take it all back in a second, part of moving forward is looking for the positive aspects that are borne out of tragedy or the unexpected.

It's meeting and getting to know people like Erik that has taught me the true definition of sacrifice through their actions, examples, and humility.

When you finally close the pages of this book, I guarantee you will feel a little lighter. You will also understand that anything is achievable if we set our minds to it.

No Barriers: A Blind Man's Journey to Kayak the Grand Canyon made me think about myself in new ways. And not only is it a great story and a riveting read, but it will challenge you to look at your own life and your gifts in new ways.

Erik's incredible story and his commitment to be a beacon for others demonstrate how one person can make a difference in the lives of others. For him, there are many more mountains to climb, side by side with those of us who have become not just his admirers, but also his friends.

Winter Solstice

The man looked my friend straight in the eyes and said
"You've been through a lot."
My friend started sobbing
Who has not been "through a lot"?
It is when we recognize it in each other that we know love.
We unite in our endurance
As our minds embrace, our histories mingle
We lean in to share the experience
We lean in to touch one another
And we know we are alike.

—Patrick Foss

NO BARRIERS

PROLOGUE

The Colorado River running through the Grand Canyon is known for big iconic rapids, and the biggest of them all is Lava Falls, a storm of energy that churns, tumbles, and explodes in its headlong rush toward the Sea of Cortez. Standing on the banks, I couldn't see Lava, so instead I listened to its colossal roar as my guide, Harlan, talked me through the rapid. In my six years of learning to kayak, of slamming into rocks, of bleeding, of pulling the skirt on my kayak and swimming for my life, I had come to realize, if you deciphered the river carefully, you could discover a hidden map through the chaos. Boaters called this map "the line," the safest and easiest way through.

Harlan took my finger and traced it along Lava's line, stopping to point out the obstacles to be avoided. As you enter, you set your angle, approaching from the right, but not too far right because fierce upsurges of water are piling against the right shore and boiling back underneath your boat, whipping you like a monster's tail toward the left. You paddle furiously only a few inches to the left of the eddy line separating the bullet trajectory of the river and the pulsing boils. You fight the spin because just to your left is the notorious Ledge Hole, a chunk of rock under the surface spanning almost half the width of the river. Water pours over the lip and collapses under its own weight, recirculating in a maelstrom of white water like an enormous washing machine. It's the most feared place in all the 277 miles of the Grand

Canyon, because it will suck you down and hold you there for a long time. Squeak by the Ledge Hole and you drop off the horizon into the entry waves, two walls of water, the right being the biggest and coming at you in the shape of a huge rooster tail. Next, you line up for the V-Wave, two massive lateral waves that slam together. You need to strike the V slightly left of center and punch through with everything you have; otherwise, you'll be launched skyward and cartwheeled into a backflip. If you manage to bust through, you turn left, angling out into the river to avoid the Cheese Grater Rock, a wicked peninsula of jagged black basalt that will tear apart anything that comes into contact with it. You then square off against the Big Kahuna waves, a thundering series of whitecaps over ten feet tall that break over you, crushing you under hundreds of pounds of liquid force. Finally, you ride the tail waves, boils, and whirlpools like a roller coaster toward the exit of Lava.

Staying on the line is no guarantee of success, but if you manage to stick to it, your chances of emerging on the other side upright and unscathed are dramatically increased. Fall off the line, and your chances exponentially decrease, and once you're off, it's a cascading series of circumstances going from bad to worse. And you can't trust the current either, because sometimes the wide, smooth tongue will lead you right into a hazard you need to avoid: a sharp rock ledge or whirling hole that can trap you. As you try to navigate that turbulence, sometimes trusting it, sometimes desperately fighting it, you realize you're merely experiencing the effects of inexorable forces swirling and colliding. What creates the surface energy are the features far below, a million pounds of water surging against boulders of every size strewn across the bottom: steep drops, undercuts, and narrow grooves between unseen rock.

I had become spellbound by rivers, by the roiling energy at the surface, that, at first, seemed impossible to navigate; but I was equally fascinated by the landscape beneath, those hidden shapes and forms that dictated the map I needed to follow. As a blind man, I knew I could never fully comprehend that power without experiencing it firsthand, to feel and hear the essence of the river, to face that cacophonic mix of forces, and to see if I might hit the line and find a way to ride it through.

After two weeks of kayaking, we were finally here: mile 179, directly above my nemesis. Lava Falls was rated class 10 out of 10 on the Grand Canyon's difficulty scale. Here, Prospect Canyon converged with the Colorado from the south, its debris flows dumping boulders the size of cars into the main river and constricting the channel by as much as 50 percent. That, combined with massive lava flows pouring in and hardening over 750,000 years ago, had created a dramatic, dangerous rapid.

We'd been scouting Lava for too long. The sun's heat scorched the volcanic stones and permeated through the bottoms of my paddling booties. Dry wind, superheated between high canyon walls, blew upstream, burning my face to leather and sucking the moisture from my mouth. My arms were leaden, heavy with fatigue from the day's fourteen-mile paddle. I had been thinking about this rapid ever since we put in upstream at Lees Ferry, this monster that routinely swallowed eighteen-foot, fully loaded rubber oar boats, spitting the passengers out to swim for their lives. But honestly, I'd been thinking about Lava for eight years now, ever since I had pondered the idea of solo kayaking the Grand Canyon.

"You ready to do this?" Harlan asked.

"I think so," was all I managed to say.

We hiked back upstream to our boats at the put-in. I squeezed into my kayak and sat down, adjusting my seat, getting the distance to the bulkhead, where my feet touched, just right. Continuing my pre-paddling ritual, I stretched my neoprene spray skirt tightly over the top of my cockpit and felt for the grab loop, my means of escape. I shook sand from my helmet, pulled it over my forehead, and adjusted the mouthpiece and earpiece. We tested the radios once more, and they seemed to be working. I pushed off from the shore into calm water above the rapid. Harlan tucked in behind me.

His voice was comforting. "We're here, right now, in this moment; nothing else matters. Be clear and calm and concise." But instead of feeling confidence, I was tentative. I wasn't ready.

"We're about to cross the eddy line, on to the tongue," he continued, "and we're going to hug that eddy line. It's not going to mess with us too much. When we get near the rapid, these boil lines are going to form, and they're gonna feel like they want to spin us one way or the other, and once we're on them, I'm going to call for a left-hand turn, and that's going to set our angle and bring us in. We'll have the two entry waves, the V-Wave, straighten up into the Kahuna waves, then the tail waves, and you're through."

"That's all?" I asked. It was a lot to process. The current gripped my hull and slung me forward, toward the rumble of an "earthquake," the deep vibrating echo of frenzied water ricocheting off the surrounding walls. It sounded more menacing than anything I'd ever paddled. All those rivers—the Usumacinta in Mexico, the Apurímac in Peru, and the Ottawa in Canada—had led to this moment. The air felt suddenly cold, the sun gone behind the canyon walls. My upper body had grown stiff and sluggish from the waiting. I shook my arms loose, knowing that mental anxiety translated to physical tension, and physical tension meant imprecise paddle strokes and mistakes. I whispered Harlan's familiar words: "Relax. Breathe. Be at peace with the river."

"We're about a hundred yards above now. Small left, hold that line, hold that line . . . we're getting closer to that first boil, calm strokes, good thoughtful strokes, fight the spin, fight the spin . . ." Harlan's voice was serious, and I knew this was no time for a mistake.

The boil hit my boat from the right; the main channel surged from the left, and I fought the spin. But tension gripped my upper body, and my strokes were rigid. I felt myself leaning the wrong way, and then I was over, upside down underwater at the top of the hardest rapid on the Grand Canyon. My mind spun with the turmoil of water surging around me, and I thought, *You've got to be freaking kidding me. This can't be real; this can't be happening.* I dug with my paddle, snapped my hips, and rolled back up to the surface. Harlan was yelling, "Hard left!" then immediately, "Hard right!" I knew the V-Wave was approaching. The colliding surges beneath and around my boat felt violent and confusing, but I tried to follow his commands as I dipped down inside a deep trough and into the snarl of two giant pounding waves, like jaws closing. My angle was crooked, and before it even registered in my brain to react, I was slammed over once more, my boat spinning crazily above me. Years of training took over, and I stuck my roll, emerging upright again. I was totally disoriented. *Where am I pointing?* I thought desperately, yet Harlan was right there in my ear, his voice loud and definitive.

"Charge, charge, left turn!" he yelled. "You're good, you're good! Charge!"

But as I was yanked backward, I sensed I was facing upriver.

"Hard right!" Harlan yelled. A massive surge then slammed me in the back and side of my head, water tearing at my helmet and throwing me over again. In the midst of the roar and spray, I rolled up. I couldn't hear anything from Harlan. Then more waves broke over me from the left. I felt my boat tipping and fought with a hard brace. I tried to take a gulp of air, but swallowed mostly foam and water as I slipped under for the fourth time. The rush and roil became a gurgle, great bubbles exploding underwater. The power of the conflicting currents beat my paddle against my boat and then attempted to rip it out of my hands.

Crashing waves pounded on the hull of my kayak, shoving me farther down, and I had no idea which direction I was facing. Each roll attempt grew weaker, and I was running out of air. Swimming in raging white water was bad enough for a sighted paddler—but swimming blind—that was the last thing I wanted to do. But I was almost out of oxygen, my arms heavy with fatigue. Finally, clenched by fear and instinct, I reached for my grab loop and yanked hard, releasing my spray skirt. I launched out of my boat, clawing for the surface, for safety, for air, and now my body spun and shook with the swelling waves. I groped for the surface, with no clue whether it was above or below me.

Finally, my head popped up, and I gasped for breath, floundering in the tail waves. I felt a boat next to me and grasped for it, trying to hold on, but it didn't feel right; it was smooth and rounded, and when I couldn't get a grip, I realized it was the bottom of Harlan's boat! My guide was upside down, and I was holding him down. I released his boat and pushed away. Another safety boater skirted up next to me and called for me to hang on.

As he furiously paddled toward an eddy, with me clinging on to his stern, I heard Harlan's voice nearby. He was breathing hard. "Damn, that big wave hit me head-on and snapped my paddle in two. With half a paddle, it took me a bunch of tries to roll up." I could hear him clacking the pieces together.

Reaching the calm water, I found the shore, clung to a pile of slick rocks, and pulled myself onto the river's edge. At first, I was just relieved to be out of that terrifying carnage, but soon relief changed to shock and anguish. It was so crushing, I thought I might still be spinning under the weight of the

Kahuna waves. I sat on a rock, surrounded by giant volcanic boulders. My team, still in their boats, swirled around in the eddy. My helmet was shoved sideways. My radio earpiece was pushed around the back of my head. My hands shook as I fumbled with the buckle of my helmet. I yanked it off, and silty water poured over my face. My body felt beaten, and I labored to slow my breathing. With my head in my hands, I leaned forward, shattered. The feel of sharp rocks, the echoing sound of canyon walls and sky, the dry smell of sand and desert, all of it faded until there was nothing but the unrelenting surge of the river, moving ever forward and shaping everything in its path. And with its all-consuming roar, I knew it was speaking to me. I tried to listen to what it was saying, but in that moment, it was impossible to understand.

1

VISION

I wasn't always completely blind. Even though I couldn't see well from birth, I could still play basketball, ride my bike, and jump off rocks in the woods behind my house. Then, when I was three years old, I was diagnosed with a rare disease called juvenile retinoschisis. The odds were about the same as winning the lottery. The disease causes hemorrhaging in the eyes and makes the retinas split away over time; and just like my retinas, my life split away from everything I'd thought was normal one week before my freshman year of high school.

On my first day, I was led into the building by my teacher's aide—not the ideal way to begin freshman year in a sighted school. She guided me from class to class and even to the bathroom. At lunchtime, she led me into the cafeteria, where I sat at a table alone, thinking about everything I had lost. I was afraid of going blind and seeing only darkness, but I was even more afraid of what I'd miss out on. I could hear the other kids around me, their laughter and wisecracks, their horsing around. A food fight broke out, and from what I could hear—all the yelling and screaming—everyone in the room except me was in the thick of it. The darkness was the easy part. The hard part was realizing I would never be in the food fight. I'd been swept aside, shoved into a dark place, and left alone there. Blindness descended upon me with such force that I thought it would swallow me.

I've heard people say we shouldn't be motivated by fear. Even Yoda said it in my favorite movie series, *Star Wars*: "Fear is the path to the dark side."

But that day in the cafeteria was my first bitter taste of fear. It caught in my throat like bile. It writhed in my gut, intertwining itself through every action, every decision. No matter how I fought it, fear was ever present. It was a tug-of-war, the fear of pushing forward through darkness against barriers you can't see, tugging against the fear of sitting quietly and safely in a dark place.

Earlier that summer, right before the last traces of my eyesight were gone, I was watching TV. I could barely see out of my right eye, with just a little peripheral vision remaining. To see what was happening, I had to put my face almost against the screen, so close I could feel static electricity crackling on the tip of my nose. I was watching my favorite show, *That's Incredible!* That night, they were featuring the story of a young Canadian named Terry Fox. He was nineteen years old when he was diagnosed with cancer. A tumor appeared in his right leg, and he was rushed in for surgery, where his leg had to be amputated six inches above his right knee. In the hospital recovering, Terry watched children even younger than he was succumbing to disease, and their deaths were a searing pain, sharper than the saw that had taken his leg. Of course he felt for their pain, but his next act was the most surprising thing I'd ever seen. After enduring eighteen months of chemotherapy and witnessing all that death and tragedy, he should have been reduced. As he contemplated his own mortality, he was supposed to retreat, curl into a ball, and protect the precious little he had left. Who would have blamed him? Yet instead, Terry did the exact opposite. He made the astonishing decision to run, and not just for a day, or a week, but from one shore to another, through every province, across the entire country of Canada. It was a marathon a day for thousands of miles.

I pressed my face against the television watching Terry hobble mile after mile in his Marathon of Hope. This was before the days of high-tech flex feet and "smart," computerized prosthetics. His clunky, old-fashioned steel and fiberglass prosthetic leg created a herky-jerky gait, an awkward double-step, and a hop on his good left leg as his prosthetic right foot went back and then swung forward, almost like he was skipping. The look on his face was a contradition, exhaustion mixed with determination. In his eyes, I sensed something I could only describe as a light that seemed to give intensity and power to his gaunt expression. At first, as Terry ran from town to town, only a few people paid attention, but soon, as news of his daily marathon spread, supporters began to line the roads to cheer him on. By the middle of his journey, throngs were showing up in the thousands.

Later in the piece, the host came back on and said that on day 143—after running an average of twenty-six miles a day for over four months and 3,339 miles through six provinces, Terry was forced to stop his run. Cancer had invaded his lungs, causing him to cough and gasp for air as he ran. Terry cried as he told the crowd of reporters that he wouldn't be able to finish, but through his tears, he said, "I'll fight. I promise I won't give up."

Terry Fox died seven months after he stopped running. It wasn't fair. He'd only gotten twenty-two years on earth. But in that short window, he had made a decision to run, and that decision had elevated an entire nation. Instead of shrinking away, Terry had gotten bigger. He had lived more than he had died. Donations to his Marathon of Hope fund poured in and reached $24 million, equal to a dollar for every Canadian citizen.

I knew that my blindness was coming. It was a hard fact, and nothing I did would prevent it. As Terry's story concluded, I knelt with tears pouring down my face. I yearned for that kind of courage, and I dared to hope Terry's light existed in me.

I eventually climbed out of my dark place, with the help of my father, Ed, and the rest of my family. I joined the wrestling team, going from a 0–15 record my first year to becoming team captain my senior year and representing my home state of Connecticut in the National Junior Freestyle Wrestling Championships in Iowa. At sixteen, I also discovered rock climbing at a summer camp. I learned to scan and feel for holds on the rock face, using my hands and feet as my eyes. Through trial and error, by thrashing, groping, and bloodying my knuckles and fingers on the rock—I learned that the beauty of climbing was discovering the clues in the rock face, the nubs, edges, knobs, and pockets I could hang on to and remain on the vertical wall. When I successfully made it up a difficult climb, I was overwhelmed by the wonderful sensation of being in the mountains: the wind at my back, the brilliant textures in the rock, the intermittent patterns of coolness and heat under my touch. My senses awakened. Every sound, smell, and touch was so vivid, so brilliant, it was almost painful. One hundred feet above the tree line with the sun in my face and the wind and elements all around me, I felt an intoxicating freedom and the possibility that the adventure in my life was just beginning.

During high school, tragedy struck a second time. Two years after I lost my vision, I lost my mom in a car accident. I was only a sophomore in high school, and my mom, who'd spent years protecting me, driving me to and from eye doctor appointments, and giving me the inner strength I needed to confront blindness, was gone. How can I explain that pain? If I had gone blind a thousand times, it would not compare to what I felt in losing my mother.

After her death, my father wanted to take my two brothers and me on a trip that would bring us all closer together. In school, I had listened to an audio book about the Spanish conquistadors and the lost city of the Incas, and I suggested Peru. Dad agreed, and we set off for the Inca Trail. The trip, which included a hike to nearly fourteen thousand feet, started a tradition of annual family treks to remote parts of the world and fueled my love of the mountaineering life. As I sat with my older brother Mark at the Sun Gate, he described the ancient city of Machu Picchu, with immense rock structures terracing down the valley. I could hear the lost city, far below us, hidden in a deep cleft between high mountains, and I felt like an explorer, with the possibility of new lands to discover.

I went on to graduate from high school and then from Boston College, where I got a degree in English and communications. I ended up teaching middle school English and coaching wrestling at Phoenix Country Day School in Arizona. That's where I met and fell in love with Ellie Reeve. When she learned about my passion for mountains and adventure, she supported me wholeheartedly, and I continued climbing and mountaineering. My confidence in climbing led to other adventures—skydiving and paragliding, skiing, and ice climbing.

But it was the challenge of big mountain summits that most intrigued me. Between 1995 and 2000, urged on by my Phoenix climbing partner Sam, I trained hard, developed strong teams, and started climbing serious peaks.

First Denali—"the great one" in the Inuit language—at 20,310 feet, the highest point on the North American continent. For weeks we slogged over minefields of hidden crevasses and upward through a region ruled by the diabolical Coriolis effect, a phenomenon—connected to the mountain's proximity to the Arctic Circle—which results in fierce storms with heavy snowfall, high winds, and biting cold. During those years I also climbed Aconcagua, at 22,841 feet, the highest point in South America, and the Vinson Massif in Antarctica—16,050 feet and one of the world's remotest peaks. Vinson was also one of the coldest I'd ever experienced, with summer temps plunging to minus forty-degrees Fahrenheit. On top, I took a leak, and the stream froze in midair, clinking to the ground as yellow ice.

A couple of years later Ellie and I were married at thirteen thousand feet on the Shira Plateau of Mount Kilimanjaro. Ellie didn't have a wedding dress, so we wrapped her up in Tanzanian fabric we'd been using as a tablecloth! Our friends built a rock altar and collected beautiful mountain flowers, which Ellie held in a bouquet. At the end of the ceremony, we walked through a gauntlet of Tanzanian porters as they threw rice over us; the only slight glitch to this time-honored ceremony was that they had boiled the rice, and it stuck all over our fleece. Glacial-capped Kilimanjaro stands alone on a flat plain, formed by a massive volcanic explosion that deposited magma in the shape of a gigantic cone called a stratovolcano. It's the only place in the world where you can pass so quickly through five of the earth's distinct vegetation zones: farmlands on the lower slopes, forest, heath and moorland, alpine desert, and arctic. When you arrive at the summit, you're met with the profuse smell of sulfur emitting from the crater. A few days after our idyllic wedding, we left for the top. I told Ellie it was our honeymoon, but she disagreed, describing our twenty-one-hour summit day as "an endless nightmare."

These expeditions prepared me enough, I believed, for an even greater challenge: Mount Everest.

At 4:00 A.M. on May 25, 2001, I stood at 28,000 feet, still more than a thousand feet below the summit of Mount Everest. I sensed the first beams of sunlight breaking over the Himalayas, and unbelievably, despite the time and the altitude, I could feel warmth on my face, on my chest and shoulders. I was so high up; no other mountain blocked the sunrise. The good weather was a small miracle considering we had been climbing all night through intermittent spells of blasting wind and horizontal snow that caked our down suits with a layer of ice. As we labored toward the Balcony, a small flat shelf at 27,700 feet, lightning had begun exploding nearby, like a terrifying version of a Fourth of July fireworks show. We'd stopped and huddled together in the deteriorating weather, wondering what to do, debating whether to keep going up or to descend. Doubt and fear had swirled in my head like the wind that whipped around us. More than 170 people had died on Mount Everest. Earlier, I'd walked right by a frozen, mummified corpse lying next to the trail, and I tried not to think too deeply about his last moments, his suffering, and his regrets.

Stalled out for almost an hour, I was so cold I bounced up and down, windmilled my arms, and swung my legs back and forth, trying to raise my body temperature and return blood flow to my numb hands and feet. I'd been preparing for this climb half my life; I'd been training intensely for two years, and I'd been toiling up and down the mountain over the last month and a half to acclimatize. And now, hostile weather was going to turn us back. Although desperately wanting to make it to the top, I also wasn't willing to go bullheadedly forward and throw my life away. I pictured my wife, Ellie, and my little one-year-old daughter, Emma, at home, bundled together under warm blankets, reading a storybook. My mind started to settle on the grim reality of heading down when a voice from our team at base camp crackled over the radio.

"The storm's clearing down here. It's on top of you now, but I think it may pass over."

Sure enough, one of my teammates had looked up to study the night sky and reported that stars were beginning to shine through the clouds. That was just the confirmation we needed to push forward. Later, he described the sunrise breaking, cirrus clouds streaking above in the jet stream, and the skies turning a spectacular, electric blue.

By 8:00 A.M., we had struggled to the South Summit, 28,700 feet above sea level. As I knelt in the snow, my brain felt as numb as my hands. A heavy weight took hold of me, a weariness that seemed to oppress every muscle in

my body. I adjusted my mask securely over my mouth and nose, then checked
the knob on my oxygen tank exactly as rehearsed: twelve clicks to provide
me with two liters of oxygen per minute. I'd contemplated this place a thousand times, and now the moment had arrived. If I was going to turn around
and descend, this was the time to do it. From a tactile map I'd once felt, I
knew that the true summit of Mount Everest still loomed nearly a half mile
away, protruding like an island in the sky. Beyond was a rappel down the
backside of the South Summit, a treacherous four hundred–foot crossing of
the knife-edge ridge, and finally the wildly exposed forty-foot spur of the
Hillary Step. If I proceeded, it meant unwavering, absolute commitment. I
gathered my will, stood up, and stepped forward, falling in behind the boot
crunches of my team. We lowered down the twenty-foot vertical snow face
onto the severely sharp ridge, the width of a picnic table and heavily snow-
corniced. To the left was an eight thousand–foot drop into Nepal, and to the
right, a ten thousand–foot plunge into Tibet.

I slowly, carefully probed my ice axe in front of me and found the frozen
boot steps that ran along the leftmost side of the ridge: Scan and step—scan
and step. Despite the thin oxygen and my exhaustion, I tried to stay focused,
or as the Buddhist Sherpas said, to keep my mind "still like water." This was
a No-Mistake Zone.

At last, I came to the base of the vertical Hillary Step. Feeling the rock
under my gloves, I was suddenly in my element. I stuck the crampon points
of my right foot tenuously into a thin rock crack, the left points into a snow
cornice, slid my ascender as high as it would go on the rope, stood up quickly,
and reached for the next bulge of rock to hang on to. At the top, I pulled
myself onto a flat ledge and splayed out in a belly flop, resting, breathing. I
slowly rose to my feet and began trudging up the last slope.

Each step felt like I was pushing through half-hardened cement. Six deep
steady breaths, then another solid step. *Just keep moving*, I thought. Six more
slow breaths, another step. Time blurred around me, and inside the layers of
hats and hoods, all I could hear was my heart pounding in my chest and the
heavy, guttural breathing in my mask.

Then I sensed a teammate pausing in front of me and felt thin, wiry arms
beneath a puffy down suit wrapping around my neck. "Erik," the voice rasped,

hollow, wispy, and strained from calling commands to me through the night, through the storm. His voice tried to say more, but his quaking words dissipated in the wind. Then he leaned in close, pressing his face against my ear. "Big E"—his voice gave way to tears, then struggled out in an immense effort—"you're about to stand on top of the world."

A few steps later, the earth flattened out and there was nowhere else to go. I hugged my teammates. They'd believed in me fiercely, even when I tried to count myself out. "Thank you," I said, the tears flowing and freezing on my face. Then I was handed a radio.

"This is Erik," I called into the transmitter. "We're on top. I can't believe it; we're on the top. Tell Ellie I love her, and we'll be home soon."

Kami Sherpa's voice came back clear and serious: "Congratulations, but Summit is not real summit. Only halfway summit. Weather changing. Go down now. Go down now."

I knew that most accidents happened on the descent, when bodies were spent, legs were shaking, and climbers were trying to beat the afternoon storms that inevitably rolled in. The clouds were lowering again, and the temperature was dropping. Jeff Evans, standing next to me, called out, "You'll never be here again. Look around."

The irony of his words wasn't lost on me as I knelt down and touched the snow with my gloved hand, heard the Sherpa prayer flags flapping in the wind, and listened to the empty, infinite sound of the sky enveloping me. Against this powerful, cold, and rugged mountain scape, I felt fragile and vulnerable. Summits, I thought, were rare and sacred places, but they were only meant to be visited for a moment. It was time to go down.

We descended through increasing snowfall, lowering down the Hillary Step and again traversing the knife-edge ridge. Finally, after eighteen hours of climbing, we reached our tents at 3:30 P.M. For the next few grueling days we picked our way through the anvil-shaped rib of black rock called the Geneva Spur, crossed the treacherous Yellow Band, and inched down the steep, sun-glazed Lhotse Face, now streaming with rockfall.

As I creeped downward, it began to dawn on me what we'd accomplished. For months my teammates and I had traveled together as one, our lives inextricably linked. I'd pushed past my known physical limits, learning much about what my body could endure and what my mind could achieve. Climbing experts had doubted us and questioned my abilities. But on May 25, 2001, nineteen from our team had made it to the summit, the most from one team to reach the top of the world in a single day. And I had made some history of my own. There was much to celebrate. But not quite yet. We reached the deadly Khumbu Icefall—the two-mile-long glacial jumble of shattered seracs and explosions of afternoon avalanches. My legs rubbery and my body weak from the thirty pounds I'd lost, we navigated once more the thirty rickety aluminum ladders spanning wide crevasses, some nearly two hundred feet deep. It was my tenth and final time through the icebound labyrinth.

After crossing the last crevasse, we kept walking downward. Streams ran in little gullies over the ice, and then the ice morphed into expansive slopes of snow. With the last of the icefall behind me, I knew I was going to live.

Just then, as I heard the hoots of our team below, our expedition leader, Pasquale—"PV"—strode up next to me. He grabbed me by the shoulder and stopped me, and I felt him stare into my face for a long time.

"Your life's about to change," he pronounced, patting me on the back. Then he laughed, but underneath, his tone was serious. "Don't make Everest the greatest thing you ever do," he said.

"Don't make Everest the greatest thing you ever do."

Those words sank into my brain and rattled around. At first, I was taken aback. I had just done something that many critics thought was impossible. They'd said I'd be a liability, that I'd subject myself to horrendous risk, that I'd slow my team down, that I'd draw the whole mountain into a rescue. They'd said a blind person didn't belong on the mountain. The secret was that, at times, I had been one of them, doubting, wondering, and second-guessing myself. I was almost as bad as the naysayers themselves. The difference, however, was that I managed to shove out some of that clutter, to train hard and to move forward step by step, regardless of what my brain was telling me. And so I'd found myself at the summit with my team, standing on an island in the sky the size of a two-car garage. And although my body was there, my mind hadn't caught up. A voice kept asking me, *Is this really true?*

Are you really here? Standing here? Later, a reporter had said I'd shattered the world's expectations about what was possible, but what he didn't know was that I'd shattered my own expectations even more than the world's.

So not even down to base camp yet, how off-putting for PV to get in my face and try to ruin the achievement. Or at a minimum, it represented terrible timing. I pushed his words out of my mind. It was easy, since the next six months were a constant blur of celebrations reliving the triumph. I was on the cover of *Time*, and our entire team met the president in the Oval Office. We went to Disney World where I climbed the outside face of the Matterhorn, roped to Mickey Mouse with Goofy belaying us. My photo was fifty feet tall in Times Square, and I received an ESPY Award, meeting celebrities like Tom Brady and Derek Jeter. I even got to shake hands with Muhammad Ali and have a beer with Carl Lewis. Back home in Golden, Colorado, I was chosen as the Grand Poohbah of our Buffalo Bill Days parade; my wife and daughter got to ride with me in the front of a horse-drawn carriage waving to the crowd and throwing candy to the kids. On one of my media tours, I was in a fancy restaurant hotel eating breakfast. I'd lost over thirty pounds on the climb, so when I felt a chocolate croissant on the buffet table, I snapped it up. I finally stopped after seven of them. I was so busy; there wasn't much time to reflect on the future. I was also speaking to a lot of groups. It was weird, because before Mount Everest, people constantly asked, "What's next?" I'd make a joke, like, "My next climb will be to climb into bed for a nap."

But after Mount Everest, not many asked me the "what's next?" question, as if to say implicitly, of course there's nothing else to do, there's nothing bigger on earth. But in those brief moments of quiet, I'd relive PV's words. "You know what the biggest problem with this mountain is?" PV asked soon after we'd made it down to base camp. "You hang your pictures up on the walls. You set up your trophies, and it becomes a museum, even worse, a mausoleum."

As PV talked, I could feel the cuts all over my hands that had been oozing for two months; above eighteen thousand feet, the Death Zone doesn't provide enough oxygen in the atmosphere to heal injuries. My hands were so puffy that I could barely get them into my gloves. Muscles suffer from the same affliction; my legs felt like rubber bands that had been stretched too many times. My face was fried from the sun that, on the surface of the glacier, topped over one hundred degrees; my cheeks and ears were raw from the wind and cold that fell to thirty degrees below zero. My lips and tongue were blistered and swollen from the ferocious sun reflecting off the snow and burning my open mouth. Speaking was difficult.

"Just let me revel for a while," I replied softly. Then in my mind, I added, *Let me go home and shuffle down smooth sidewalks, lie flat on my back in the grass and feel the soft Colorado breeze on my nose, drink hazelnut lattes and eat chocolate croissants, and let me, as a very old man, tell my grandchildren the amazing thing I had done when I was thirty-three years old.*

During that late spring, I especially loved soaking in the hot tub on my back porch, enjoying the still, peaceful nights. It was a luxury I'd always dreamed of while shivering on mountains. So we'd splurged, justifying it as "expedition recovery." The hot tub was also where Ellie and I talked and went over the events of the day. One night, I asked Ellie to join me in the tub, but she was too tired and was going to bed. "But what if I slip on the ice out there," I said, "and crack my head on the side of the tub and I slide underwater and drown?"

"Seriously?" She laughed. "Didn't you just get home from a very big mountain?"

My persuasion finally paid off, and we sat with the steam rising and soft snowflakes landing in our hair. I told her about all the e-mails I'd received that week from people around the world sending congratulations. "One guy wrote and says I should be the first blind man in space," I said. "Another guy invited me to go run with the bulls in Pamplona."

"You could be a blind Evel Knievel," Ellie said. "You could be shot out of a cannon or be catapulted against a wall in a Velcro suit."

I laughed. Her point was clear. It couldn't be as shallow as that, my life a series of harder and harder stunts that quickly lost their meaning. And a lot of people who had followed that path were dead. Besides, I didn't get to the summit of Mount Everest as a daredevil. I was methodical; I trained like crazy. I planned. I developed systems to keep me safe and surrounded myself with a superlative team. Everything fit into a careful risk equation, and I was not fearless. A lot of things, in fact, scared me. Feeling the night breeze on my face, I thought about my little Emma, sleeping upstairs in her crib. Through the baby monitor lying on the side of the tub, I could hear her soft breathing, interrupted by an occasional sigh. Then I reached out and found Ellie's hand. "I have a lot to live for," I said. And I knew that whatever came next, it would have to mean something.

Over the next year, I worked my way around the world, attempting to finish the Seven Summits, the highest point on each continent. I climbed Mount Elbrus, the tallest mountain in Europe, and skied down ten thousand feet to base camp. I went to Australia and climbed little Kosciuszko. I even headed over to New Zealand and climbed infamous Mount Cook, a twenty-four-hour push from hut to summit to hut again. Back home recovering, I was in front of my computer and heard the familiar ring of an e-mail coming in. The subject was "Congratulations from Tibet." I'd received plenty of e-mails of congrats, but none from Tibet, a remote region just over the Himalayas from Nepal where I'd embarked from for most of my climbs. It was from a teacher of the blind, a woman from Germany living in Tibet, and read as follows:

Dear Erik,

After you reached the top of the world our Tibetan neighbor rushed into our center and told the kids about your success. Some of them didn't believe it at first but then there was a mutual understanding: if you could climb to the top of the world, we also can overcome our borders and show to the world that the blind can equally participate in society and are able to accomplish great things.

Since my boyfriend Paul and I had read your book with great pleasure, I decided to tell the children about your life. Just one week ago I told the children in our center all about your childhood, how you became blind, how you threw your canes from bridges in anger, how you finally met other blind people and then how you became confident in wrestling. All of them were very impressed by all these experiences you had and they compared your experiences with their own ones. Again they realized that it does not matter much if you are a blind child in Germany, USA or Tibet, the experience one has who becomes blind, the embarrassment at first, the confidence which builds up slowly but steadily, the reaction of the sighted surrounding is probably for every blind person the same.

After I had told your story to the children, the boys were walking together with some of our sighted colleagues through the inner part of Lhasa. Lhasa is not the blind-friendliest city in the world. There are lots of holes in the street, which sometimes are a few meters deep. Construction sites are never protected with fences. It can happen that you step in huge puddles of dirty water or even excrements. Most of our children know their way through this chaos. I teach them mobility and they are quite confident in using their canes. They always think that if I could find my way around they also have to try. The only problem is that they are sometimes very embarrassed to show their canes since nomads and pilgrims who never saw a cane before often make fun about them. They call them "blind fools," imitate them and laugh about them. One of the boys however once turned around and said: "you cannot talk to me like that, I am blind but I am not a fool! And did you ever go to school, do you know how to read and write? Can you find the toilet in the middle of the night without a flashlight?"

Not all of these children have this pride and confidence to react in such a strong way. I often tell them, that they should understand that these people are just stupid. And if they can, they should say something back. Most of them now like the idea to defend themselves in a verbal way. First they try to reply in a rather friendly way and if this does not help, they are starting to shout back, make fun of them and soon they have the crowd on their side.

And still, if a sighted friend is around, they try to hide away their canes to walk invisible and convenient on the arm of the sighted.

And at this day when I ended your story by saying: "This man, who is blind like you climbed the top of the world, not by holding the arm of a sighted friend, but with the help of some strings and two canes," they all proudly decided to walk on their own, without the convenience of walking with the sighted. Stories like yours change their lives. Most of them now understand that there is nothing to be embarrassed about. They can be very proud little people, and they say quite often: "We are blind, so what? We can speak English and Chinese, we can find our way in the labyrinth of Lhasa's walkways, we are able to read and write in three different Braille scripts and we read and write without using light."

In a way, we are something like colleagues, maybe in encouraging the blind to stand up and to find and overcome their own borders. As I read from your book we have the same philosophy, similar history and a similar way of approaching ideas.

Right now I am sitting in our computer room. Next to me is Gyenshen, a brilliant young student who became blind at the age of 9. He together with two other girls gets computer lessons.

Gyenshen comes from a very remote and poor farmer area. After he became blind his family kept him away in a dark room for three years. The family was embarrassed having a blind child. In Tibet people believe that blindness is a punishment for something which the person has done bad or wrong in his/her previous life. People also believe that blind people are possessed by demons.

When he came to our project he was very shy. Now he is one of the best students and is quite confident with handling the computer. He is probably the only one of his village who knows that the world is round, and that one can communicate through just a wire. He is able to tell the other children of the village that "iron yaks" are Toyota Land Cruisers that drink gasoline instead of water.

The blind that grow up in Tibet have certainly a totally different life than we in Germany or you in the US. But they feel a close solidarity with blind people from other countries. This connection and solidarity gives them a lot of strength and power to manage their lives.

We all would be very excited if you could visit our project. Today is the international day of the white cane and you help us to fill this day with pride. Greetings from a sunny and cold Lhasa, greetings from all the children, the staff and from Paul.

With lots of good wishes,

Sabriye Tenberken

By the time my speech synthesizer had finished reading her letter, tears were pouring down my face, and I knew I would find a way to get to Tibet.

2

THE DREAM FACTORY

The jetliner dipped and yawed, jolting me from my half slumber and bouncing me into Jeff Evans, whose head was resting on my shoulder.

"Get off me," I said. "I'm not your pillow."

"Yeah, you are," he said. "You jacked mine when I was sleeping."

Jeff had been with me on Mount Everest, and I trusted him with my life. We'd slept in many tents together, but using my shoulder as a pillow was too much.

"My shoulder's all wet," I protested. "Have you been drooling on it?"

"Nah," he scoffed. "That's not drool. I spilled my Jack and Coke on you in the turbulence."

"Please return to your seats and fasten your seat belts," the captain's voice said through the speakers. "We're heading into some rough air again."

With that, I heard the movie come back on. It was *Vertical Limit*, ironically, a mountain-climbing film set in the Himalayas. As the plane bounced and dipped, Jeff began describing the entertaining yet absurd action scenes, avalanches thundering down the slope and climbers falling to their deaths.

Jeff chuckled and nudged me in the ribs. "The rescuers just leaped over a thirty-foot-wide, gaping crevasse and caught on the other side with the points of their ice axes." He laughed. "Like that could ever happen!"

"I've done that a lot of times myself, dude," I replied and then listened to a giant explosion on the screen. "What the heck was that?" I asked.

"A guy just threw a bomb made out of nitro, and the mountainside disintegrated," Jeff answered. "Don't ask me why. It doesn't make any sense."

"Can't remember if we brought any nitro," I said.

"Yeah. Think we forgot that on the equipment list," he retorted.

As overly dramatic as it all was, the high-altitude scenes got me thinking about the gravity of what we were about to do. I'd agreed to lead six of the teenagers from Sabriye's school, Braille Without Borders, on an expedition, and this would be our first of two trips to Tibet. We couldn't bring all thirty of Sabriye's students, so she had handpicked four boys and two girls who had adventurous spirits, those who she thought were poised for great things in their lives. We would train the team in all the skills they'd need to know, and five months later, we'd return to make the climb together.

Ever since reading Sabriye's letter, I had been struggling to find the bigger picture behind our goal. These blind kids were looked down on, shunned, and called blind fools. From Sabriye's words, I knew this prejudice was based on ignorance and superstition. I had also witnessed something similar when I went to Mount Everest. We had climbed from the Khumbu region on the Nepal side, forty miles through remote Sherpa villages. At first the Sherpas didn't want to climb with me. They thought I'd be unlucky, that my presence on the mountain could bring bad fortune to their families. One brave and well-respected Sherpa, Ang Pasang, who'd already climbed Mount Everest twice, finally stated, "I think we make our own karma," and signed on with us. After that, other Sherpas quickly followed. The folklore of Mount Everest had progressed similarly. Up until the '50s, no Sherpa would dream of even stepping into the high mountains. Their presence would anger Chomolungma—"Goddess Mother of Mountains," into sending down a massive avalanche or unleashing an earthquake on the villages. And it worked the opposite way as well. Famine, drought, natural disasters, children being stillborn all could be attributed to the mountain god's displeasure. It became the way to explain all the pain and suffering of a harsh, high-altitude existence. But in 1953, when Edmund Hillary and Tenzing Norgay came back from the summit of Mount Everest with no divine repercussions, the mythology began to collapse. The Sherpas who climbed Mount Everest in the modern world had become revered, like rock stars or professional athletes.

Tibet was at least fifty years behind Nepal, and life was still largely guided by superstition, especially the beliefs around disability and blindness. From what I'd read, Sabriye's work had already begun paving the way out of ignorance. Her school and training center provided education and vocational preparation for a hundred blind students and adults. Education for the blind was still a revolutionary idea in the high plains of Tibet. I thought, *What if we did something that could serve as a dramatic extension to Sabriye's work? Something big, something that no one in the local villages would have ever dreamed of?* So we'd hatched the goal of climbing Lhakpa Ri, a twenty-three thousand–foot peak on the north side of Mount Everest. Lhakpa Ri was considered one of the easier seven thousand–meter peaks in the world—but that was like saying you were going to swim with one of the friendliest great white sharks in the world. Still, I knew from my own experience that climbing a tall mountain and standing on top could take those perceptions about what was possible for the blind and break them apart. And maybe the bigness of that achievement could sink into the minds of Sabriye's students and affect the trajectory of their entire lives. The boy in Sabriye's letter, Gyenshen, was the only one in his village who knew the world was round, so maybe he could also be the only one to stand on the top of a twenty-three thousand–foot peak.

It was an ambitious plan, but I'd brought together the best team imaginable to guide these kids. Jeff Evans, sprawled out to my right, was a wild man, boasting 107 Grateful Dead shows and over 300 Widespread Panic shows, but I wanted him on my expeditions. He'd worked for the National Park Service on Denali rappelling out of helicopters into crevasses to retrieve injured climbers and, unfortunately, sometimes dead bodies. He was an emergency room physician assistant and also one of the most experienced people in the world in high-altitude medicine.

Across the aisle from us were mountain guides Charley Mace and Michael Brown, both also with me on Mount Everest. Charley had climbed K2—one of the most technically difficult climbs in the world, and Michael had climbed Everest three times. A year earlier, they'd gotten a blind guy to the summit of Mount Everest, through the two thousand feet of jumbled up boulders of ice called the Khumbu Icefall—a blind person's worst nightmare. So if it could be done, these guys were the ones to make it happen.

I wanted to have a one-to-one ratio between guides and students to increase their safety, so I'd brought along three more mountaineers: Gavin Attwood, a loyal friend who had helped me train in the past and was great with logistics; Sally Berg, who'd done many Himalayan climbs; and Stefani Jackenthal, a well-traveled adventure journalist.

The other coup was that on hearing the idea, a friend had introduced me to Stephen Haft, one of the producers of the film *Dead Poets Society*. He, in turn, had introduced me to Sybil Robson, an aspiring filmmaker and philanthropist who had been so inspired by our project that she'd decided to fund a film, as well as the trip itself. I was on a high, excited that we could do this important work and also come away with a film that would bring attention to Sabriye's work and our adventure together. A film would help a lot more people.

We entered our approach to Lhasa, and I heard, then felt, the landing gear release, as *Vertical Limit* ended with triumphant music. "If you didn't notice," Jeff said sarcastically, "they saved the day."

Inside the Lhasa airport, I was excited to finally meet Sabriye Tenberken, Paul Kronenberg (the school's cofounder), and the six students chosen for the expedition. The students were waiting just outside customs, separated from us by thick Plexiglas. "Hello, hello, Erik!" they screamed eagerly as they rapped their canes against the glass.

We rapped the glass and waved back.

We took a bus from the Lhasa airport down a long, straight avenue of honking horns, whining mopeds, and the whir of bike rickshaws as all the kids peppered us with questions. My long white cane was a topic of fascination, since it was a full head higher than the tallest of the teens. The bus slowed down and crawled through the city center. The two girls who would be on our expedition, Kyila and Sonam Bhumtso, surrounded me on my seat, already clinging to my arms. They must have had the route memorized, because they cheerfully called out destinations along the way.

"Jokhang Monastery," they chimed, almost in unison.

Sabriye told us the Jokhang was arguably the most sacred monastery in Tibet and situated in the busiest section of Lhasa. The school was only a few hundred yards away. "This is by design," she added. "If we want to change the way blind people are viewed and treated here, our school is perfectly located. Every day, thousands of pilgrims walk the Barkhor, a circle road around the Jokhang Temple. When the pilgrims see our students walking by themselves with their white canes, news of their ability to travel independently spreads across Tibet."

We parked and walked a short distance, ducking under low-hanging wires. Dogs yipped at us from small courtyards in front of houses. At the entrance to the school grounds, Sabriye had me run my hands up the ornate Tibetan gate. I touched the two wooden pillars, about six feet apart. High above me, I could hear a solid archway, a confined sound that seemed to block the sky. On the left pillar, carved into the smooth wood, were the indentations of the Roman alphabet, the letters running downward. The Braille equivalent of each letter was carved beside it. On the other pillar were strange symbols that swooped and curved in shapes I didn't recognize. Sabriye told us this was Tibetan Sanskrit. To the right were the corresponding Braille symbols. The Braille dots felt familiar, but the arrangements made no sense to me.

"That's Tibetan Braille," she added.

"Sabriye studied Tibetology at the University of Bonn in Germany," Paul said. "When she discovered that there was no Tibetan script for the blind, she invented one. She combined the principles of the Braille system with the special features of Tibetan syllable-based script. Tibetan scholars have now adopted it."

Once inside, we all stopped at the edge of a courtyard, and I could hear a group of kids kicking a soccer ball with a bell inside it. I listened to shouts and laughter as the jingle moved back and forth.

"When I first came to Tibet in the summer of 1997," said Sabriye, "I rode horseback across the Tibetan Plateau. Everywhere I went, camping outside of villages, sleeping in barns, I met lots of blind people, but many were hidden away. Their houses were poorly ventilated, and they heated and cooked with blocks of yak dung. The smoke and soot from the fires, the extreme ultraviolet rays, plus cataracts and poor medical treatment contributed to a high percentage of blindness. But I learned there wasn't a single school for blind people in Tibet. I decided that I would change that."

"I met Sabriye that summer," Paul chimed in, "when I was backpacking through Tibet. Most people back home thought her plan was ludicrous, but I was sold. When she was finally headed to Lhasa to start the school, she called to thank me for the support and say good-bye. I said, 'What do you mean, good-bye? I'm coming with you!' I quit my job as a mechanical engineer the next day and a week later joined her."

Sabriye told me that, at first, getting through all the red tape was difficult because the Chinese government was suspicious of foreigners. She and Paul were forced to leave the country numerous times to renew their visas as they attempted to prove their only goal was to support the blind.

"There was suspicion from the Tibetan community as well," she said. "They thought we might steal their children, but one morning we woke up and a blind child was dropped off at our doorstep. After that, word spread that a place existed where the blind would be cared for and educated, and many more began arriving."

"In the beginning," Paul reminisced, "we only had a bedroom that functioned as an office, a dormitory that also functioned as a dining hall, and a kitchen. We taught the students in a tent in the garden. But two years ago we built a new building that contained two dorms—one for girls, one for boys—three classrooms, a Braille production room, a medical massage training room, and a large terrace. It has been quite a transformation."

They had made it seem so simple, so matter-of-fact. No Tibetan Braille code in existence? Then just invent one from scratch and open up literacy to a whole new population. No school for blind children? Then teach them in a yak herder's tent. Get kicked out of the country by a suspicious bureaucracy? Then simply drive the thousand kilometers over pitted dirt roads and high mountain passes to wait it out for months in Nepal, and repeat this a half dozen more times until you've gained their trust. I was awestruck.

"Erik, why don't you show the boys some of your wrestling moves?" Sabriye asked not ten minutes after stepping into the courtyard. She'd apparently told some of the boys about my high school wrestling career, and instantly, Tenzin, Dachung, and Gyenshen attacked me from all directions. They'd clearly planned the ambush. They were light and small and young—

so I toyed with them, throwing them off pretty easily. But they kept coming. As we spun and battled, dogs yapped and younger kids cheered the three boys on. Two of them shot in on my legs, and the other leaped on my back, and I had to double my efforts. Then they released me, and it got quiet—*too quiet*—so I readied for another assault. They attacked again, but this time they wound one of our climbing ropes around my legs. Soon they got a few coils around my feet. They yanked the rope. It went tight, and I toppled over.

"Dude, you're getting yak-tied by three little Tibetan kids!" Jeff called out, laughing.

With that, I began pouring it on, one hand fighting them off while the other furiously pulled the coils from around my ankles. *These kids play to win*, I thought. I popped up, arms outstretched in defense. Panting, I said, "Okay, I'm good. I don't want to hurt you guys."

One of my knees was skinned up, and wiping the grit out of the wound, I thought how tenacious and scrappy these guys were. Tenzin was deceptively strong for his diminutive size. He was all sinew, without an ounce of fat on him. His hands were vise grips, like he'd been doing hard physical labor all his short life.

"They got some moves," I said, still fending them off at arm's length.

"We stress mobility, orientation, and independence," Sabriye said. "They should be able to look after themselves." Her voice went higher with a little laugh—probably at the image of me being tied up.

I'd now spent time with the two girls, and the three bruisers I'd just tangled with, but the sixth teenager in the group, Tashi, had hung quietly in the background.

"Tashi," Sabriye urged, "come over and talk to us."

As if waiting for that prompting, Tashi stepped to my side. He was nineteen and the oldest of the group. His name meant *Lucky*. He was rail thin, gangly, awkward, and shy. It took him a while to stutter out his broken English. I learned he came from far away—according to Tashi, "A thousand miles away"—from a small village in China.

When Tashi left to begin his lessons, I asked Sabriye more about him, and she explained his background. When he was ten years old, his father took him on an outing to another village, but while there, they met with a Chinese couple. His father struck a bargain, and the couple whisked Tashi away. Over the next week, the couple drove him to Lhasa to beg for them on the streets. However, when he didn't make enough money, they beat him and refused to give him food. This went on until Tashi couldn't stand it anymore, and one evening after a day of begging he didn't go back to the Chinese couple. He decided to take his chances alone on the streets of the Barkhor. Homeless, with no family, he roamed Lhasa, malnourished and in tattered clothes, until a Tibetan woman found him, took pity on him, and brought him to Sabriye's school. I listened to the ball jingling across the courtyard and the stomp of small feet, and I knew there were a hundred more blind children with similar stories, whom Sabriye and Paul had saved from tragic fates.

Next, Sabriye and Paul toured us through the classrooms, designed by age groups: *Tsitsi Dsindra*, Mouse Class; *Dah Dsindra*, Tiger Class; and *Rebong Dsindra*, Rabbit Class. The classrooms were tidy, with neat rows of small desks with children plunking away on Braille typewriters. The walls were shelved with thick Braille books. Thumbing through them, I asked, "Where do you get all these books?"

"At first they were donated from Germany and America," Paul replied, "but then we decided to create our own Braille printing press. The first step was easy, scanning the Tibetan books into digital text, but the second step was much harder. We had to develop a software program to translate digital Tibetan script into the Braille code Sabriye created, and it all prints out on a Braille embosser. With our Braille printing press, we now print books in English, Chinese, and Tibetan Braille."

Gyenshen was already back working at his desk, manipulating the Braille keyboard on a computer, learning word processing and desktop publishing. Dachung, also adept at computing, was researching techniques of medical massage, an interest of his. Sonam Bhumtso was sliding her fingers across a Braille book written in Tibetan and working to translate it into English, while Kyila patiently helped the younger kids with their lessons.

"Our philosophy is very simple," said Sabriye. "Blind people are discriminated against, and we try to give them an opportunity to learn. By learning, they get skills, and these skills give them value. When they are ready, they will leave here and integrate back into their villages. And when they are the only ones who can read and write, or can use a computer, or can translate three different languages for their families, they will no longer be disposable; they will be indispensable."

As I listened to the busy sounds around me, I was hearing Sabriye's philosophy coming to life. It was in the echo of long white canes tapping, in the clanking of Braille typewriters, in the mechanical drumming of the Braille printers, and especially in the whispering voices of children discussing their lessons and preparing for their futures.

The next morning, we began the preparation for our expedition. A sighted guide was assigned to each student, and we broke up and practiced navigating with trekking poles and following bear bells through an obstacle course we set up in the courtyard. Desks became boulders; two chairs with a broomstick laid across became a fallen tree to step over; a rolled-up Tibetan carpet became an open crevasse to leap over. Two children facing each other held the two ends of a white cane and lifted it up and down, simulating a dangerous rockfall zone where we'd need to hurry through. The game was for each duo to maneuver together through the course without touching any obstacles, stumbling into a crevasse, or being pegged by falling rocks. Teams would stop in front of the horizontal cane being raised and lowered, and the guide would scream, "Now!" and the kid would sprint through the gauntlet. The whole time, Jeff gave a string of running commentary like, "Dachung, you just disappeared down a slot . . . Tashi, too slow. That rock just took you out."

Next, we unloaded piles of duffel bags and fitted the kids out with all the gear they'd need for the trip: layers of fleece, gloves, hats, and socks, down jackets and pants. We taught them how to strap crampons to their boots so they could walk on steep ice once we got high up on the glaciers.

The next three days, we visited the hillsides outside the city, assessing their skills and abilities and getting to know each other. We practiced setting up tents, packing and unpacking our backpacks, and tying essential knots. We demonstrated roping up and trekking as a unit. While roped together, we taught the kids how to do self-arrests. In case of a fall, the other members of the rope team needed to throw themselves down on the steep slope, dig their ice axes into the snow, and bring their rope mate to a stop.

Around a small juniper campfire that night, I sat next to Sonam Bhumtso and asked her questions about her life.

"She has very round cheeks," Kyila said from the other side of the seat. "She like it when you squeeze them."

I reached out, and Kyila was absolutely correct. I felt soft, round cheeks. They lifted, and I knew a broad smile had creased the space between them. Sonam was tiny, a full head shorter than Kyila. She came from the Gompo district in eastern Tibet, from a village of only seventeen families. Sonam Bhumtso meant a *Hundred Thousand Beautiful Lakes*, which she said was strange because she hated water and never learned to swim. "Lakes and rivers may be beautiful," she said, "but I prefer to stay on dry land."

Sonam went blind when she was four months old. Like Gyenshen, her family believed a Lu, a water demon, cursed her. "One day my uncle went fishing," she said. "He caught two fish, and when he got home, he threw them into a container of water. My mother ladled some water out of it while she was cooking, but by mistake she also got hold of the fish, and they fell onto the cook fire. She looked for the fish everywhere but couldn't find them. She said they burned up in the fire. This offended the gods, because right after that, I went blind. It was my uncle's fault, because he caught the fish, but I was the one who had to pay. When I was little, I cried a lot. I was sad and angry because I didn't belong and because I was different from the other children in my village. Before I went to school in Lhasa, I had few friends. The children teased me and threw stones at me. When my grandmother and the others went to tend the yaks, I stayed behind by myself. I cleaned the house, fed the other animals, and then I would sit in the garden to guard the cheese where it was laid out to dry. The crows love dried cheese. If they got too close, I chased them away. In the mornings I often heard the other children laughing and whistling on their way to school. I would get especially angry when they came back and held a book in front of my face and asked me to read it to them. Sometimes I played school all by myself. I would collect flat stones and scratch things on them. I pretended they were the letters of the alphabet. When the other children saw what I was doing, they laughed at me, took my stones, and threw them at me. After I went to school in Lhasa for one year, I was looking forward to going home again. I did not miss my family, but for a different reason. I took my Braille book back with me and held it up for the other children to see. I held it to their noses and said, 'Why don't you read something for me if you're so smart?'"

At the punch line, the entire team actually cheered. I grabbed her small hand, folded her fingers under her thumb and into a fist, and guided my clenched knuckles to hers. "That's a fist bump," I said. "Then you open your hand, spread your fingers and palm upward, out to the sky, and go 'Pow,' like an explosion." She tried a couple of times until she got it, and we all laughed.

On our return from the countryside, the six teens took us on a tour of the nearby Potala Palace, just a twenty-minute walk away, up a long series of stairs to the top of a thousand-foot hill overlooking the Lhasa Valley. This was the seat of the Tibetan government and where the Dalai Lama lived until 1959, when he escaped to India during the Tibetan uprising. It was a complex network of towers, temples, libraries, and golden stupas where the bodies of past lamas were enshrined. It comprised over a thousand rooms. The stone fortress sloped up at an inward angle, with walls more than fifteen feet thick at the base. The foundation was filled in with molten copper that had solidified to protect the palace from falling down during Tibet's regular earthquakes.

Inside, we circled the monastery clockwise, spinning an endless chain of giant sacred prayer wheels, all intricately embossed on sheets of copper. Incense perfumed the air. The practice was supposed to unleash unlimited wisdom, love, and compassion and awaken one's own highest potential, one's Buddha nature. We all recited the mantra OM MANI PADME HUM—signifying the indivisibility of compassion and wisdom—and we were supposed to visualize pure white light rays emanating out from the spinning prayer wheel and spreading out to all sentient beings on its way to the universe as the light rays purified and healed the world. In Buddhism your level of success and happiness was enhanced, or harmed, by behavior in a past life.

So as we spun, we also built up our karma, a kind of cosmic merit system along the chain of many lives as we worked toward enlightenment.

During the tour, we learned the palace had been built over the ruins of a far more ancient temple, founded in A.D. 637 by the Chenrezig, the embodiment of love and compassion in Tibetan Buddhism. He is believed by Tibetans to be their "Adam," the actual progenitor of their people. Legend said that when he attained enlightenment, he ascended to the top of Mount Pitaloka, a mythical mountaintop that means *brilliance* in Tibetan, where he dwells eternally. Before his ascent, he vowed that he would not rest until he had liberated all beings from all the realms of suffering. After working diligently at this task for a very long time, he looked out and realized the immense number of miserable beings yet to be saved. Seeing this, he became despondent, and his head split into thousands of pieces. Amitābha Buddha put the pieces back together as a body with very many arms and many heads so that Chenrezig could work with myriad beings all at the same time. Jeff described a painting of Chenrezig with eleven heads and many arms spreading out from his body.

After the tour, we relaxed for a while at the palace gardens, at the foot of the palace, beside a small lake. Prayer flags flapped in the wind up high, sending yet more prayers to the heavens. Ducks splashed and swam in the water just behind us. I sat down on a bench with seventeen-year-old Gyenshen. He told me he became blind at nine years old, unfortunately right after he'd received a scholarship to attend a prestigious school in Beijing. When the school learned he'd lost his eyesight, his scholarship was revoked. His family believed a serpent had cursed him, and they were so ashamed they locked him away in his home for three years. "My mother say I was the cleverest boy, but now the cleverest child has gone to waste. Without eyes, she say, a man is not complete. Once the school took me away, life was much easier for my family."

I thought about the founder of the Potala Palace, Chenrezig, and the fact that, almost 1,500 years later, his mission was far from realized. Tibet seemed like a strange and contradictory place, a clash between sacred ideals and the harsh cruelties of the real world. Societal and cultural barriers in Tibet still demonized the blind. They were at the bottom of the caste system, often believed to be murderers in their past lives. They lived in a world where you could be enslaved, thrown out on the streets to freeze and beg, and locked in a dark room for years because your family was embarrassed by you. Hearing Gyenshen's and the other kids' stories, it was easy to understand how Chenrezig's head split open with frustration and pain. Sabriye and Paul were one of his many arms, rescuing these kids, in many cases literally from the streets, and giving them hope, giving them something real, a sanctuary where they could feel loved and safe and connected, part of a family. It dawned on me that Sabriye and Paul were not just educating blind children; they were challenging an entire belief system.

Later, I sat in the center's small office, drinking a cup of milk tea with Kyila and Sabriye. Kyila told me her name in Tibetan meant *Happy*. It seemed to fit her; her voice was light and expressive, like a smile was dancing through her words. She came from a small village ten hours by bus from Lhasa, and she had twin brothers, also both blind, who entered the school with her at the same time. Her father had lost his sight as well.

"It was very hard at home," she said. "I sat around doing nothing. I couldn't dress myself; I couldn't eat by myself. My mother took care of all of us, but she went to hospital. She had a heart problem. She worried too much about my brothers and me. After one month in hospital, she wanted to tell me something, but she couldn't speak anymore. I wanted to know what she was trying to say, and I wished, maybe for just five minutes if I could become sighted, I could see her face, and what it looked like just once. Then she died."

Sabriye and I sat silently. There was nothing to say, and I thought that her name, Happy, contrasted with her stark early life.

"Then at twelve," Kyila finally continued, "I learn about Miss Sabriye's school, and my life change. I am here three years now."

"It's incredible what you've built here in just a few short years," I added.

Sabriye reached out and touched my shoulder. "I feel like it was a long chain of events that have brought us all here," she said. "When I went blind at twelve, my greatest fear was not having friends anymore. I still attended a sighted school and hadn't learned to use a cane yet. I would ask the other children directions to class or to the bathroom, and they would tell me to keep walking straight. Then I would walk off a flight of stairs and fall to the bottom. I would hurt my ankle. Sometimes, I hit my head. Then they would laugh and hiss at me, calling me '*Blindschleiche*,' a German curse word. It translates to *blind snake*."

You didn't have to live in Tibet to face hardship, I thought as I listened. I remembered a day after I'd gone blind, tapping my cane into the high school cafeteria. I always sat at the same table with my friends, but as I approached the table, they'd played a game and remained totally silent. I knew they were there from their quiet breathing, but I just walked away and sat alone at another table. Pain and humiliation had flushed from my head and through my entire body, like a poison. *Cruelty was a trait that all humankind shared equally*, I thought.

"After all the teasing and bullying," Sabriye said, "I became so depressed, I was barely even speaking. I withdrew into my interior world. My mother decided that something had to change, and she took me out of school, far away, to an island on the North Sea. I remember sitting at the end of a dock overlooking the harbor, listening to a fierce windstorm. There were boats moored nearby, and their sails were snapping. Waves crashed against the shore, and I knew the storm was also inside of me. It was raging. That inner rage turned outward. It was the anger about myself, anger about my victimization, and anger about my former friends and teachers who didn't understand that I was still the same person."

At the end of that week, Sabriye and her mother agreed she would be better off at the Carl Strehl-Schule for the blind and partially sighted, where she quickly learned the teachers were far from overprotective. She rode tandem bikes, windsurfed, skied, and rode horseback, even jumping over fences.

Then Sabriye stood up from her desk chair and said, "I'd like to show you something," and then led me down the hallway and across the courtyard. We stopped at the doorway of a quiet room, and Sabriye picked up her story where she'd left off.

"It was at the school for the blind that one of my teachers asked us what we wanted to do with our lives. What dreams did we have? The teacher encouraged us to think about it for a long time. I was sixteen and nearing the end of high school. I thought about my life, about people's expectations of me. In Germany, people have very clear perceptions about what blind people can or *cannot* do. People kept telling me to go into psychology, or become a lawyer, to do something that had been done before by other blind people, but to me, it felt suffocating. I wanted to really *live*, to take risks and push toward unknown territory. I had read about Tibet, and for me, it was the most adventurous place I could imagine, undiscovered and filled with wilderness.

And I determined to risk something, to live that kind of adventure, and do something meaningful. I didn't know what that would look like exactly."

Then she took my hand and pointed my finger into the room. "We do something similar here. We call this the 'Dream Factory.'" We walked inside, and I touched the tapestries hanging on the walls that the kids had made; the woven patterns felt like hourglasses or figure eights. I could feel a big south window enveloping me in warmth as the sun climbed upward, and, outside, I could hear the honking of traffic and the markets coming to life. "Here in our Dream Factory," Sabriye went on, a deep pride edging her voice, "we encourage our students to dream about what it is *they want* to do. They should not limit those dreams in any way. We then try to find ways to turn these dreams into reality."

Sabriye, Kyila, and I sat down and leaned back against a soft Tibetan carpet laid over a thick mattress of straw. My arms rested on ornately stitched pillows. "We did Dream Factory," Kyila said, "and Sabriye asked us what was our dream. It was such a strange question to me, because I didn't know what was a dream. Sabriye made me think about it and answer, and I said I wanted to start a kindergarten, because I think every child should have a special childhood memory where you can make friends, be naughty, and play with other children. And not be home all alone, with no one."

Like Sabriye, I'd grown up with defined rules of what a blind person could and could not do, and I knew what that blanket felt like as it lowered down and began to suffocate you. My whole life, I'd been trying to break free of it and do something bold and unexpected. After college, I'd traveled by bus across the United States to Phoenix, Arizona, to begin a job as a middle school teacher. It was exciting to be in charge of a classroom full of twenty eleven-year-olds. Many school principals had turned down my application on account that a blind teacher wasn't safe, couldn't maintain order, and wouldn't be able to keep up with all the grading, but I'd thrived, teaching for six fulfilling years and feeling I just might do this forever. At the same time, I also got my first taste of climbing, ascending vertical rock pinnacles in the desert outside the city, and that had led to a dream even more on the edge. I was on the summit of one of those desert towers when I decided to pursue a life as a mountain climber. It was a bet that no venture capitalists would have banked on. However, Ellie had cashed in her life savings, $20,000, and moved with me to the Colorado Rockies where I'd begun training and trying to eke out a living as a full-time professional athlete and adventurer. I was able to get the attention of some outdoor sponsors, and those, combined with some paid speaking engagements, I hoped could support my expeditions. "It was my dream to climb the tallest mountain in every continent," I said. "When I finished the Seven Summits, I read Sabriye's letter, and then it was my dream to come here, to meet you, and be a part of this dream."

In the distance, I could hear the rhythmic chug of a Braille printer. *Ka-chung . . . ka-chung . . . ka-chung.*

I saw it in my mind, rolling out thick stock paper embossed with Sabriye's Tibetan Braille, thousands of Braille dots secretly lifting up off the pages and escaping out the window. I imagined them rising up into the sky and dissolving into the pure white light of the prayer wheel. And as that light spread through the world toward the heavens, hopes and dreams were born.

3

BLIND SUMMIT

After months of training and two separate trips to Tibet, it was finally time to embark on our big adventure to summit Lhakpa Ri. As our bus left the busy streets of Lhasa and rattled up toward the Tibetan Plateau, it felt sort of like we were going on a family road trip. Sabriye was the mom; Paul and I shared the role of the dad, and our kids would go wherever we took them. Sonam Bhumtso and Kyila sang American pop songs from the '60s. They were the Tibetan Supremes, raising their hands and belting out classics like "Stop! In the Name of Love," then the mood got dreamy as Kyila became Sonny and Sonam became Cher:

Kyila: "They say we're young and we don't know."

Sonam: "We won't find out until we grow."

Their voices harmonized in perfect sync for the chorus, "Babe, I got you babe."

Sonam said the whole school got together and conducted nightly sing-alongs, and it showed. It sounded like they practiced all the time, like they'd memorized an endless songbook. Their singing was nearly constant, and it annoyed the boys. "Sonam Bhumtso is your wife," Tenzin said, turning to Kyila, and the boys laughed.

"No. You are my wife," Kyila replied in a sly smiling voice, "and this is our honeymoon. Gyenshen and Dachung are our children."

That shut the boys up for a while, and the girls went back to their routines. I found myself singing along to my favorites. The bus filled with excited chatter and expectation—the boys jabbing each other in the ribs, smacking each other.

The trek and summit attempt of Lhakpa Ri would take us about three weeks. We'd start by crossing over the Tibetan Plateau by bus three hundred miles southwest toward the village of Tingri. From there, at fourteen thousand feet, we'd start hiking up through a series of high camps, eventually reaching the same base camp shared by Mount Everest climbers. There, the real mountain terrain would begin, thirteen miles up a steep circuitous trail of boulders and ice, through increasingly thinning air, to advance base camp, or what's known as ABC. At 21,500 feet, ABC would lead us across a heavily crevassed glacier to a high camp positioned at the head of a snowy valley. If all went well, from that point, we'd climb a steep, thousand-foot slope and gain a long ridge to the top of Lhakpa Ri. Charley told me the peak appeared as a dramatic three-sided pyramid, with its even taller cousin, Mount Everest, not so far to its west.

Paul drove the large van packed with fourteen people and a stack of duffel bags piled on the roof. The film crew followed behind. It was dry and dusty as we bounced over rutted dirt roads for seven hours, crossing over a seventeen thousand–foot pass. We finally pulled over and unloaded for a break near Shigatse. Sabriye took me by the arm. "You've seen our center in the city," she said, "but you haven't seen the most beautiful part of the project. This is our vocational center."

Before us was a large working farm with orchards, crops of wheat and barley, and grazing land. She introduced me to one of the elder farmworkers, and I shook his leathery hand. Sabriye explained, "Nomads, farmers, and herders here, many become blind at a later age. We provide them an opportunity to perform their old professions again. And younger blind people, they can learn new skills in agriculture and animal husbandry." After four years of requests, denials, and ongoing negotiation, the government had finally acquiesced and given Sabriye and Paul scrap land, deemed unusable. However, in typical Sabriye fashion, they'd managed to carve something out of nothing here at over thirteen thousand feet. They planted one hundred apple and one hundred peach trees. "After the trainees learn how to plant the trees," Paul said, "they can take the seeds home to their own villages and plant them to sell the fruit to generate income."

"But that's not all," Sabriye said. Her voice was dancing a little, like she had a secret. We entered a large wooden building, and I immediately brought my hand to my nose. "What's that smell?" I asked, crinkling my eyes and sniffing the sharp, pungent air. Sabriye and Paul just laughed. "You saw our Dream Factory. Well, this is our cheese factory," Sabriye answered. "In Tibet locals only eat cheese made from a nak, which is a female yak, but that is an acquired taste. Most Westerners think it tastes very gamy. Many foreigners pass close to here, on their way to the Everest base camp. So we thought we could bring in cows and produce cheese for the tourists, but everyone told us that cows could not produce milk at this altitude. Then we brought in a specialist, a friend of Paul's, who challenged that thinking. He felt it was possible, if we radically changed its diet. It turns out, he was right. The specialist also taught the highland farmers how to make the cheeses, and they now sell to the area restaurants. We have a soft cheese like brie we call Tibetino, and our favorite, a famous cheese that is good on pizza. We call it Lhasarella."

I smiled. She'd even pronounced *Lhasarella* with an Italian accent.

Later, as we walked the perimeter of the farm, Sabriye said, "The goal of this vocational training center is not just a way to keep blind people busy, but a chance for the blind trainees and workers to contribute economically, to have value and to add value through their work."

Experiencing the cheese factory, and hearing her now, enabled me to put the finishing touches on her philosophy. It felt like putting the last piece of a puzzle in place and getting the first glimpse of the full picture. The last two weeks had been a crash course in Tibetan culture, history, religion, beliefs, and superstitions—all swirling and intersecting in confusing and subtle ways. But there was a way to cut through it, a possible solution, and perhaps Sabriye and Paul had discovered it. I had understood the importance of education, but I hadn't fully grasped the end goal. It came down to economics.

Life was hard in Tibet. People lived and died by what they could produce with their hands. They scraped out a meager living by planting a couple of rows of potatoes and barley and owning a nak for milk and cheese. If one family member was born blind, he couldn't thrash the grain; he couldn't watch the yaks. The perception was that he could not contribute to the hard-nosed work of keeping the family alive. Even further, he was another mouth to feed, a dangerous burden, another weight tipping the scale toward starvation. This was not an indictment of Buddhism or of Tibet. It would happen in any society, if the recipe of circumstances were repeated.

When people were born imperfect and unable to contribute, there had to be an explanation other than the random and unfathomable cruelty of life. It was much easier and more rational to create cosmic reasons to explain it away. They must be cursed. Surely they must have deserved their fate. The next step was natural: Those people born imperfect fell to the bottom of the caste system and became pariahs, outcasts, spit on and shunned.

So now, after observing the blind workers happily tending crops, pruning fruit trees, and tending to the cows, I realized how brilliant their strategy was. They had figured out the tenuous trail that led to acceptance and dignity. It wasn't about asking for it or even demanding it. Dignity was earned. Education led to skills. Skills led to making a living, and making a living led to value. When the blind were no longer burdens but instead began sending money back to their families and were now the ones keeping their families alive, it was impossible to view them as cursed any longer. It was a clear and concise worldview: education and economics could change an entire culture.

After another endless bounce-session in the van, we arrived at the small village of Tingri, with its dirt streets and packs of snarling stray dogs. Smoky yak-dung fires burned our eyes. We left the van above the village and began our trek, moving closer toward the high mountains, crossing through knee-deep rivers and stumbling over rocks and scree. We passed through a series of highland herder villages. Jeff described the herder's garb to me. "The women are all decked out in multicolored, hand-woven coats and ankle-long dresses," he said, "their hair tucked under turquoise and red and purple woolen scarves, like do-rags. The men sport broad-brimmed hats to shield the sun, and a few of them have what look like braided yak tails wound around their foreheads, and they pull them down and peer through little gaps of hair, like makeshift sunglasses. Pretty ingenious, but I'll stick to my glacier glasses," he said.

The locals waved at us from their fields; women came out of smoky huts to watch us; throngs of children laughed and followed us through the mud streets and out of the village in a procession, singing, "*Kha-leh shu*" and "*tashi delek*"—good-bye and good fortune.

The grunts of yaks and the bleating of sheep competed with the voices of Kyila and Sonam as they sang. The strange combination rang across the valley: "Me and you, and you and me, no matter how they tossed the dice, it had to be, the only one for me is you, and you for me, so happy together!"

At one village, I sat with Sonam Bhumtso. She was giggling and giddy as she whispered with Kyila. "Why are you so happy?" I asked.

"There are thirty students in our school," she replied. "Six of us children have been given a golden chance. So I am very happy."

I laughed. It was like she had just opened the winning Wonka Bar in *Charlie and the Chocolate Factory*. She had gotten the "golden ticket."

High above us, I could hear Gyenshen and Tenzin at the edge of a grassy ridge. They leaped and danced, and their voices were full of exuberance as they sang out a traditional nomad's song: "*Alasso, alasso, tashi sho, alasso! Chung se mo, chung se mo!*"

Despite the laughing and dancing, the kids' grim backgrounds were never far from the surface. Tashi was our biggest concern. Though he was the oldest at nineteen, he was already struggling, far behind the other children, and often appearing exhausted. I was increasingly worried about his health, both physically and emotionally. He'd be tromping happily along, joking and singing songs, but in the next moment, he'd shut down, become completely uncommunicative, and withdraw inward. I noticed he was also an outcast. At breaks, he'd always sit just outside of the group. One afternoon, he took his shirt off as we washed in a clear stream. Gavin took me aside later to tell me Tashi had twenty or thirty dark, round pits and scars across his chest and back.

"They look an awful lot like cigarette burns," he said.

Given his past, Tashi had plenty of reasons to feel like an outcast, but he was a survivor too. In the summer between our first trip to Tibet and our expedition, Tashi had come to Sabriye and Paul with a revelation. "He was so nervous, he almost couldn't speak," Sabriye told me, "but finally he admitted that he wasn't Tibetan. He was Chinese, and his real name wasn't Tashi Pasang but Fang Qing Hong. He had learned Tibetan and pretended to be from Tibet because he thought our school would only accept Tibetan children."

Without his identity papers, Tashi couldn't start his medical massage clinic, an idea conceived in the Dream Factory, so he needed to go back to his home in China and get them from his parents. Sabriye and Paul agreed to take him to his village, a thousand miles from Lhasa, near the city of Chengdu in the province of Sichuan. He had been gone for eight long years, so he wasn't even sure his parents were still alive. He wasn't sure of the name of his village either, so they flew to Chengdu, rented a car, and drove in a direction based on distant memories. The three finally stopped on a bridge over a river, and Tashi thought its name sounded familiar. From there, based on the names of relatives Tashi remembered, they started asking around, and eventually their inquiries led to his town and to his family.

"The reunion was a strange mixture of joy and awkward tension," Sabriye told me.

At first, Tashi's father cried out, "My son, my son, where have you been?" Then his mother and brother arrived, and they all hugged and sobbed. However, when Sabriye confronted the father with the story of how Tashi arrived at the school, he became nervous and defensive. He began to contradict himself, at one moment admitting he'd given Tashi over to a Chinese couple and in the next claiming he'd lost Tashi at a bus station. "I searched for you a day and a half," he claimed. "Finally, I gave up and returned home without you."

Tashi was heartbroken. He clearly remembered his father making the deal. He even remembered what he was worth: three hundred yuan, the equivalent of fifty dollars.

The worst part came when Tashi learned his younger sister had also been sold—or, in his father's words, had "been lost."

Now he was enraged. He stormed out of the house. "My father is a shit bag and a liar!" he yelled to Sabriye. "I don't want to spend another minute here. I want to go back to Lhasa now. I want to be with you and Paul and my friends from the school. That is where I belong. That is my real home."

At Rongbuk Monastery, we rested in a sprawling valley below the Mount Everest base camp. At 16,340 feet, it is said to be the highest monastery in the world and is the sacred threshold to Mount Everest. Inside, the monks chanted an unearthly deep-throated song, like the guttural growl of a wild beast. The chorus was part of a tantric ritual that was a manifestation of divine energy, uniting the singers in a web of universal consciousness. It was haunting and a bit menacing too. Every now and then, the nuns, called *bhikkhunīs*, would bang a giant gong that accompanied the chant. The deep rumble would begin slowly and spread out and engulf the room.

We all lined up to have the monks bless our climb in a traditional *puja* ceremony, but they only gawked at us. "*Nyingje nyingje*," the nuns said. "What a horrible fate is yours." The chanting and trumpeting ceased; the gong stopped banging. A couple of the nuns were sobbing. It seemed as though a depression had fallen over the monastery. Kyila translated for us. "They say, 'How sad that none of you can see. You poor, poor blind people, and now you are being forced to climb a tall mountain.'"

But it was obvious our team of Tibetans had confronted this scenario before. They smiled broadly and laughed. Sonam said, "We are not sad. We are happy. We have a good life. We have friends. We can read and write, and we can climb a tall mountain."

The tiny nuns began shooting questions at the kids, and soon, they were smiling and laughing too. The chanting and trumpeting started up again. The gongs banged again. The monks bowed and rang bells to bless our climb, and one of the nuns began draping *khatas*, sacred white scarves, over our necks.

In the courtyard outside the monastery, the kids sat in a clump as Jeff stood and reminded everyone about the early signs of altitude sickness, like headache, loss of appetite, and nausea. "You might feel a little dizzy," he said, "and you may not sleep that well."

With each sentence, he'd stop to have Sabriye translate.

"Symptoms are very similar to a really bad hangover," he finished, and he paused. I'd been around Jeff long enough to know he was looking over at Sabriye with a smile. She mumbled something under her breath and didn't bother translating. Then he launched into the more serious phenomena of pulmonary and cerebral edema, in which your lungs fill with fluid or your brain swells, both dangerous problems.

"From here on up," he said, "things will get much more serious. The oxygen will get thinner, and that can affect your motivation and judgment. We'll need to stay very focused."

He ended his warning with, "Do you understand?"

All the kids nodded in unison and responded, "Yes," but when he asked if anyone had questions, they were utterly silent, as if witnessing an alien diagramming the atmospheric ratio of nitrogen to hydrogen on his planet.

Next, I took over, and the kids huddled around me as I showed them one last time how to organize everything in their backpacks. I told them it would be very cold where we were going, and knowing exactly where a glove or hat was in their pack was vital. The boys were goofing around, poking each other and not paying attention. I pressed a glove into Tenzin's hand and kept the other one away. "You lose one glove up there," I said, "and you lose your fingers to frostbite." That got their attention.

Afterward, I asked Sabriye if she thought they understood the extent of what they were about to do.

"These children are very fit and tough," she answered, "but you should understand, the mountains are a foreign concept to them. These kids come from Tibetan villages where no one climbs mountains, not like the Nepali Sherpas. They are a people of necessity, a practical people. They thresh grain to make the barley porridge called *tsampa*. They dig potatoes out of the hard ground to make their stew. They might walk over a high pass to bring supplies to another village or chase their yak through the high pastures into the mountains if it escapes, but a climbing expedition to stand on top of a mountain, this is outside their experience." Then she added, "Even for me, a high mountain is an abstract idea. Only you can truly know its magnitude."

What she said made sense. I thought we'd been crystal clear about what we were attempting. We had gone through it all on a map, the guides tracing the kids' fingers along our route up the mountain, pointing out the mileage and altitude gain each day. We had tried to define what an expedition was; we had used all the same words, but despite that, the kids didn't have the context or the background to comprehend what it all meant. They were there primarily based on us, these strange foreign climbers, led by a blind man who had flown over the vast ocean; and their foreign teacher, also blind, who had flown across that same ocean to educate them and spend time with them—with blind children who had been cursed. It was the same kind of trust you placed in your dad and mom. The mountains fell a far second to that.

I sat cross-legged in the dirt outside Rongbuk Monastery. I knew Mount Everest rose up far above me, casting its massive shadow over the valley. It was hard to believe that my team and I had stood up there, and now, just two years later, we were about to return to its base from its other side. It was so cold, clear, and peaceful. Distant ravens cawed in the immense skies overhead, and the wind wailed mournfully through the deep valleys. The intense, bitter smell of yak butter burned in my nose, and I could hear the candles spitting.

The next morning, we'd be ascending to base camp, and then, up higher, the environment would dramatically change. Our team of six Tibetans had already faced more than their fair share of hardship, and what we were about to do, to take these teenagers up into the high Himalayas, seemed, at the surface, like simply piling more suffering and hardship on top of them. The trails would be increasingly rough, steep, and rocky—with real consequences. There'd be cold, long days with storms to endure. I couldn't dismiss the truth that this would be a high-stakes endeavor, but I crossed my fingers and hoped this adventure together wouldn't become another brick wall in their lives.

Two days later, we all left base camp and followed the jangling bells hanging from our long train of yaks snaking up the mountain, carrying our tents, cooking equipment, and food. It was easy to distinguish the bear bells that the guides rang from the deeper clang of the yak bells. The kids plodded along, jabbing their trekking poles in front and to the sides to feel their way up a dry riverbed. The going was very slow. The Himalayas were a place of extremes, either intense scorching sun or bitter cold. So we'd stop often to drink and to add or shed clothing layers.

"Stay hydrated!" Jeff would yell. "And don't sweat too much, or it will make you very cold!"

Sabriye translated his instructions.

"And make sure you're wearing your sunglasses," he added. "The UV rays up here are strong and will make you go blind."

Sabriye huffed and didn't bother translating. I got the impression Jeff irritated Sabriye. I figured he'd brought it on himself. Knowing her less than an hour, he'd said, "I know you can't see me, but you should know, I'm a good-looking man." Climbing with Jeff for over ten years, I knew he said it with a smile on his face, but I think the joke was lost on her. It didn't help his cause either, when he began describing his tattoos.

As we started up the trail again, I hiked behind Sabriye and Paul as they weaved around and scrambled over giant piles of boulders strewn across our path. "Where do all these boulders come from?" Sabriye asked.

Looking up, Paul replied, "They come from the upper mountain. Just be glad you can't see it."

I refrained from saying anything, but I worried Sabriye was getting the wrong impression. Although most mountains, including this range, had loose rock to contend with, our trail was comparatively safe. We were here in the fall, which was the off-season, so we had the mountain completely to ourselves, but in the spring, hundreds of climbers hiked from base camp to ABC, the point from which they staged their Everest expeditions. Our route was considered physically strenuous but not actually part of the objective dangers of the mountain. It was a relatively straightforward trail, and I had never heard of anyone being hit by falling rock on this approach, but I worried Paul's description might send her imagination soaring.

I hiked for a while behind Gyenshen. He was one of the strongest in the group. Of the six, I thought he had a good chance of reaching the summit of Lhakpa Ri. "I'll be so happy if I get to the top," he said. "I'll prove I can do all sorts of things in my life."

He and Tenzin especially seemed to have boundless energy. Often, they didn't even bother following the bells. Where the trail widened out into flatter tundra, their guides would say, "Now," and they'd sprint out ahead, making their own course through deep ruts filled with mud, over tall tussocks of grass, around and over scattered boulders. It didn't really matter where their feet landed. They plowed forward through everything in their way, like four-wheel jeeps with big knobby tires.

As Gyenshen and Tenzin cruised ahead, Jeff ran along behind them. "Wow. You boys are impressive. Our old blind guy's getting pretty worn out," he joked. "You guys are going to replace him. You know what we say—out with the old, in with the new."

I laughed from behind, huffing and puffing to keep up. "Maybe on our next expedition, we'll climb Everest," Jeff said.

Sabriye pulled me aside at the next break to give me an earful.

"When you climbed Mount Everest, we all applauded because you showed that blind people did not need to live by others' expectations. Your climb opened doors, but I do not like your team pushing these boys into needless and risky pursuits. Everest has already been climbed by one blind person, and that is enough."

"I think it was mostly a joke," I protested and tried to reassure her again. "What we're doing is really a walk uphill on snow, and the summit of Lhakpa Ri is more than a mile below Mount Everest."

"I'm not sure the boys knew it was a joke," she said. "They already asked me if it would be possible for them. I told them they did not need to waste their time attempting to break records. Their hands can be spent in better ways than getting frostbite."

After lunch, the trail wound up a steeper, narrower side canyon that rose progressively higher above a mountain creek. We could hear it far below us, and although the drop-off was severe to our right with some loose rocks, the trail was relatively wide and smooth. On this section, Gavin was holding one end of a trekking pole and Tashi the other end, so he could direct Tashi where to step. Tashi slipped a few times, sending rocks clattering down the cliff, echoing like rifle shots as they shattered against boulders far below.

"Everything's okay," Gavin called out.

"What if Tashi were to fall and break his leg?" Sabriye asked anxiously. "Or worse? I get a pit inside my stomach to think of it."

As everyone collected on the trail, we sat down on a boulder, and I tried to calm her nerves. "I understand your concern. The guides are always near the kids. If they slip, they'll be there to grab them. Where it's very narrow, the kids will be short-roped, and the groups will move together. And Jeff is here, constantly assessing how the kids are doing. He has a bagful of high-altitude medicine, and if anyone has serious problems, we have the resources to get them down quickly. We can carry them down if it's really bad."

Sabriye now gave up her composure and began to cry. Through her tears, she said, "This isn't just a stroll anymore. It's too dangerous for me. I can just imagine the kids getting too close to the cliff and stumbling. Then what?"

All the kids were surrounding us, watching in silence as their revered teacher shed tears over all the possible scenarios of death and doom, and I feared her apprehension would project onto them. I could empathize with her. In a way, these were her children, and it was a mother's responsibility to keep them safe and healthy. I remembered my own mom watching me wrestle from the bleachers. My dad said she dug her long fingernails so hard into his hands, it left traces of blood. It must have been torturous watching her blind child get his head drilled into the mat. My father had been like a broom, constantly sweeping me out into the world, and my mother was like the dustpan gathering up the shattered pieces and rebuilding me, only to have my father sweep me out again. So now we were going ever higher up a mountain. Even though we had done everything humanly possible to stack the odds in our favor, we couldn't totally eliminate the objective dangers of the mountains.

"None of us are adrenaline junkies," I told her. "We don't love risk for risk's sake. But risk and uncertainty are simply part of any adventure."

Sabriye kept persisting. "But why is it important to risk something," she asked, "to have this unnecessary danger?"

"You're right. There are risks to this expedition," I blurted back. "It's unlikely, but an avalanche could take us all out tomorrow. Someone could fall in a crevasse. One of us could get frostbite or cerebral edema . . . but they could also be taken out by a motorcycle or rickshaw crossing the street in Lhasa; I don't recall any stoplights. They could fall into an open construction hole or run into one of the live electrical wires that are hanging free in the alleys. There are risks to everything, but we're going to do everything within our power to keep everyone safe and to make good decisions. Stop worrying and relax. It's going to be fun."

"I'm not so sure where is the fun," she said with a wrinkle in her voice as we moved upward.

When we arrived at Old British Camp that evening, we had our first revolt. Normally teams take two days to ascend the four thousand feet from base camp to ABC, but we negotiated with the yak herders to extend to four days in order to give the kids plenty of time to acclimatize to the thinning oxygen. But now, the yak herders were angry about the slow pace and were going back on their word. The terrain was too high for any grass or shrubs, and the yaks had to carry all their hay on their backs. They were already low on food, and the herders wanted to hurry up and get the piles of gear to ABC and get down again to lower pastures. Along with us were four of the Nepali Sherpas who had been on my Everest team; they had lots of experience with climbing teams, and I knew we could fully trust their decisions. Kami, the head Sherpa, squared off with the head yak herder outside our kitchen tent. Their arms waved wildly in each other's faces. They yelled back and forth angrily, their voices growling in Tibetan. Then the rest of the yak herders piled forward, and the Sherpa team rushed in to meet them. It was like two baseball teams clearing the benches, yet instead of holding baseball bats, they clutched ice axes. I was convinced there was going to be a fight. Kami eventually calmed everyone down and mediated a settlement. We would need to pay a little more money, but thankfully it wouldn't end the expedition. Kami took me aside. He was still fuming. "These yak herders are worthless," he vented. "The Tibetan guides are worthless too."

As part of our negotiations with the China-Tibet Mountaineering Association, we had been compelled to bring four Tibetan guides as well. They had much less experience climbing than the Sherpas and were known for being unreliable.

"They do not help set up tents. They do not even carry their own packs. They put them on the yaks." I knew this was a big point of pride for the Sherpas, who had left Tibet hundreds of years ago and crossed over the Himalayan passes into Nepal, searching for a new life. They were distantly related to the

Tibetans, sharing some common customs and some common words, but they considered themselves a separate people, more modern, and definitely better mountaineers.

We had another problem too. The guides were worried again about Tashi. He was constantly falling way behind and was straggling into camp two hours after the other five. "I think we have to face the fact that Tashi may not be able to continue," Charley said. "It's only fair that we tell him."

I was alarmed. I knew once you started splitting teams, it was a complicated business. You had to separate enough food and fuel, cooking utensils, sleeping gear, and perhaps a couple of yaks to carry it all. It was demoralizing for the climbers too. Splitting people and resources usually meant the beginning of the end. I also objected to the idea of writing anyone off. When I was hiking with my older brothers and father as a kid, I desperately tried to keep up, stumbling along the trail with my long white cane and hating the fact I was falling behind. So I stepped in and said, "I don't think this should be like an episode of *Survivor*. There's no elimination. We've opened a door, so let's not close it so soon. This isn't the weaker kids or the stronger kids. We are one team. So let's get the whole team as high as we can, as safely as we can. We don't have to make any decisions yet. We can reassess at ABC."

The guides mulled this over, but I could tell they still had doubts.

Our evening's camp was less than ideal. It sloped down at a steep angle. We spent an hour moving rocks and flattening campsites. The hill was so steep, the yaks had to be tied up. The yak herders told us that the yaks were easily spooked and to not make sudden movements near them. All night long, we could hear their hooves stomping and bells clanking right outside the tents. Sabriye and Paul had a yak that decided to settle down in their entranceway. The kids were afraid to go outside their tents to pee, so most lay awake suffering. Later, we awoke to the crash of a huge rock that had dislodged somewhere in the distance. People popped their heads out of their tents to ask if everyone was okay. Even though the boulder was far away, I knew it only added to Sabriye and Paul's growing anxiety.

The next morning, biting winds hurtled through the camp as the temperature dropped. The team layered up, climbed out of the tents, and pushed out of camp, all lined up in rows, guide to student. Then I heard a familiar request. The film crew called out, "We missed it. Can you have everyone do it again?"

"What again?" I replied, already annoyed.

"We need to get a shot of the kids leaving camp, so have them all line up in front of their tents, and we'll give the signal to leave."

We all stood there, hopping up and down and swinging our arms to stay warm while the camera crew set up. Their cameras were acting up again in the chill. Their batteries were so cold that they were constantly losing their charge. This seemed like the culmination of a long, ongoing tug-of-war. The film's funder had hired a director who had turned out to be frenetic to the point of obsessive. She told her crew to keep the cameras rolling from dawn to dusk so she missed no bit of action, drama, conflict, or triumphs. She told us directly that she didn't know where the story would lead, so the cameras had to capture absolutely everything. When she happened to miss something, she went into a fit, Jeff said, with her face in her hands. And it would result in a surly mood for hours as she harangued her crew, drove them even harder, and told them they were letting her down and ruining the film. At base camp, she actually got into a physical altercation with a crew member. We all stood in amazement and shock, not quite sure what to do, as the two circled around each other, pushing and shoving. It was surreal hearing two grown-ups tussling at over seventeen thousand feet. Her crew was exhausted and demoralized. One cameraman told me that because of the director, this was hands down the worst production he'd ever been on, and they were very close to revolting and walking off the job.

"One more minute," the director called from above the camp, and twenty minutes later, "Just one more minute."

An hour later, we were still waiting in line, the kids shivering, beating their hands against their sides and kicking their legs to warm up. I was about to lose it. The kids were in danger of getting frostbite. I yelled up, "Hey! We can't have the kids going hypothermic here! We gotta move!"

The director replied, "We're making a film here!"

I yelled back, "No, we're making an expedition, and you happen to be filming it. Big difference!"

I gave the signal, and we started up. I stormed past the camera crew who had missed the shot. I could hear the director groaning, stomping her feet, most likely fuming.

Higher up, I came across Jeff and Charley, Jeff guiding Tenzin and Charley guiding Dachung. They were arguing. Dachung had slowed up, and Jeff was insisting that he unload his pack on one of the guides.

"He's fine," Charley insisted, and they went back and forth, the exchange getting more heated by the minute.

"Look at his pack," Jeff insisted. "It's almost as big as he is."

"But he's doing fine," Charley shot back.

"But for what purpose?" Jeff pushed back. "This isn't about who can carry the biggest packs."

Tenzin, who was usually pretty quiet, yelled, "Guys, you stop arguing!" The two didn't hear him but kept sniping at each other, as if the conflicts between the yak herders and the camera crew were a virus that had now begun to infect the climbing team.

In the afternoon, we ascended a broad, rounded ridge that dropped away hundreds of feet on both sides. The top of the ridge was twenty feet across, consisting of chewed-up glacial sand, so it was easy walking. However, Sabriye was nervous again. She could hear the echo of the surrounding drops and kept imagining herself or one of the kids sliding off the edge.

A yell from Paul made us all perk up. A large black bird had swooped overhead and landed on a frozen petrified yak that had once stumbled off the side. Its legs, now mostly bone, pointed skyward.

As we walked, the guides described to the kids the stunning views. To our left and right were the remnants of the retreating glacier, a labyrinth of human-size ice pinnacles stabbing upward like twisted spears, and sheets of ice plastering the vertical gray-and-black cliffs, some hanging in space like curtains, glittering in the sun. Charley described the surrounding peaks, the color of chocolate, piled at the tops with whipped cream, spilling over the sides. He took Dachung's finger and traced the ridgeline. As we rested, Sabriye said, "That is a beautiful image, but the children and I are blind, and we need more time to process this beauty. It is hard to notice it when we are concentrating so hard with our poles, listening to the bells, and making sure not to fall."

I agreed with her wholeheartedly and had heard this same complaint from sighted people, even from my wife, Ellie. When we had trekked Kilimanjaro together, she had said, "I want to stop, look up, and look around. I want to take it all in, but all I ever do is look down at my feet on the trail."

I would have loved to sit all day and have the grandeur of our surroundings described to us, to stop and play on the different rock formations, to throw stones into the gorge and listen to their echo against the edge of the glacier, but that was the dilemma of a mountain expedition. I had the pressures of logistics on my shoulders. There was only so much food and fuel; yaks could only carry so much weight on their backs, and there was the finite math equation of how many miles and how many hours it would take us to reach camp. An expedition had rewards, but it wasn't a school field trip.

In the last thirty minutes of light, we reached Changtse Camp, 19,600 feet. Paul described the pinnacles of ice, now morphed into fifty-foot towers, glowing orange in the evening light. Even though the scenery spoke of a fairy tale, the mood of the team had degraded and seemed just the opposite.

In our big dining tent, Paul, Sabriye, and Sonam held their heads with splitting headaches. Everyone was tired and suffering from the effects of the altitude. Dachung finished his bowl of noodles, curled up, and fell asleep. Trying to lighten the mood, I asked the kids their favorite part of the trip so far.

Kyila said it was singing pop songs with Sonam Bhumtso. Gyenshen said it was rushing ahead of their guides with the other boys through the high valleys and roaring from the cliff tops. Tashi said it was sitting next to Sabriye and me, drinking tea, and listening to stories of Germany and America. Tenzin said that he liked climbing, but then he said, "But when does the climbing begin? Today was a long walk." He hesitated and then added, "And a little boring."

Listening to their highlights, I silently questioned whether we were doing the right thing. Maybe we were pushing too hard and should have settled for something less grandiose.

Paul broke the silence. "I don't think the youngsters are getting very much out of this."

"I think this is not so good for them," Sabriye backed him up. "Maybe we've done enough. Maybe we should go back down."

"I know we're all suffering," I interjected, "but that's not a reason to turn back."

Paul replied, "But I wonder if we are going up for the sake of the kids, or so we don't disappoint Erik or hurt the film?"

"Whoa. Hold on now," the guides interjected, taking major offense. It was one thing to have an opinion, but another thing entirely to question motives. These two, who I had so much respect for, seemed to be sabotaging us every step of the way. It was at that point when I lost it. I yelled, "The goal here is to summit a mountain! An expedition has a clear definition, with clear expectations. We leave the city, we drive to the mountains, and we hike every day until we arrive at camp. Then we repeat until we reach the summit. We all knew we wouldn't be sitting around the campfire, roasting marshmallows, and singing camp songs."

Through the heated exchange, the kids sat silently, confused and torn between these two opinions, between the teacher they loved and their expedition leader.

I took a deep breath and tried to keep my voice under control as I said, "Climbing a mountain involves some suffering. There's no denying that. Every step is hard. It's too cold or too hot; you're exhausted, have a headache, and can't catch your breath. When you're calling on your last reserves, it's easy to lose motivation and wish yourself back home again. To be honest, over the last few days, when I'm eating canned sardines, I was dreaming about a blueberry muffin. But all that physical exertion and pain is not the end goal, and it's not why we are here. That struggle is just what you have to go through to earn the gifts that the mountain offers. Despite the discomfort and the fear, you have to keep your heart open, or you miss them. Sometimes you can't even understand what they are until you are back home again in your regular life, and at that point, all that apprehension will turn to pride. So I'm asking you to hang on a little longer. Just give it a few more days."

I left for my tent dejected. I had come to Tibet to break down barriers and contribute to Sabriye's work, but it seemed like all we were doing was creating more barriers. They were all around us: language and cultural barriers with the kids, a competing set of agendas from the film team and yak herders, and severe philosophical differences with Sabriye and Paul. As if the mountain were agreeing with Sabriye, that night was the coldest yet. The inside walls of the tent froze from the condensation of our breath. A thin layer of ice covered our clothes and sleeping bags. The water bottle sitting next to me froze solid. There was even a tremor in the earth, a rumbling, like the harbinger of an earthquake.

As I lay awake, I thought hard about what we were doing here. All six kids had been thrown into a harsh world that could have easily crushed them, but Sabriye and Paul had introduced them to an array of new skills and tools to confront those challenges. They'd learned to read Braille, navigate with long white canes, and interface with talking computers. But more importantly, Sabriye and Paul had introduced the teens to a new mind-set. It was the belief that they could take on that world and flourish in it and even leave their mark on it. A mountain was a very different setting, yet with similar threads running through it. Above the tree line was a harsh environment, indifferent to human suffering and desires, but in a way, it was clearer than regular life, which didn't always have finite summits to point to. The map was more straightforward and the risks and rewards more defined. Equipped with the proper tools, supported by a strong team, and with the right mind-set, you could enter that realm, flourish on its flanks, and have a chance to reach the top. I had discovered this on my first of the Seven Summits, Denali, in Alaska. Standing on top, I felt like I had done more than survive this austere and wild place. I felt like it had ingrained itself inside me and become a part of my body, my brain, my bones—my entire being. So why couldn't I convince Sabriye and Paul it was all the same mission?

It was so easy to be crushed by hardship, but equipped in the right way, I hoped this great adventure together could burrow itself into the kids' minds, consolidate their will, their resolve, their insights and beliefs, and propel them forward into a new kind of life. Sabriye had helped the children to dream, but the mountains could harness those dreams and give them substance and energy, like the glaciers that carved out the valleys, the fierce wind gusting through the narrow canyons, like the mountain rivers raging through the deep gorges. Yet so far, I admitted to myself, this experience had been just as messy and ambiguous as life off the mountain.

The next morning, over oatmeal and tea, Michael rushed into the tent and asked for a meeting among the team outside. Michael had majored in meteo-rology in college, and his GPS tracker was predicting a storm hitting the north side of Mount Everest, including Lhakpa Ri. "These things are hard to predict, but it looks like it may come in a couple of days from now," he said.

"Well, then, we should all head down as soon as possible and get to some-where safe," Sabriye said.

"We've been in this situation before," I stepped in. "If the storm hits, it will most likely bring some wind and snowfall. At worst, the yaks may have to go down and come back for us in a few days. But we have enough food and fuel to wait it out, so let's not panic. I think we should keep going as scheduled."

Sabriye and Paul were now visibly angry. "We aren't mountain experts like you and your team, but when we hear the words *storm* and *snow,* we feel this is the time to turn around."

Michael tried to explain. "An expedition is a tricky balancing act. Nobody's interested in pushing into the face of a storm, but if we turned around at the first threat of bad weather, then nobody would ever stand atop anything."

"So it sounds like we will go up at any cost," Paul accused.

"We would like a second opinion," Sabriye answered. "Let's bring in the British guides to see what they think."

The film team had brought with them two British guides to watch over their crew. I had tacitly approved this, knowing we'd need to direct our full focus on the kids and not on the camera folks, editor, producer, and director, none of whom had much experience in the mountains. The Brits would make the camera crew self-reliant, a separate independent entity, and wouldn't drain our resources or detract from the climbing expedition. It was all under the condition that the British guides would not interfere with our team deci-sions.

I had learned some hard lessons in my early days on climbing expeditions: democracy didn't work in the mountains. When the situation became serious, when rescues needed to be assembled, when people were sick or in-jured, when storms raked the mountain, decisions needed to be made swiftly and decisively. Those decisions, or lack of decisions, meant the difference between life and death. There wasn't time for endless debates or second-guessing. Teams enter an expedition with a leader they trust. Everyone has the ability to express their opinions and give feedback. The leader listens and takes that information but ultimately makes the call. A good team then falls into line and executes to the best of its ability, whether its members agree or not. This was the code of the mountains.

I came into this trip as the expedition leader and had been making those hard calls from the beginning. I had outfitted the kids from head to toe and had provided tents, sleeping bags, and mats and a mountain of food, kerosene, and cooking supplies; I'd negotiated an extra yak just for our medical kit and fifty pounds of high-altitude medication; I'd broken a normally two-day hike into four for the sake of the teens, which had almost led to a fist-fight. I'd resisted the team's push to split off the strong from the weak, and along the trail, I'd fought the camera crew and managed Sabriye and Paul's fears and apprehensions. It was exhausting work, both physically and emotionally, to juggle so many competing expectations and interests. I had just come off the heels of Mount Everest in which we had been such a cohesive group that it had taken on a collective energy, propelling us to the top. But this team wasn't the same. Our different factions sucked the energy away from the whole, and personally, I felt as if I were tied to four different yaks, each pulling my limbs in different directions. I had already reluctantly given in and allowed Sabriye to go against our judgment by bringing aboard their own physician. Even though Jeff was one of the most capable high-altitude medical experts out there, Sabriye and Paul had insisted on bringing their own school doctor. I strongly advised against this. "He's never been tested at altitude, so he's a total wildcard," I said. "The doctor may very well become the patient and take our attention away from the kids."

So now bringing the Brits in for a second opinion was another break in the code, yet the more serious insult was that they had denied me their full trust. It hurt even more, considering it was Sabriye turning to these near strangers rather than to me.

Thankfully, the result was anticlimactic. The Brits agreed completely with the team's assessment. "As long as everyone's doing okay, this isn't a matter of safety. We should keep going."

When we trudged out of camp, nobody was in a talking mood. We moved for two hours over undulating terrain. Jeff ran up and down the line urging everyone to drink and put on more sunscreen. Charley passed out candy bars. Up higher, we came across a series of high frozen lakes, and some of the kids stopped to throw rocks across the ice. We could hear the echo reverberating off the cliff on the far side. "I can hear how big the lake is," Dachung said, amazed.

Jeff softly stepped onto the ice, and the surface cracked. It was plenty cold, and there was no chance of breaking through, but the surface of the ice was old and brittle, and his foot caused the crack to zigzag across the ice, making a zipping sound as it traveled. There was also a deeper *woomph* and warbling sound as the embedded layers of water sloshed around far beneath. It sounded foreboding. The kids gathered around and wanted to know the source, and I told them a story of the frozen serpent that howled from beneath the ice. I envisioned their eyes bulging as they considered sprinting for their lives. Then Jeff cracked up and bounded out onto the lake.

"Follow me!" he yelled, and I leaped out behind him. I heard the kids tentatively step forward onto the perfectly smooth ice. Soon the kids were jumping and sliding around. They held each other's hands for reassurance and skimmed across on their boots like ice-skaters. Dachung sat on his butt as I pulled him by his trekking poles, spinning him around, making him dizzy. I was going anaerobic with the effort, since we were now at about twenty thousand feet. Then the guides began using the poles to spin the kids in circles. One of us would say, "Now!" and the kids would let go, gliding across the ice. Of course, it became a game to see who among us could slingshot the kids the farthest. Later Tenzin and Sonam sat in the center of the pond that still had a layer of snow over it. They drew pictures with their gloves; both could still see a tiny bit, and the dark green and black ice contrasted the white snow.

At the next little frozen pond, there was a shallow ice cave with an entranceway formed by a curtain of ice stalactites. The guides described them hanging down at different angles and all different sizes from pencil thin to the width of an arm. Then Jeff took a rock and hurled it toward the cave. It hit the huge chandelier of ice that shattered and sent a thousand shards of ice particles down onto the frozen pond. The larger spears calved off, popped, and exploded. The sound thundered against a nearby alcove of rock and echoed across the range. The smaller pieces followed, continuing to tinkle down like delicate bells, and then the sound grew even softer as a spray of fine snow feathered the ground like falling rain. "*Ki bu la*," Sonam whispered. "How beautiful!"

As the echo vanished into a cold, still silence, we all stood there listening, transfixed by the mountain's performance.

Coming out of the spell, I pushed my watch, and it spoke: "11:00 A.M." I knew we had a long way to go to ABC. "Hey, guys!" I yelled to them. "I'd love to stand here, to stay and skate too, but we need to get to ABC before nightfall and the temperature drops."

We crept upward, the mountains beginning to exact their toll on our team. Tashi's legs grew rubbery, and he fell a few times. About three hours from ABC, Jeff sat with him among the boulders and scree, and we contemplated Jeff descending with him. We wrapped Tashi in a down jacket, and Jeff held his wrist, checking his pulse. Next, he put a pulse oximeter device over Tashi's finger, which measured the oxygen content in his blood. Finally, he put a stethoscope to Tashi's chest. "Heart and pulse and oxygen levels are all normal, and lungs are clear," Jeff said. We huddled and debated. "I don't think this is altitude sickness," Jeff concluded. "I think he's just exhausted."

I relaxed a little, knowing he wasn't in any immediate danger. We were so close to ABC, and I desperately wanted him to reach camp with the other kids, to feel like part of our team. Plus, splitting the group and supplies on the middle of the trail would be a nightmare. "Tashi, do you think you have the strength in your legs to walk up for three to four more hours?" he asked him.

Tashi breathed deeply, nodded, and then said stoically, "I walk up."

Hours later, Tashi finally trudged in and collapsed on a camp chair. As we applauded, he slumped silently, grimacing and pointing to his temples. That night, squeezed into the mess tent, we tried to celebrate.

"Let's hear it," we said. "You've all made it to Advance Base Camp—twenty-one thousand feet. The summit is only two thousand feet above us."

Everyone cheered and raised their tin cups of hot tea, but the celebration felt a little forced.

The first to be brought down by cerebral edema was the school's doctor, Toan. I was irritated, because Michael would now need to walk with him all the way back to base camp, thirteen miles away. As I had feared, this detracted from our goal, and we'd now have to split our people and resources. Michael cheerfully geared up in his warmest clothes and left that night with Toan.

Kyila and Sonam Bhumtso were also struggling with altitude. In their tent, Sonam held her head in her hands, complaining of a headache. Kyila was growing nauseous and feeling faint. Jeff switched into full-on doctor mode, no longer a trace of the laid-back joker. He monitored the situation carefully, moving purposefully between the mess tent and the girls' tents with his bagful of high-altitude medication and monitoring devices. We now faced a difficult decision. Some of us, a part of the team, could still potentially make a summit bid. But it was looking like three of the kids needed to get lower. In the end, we all begrudgingly agreed that the next morning, Jeff, Stefani, and Sally would walk down with Tashi, Kyila, and Sonam Bhumtso.

The sun rose over the camp, but the mood was gloomy. It was a hard call as to what to do, because none of them wanted to go down. With rest, they were starting to feel better, and their headaches were improving. The two girls sat sobbing. They felt they had failed. Kyila was so upset at the prospect of going down that she collapsed and began writhing on the ground, crying and muttering in a kind of delirium. Just in case it was the start of something dangerous like cerebral edema, Jeff appropriately gave her an injection of dexamethasone, a steroid to stop her brain from swelling. The kids had so much pride and wanted to keep going. As throughout the entire expedition, they were torn between Sabriye and me. They had listened as Sabriye and Paul insisted that we turn back. They didn't want to be disloyal to them, but also didn't want to give up the dream of making the summit with their team.

I knelt in front of Tashi's tent, holding his hand and helping him change into warmer clothes. He cried as I told him he had to go down. "But you'll feel better down lower," I explained. "You'll be warmer and stronger, and your head will stop hurting. Then in a few days we'll all come down and meet you, and we'll be together again."

He squeezed my hand hard, and through his tears, he said, "I am no good."

"Do you know how high we are?" I asked him. "Do you know where we are?"

"I don't know," he said as the wind whipped down from the glacier.

"Twenty-one thousand feet," I said. "At the advance base camp of Mount Everest. You've worked so hard, and we are very high. You are very strong. You should feel proud."

He paused for a long time, and I held him close to me, patting his shoulder. Prayer flags snapped in the wind around the camp.

"Twenty-one thousand feet," he repeated as if trying to make some meaning out of that number. I wiped freezing tears from my cheeks with my sleeve.

We hugged and said our good-byes, and I listened to the sounds of their boots crunching away as Jeff and the other guides led Tashi, Kyila, and Sonam down the mountain.

Back in the mess tent, I tried to rally the team that remained. Tenzin, Gyenshen, and Dachung were still feeling strong and optimistic. The summit of Lhakpa Ri was less than two thousand feet above us, through a crevasse field, across a short glacier, onto the ridge, and straight to the summit. The plan was to set up one last high camp in the glacial basin. Charley said the summit could be seen right above us.

"It was never a guarantee that all the kids would make it to the top," I said again. "Getting a few of the team, even one, to the summit would be a successful expedition."

"There is nothing left to prove," Sabriye insisted. "The kids wanted to make new friends, to be with us, to be with Erik, and they've done that. For me, the most important thing left is that the kids learn about solidarity. That we should look out for the weakest."

"So let's all get out of here," Paul seconded.

That afternoon, the remaining guides geared up and left camp on a scouting venture. We hoped there would be an alternative bump on the Rongbuk glacier, closer and less strenuous than Lhakpa Ri that could serve as an alternative summit, but no luck. The other ridges and towers were much too steep and technical. That night, there was more bad news when Paul began going downhill with AMS, acute mountain sickness. We all organized another evacuation, and Paul went down. Then, amazingly, Michael returned to camp, having taken Toan down and returned all the way back to ABC—a twenty-six-mile trip that took him thirty-six hours with only an hour of sleep. It was a feat of incredible strength and fortitude. He said that the latest weather report on his GPS wasn't good, and he'd pressed through exhaustion because he wanted to help the team. It looked like a big storm would come in sometime the next afternoon. With the three evacuations, we'd lost too much time, and with the loss of four guides, we'd lost too much expertise for our safety margin. As a precursor, the temperature had already plummeted to zero degrees. Even in my thickest down parka, I shivered and had to constantly swing my feet to keep warm. I knew we were done. There would be no summit for any of us.

I left the mess tent and sat down outside with a cup of tea. I felt broken. Everything caught up to me, all the wreckage, all our objectives that had hideously backfired. We were supposed to be helping these kids, making them understand their dreams were real. Instead, they felt like failures. I felt like a failure too.

After an hour, I walked over to Sabriye's tent and sat down in her entranceway. "What do you think we should do at this point?" I asked.

Sabriye thought for a couple of minutes. I could tell she was weighing all the possibilities. "As I have been walking," she said, "I listened to a waterfall that created a soft breeze. It was a rain of cool spray against our faces. There were foaming brooks and meadows with sweet and bitter and even spicy herb smells, as well as quite a few fresh, pungent-smelling yak piles that my foot squished in," she added. "I've heard eagles screaming above and yaks bellowing. One put his head in my tent, you know." She laughed. "There was even a herd of antelope galloping away as we rounded a bend. I lay awake at night, listening to the thunderous rumblings of distant rockslides and the wind when it whistles through the narrow openings in the canyons. It sounded like a ghost. There are so many other beautiful things besides the summit to experience. Perhaps even more beautiful."

It seemed like such a long time ago when I had told Sabriye that the mountains offered up gifts, that you had to keep your heart open to them, but I had held a secret bias that the summit was the most prized of those gifts, that standing on top together would solidify their dreams and make the kids understand that those dreams were real. But I hadn't really kept my own heart open to the idea that after all our struggle and hard work, the summit may not lie on the top of Lhakpa Ri, that it might have to reside in another place entirely. There had been so much wreckage in our path, but I still had Gyenshen, Tenzin, and Dachung to consider. Was it still possible to take the splintered remnants of this team and forge something meaningful? I thought about the cold spray on Sabriye's face and the cry of an eagle above. I thought about the pointed spears of ice left in the wake of the retreating glacier and Jeff's rock hitting the chandelier of ice, the collage of sounds brilliant and distinct, like the colors of a rainbow. "*Ki bu la*," Sonam had said, like she was whispering a secret. Perhaps there was an alternative summit, I thought. During our scouting venture the afternoon before, we'd passed near a miniature version of the Khumbu Icefall, which lay on the other side of the mountain in Nepal. I'd crossed through it many times on my way to the summit of Mount Everest. "I have an idea," I said to Sabriye, my voice coming alive again.

The next morning, the storm had still not materialized. The sun shone, and the wind had actually abated. We hiked twenty minutes up a short scree hill, and on top lay a magnificent world of ice, just on the edge of the glacier. Weaving through it were deep canyons with tall walls surrounding us. The kids took off their gloves and ran their hands across the faces, some as smooth as glass. Farther in, it turned into a thick jungle, with giant icicles hanging from the walls and tree-size pinnacles protruding into the sky. There were jumbly formations shaped like castles with holes for windows and others like the snouts of dragons with mouthfuls of jagged teeth. Other structures were delicate and crisscrossing like antlers, and some resembled fish. Some felt like humans with blobs for heads and long, curving arms. I imagined it all looking like Superman's Fortress of Solitude in one of my favorite movies from the '80s when I could still see. When Superman was facing a big decision, he'd escape there to reflect. It was a blind person's ice palace, the mountain's gift of touch and sound.

Charley took Sabriye's hand and placed it in a small cave-like opening. Inside, she felt wafer-thin leaves of ice that broke away when her fingers touched them. As each piece collapsed, it sounded like she was playing a frozen xylophone. Everything around us crackled, clinked, and crunched, and Sabriye smiled for the first time in several days.

The boys followed each other, squeezing through narrow passageways and crawling through expansive caverns, howling and listening to the amazing acoustics. Then they used their ice axes to climb to the tops of the huge formations and made up imaginative stories. Gyenshen straddled an ice elephant. "Get out of my way!" he yelled to Tenzin, who drove an ice chariot. "I'm off to slay the lake serpent."

Dachung trotted along behind on an ice camel, shouting back, "We'll attack from all sides!"

They wore elaborate robes, woven from silky threads of ice. They broke off long icicles and used them as swords and lances, fighting off their invisible enemies. Gyenshen placed a hard chunk of snow on top of his head and proclaimed himself king. The three played in their frozen world until the sun sank low in the sky. Finally, Tenzin climbed to the top of the palace and wielded his ice axe. When he came back down, he said quietly, "Because I could not climb to the summit, I wrote my name in the snow. And in the future, I will come back to climb, and I will try again."

The next morning, the storm hit for real, with wind and blowing snow, and we waited it out in the kitchen tent, huddling together, sitting on our duffels of provisions that had dwindled substantially. The kitchen tent was by far the warmest, with the big kerosene stove burning, but it was still one of the coldest mountain storms I'd ever endured. When the yaks arrived again, we descended in a foot of fresh snow, pushing out all thirteen miles to base camp in a long day. I arrived at the teahouse a few minutes before Sabriye and the kids, and when she came through the door into the smoky room, I couldn't resist teasing her. "You smashed the record," I called out. "The first blind female one-day descent from ABC to base camp. Congratulations!" Sabriye managed a laugh as I gave her and the boys a big bear hug.

We met up with the girls, Tashi, and Paul at the farm in Shigatse, and it was an emotional reunion. The weather felt tropical compared to the frigid mountains, and I was filled with relief that the team was safe and healthy. Everyone crowded around as the boys excitedly recounted their adventures in the Ice Palace, and I smiled because the stories seemed to be accompanied by a good amount of reenacting. They ran around, crouching, crawling, and climbing hand over hand into the air. They trotted, galloped, cracked the reins, and swung their arms around crazily, parrying and thrusting their swords against imaginary foes. "It was a magic palace," Dachung said. "Gyenshen was the king; Tenzin was the prince . . ." He hesitated. "And I was the princess." He giggled.

We all made the long drive together back to the center in Lhasa, and the homecoming was repeated with the little kids who swarmed around our team and greeted them reverently like returning heroes. The boisterous little ones quieted down and hung on every word as the six teens described trains of fifty furry yaks jangling up the trail, snowball fights in such thin air that you couldn't catch your breath, frozen lakes that popped and groaned with the calls of mountain spirits, and bridges of ice spanning over deep crevasses.

Then Gyenshen stepped forward and began to tell of the Ice Palace. The children gasped and sighed with envy. After he finished, he sidled up to me.

"Lhakpa Ri was the summit," he said softly, "but the Ice Palace was the blind summit."

I had started this journey with a letter from a stranger on the other side of the world, and it had carried me through a challenging journey and ultimately to this destination. It had also brought us all together. I remembered the actual words that had drawn me here: "Gyenshen is probably the only one of his village who knows that the world is round, and that one can communicate through just a wire. He is able to tell the other children of the village that 'iron yaks' are Toyota Land Cruisers that drink gasoline instead of water."

With Sabriye and Paul's help, he was also the only one in his village who could decipher tactile bumps beneath his fingers, who could speak three different languages, and the only one who could define a dream. And now he could tell the village children that once he had discovered a magical palace high up on a mountainside, where he was a king who had ridden an elephant made entirely of ice.

"It was a good summit," I finally said, "a very good summit," and I felt the tears beginning to roll down my cheeks again. Suddenly, I felt the exhaustion of the three weeks pour over me, and I sat down on a bench in the courtyard. Tashi sat down on my lap; Tenzin piled on top of Tashi; Gyenshen climbed to the top, then Dachung, and finally the two girls. They were all shifting, elbowing each other, and exploding with laughter. "The boys had their summit," Sonam called out, "but this is my summit." And although I was being crushed, and the bench was nearly buckling, I felt the pressures of the expedition melting away. I laughed right along with the kids and felt truly happy.

As we untangled from the pile, Kyila announced, "We all want to know if you will come back to take us to the top of Mount Everest."

"I thought you didn't like climbing," I responded playfully.

"We love climbing!" they all yelled in unison.

"You can't climb mountains," I teased. "You're blind."

"We can do anything," tiny Sonam shot back, slugging me in the arm.

That evening, Sabriye and Paul had two surprises for us. First, the entire school of fifty blind children, from ages five to nineteen, performed an exuberant and near-perfect rendition of "Happy Together." We all sang along, Kyila and Sonam of course singing the loudest. "Now for the second surprise," Sabriye said excitedly. The kids, Paul, and Sabriye led me and the guides down a steep, narrow stairway into the basement of the school. "The lighting's horrible down here," Michael remarked.

"Don't worry," Sabriye responded. "It gets even better."

She instructed each of the Westerners to line up and grab the arm of the blind student he or she had been guiding. Then each student led his or her sighted partner through a slip in a curtain. "It's pitch black in here," Jeff said. "I can't see a damn thing."

"That is the point," Sabriye replied cheerfully. "We call this Dancing in the Dark."

"We've customized this room," Paul added. "There's padding around the pillars and walls so you can't hurt yourself."

"I have to admit," Jeff commented, "I'm a little freaked out right now."

"This is really cool," Charley said with awe.

I felt around, and I could feel the padding surrounding, even on the low ceiling, in case someone jumped up. One of the kids cranked up a stereo, and the bass vibrated through the tight room, thumping off the walls, the roof, through the floors. The sound rose up, and it was no longer '60s Motown but thumping Euro-techno dance music. Predictably, Jeff used the occasion to pinch Sabriye's butt with anonymity, and she immediately called out, "I know that was you, Jeff."

It didn't take very long for everyone to let go of their fears and allow the darkness to take their inhibitions. Soon, we were spinning and swirling around each other in a tight circle. It was a little cheesy, but when Bruce Springsteen's "Dancing in the Dark" came over the speakers, we all cheered and sang along, bumping, laughing, sweating, and dancing in the dark late into the night.

4

ALCHEMY

Still jet-lagged from Tibet, I was relaxing on my couch in a half daze when I got a call from an old friend. Mark Wellman was a world-famous adventurer and a personal hero of mine who had skied across the rugged Sierra Nevada in California and the heavily crevassed Ruth Glacier of Alaska. His most well-known feats, however, were the stunning ascents he had completed on some of the most difficult rock faces in North America. Mark was also paralyzed from the waist down.

Recently, Mark and filmmaker Eric Perlman had produced a series of documentaries featuring a host of unusual athletes: a leg-amputee surfer, a paraplegic hang glider, and a quadriplegic, Larry Boden, who sailed independently by using an ingenious "sip 'n' puff" system through which he lightly blew out or drew in air through a mouth tube to maneuver the mainsail and jib. "I went from a viewer to a doer," Larry had said.

Mark was now planning some kind of festival and wanted me to be a part of it. Honestly, he could have asked me to wash his dirty socks, and I would have agreed readily, but fortunately what he had in mind sounded way more intriguing. "I'm calling it 'No Barriers,'" he said. "I want to change people's perceptions of what's possible, but not in a gentle way. We need to come together to blast through one barrier after the next, until there are none left. It'll be a gimp revolution."

I chuckled. The word *gimp* was one of Mark's favorites, one that, only by virtue of being blind or in a chair, could you get away with using without being scorned.

"Sounds ambitious," I replied, picturing Mark in his wheelchair, leading an army of gimps—surfers and sailors and hang gliders—and Mark like the giant Kool-Aid guy, cranking forward and exploding through a solid wall, the boards and plaster splintering around him.

When Mark was twenty-two years old, he was hurrying down the Seven Gables, a thirteen thousand–foot peak in the Sierras, jumping from rock to rock, trying to beat the darkness that was coming on quickly. A rock shifted under his foot, pitching him forward, sending him somersaulting a hundred feet down the steep talus. He landed with a sickening crack on a small ledge above a sheer, one thousand–foot vertical drop. Blood poured from the back of his head, and his clothes were shredded. His body was battered, with electric shocks of pain shooting through his chest and arms. But worst of all, he obsessed over his legs that he could no longer feel.

Mark's climbing partner covered him with a pair of pants and a sweater, staunched his bleeding head wound, gave him some water and food, and made the difficult decision to go for help, leaving Mark alone high on the mountain with darkness coming on. For an agonizingly long night, in which he worried about freezing to death, and most of the next day, Mark lay on his back, waiting for the rescue party, or for death to take him, whichever came first. He hadn't died in the fall, but after being rescued, the diagnosis that he'd never walk again felt worse than death. "My hospital room was on the sixth floor," Mark said. "If I could have crawled to the window, I would have jumped for sure."

But then another patient showed up. He was a quadriplegic in his late twenties who'd broken his neck eleven years earlier and was now back for a bone spur surgery. He told Mark that he drove race cars, including a souped-up Mustang, using hand controls. He was confident and moved around the room in a sporty, lightweight wheelchair. "I have no time for self-pity," he said to Mark. "It's all up to you. If you choose to live, get off your ass and live. If you choose to die, lie down. Don't get out of bed."

Mark chose to live, inspired to attack his painful rehabilitation with drive and purpose. He built up his shoulders, back, and arms to such a degree, he eventually resumed climbing again with a special rope ascension system that no one had ever seen before. Seven years later, Wellman climbed the infamous three thousand–foot rock face of El Capitan with his new climbing partner, Mike Corbett. He'd inched his way up the vertical wall with the force of his will and the massive power of his upper body.

To thousands of people like me around the country, Mark became an overnight hero. He'd met presidents and wherever he went was accorded the respect of a visiting head of state. He was even lauded by the Paralympics when he opened the games by climbing a 120-foot rope up the Olympic tower with a torch strapped to his legs. Reaching the top, Mark touched the flaming torch to the Olympic cauldron and set the night ablaze to the ecstatic cheers of sixty thousand fans.

As I listened to Mark describe his latest project, I thought back to our last adventure together, one of the strangest and most magical experiences of my life. Mark had been making another film and wanted to lead it off in a one-of-a-kind way. "Well-meaning people use words like *physically challenged*," he said, "even *differently abled* or *handi-capable*. But the term I like is *gimp*. Among my friends, it's a badge of honor. So I want to begin my next film with an 'all-gimp climb.'"

Hugh Herr would be our third partner. Hugh was another legend with an illustrious climbing career. On the surface quiet and introspective, when he talked about climbing or the doctorate program at Harvard in biophysics he had just finished, his soft words sparked with intensity. That intensity had burned his whole life, giving him the tenacity to power through immense challenges but also contributing to his life's lowest point. When Hugh was seventeen years old, already a brilliant rock and ice climber, he and a friend had pushed to the top of a steep ice gully called O'Dell's on New Hampshire's Mount Washington in the midst of winter storm conditions. They decided to try for the summit, but after going only a few hundred yards, the winds increased to ninety miles per hour, and temperatures plunged below zero degrees. They turned around to descend, but in the whiteout they went the wrong way, accidentally entering a vast wilderness area called the Great Gulf. They were hopelessly disoriented.

They walked for what seemed forever until Hugh broke through snow and ice, plunging him thigh deep into a river. His boots and feet were soaked and soon froze. He told me it was crazy looking down at his feet that he couldn't feel, willing them to move and realizing the circuit between his brain and his legs was broken. His legs refused to respond. He'd try to take a step and simply fall on his face. Their only choice was to hunker beneath some boulders, covered with a few spruce boughs, and wait for help. As the storm raged, mountain search-and-rescue teams scoured the area for three full days, and miraculously Hugh and his climbing partner were found by a snowshoer who happened by their makeshift shelter. After a difficult helicopter rescue in dangerous winds, they both lived.

Doctors confirmed the first news, something he had already feared. Both legs had suffered frostbite and would need to be amputated below the knees. His family told him the second tragic news. During the search, a young member of the rescue team named Albert Dow was caught in an avalanche and killed. Albert was a beloved climber and resident of North Conway, New Hampshire, and Hugh became deeply depressed and angered that his poor decisions had cost a human life.

Hugh had believed with certainty that he would die on the mountain. When he survived, he became fueled by the memory of Albert Dow, and he vowed not only to walk again but to climb and maybe climb better than he ever had before. The prosthetics then available were crude, passive limbs unsuited to the mountainous outdoor adventures that Hugh envisioned. So, having an engineer's mind, he began experimenting in a machine shop at a local vocational school, attaching composite polymer, wood, and rubber-coated feet to aluminum legs, with padded suction-cup sockets affixed to his stumps. He tested different-size legs and various versions of climbing feet. One pair had squared-off toes that could balance on rock edges the width of a dime; another set were pie shaped and could wedge into vertical cracks; a third pair were thin blades that could stand inside shallow grooves in the face. Less than a year after he'd had both of his legs amputated, he was scaling routes more difficult than he'd ever been able to climb on his biological legs. Even more surprising was that, despite being viewed as a pariah in the town of North Conway, Hugh eventually faced his colossal mistake head-on and moved back to the little town for a time.

At a rest-stop diner near Moab, Utah, Mark described our route—a steep, five hundred–foot sandstone tower jutting fiercely out of the desert. I had heard of the Ancient Art tower, one of the desert-climbing classics known for its corkscrew summit. Mark was a laid-back climbing bum who laughed easily, and I liked him immediately. He lent help just like he laughed, with an easy confidence. He wheeled behind me in the diner and said, "Big scary sign ready to clock you in the head on the left," or while I was eating my dinner, Mark chuckled and said, "Dude, you're about to eat the garnish." He knew what it was like to need help, especially in his days recovering in the hospital. Mark wasn't shy about receiving help either. As I sat in the passenger seat of his truck, he'd ask me to jump out and pull his chair out of the back. I learned to unfold it, pop the wheel on, and place it near the driver's side so he could use his arms to shimmy on.

Along the mile-and-a-half trail to the base of the rock face, I got the privilege of carrying Mark on my back, piggyback style, his legs resting on my curled arms as they strained to jab my trekking poles out in front of us. With all 165 pounds of him on my back, his head protruding over my shoulder and his muscular arms clutching my neck, we were an out-of-control video game in which this sputtering, slightly defective vehicle tottered and swayed while Mark desperately worked the joystick. Knowing that if I bit the dust, he would too, Mark's directions were urgent. "Deep ruts in the trail." I jerked to the left to avoid them. "Cliff on the left!" I jerked back right and bounced jarringly through the ruts. "Whoa! Rock straight ahead." With Mark's directions and the sound of Hugh's footsteps a few feet ahead, we managed to progress up the trail. Near the base, Mark directed us to a large boulder where I turned around and lowered him onto it with relief.

As the three of us sat side by side, I listened intently as Mark and Hugh shared their epic stories of loss on camera. I had gone blind from a boring genetic disease and, at that moment, longed for my own cool disaster story. When they turned to me, the words began to spill out of my mouth. "I was five hundred feet up on an ice face," I started, building steam as I went. "At that very moment, two giant stalactites simultaneously broke off and plunged into my eye sockets. I hung there, flailing in pain for . . . four days until help arrived!" They both hesitated and then laughed awkwardly. With Mark's cameraman shooting video, Mark said, "My accident was in 1982."

"That's weird," Hugh said. "Mine was too."

And again, I plunged forward, blurting out, "Mine too," and waited through the next few moments of uncomfortable silence as the cameras rolled.

Hugh then pulled a small tool kit out of his pack and proceeded to pop off his prosthetic legs, unscrew his walking feet, and screw on his smaller plastic and rubber climbing feet. He made it seem as normal and commonplace as changing shoes. Mark donned his chaps and assembled his rope ascension system. I laid out the ropes and slung my harness with gear, and up we went. Hugh led the five-pitch climb. I seconded, followed by Mark. As I played out rope for Hugh, I heard him make delicate face moves up thin, sloping holds. He told me that he had learned to feel the rock through his feet.

"I'm a better climber now," Hugh laughed down from the face, "because I'm lighter, about twenty pounds to be exact. In fact, when I first started climbing with prosthetics, I was making it onto the cover of magazines like *Outside*. Some people wrote that I should be banned from entering climbing competitions, because I was cheating. They thought my prosthetics gave me an unfair mechanical advantage. When people started complaining about my unfair advantage, that's when I knew I was back on top."

Hugh's prosthetic legs were designed to suction onto his stumps. His climbing tights acted as another precaution to hold them on while he dangled in midair. "I'm glad you're wearing a helmet!" Hugh yelled down. "My climbing tights have a rip in them, and I'm not sure if my left leg's gonna hold. It's happened to me before. I was climbing Skytop, in the Shawangunks, working on a new route; I took a fall and spun hard into the wall. One of my feet snapped off and fell a long way, clattering in the boulders below. A freaked-out hiker down at the base retrieved it for me, and I named the route 'Footloose and Fancy-Free.' So if you hear something whizzing past your head, it's probably my leg."

On the top of the first pitch, we were starting to feel comfortable around each other, and I asked Hugh if he minded if I felt his prosthetic legs. He didn't, and I touched the thin metal shafts like stilts. I knocked on them with my knuckles, and they made a hollow sound. "When I was seventeen, I was five eleven, but with these things, I can be whatever height I want. On an overhanging, gymnastic climb, I can be short, so I can crunch my body up. On a blank face, with the holds far apart, I can make myself as tall as I want." Hugh told me he liked to shock people at weddings by extending his legs as far as they would go, so he was about seven feet tall. Then he'd hit the dance floor, grabbing various unsuspecting women and throwing them over his shoulder and swooping them through the air.

The day was growing colder. I wished I had brought my gloves. I yelled down to Mark, who was just beginning to climb, "You got an extra pair of gloves? It's so freaking cold, Hugh can't even feel his legs." Hugh humphed, and I got the impression that my joke wasn't that original.

With that, Hugh yanked up the rope, and I started climbing. Reaching the top of the pitch, Hugh and I secured one end of the rope to an anchor in the rock, so that the rope dangled down to Mark. "We're finally doing it!" Mark yelled up a few feet off the ground. I could hear the rope twanging with Mark's weight. He had invented an ingenious climbing system. He wore a body harness attached to an ascender, a mechanical device that bit into the rope like teeth, making it possible to slide up but not down. Above, Mark used another ascender to attach a modified pull-up bar to the rope. He'd then slide the bar up, and when it locked off, he'd hang from it and do a pull-up to its base. Afterward, he would hang from his ascender, rest for a second, and repeat the whole process. With the stretchy rope and the wobbly bar, each pull up only gained Mark about seven inches. He'd climbed El Capitan in this same way, doing over seven thousand pull-ups in eight days.

Around Mark's legs, he wore a pair of ballistic nylon chaps to protect them from the continuous abrasive sliding against the rock. Surprisingly, for Mark, the steeper the climb, the easier it became, since that meant the rope was mostly suspended in space, away from the rock, eliminating the added resistance of sliding and scraping. But the second pitch of Ancient Art forced us to climb inside a narrow, three-sided chimney containing a hodgepodge of deep grooves, overhanging bulges, and needle-sharp spears of rock. Inside the chimney, Mark yelled up, "What a scrape fest!" and he couldn't have been more right. Mark constantly had to stop, reach down, and free his feet from an unending series of tight slots. Since he couldn't feel his legs, he'd heave on the pull-up bar to no avail, look down with growing frustration, and see that one of his feet was wedged again. When he finally moved up, his rope would rub against the loose sandstone, sending down a spray of pebbles and dirt that bounced off his face and collected in his eyes, nose, and his open mouth. Halfway up the chimney, I heard Mark grunt. As a paraplegic, Mark had no bladder control, so he wore a pee bag strapped to his leg. While struggling up the wall, the bag had ripped off and spilled all over him. Covered in his own urine, his hands and elbows torn and bleeding, his face marred with grit, Mark just kept hauling himself up the sheer sandstone face.

Finally, above the chimney, Mark dragged himself onto our ledge and said, breathing hard, "Wow! I'm pumped, but it sure is good to be out of my wheelchair."

The top of the climb was even worse for Mark. A long rock ridge, as narrow as the saddle of a horse, spiraled to the top like a corkscrew. I put my hands flat on the middle of the ridge and, with my legs straddling the sides, shimmied across. Mark laid his whole body flat on the ridge and pulled his way across, adding significantly to his assortment of scrapes and gouges. Beyond the ridge was a formidable obstacle—a flat, protruding shelf of rock about chin height that climbers call the Diving Board. I reached up and laid my hands on the edge, then used my legs to spring myself up and give me the momentum needed to heave my body over. I honestly couldn't perceive how Mark would do it. I got ready to say, "Good enough. We'll just call this the summit," but fifteen minutes later, I heard the familiar scrape and the sound of Mark's heavy breathing. "I've gotta get in shape," he panted as he arrived at the large boulder that signified the very top. "Not bad for three gimps, huh?"

Each of us was incomplete, missing eyes, legs, even the use of half a body, yet I had carried Mark on my back up the trail; on the face, Mark had told me where to reach when the holds were just out of range, and Hugh had led the pitches using his miniature rubber feet. Together, we were a brotherhood, like those flawed, dejected, pimply characters I'd read about in comic books who came together to form an invincible fighting force. We were the

X-Men. We were Teenage Mutant Ninja Turtles. Even better than that, together we had become Super Gimps.

The wind blew, and it snowed heavier than before. "What does it look like?" I asked, waving my hand out into space.

"We're at the highest point, as far as I can see," said Hugh in his quiet, understated voice. "The desert floor is flat, with hundreds of sharp reddish-orange pinnacles piercing the sky."

I thought about those pinnacles, rock eroded and sculpted by wind and rain over thousands of years. The result of that process was sometimes miraculous. The three of us had only spent a couple of days together, but I already felt a deep connection, born not from our triumphs, but from our common experience of loss and challenge, of being pulverized by those forces, and the arduous journey of reemerging.

The experience had awakened me to that process, to all the gritty sensory images that lay beneath the summit: the wild roller coaster of a blind/para/piggyback team, the chalky taste of desert sand grinding between your teeth, the violent scraping of rock tearing bloody gouges into skin you couldn't feel, and the acceptance of a bursting pee bag and the stench of urine. I wanted to understand the impetus behind all that flailing and suffering. It had to be something deep and internal.

The question brought me back to the visceral memory of being thirteen years old and watching Terry Fox limp and shuffle across Canada on a clunky prosthetic leg. The miles had taken a terrible toll on his body, on his blistered stump. His thin face and his burning eyes had been the last clear image I had taken with me into blindness. In the hospital, Terry watched children dying of cancer around him, but that darkness hadn't ultimately destroyed him. Instead he'd gathered it up, harnessed it, and converted it into something else. I felt like those burning eyes had reflected something deeper, a blazing internal light. In college history, I'd studied the Middle Ages when medieval alchemists toiled to turn lead into gold; they had never succeeded. Now, I wondered if there was another kind of alchemy, turning pain into purpose, darkness into light. It was a never-ending fuel source to struggle forward. A rare few had learned to tap into it, but for many, that light had dwindled and even flickered out. I wondered if you could grow it, nurture it, and ignite it in others . . .

"Hugh's already agreed," I heard distantly. "So are you in?" Mark's voice came back into focus. "Dude, are you still there?"

Not having heard any of the details, I finally said, "Yeah. I'm in!"

Later, I was delighted to learn the details. The No Barriers Summit would be held in a storied place, in the heart of the Italian Dolomites, Cortina d'Ampezzo. This was the birthplace of climbing itself, where legends like Walter Bonatti grew up and trained to climb giants like K2, the second-tallest peak in the world. And it was where Reinhold Messner had gained the experience to eventually become the first person to climb the fourteen eight thousand–meter peaks of the world without oxygen. I even convinced Ellie to come along with Emma, who was a toddler now. We'd make it our first family vacation.

When I arrived in Cortina, we had dinner with Mark, Hugh, and the many supporters who had helped organize the event. Jim Goldsmith was a retired businessman who had met Mark at an event where he spoke about his historic climb of El Capitan. Jim was enthralled by Mark's message, and the two of them had begun brainstorming. The idea had eventually led to this region of Italy where Jim had ties through family. I met the members of the city council who had invited us over to stage the summit and bring disability awareness to the community. Cortina was a beautiful resort town, yet it was poorly designed for those with disabilities. The cobblestoned sidewalks were narrow, twisting, and had few wheelchair ramps into buildings. Elevators had no Braille labels. Hotel room showers were cramped, slippery, and treacherous for those with mobility issues. And although Cortina had been the location of the 1956 Winter Olympics, the chairlifts were inaccessible, and the lift operators were untrained in how to help. The result was that people with disabilities didn't venture out, especially into the mountains.

That week Hugh, Mark, and I gave talks and showed our adventure documentaries. We introduced Cortina to an array of adaptive sports like goal ball, a popular sport for the blind in which you dove for a ball with a bell inside and tried to huck it past the opposing team. It was all about hand-to-ear coordination. We showcased sled hockey in which paraplegics on sleds propelled themselves across the ice using two sticks, one side with curved blades and the other side with sharp metal teeth for pushing the sleds.

The second day, Jim Goldsmith, who had written a trekking guide to the Dolomites, led a few of us on a hike to a high mountain hut called a *Rifugio* in Italian. Jim was an amateur geologist, and he described in detail the Dolomite rock, a kind of limestone, porous and filled with a calcite that painted the rock with distinct hues of rose, yellow, and grays. He described the ring of high, jagged peaks, spires and towers and the continuous, sheer walls— some nearly three thousand vertical feet above us. Near the top, he took my finger and pointed it directly above us to the rock route Mark, Hugh, and I would be doing in a couple of days to close out the festival. It was the Cinque Torri (meaning *Five Towers* in English), a formation of five distinct limestone towers of varying heights and shapes that ruptured the skyline.

When it was time for our demonstration, everyone rode chairlifts up to the Cinque Torri despite a sketchy weather day in the Dolomites. Hugh and I lifted Mark piggyback style off the lift and carried him along the trail to the climb. As we ascended the five hundred–foot sheer, vertical limestone, we climbed into mist and clouds, and by the top it had begun to pour. This time, however, we weren't climbing alone; we had an audience of a hundred observing through the giant bay window of the nearby Rifugio. When we rappelled down and entered through the large wooden door, we were surrounded by a group of children with Down syndrome, kids in wheelchairs, and some on prosthetic legs. They gathered around us, crowding in to check out Mark's pull-up equipment and Hugh's prosthetic feet. Jim said, for most of the kids, it was their first time in the mountains. We laughed and high-fived, trying to communicate despite the language barrier. It was a special moment, but I couldn't stop thinking about these children watching us climb the Cinque Torri through the bay window like I had watched Terry Fox through a TV screen many years ago. It was a good start, I thought, but it felt like only the faintest beginning of something bigger. I wasn't satisfied with these children standing inside, separated from all the adventure. They should have been outside, running and wheeling, soaked by rain and covered in dirt, right in the thick of it. I already knew this idea of No Barriers wasn't just about disability awareness, accessibility, or even extreme sports. No Barriers was about bridging that dark expanse between the dry, cozy Rifugio and the wild mountaintop, and all the alchemy needed along the way. It was tantalizing to ponder all that it could become, but the prospect felt a long way off, like Mark scraping and bleeding toward a distant summit.

After everything concluded, we got together in the lobby of my hotel to debrief. Mark, always direct, cut to the chase. "This was a good start, but No Barriers is not a spectator sport. As my old friend Larry Boden says, 'It's about going from a viewer to a doer.' So I don't think we're finished here."

5

DÉSÉQUILIBRE

The next summer, July 2005, we were back in Cortina for our second install-
ment of the No Barriers Summit. It was great to return to the stunning mountain setting, the village situated in a natural amphitheater ringed by jagged
peaks. This year, Hugh Herr had seriously ratcheted up the technology and
innovation, and he'd be running a whole new component called "Technology
Meets Physical Disability." Hugh was now leading a major biomechanical research lab at MIT, and he'd invited scientists and representatives from companies like Össur and Ottobock, both making advanced computer-controlled
prosthetic limbs. All the technologies would be featured at our expo tent in the
village center. The year before, we'd mostly been about showcasing, but this
time, we were shifting into full-on active participation. Attendees would get
the chance to test equipment and ideas and see what was possible.

Some of the clinics seemed more like science fiction. Mike May, a blind
technologist, led tours on the mountain trails outside town, using a talking
GPS device he invented that speaks with a computer-synthesized voice. He'd
previously plotted waypoints at intersecting trails, picnic benches, and a scenic waterfall, and those auditory outputs guided the large group of blind
hikers. At the end of the tour, he said, "Identifying beautiful waterfalls is
one thing, but next year's model will be even better. It will identify beautiful
women."

Mark Wellman was just off another adventure, a six-day mountain bike ride of the 103-mile White Rim Road in Canyonlands National Park. In places, the trail was so soft and sandy his wheels spun out, and he had to drag himself through the desert on his elbows while towing his mountain bike behind him. Mark had brought some of these three-wheeled, hand-cranked bikes and led outings with other paraplegics over rocky trails no wheelchair could ever access. A group called DRAFT (Disability Rights Advocates for Technology) brought Segways adapted with special seats for people with mobility and balance issues.

As I tapped my white cane toward the expo, I could hear the group whirring by and whooping as they performed 360s in the parking lot. To broaden the appeal beyond physical pursuits, we'd even invited a well-known artist to the No Barriers experience.

That morning, we all convened at the expo tent where Hugh Herr gave a short presentation to formally kick off the summit. We sat in folding metal chairs as he took the podium. His voice was low and measured. "There is no such thing as a physically disabled person," Hugh began. "There are only physically disabled technologies." He let this heady proclamation sink in, and then he went on. "What are the characteristics of an innovative person or an innovative community? The No Barriers framework that you'll see and experience here over the next few days is all about exploration. At MIT, I've had straight-A students, but when they get work in the research laboratory, they're paralyzed, because they view an unexpected outcome as failure. When you look at the great creative minds throughout history, there's a characteristic of fearlessness."

There was a collective quiet in the room. People leaned in, listening to Hugh's soft voice growing in volume and confidence.

"Thomas Edison, for example, did not care if he was laughed at or if people thought his ideas were stupid or silly. That fearlessness enabled him to try things, to conduct experiments that a normal person would never try. One of his experiments was to take a rubber tube, and place one end of the tube near his ear or forehead, and the other end of the tube at the base of a pendulum. The experiment was to see whether he could think and move the pendulum. Even in his day—probably especially in his day—people would think that was very, very silly."

The group chuckled at the image, and Hugh waited for the laughter to subside.

"But we have a representative here in this tent from a group called Cyberkinetics, whose new BrainGate System does essentially what Edison was trying to do—to turn thoughts into actions. The technology will allow people with traumatic spinal cord injury and loss of limbs to communicate and control common, everyday functions literally through thought. This is happening—as are many other remarkable advances that you'll see in this exposition area—because of that childlike exploration. I believe that it's important to explore, and if the world turns out to be different than you expected, to view that as adventure and not failure."

We all applauded, and Hugh closed by inviting everyone to visit the booths and talk to the scientists and product developers. He encouraged the end users, those who would actually be putting the technology into daily use, to engage in dialogue with the creators, because No Barriers was the only event that brought these groups together in one place. Hugh's talk made me consider all the days he had spent in the machine shop, intricately shaping wooden feet and slowly layering on the stealth-rubber coatings until they were works of functional art. I thought of Mark experimenting with different bars and grips for the pull-up system he'd conceived. Their initial inspiration to climb again had been followed by a lot of trial and error to develop the right tools and techniques. And now we had all these elements here in Cortina.

As the audience dispersed, I headed over toward Hugh. I flicked my cane in front of me, found the table Hugh was behind, and greeted him with a handshake. Though we'd climbed Ancient Art together and I felt a deep connection with him, he wasn't much of a hugger, at least not in public when he was in his professional mode.

"This is what I've been working on," Hugh said, handing me a solid, heavy device that was about a foot in length, four inches by four inches, rounded and circular at the top. It was smooth and dense and felt sort of like a car part.

"That's the Rheo," he said, his voice rising with enthusiasm as he described his creation. "The first artificially intelligent knee." He guided my hand to the top, rounded section. "The muscle, if you will, is up here, and there's a magnetic field inside that changes the resistance as a person walks and moves. The part you're holding, the knee, gets bolted to a socket interface above that attaches to the user's residual leg or stump. And a pylon and foot attaches to the bottom of the knee. Inside, it has a microprocessor that responds to input at one thousand times per second, integrated sensors, and a fluid actuator, all allowing the user to walk more naturally, even over rough terrain, and up and down hills. It's a major breakthrough—a bionic knee."

I laughed, then did my best voice-over impression: "A man, barely alive. We can rebuild him. Better, stronger, faster." Like most American boys in the mid-'70s, I'd been a fan of *The Six Million Dollar Man* series in the years before I lost my sight.

"That's right," Hugh said with a modest laugh. "Electromagnetic artificial body parts. That's bionics, and that's what we've been focusing on at the MIT Media Lab. Only problem is that, with all the R&D, he'd be closer to the Sixty Million Dollar Man."

I handed the Rheo knee back to him, very carefully, totally impressed. I thought how far his designs had come since the first legs and feet he'd created and could not imagine what he would come up with next.

"These are going to change lives," he said. "With the number of vets we have coming home injured—especially those with above-the-knee amputations—these knees will be instrumental in getting them up and out of wheelchairs and even walking with a natural gait."

I could feel people pressing in behind me, wanting to talk with Hugh, so I moved on.

In the far corner of the expo tent, Andy Parkin was displaying his paintings and sculptures and giving a talk. I could hear his distinctive Yorkshire dialect that I had to work to understand—he pronounced the name *Doug* as *Duke*, the word *love* as *loov*.

I'd met Andy the year before, while I was climbing Les Droites, a mountain face above Chamonix, France. We didn't get the chance to spend a lot of time together then—just a dinner and a quick tour of his workshop and studio—but I was immediately drawn to his passion and drive. Climbing friends of mine told me that in the early '80s, Andy had been one of the most respected alpine soloists in the world, known for taking on extremely difficult and dangerous routes throughout the European Alps, South America, and the Himalayas. In 1995, he'd won the coveted Piolets d'Or award—the Golden Ice Axe—for pioneering a new ice and rock route up the Esperance Col on Cerro Torre in Patagonia.

"I wasn't always an artist," he began as the audience of about thirty people settled in and listened. "I dabbled some as a young lad, sketches of the countryside and such, but nothing serious. Growing up, I read some about the famous British alpinists—like Mallory and Irvine—and started to dream about life as a climber. By 1984, I'd moved to Chamonix and was living full-time as a climber and mountain guide. That year, I had a serious climbing accident. The doctors all told me that I'd never climb again. I remember getting very angry when they told me that—I thought, *But you don't know me!* I developed my painting in that time while I went through surgeries and physical rehab and all the rest of it. Painting saved my mental health. Honestly it did. And I got my climbing back through art. So now I think of myself as an artist/climber."

That was the end of his talk, and he started chatting with people about his art and sculpture. He'd been unsatisfyingly brief, though I knew that he was more about action than words. But I also knew there was more to his story, parts he'd revealed to me in France. He'd been leading a client up a route on the Riffelhorn, near Zermatt, when a huge slab of rock he was standing on cleaved from the mountain, and he catapulted thirty-five feet down, slamming onto a flat belay ledge. His left pelvis shattered in thirteen places; he ruptured his spleen; one arm snapped like kindling, and he fractured a bunch of ribs. His client was able to call for help, and a helicopter came and whisked Andy off the mountain. But the horrid detail I remembered most—a pretty important one to leave out—was that after the doctors performed open-heart surgery on him and saved his life, they said that his heart had literally "exploded out of its casing"!

I headed straight over and greeted him warmly, thanking him for coming.

"I'm just over the mountain in Chamonix." He laughed. "It's no bother at all."

I asked him to talk about some of the paintings that were on display.

"Ah, well, there are a few just here from my early days right out of hospital," he said, pointing my hand to a wall behind him. "The critics quite rightly call this my 'dark' period. I saw the mountains then, immediately after my accident, as dark and somber and foreboding. And life was like that for me too. They are images of mountains drawn in dark pastels and charcoals because that's the way they can be, if you spend enough time in them— not some pretty, lovely mountains the way people like to think of them, but mountains with dangerous, dark moods as well. The dark side of the mountains."

I'd been in mountains when they were ominous and stormy, so I knew what he meant.

"But I've lightened up some." He laughed. "And my painting has too. Say, we're set for the Hexenstein tomorrow, yeah?"

We'd made a plan for him to take me up a classic local crag while we were in Cortina. I still had so many questions for Andy, and an ascent together would be the perfect opportunity.

The Sass de Stria Hexenstein is a classic Dolomite crag rising at the junction of the Falzarego and Valparola passes, just a short drive west of Cortina. I felt the morning sun on my face as we made the twenty-minute approach to the South Arête for eight roped pitches of climbing. I followed the sound of the bear bells we'd mounted on Andy's trekking poles as he hiked ahead of me up a steep mountain trail for about a mile. I could hear Andy's shuffling, herky-jerky gait in front of me, his left side just a beat behind. It made me envision the Frankenstein monster in the old black-and-white movies. As if reading my mind, Andy remarked, "I'm not as fast as I once was. My hips and pelvis have lost the free movement they had before, and I drag a bit. One of my climbing friends calls my walking 'the movement of a very graceful crab,' and I s'pose that's about right. But I still get on, don't I?"

I laughed. "We're even," I added. "Because my friends tell me that with my trekking poles jutting forward, I look like a giant praying mantis and that my walk looks like a controlled stumble."

As we walked, I asked him how he'd been able to start over, to start from scratch after being so badly broken.

He came to a stop ahead of me.

"It was fits and starts, really," he said. "After my accident, I was in the hospital for a long time, surgeries on my pelvis, hips, and elbows. I got very depressed, thinking about myself as a cripple, really. I couldn't imagine a future. It was soul-destroying. But in the hospital, I never stopped thinking about climbing mountains. Out of boredom, I got some sketchbooks, paints, and pencils and started sketching and painting from memory. At some point I rolled my wheelchair over to the window and started looking out at the mountains and painting. After the hospital, I was on crutches for four years. I threw myself into painting then. I was hobbling around, riding up on the *teleferique*, limping about a hundred feet from the cable car and painting—that was my only contact with the mountains. It was the closest I thought I might ever get to them again. But I kept scrambling around, testing my capabilities, getting stronger. Remaking my body. Remaking myself, really. Anyway, I s'pose you could say I painted my way back into climbing. I started trying short routes, new routes that were hard for me at the time, and each route for me was a healing process."

It was the most I'd ever heard him open up. We started up the trail again, and the ground changed from dirt to looser scree that skittered down the hill below us as we went.

"Almost there," Andy said. "Just a couple of hundred yards ahead. I can see where the trail ends and the crags begin. It's funny, what people tell you that you can or can't do and what you are willing to believe," he went on. "After the accident, secretly, I did actually believe that my climbing days were probably finished. But it turns out they weren't. And here we are."

The two of us geared up, and Andy led the rope upward. The beginning of the route followed a long arête—a ninety-degree edge like the corner of a tall building. Andy called down to me, "It's exposed but comfortable climbing."

The morning sun warmed the rocks, and it felt good to be in the mountains with Andy, whose solo endeavors—especially hard, remote, winter solos—were the stuff of mountaineering legend. "What was your favorite climb?" I asked as we sat on a ledge eating candy bars.

"That'd have to be Makalu," he said without hesitation. "Funny choice too, considering I never stood on top of it."

Makalu was the fifth-highest mountain in the world and one that interested me. It was only fourteen miles from Mount Everest, in the Khumbu region. Standing at almost twenty-eight thousand feet, it is known for its perfect pyramid shape, with four distinct ridges. Climbers said that it was one of the most beautiful peaks in the world.

"That was major for me, the whole experience," he said. "It was 1988, four years after my accident, and I was just off crutches. When I got invited along to trek to its base camp, I went just to paint, really, and I didn't expect to climb. My climbing lifestyle was finished. I brought some supplies up there, packed all my paints and canvases in my rucksack. I painted the mountains at each camp, hanging canvases inside the tents to dry and to view, and after my mates headed up to try the summit, I started venturing alone, higher and higher each day. I struggled mightily, limping, dragging my bum leg. It was slow slogging. But each go, I'd study the face of Makalu, just sit there in the snow, look at it and think about it for hours: how the shadow and light moved across its ridges, and precisely how the ice seracs cracked and broke away from the face when the sun lit them up at the perfect angle, and how late in the afternoon, the wind whipped and shifted plumes of snow over its four ridges. Then I'd go back to the tents at base camp and paint. Each day, I felt a little stronger, and I'd go a bit higher up. Always alone. Eventually, all the way up to twenty-four thousand feet."

I pictured Andy there, a tiny fleck on an endless expanse of snow and rock gazing at the mountain until he knew every inch of it, its intricacies and patterns, how it changed from one minute to the next.

"And one day," he went on, "I'd just finished a canvas. I looked at it, and the energy of the art fueled my desire to climb again. I realized I *could* climb! I could carry on; I could do this! I had come full circle. The painting brought me back to the climbing, but now in a deeper way. I was remade back into being a climber, but en route, I became an artist. I went there looking for space to find myself, but I also discovered something new."

Since that expedition, I knew that Andy had gone on to become a famous artist throughout Europe, known as much for his artwork as for his climbing. His art was in such demand that he'd expanded his studio, and he was frequently commissioned to create unique outdoor sculptural installments.

The critics raved about his work, as one wrote, "Not for its chest thumping on the top of a mountain, but for its expression of fragility."

Another two hours of easy chimney climbing and we reached a corner crack where the rock got super smooth and polished. I struggled as I scanned and groped for holds, but Andy talked me through it, and eventually we arrived at the last belay.

"There's an easier gully curving over to the right," he said. "But I like this nice slab just overhead, leading straight to the summit. Let's take that."

At the top, we sat quietly in the sun next to the large metal summit cross and ate some bread and cheese as a cool mountain breeze swept over the summit.

Finally, I said, "I didn't know how art and climbing could be so connected."

"Absolutely," he replied. "I use my paintings as a barometer to gauge when I'm ready to go climbing. When I start painting well in a place, it means I've really adapted to it. Then I'm ready. It's all inseparable: art, climbing, and life. It's less about conquering or dominating and much more about adapting in the face of change."

Later that afternoon I met Andy back at the expo tent where he was showing people his art exhibit. He'd agreed to show me some of the sculptures he'd been working on.

"I've been fabricating objects out of materials I've found wandering around the mountains," he said. "There's one I really want to show you." He led me to a display pedestal, guided my hand to chest level, and placed it on a sculpture.

I ran my hand up and down the piece to get an overall impression. There was what felt like a marble base, and then a long, skinny metal post, onto which was mounted something angular and tilted, like a rock about the size of a large book. My fingers felt holes and ridges, and on one side, as I slid my hand around trying to figure out what this thing was, my knuckles bumped into metal, like tendrils of woven wire. It wasn't big at all, but packed with a lot of movement. I touched the form, feeling what could be a leg hanging out in space, then another leg touching what I was realizing was a rock, then a shape like a body, a small rounded head, then two arms reaching upward and pulling, holding the top of what felt like an overhang.

"A climber!" I said with delight. I was certain.

"Exactly right," Andy confirmed. "I really like this piece," he went on. "The rock is mounted on that post, and there's a pretty good overhang. The climber—he's made of copper wire. You can feel the muscles in his thighs, his arms. He's hanging free, climbing up and over a steep angle."

"Like he's barely hanging on," I said.

"Yeah, that's right. Precarious, I'd say. Expressing a sort of fragility. From the time we're born, we're sort of staggering, falling into the next moment in a state of . . . *déséquilibre*, as the French say."

"What's that word?" I asked.

"*Déséquilibre*. It means . . . that point of imbalance. That moment, hinged there, vulnerable and tenuous. Maybe about to lunge toward something else."

"*Déséquilibre*," I repeated. "One foot on, one foot off."

Andy let that statement hang in the air for a few moments, like his copper figure clutching the rock. "We've all been there," he finally said.

I heard the clicking of a cane approaching behind me and a woman's voice. She introduced herself to Andy and me. I knew her from earlier in the festival. I'd tried unsuccessfully to get her to join us on the GPS tour with Mike May. Despite my best efforts, she'd declined, admitting to me she was out of shape and overweight, and being blind herself, she was really frightened by the idea of hiking or climbing. She asked Andy if it would be okay for her to touch some of his sculptures, and he led her to the same one I'd just felt.

"Put your hands on it just there," he said. "Tell me what you feel."

I wondered how long it would take her to figure it out.

After a few minutes of exploring the form, she exclaimed, "Oh, it's a mountain climber, isn't it?"

"Yeah, yeah, that's right!" Andy replied, pleased.

"I could never do that," the woman admitted.

"What do ya mean, make sculpture?" asked Andy.

"No." She laughed nervously. "Climb on a rock face. Just the thought of it makes me break out in sweat."

"Ah, but you can, love!" said Andy. "Feel the figure again and tell me what you see."

"It feels terrifying," she responded. "There's nowhere for him to go, and he's about to fall into space, to his death."

"Feel just above his left hand," Andy said.

"I don't feel anything," she replied after a minute. He allowed her to keep searching through another long pause and then said, "Do you feel a little dish in the rock? About an inch above his left hand?"

"Yes," she finally said with relief. "I feel it."

"That's where his left hand will reach next. Now feel to the right of that, just a little higher. Do you feel a ledge?"

After several more moments, she replied, "Yes. I think I feel it."

"That's where his right hand will go," he said. "Now tell me where his left hand will reach next."

"To this little knob here?"

"That's it," he said, getting excited now. "Keep finding the holds above."

"I think there's a hold here to the right," she said, also now excited, "and another ledge up to the left."

"See?" he finally said, his voice elated. "It may look like he's going to fall into space, but there's a way forward if you look carefully."

"Those holds, they're like a trail leading him up," she said.

"That's right, and soon he'll be at the top."

As they went back and forth, I chuckled to myself. Leave it to Andy, I thought, to forge a sequence of tiny secret holds in what felt, at first, like blank, featureless rock.

"We're doing a climbing clinic above town in a little bit," Andy continued. "And I think you should join us."

"I don't know if I could do it," she said hesitantly.

"Feel the figure on the face again," he said. "Feel the holds again. I think you know how to do it, and I think you want to try."

She scanned the sculpture for another few minutes, carefully tracing the figure's feet, his hands, his body position, and the holds above. Then her head lifted up, and she said softly, "I guess I could try it."

"I'll be there to guide you every step of the way," he said, beaming.

As we all walked out of the tent together toward the climbing clinic, I almost couldn't believe what had just happened. Almost twenty years earlier, Andy had painted the face of Makalu over and over until his possibilities had emerged like colors and images forming on a canvas, and now he had somehow passed that same clarity on to a total stranger, a woman who had already decided something was out of the question for her. It almost felt magical, like he'd infused himself into his art, so that it transferred on to all those who encountered it. She had touched the sculpture once, and then again and again and again, until, slowly, painstakingly, she'd been able to see the way forward, like a hidden map, leading her up the seemingly impossible face.

As the festival concluded, I was sad to say good-bye to so many friends like Andy Parkin, Mark Wellman, Mike May, and Jim Goldsmith, but I also had another adventure to look forward to. Hugh had agreed to stay an extra day to climb one of the Tre Cime with me. The Tre Cime hosted the most famous rock climbing in the Dolomites, consisting of a massif of three strikingly vertical towers standing apart from all the other peaks around it.

After breaking down the equipment, we drove forty-five minutes to the Rifugio, at the base of the Tre Cime. We arrived after sunset and had time only for a quick meal before settling into our bunks for the night. We'd be getting a predawn start the next morning to climb the fourteen rope pitches of the classic Cassin route on the Cima Piccolissima. Wind rattled against the bunkroom windows, and I heard Hugh sit up to secure the latch, then slide back into his sleeping bag. Then the wind stopped, and it grew eerily quiet and still as all the climbers in the main room also retired to their bunkrooms.

I couldn't sleep and just lay awake, with too many thoughts crowding my brain. I had met so many people at the festival who had smashed through barriers in their own lives and had introduced the world to new ideas and innovations. Their stories of moving forward seemed very different in some ways, but in others, they were the same. Hugh's and Andy's stories were at the forefront. There were so many confluences. I kept thinking about Andy trying to rebuild his life from shattered bones and a heart burst from its casing to creating art so powerful it could make a person glimpse her possibilities. I thought about Hugh's unlikely journey from lying in a freezing snow pit on the side of Mount Washington, waiting to die, to leading a bionics research lab at MIT and building the most sophisticated prosthetic legs in existence, legs that were enabling people to get up from their wheelchairs and walk for the first time since their loss. In Hugh's journey, however, there was a terrible casualty: Albert Dow, the young man from the search-and-rescue team who had died in the avalanche trying to save him. When he was rescued and carried out of North Conway, Hugh was despised by many of the local climbing community for causing this tragedy. I could hear him tossing and turning in the upper bunk, just a few feet above me, and I figured he was still awake too.

"Hugh, when we climbed Ancient Art together," I said, "I remember you telling me that after your accident, you moved back to North Conway, back to the scene. Why would you ever do that?"

I knew my question must have seemed like it came out of the blue. "I mean, why did you move toward the very thing you should have been running from?"

Instead of being offended, or pretending to be asleep, he answered, "That's a good question, one that I've also asked myself."

It was as if lying on his back staring up into the darkness had temporarily freed Hugh, and he began to speak more openly than I'd ever heard him before. "My time in North Conway was a healing time, definitely for me, and, I hope, for the community. Since I lost my legs, so much had happened in such a brief amount of time, and I think I had been building toward that decision for a while. Moving there felt like a natural extension of a process I was going through."

"But how did you summon up the courage," I asked, "to go back to a place where you knew you wouldn't be welcomed?"

"It's kind of like looking at a big face you want to climb. From a distance, it appears forbidding and impossibly steep. The rock looks featureless, with no way up. But as you hike closer, you begin to see how it might be done. You start seeing the ledges scattered up the wall, and the cracks that you can use to connect them. You start to see the places that are less than vertical, the seams and pockets you can use to surmount the roofs. I guess I knew I needed to get close up if I were going to see the way forward."

Although Hugh was casting his memory back more than twenty years, he spoke with vivid recollection. "In the hospital, after my amputations, I remember looking down at the sheets where they dropped off—the space where my legs used to be, where my legs should have been. And I just started wailing. It wasn't only the loss of my legs; it was that Albert Dow died trying to find me. I felt like a monster, both physically and because I had screwed up and my actions led to another's life ending. I was consumed by tremendous anger, and that anger became a fierce drive, a kind of fuel source. Lying in that hospital bed, I dreamed of climbing again. The first prosthetic legs they gave me were awful. There were a lot of bloody stumps. Going climbing with my brothers, there were times I barely made it to the climb. I just took off my legs and crawled through the brush and creeks for hours until I reached the rock. One time I was so angry, I just started yelling and cursing and actually threw my prosthetic legs at the rock wall."

"That anger eventually led to some good things," I added.

"Eventually," he agreed. "My first breakthrough was the realization that I didn't need human-shaped feet for climbing. Initially, I put a rock-climbing shoe on a prosthetic foot. It immediately appeared utterly ridiculous. It occurred to me that it was unnecessary to have a foot the same size and shape as an adult human foot. I realized that I didn't need to reproduce the legs and feet I'd lost: I could create something altogether new, prosthetic designs that no one had ever thought of before. Feet perfectly suited for their task, for wedging into tiny cracks and for balancing on small edges. Once I was wearing the new climbing feet and was back on a sheer rock face, there was no stopping me."

Just as Sabriye had done with Tibetan Braille—instead of waiting around for someone else to innovate a solution, Hugh did it himself. His lack of lower legs had become like a blank canvas on which he could create anything he wanted.

"My climbing reached levels I'd never achieved before, and I just kept pushing the boundaries. By 1984, just two years after the accident, I was back in North Conway. The owner of a local climbing shop hired me to help stitch harnesses and packs, so all I did was work and climb, riding my bike back and forth between the shop in town and the rock faces. I had set my sights on making the first ascent of Stage Fright, at Cathedral Ledge. It was really more like an obsession. What I'd become known for, my form of expression, was climbing very difficult rock faces with little protection, where there's a distinct possibility you'll die if you fall. It's an extraordinary mental stress to do those kinds of ascents, because you have to be perfect; there's no option. Stage Fright had all those characteristics. It was hard to even find people to belay me—it was simply too terrifying for them to witness. The climb had a very difficult move at the top requiring a lunge—I'd have to leap in the air a few feet and catch a tiny hold. I worked on the route for three weeks, climbing up to the base of the crux over and over, staring up at it, studying it, trying to map it in my mind. I'd only have one shot.

"Finally, I found myself there. My legs were shaking—I could feel them vibrating—but I was committed. My left foot had a good hold; my right foot was on a tiny ridge, my right hand on a thin flake my fingers pulled on sideways. To make the pocket hold about three and a half feet above me, I had to push off and leap upward, letting go with both my left foot and right hand." Hugh paused, reliving the moment.

Déséquilibre, I thought to myself. One foot on, one foot off.

"I sank down, lunged, and caught the pocket, locking my fingers. And then I was standing on top of Cathedral Ledge. Across the valley, I could see Mount Washington, where I had been lost and where my rescue had gone tragically wrong. I felt elation immediately, but really it was a kind of resolution in my psyche. It was as if I had gone up Mount Washington, but instead of continuing into the storm toward the summit, I descended, and Albert Dow didn't die."

I pondered how much courage that had taken. Not only the climb, but also facing the demons born in that raging winter storm.

"That's a lot to deal with at such a young age," I offered. "You were only what, nineteen?"

"Yes. And afterward I just broke down. It lasted for two days, like a nervous breakdown. I just locked myself up in my boardinghouse room, didn't eat, didn't come out; I just lay on my bed and cried. I knew when I finished Stage Fright, it would be my last ascent of that magnitude. Some said it was the hardest climb in the country."

It was getting late, and we had a big climb in the morning. The wind was picking up again outside, rushing past the Rifugio in a mournful wail.

"What did you do afterward?" I asked.

"A few days later I returned to my home in Pennsylvania and enrolled in college at Millersville University," Hugh said. "I didn't know exactly how it would be expressed, but I was going to create something new. I believed that using every cell in my body to do something worthwhile would be a way to honor Albert Dow's memory."

Hugh rolled over on his bunk, exhaled, and went quiet, signaling that he was done talking. As I lay there dozing in and out of wakefulness and dreams, I could see strange distorted images of Andy Parkin shuffling toward the base of Makalu, like a large crab, his backpack stuffed with painting supplies. I saw Hugh, crawling on his hands and knees up the trail and heaving his legs at the rock face, that rage leading him back toward the mountains, until he stood atop Cathedral Ledge, his arms stretching toward Mount Washington with exaltation, but more so in atonement. In the end, they had both found their way home. But that seemed almost secondary, because along the way and through all that struggle, they had given birth to something new. It was like an unintended summit, like aiming for the top of Lhakpa Ri and discovering instead an Ice Palace.

6

THE BUCKETS CHAMPION

On my return from the Dolomites, I was met with a family crisis: We hadn't heard from Mark, my oldest brother, for over a month, and we were getting worried. Eddi, my middle brother, and I finally got in touch with Mark's buddy Carl. "Can you go to Mark's house and call us and hand him your phone?" Eddi asked.

Carl put him on the phone, and Mark said cheerfully, "Hey, bros. Everything's cool. It's all good, man."

We knew it was a lie. Carl had told us that Mark wasn't looking that good. His slim, handsome face had gotten puffy and red with bags under his eyes. His penetrating blue eyes had dulled, no longer looking directly at you. Even worse, the water in his house was shut off again. Carl said that Mark was catching water from his roof gutters and boiling it on a Sterno burner.

This was not the Mark I had always known. Ever since I was little, his energy and prowess seemed practically mythical to Eddi and me. Mark was nine years older than me, six foot two and muscular, with wavy dark hair and very blue eyes that seemed to have a remarkable effect on those of the opposite sex.

When we were kids running around our neighborhood, he was always the one who could throw the ball the farthest and run the fastest. In high school, Mark was the captain of both the football and baseball teams. In one football game that has become family legend, we sat in the bleachers as he scored every touchdown and made the winning field goal too. Mark also had the high school record for the longest field goal in New Jersey, fifty-three yards. My dad thought he was good enough to go to the NFL someday. Even as a little kid, my vision wasn't good enough to see Mark scoring touchdowns, so I would often take his trophies down from the mantel and feel the figures, crouched down in a runner's position or arm straight up catching a baseball in a mitt. My favorite, though, was a figure wearing shoulder pads and a helmet. He was leaning forward aggressively sprinting for the end zone, with a football tucked in the crook of his elbow. The smooth metal figure was tall and lean and rippled with muscle, perched up high on a marble pedestal, and that was exactly how I pictured my big brother.

Even though he was a superstar, he'd also be the guy who jumped down an entire flight of stairs, no doubt showing off, right before the big game, and sprain his ankle, out for three weeks, when his team really needed him. When I was little, he was experimenting building a fire inside a tent in the backyard, using matches and a can of gasoline. It lit up and burned him over a third of his body. He ran by me toward the house howling in pain. I remember the smell of charred flesh, and he was out half of another season. Instead of scoring touchdowns in Pop Warner, he had to go through painful skin-grafting procedures.

To be honest, everyone in my family was pretty competitive. At Christmastime, we'd always have a series of spirited family competitions, the Weihenmayer Olympics, and Mark always won everything. However, one unusual winter vacation, Eddi won the bowling contest, my dad won a close game of darts. I'd just gotten an awesome present called Simon, an electronic disc with panels that lit up with one of four different colors and played four different sounds; you had to remember Simon's order and repeat it. I mimicked Simon's pattern through seventeen colors, eking out a win over Mark in the heated championship. Of course, we all rubbed it in for the entire vacation. "Bowling champion," Eddi said, raising his arms. "Dart champion," my father added. "I'm the Simon Says champion," I added, feeling a little lame but proud to at least claim something. Mark tried not to show it, but I could tell he was bothered. Throughout the week, he kept challenging us to games: cards, pool.

At dinner one night, he even tried to pull us into a pinball contest. He was getting increasingly desperate to win something. Eddi started goading Mark on.

"You could be the pizza-eating champion, or maybe the Hula-Hoop champion."

Mark continued to be grumpy, so Eddi finally went into the garage and started bouncing a tennis ball against the wall and trying to land it in an empty five-gallon bucket. Mark came out and was immediately interested. Soon the game had progressed into three different buckets placed at varying distances from the wall and each with increasing points. The rules became elaborate and complex, all of us, especially Mark, arguing over each score. We played for hours, and to Mark's relief, in the final showdown, he emerged victorious.

"I'm the Buckets Champion!" he shouted, losing himself, his fists pumping in the air. When we all broke out laughing, Mark's fists may have lowered slightly for just a moment, but he held a brave face. For the following year, Mark lorded over us that Eddi may have won at bowling, Dad at darts, and me at Simon Says, but he was the true champion, because he had beaten us in the most extreme gladiators battle of athleticism, concentration, and sheer willpower, the elite sport of Buckets.

As I became a teenager, Mark moved to Orlando, which was, according to him, "the coolest place in the world." Mark never crossed the line into lying, but Eddi expressed it best through a word he made up. He called it "bragadeering."

"Down in Orlando," the weather was always sunny; the girls were the hottest; the beers the tallest; and the competition on the volleyball court the fiercest.

When Mark came home to Connecticut for another holiday, I took him to a friend's house party. I went to fill our cups from the keg, and when I came back, Mark was surrounded by a group of high school kids. His arms waved wildly, and the kids around him were all laughing hysterically, as he bragadeered one of his outrageous tall tales.

"Down in Orlando," he started, "me and my friends had been out at the clubs. We stopped off at Krystal Burgers on the way home. When the lady behind the counter turned around, I lifted up onto the counter and farted into her microphone. It ripped through the speakers like a bazooka, and all the workers poured out of the kitchen to see what the explosion was. The first thing they saw were my butt cheeks hovering over the microphone. They looked pretty angry. We grabbed our fries and got the hell out of there."

Mark was the kind of older brother who would pick you up from the bus station three hours late, but he'd make up for lost time with a bag of Krystal burgers and his truck crammed with two hot girls. You'd be squeezed between them on your way to a day out at Disney World. He'd always have free passes, all scored from a friend. Your sixteen-year-old mind might have envisioned riding the spinning cups in the Mad Tea Party ride, but you never could have dreamed you'd be wedged between two exotic dancers in skimpy halter tops with their arms wrapped tight around you and kissing your cheek, all because you happened to be the little brother of Mark Weihenmayer.

To me, he also appeared fearless in all the ways I wasn't. When I was little, we lived in an apartment. Mark would come home past his curfew, and instead of walking through the front door and getting in trouble, he'd climb seven floors up the outside of the balconies and sneak into his room. One slip and he would have been a stain on the pavement. Later we moved to a Connecticut town with a river running through it called the Devil's Glen. Mark would be the one launching off the forty-foot cliff nailing perfect one and a halfs—a full flip followed by a dive—into a six-by-six-foot pool of water. On one of our annual trips to visit Mark in Orlando, Eddi arrived a few hours earlier than my dad and me. The first minute he walked through the door, Mark started bragadeering about his brand-new truck. He was in a high-energy mood, awaiting Eddi's arrival, and he had to take Eddi out on a test drive to show him all the amazing features. So before Eddi had even brought his bags inside, he was sitting in the passenger seat and Mark was revving the engine. He zipped out of the apartment complex and shouted, "Hold on, Ed Boy!" then tore across the road, bounced over the curb, and floored it up a dirt path along a canal. Mark cranked up the radio to show Eddi the incredible bass on the speakers. He raced circles around a huge, open, undeveloped area full of jeep trails. Then he spun around doing doughnuts, dust flying up everywhere, clouding the windows. Bon Jovi's "Livin' on a Prayer" blared through the cab, and Eddi clutched the handle over the window. It felt like Mark was trying to flip the truck as he steered toward a sandy, ten-foot mound. A steep narrow trail led up to the top, with orange fruit trees lining the sides. Mark skidded to a halt at the bottom of the hill, and with his foot on the brake, he began revving the engine, jumping the truck up and down without actually moving. Mark looked over to Eddi, now clutching the dashboard. "Don't you love this, Ed Boy?"

"Are you actually going to try to climb this thing?" Eddi asked, looking up at what looked like a dirt bike trail, not wide enough for a truck.

"I do it all the time!" he shouted back, letting go of the brake, gunning the engine, and rocketing and fishtailing to the top. Eddi shuddered as they shot by tree branches scraping the doors and thwacking the side mirrors. At the top, the truck stopped abruptly. Eddi went flying forward, and his head cracked the windshield. The wheels spun, and the truck became totally stuck in the soft mud. Refusing to surrender, Mark kept spinning the wheels and grinding the engine in a fruitless effort to work the truck free. It seemed like forever before he finally gave up, looked over, and asked, "You all right?"

"I'm okay," Eddi replied, wiping blood off of his forehead. "What are we gonna do?"

Eventually the two of them dug the tires out with sticks they found in the woods, and Eddi muscled the back of the truck over the top of the hill, while Mark, behind the wheel, gunned the motor, shooting sand all over Eddi. When they pulled into the apartment complex, Mark finally looked at Eddi's head. He had an inch-and-a-half-long split in his scalp and was covered with dirt. "Ed Boy, you'll be okay." Then he pointed at the tiny quarter-size crack in the windshield. He laughed. "Your hard head cracked my windshield. Don't tell anyone what happened. Just say you hit your head going over a bump."

Eddi kept the secret, even with a headache and bloody lump on his head for the rest of the vacation. Mark continued to make inside jokes about the accident and continued to bragadeer about his new truck and all it could do. "Down in Orlando" didn't seem so great after all. As time passed, Eddi's split forehead got smaller, and the crack in the windshield got bigger. "Your forehead cracked my entire windshield, Ed Boy." With Mark, you never knew what adventures awaited, Playboy bunnies on the tea cup ride or a bloody lump on your head.

The next day, we went out for pizza. Eddi, now living in Pensacola, had been given some peppers that he brought. "My friend says they're pretty hot," Eddi warned.

"Down here in Orlando," Mark jumped in, "we make the hottest peppers. They're hotter than in Mexico. I grow some myself."

"These are Red Savina habañeros," Eddi replied. "They're pretty hot. You can't even pick them up without your eyes watering."

Eddi must have still been annoyed by his throbbing forehead, because he didn't tell Mark they were so hot, the only way they were used was by drying them and cutting them up into tiny pieces for relish.

"Keep talking, Ed Boy. Yours may be hot, man, but they're nothing like the ones I grow. I know what hot is."

We ordered the pizzas, while Eddi went out to his car and got the peppers. "Hey, you want to put some of these on your pizza?" Eddi asked, returning with the peppers in a baggie.

"Yeah, put them on. I love hot stuff."

Eddi loaded them onto his pizza while Mark watched. He may have been having second thoughts, but he now couldn't say a word. Mark ate a slice, piled with peppers, and we all waited in anticipation. The image has been lodged in my mind through many retellings. Eddi said Mark's eyes began to water, and his face turned red and then purple. "His face kind of disconfigured and contorted," Eddi said. His thin lips were all pinched together in a grimace disguised as a smile, as if to say, "Everything's cool here." We kept asking Mark, "You gonna eat the rest of your pizza?"

Without saying a word, Mark actually picked up another slice and finished the rest of his pizza. When he was finished, he said, "No big deal," and then drank his beer.

"You want another pizza?" Eddi asked. "I got more peppers in the car."

"No. I'm good," Mark replied, clutching the edge of the table with white hands and droplets of sweat collecting at his hairline.

Mark had a successful small business, an aquatic lake-scaping company. He was a hard worker, spending twelve-hour days standing in murky lakes and retention ponds, hauling away tons of invasive plants and trees and replanting native species. He had tons of equipment that he was proud of: boats and backhoes, three different-size chain saws with a variety of blades, sharpeners, and chains. He'd tie a rope to the bumper of his truck and trail it behind him until he was chest deep in a forest of thick grasses and melaleuca trees. He'd use the large knife strapped to his waist to cut the huge trunks and then dive down under the water to dig out the roots by hand. Many times, the rope had enabled him to yank himself to safety after being charged by a nest of moccasins, or, even worse, a ten-foot gator. Orlando was known as the City of Lakes, so there was lots of demand. Mark's business was thriving, and he was not able to keep up, even with a team of a dozen employees. When his girlfriend, Julie, got pregnant, it was the happiest he'd ever been, so much so that he was about to get married. Every night after work, he'd sing nursery rhymes to Julie's belly and have long conversations with the baby girl inside. "Volleyball's probably the best sport for you. I bet you'll have a pretty decent vertical leap, and if you're going to serve, you got to be tall, so keep eating in there."

He dipped a carrot stick in ranch dressing and fed it to Julie.

"Your mom played softball," he went on. "Those ladies are bruisers."

He leaned down, placed his lips right up against her belly, and whispered, "Some of them are lesbians. You may wanna stay away from that crazy scene." With that, he received a punch in the arm. "Now, tennis, that's a good sport. You have to be quick if you're going to have a good volley. It's all about fast-twitch muscles. We'll need to start working on your two-handed backhand pretty soon, not right away. We'll let you learn to crawl first. And I wouldn't mind golf either. Not my first choice, but there's a lot of strategy there. I can be your caddy, because most people focus on their drive, but it's really all about the short game. Remember: 'Drive for show, putt for dough.'"

Finally, he settled down and began reading storybooks to his unborn child. His favorite was about Pippi Longstocking, a quirky little girl who lived alone in a cottage with her monkey and her horse and was constantly going on adventures with her two best friends. "'Pippi was indeed a remarkable child,'" Mark read, his voice happy and playful. "'The most remarkable thing about her was that she was so strong. She was so very strong that in the whole wide world there was not a single police officer as strong as she. Why, she could lift a whole horse if she wanted to! And she wanted to!'

"She sure is strong," Mark said, closing the book for a moment. "Just like you'll be someday. You'll be just like her. You probably won't have freckles or red hair like her, but you may have pretty pigtails. Actually, that trainer your mom is always staring at in the gym has red hair," he said, now grinning mischievously at Julie. "So maybe you will have red hair after all."

He laughed and patted her belly and received the second punch of the night.

Soon after that, we were all invited down to Orlando for Mark and Julie's big wedding, but shockingly, the night before I was to fly down, he called me on the phone. "It's off," he said angrily. "Don't fly down here."

"You're getting married, and I'm flying to the wedding in a few hours, and you're calling it all off?" I said in disbelief.

"I'm dead serious. We just got in a huge fight, and I canceled the whole thing. You can still fly down if you want. The facility is already paid for, so we'll have a big blowout. We'll call it the 'eff the wedding' party."

Despite the relationship going south, Mark was there for the birth of his daughter, Gabrielle. Of course he was behind the camera, giving a play-by-play near the hospital bed. He loved being a dad and threw himself into parenthood in his customary style, like gunning his engine up a steep embankment. He took baby Gabbi's footprints and had them printed on T-shirts, which he gave out to all his friends and family. He had those same footprints enlarged and printed on the side of his boat, and he rechristened it *Little Miss Gabrielle*.

On my next visit, I sat beside Mark as he reclined on his couch, his baby Gabbi lying on his chest. He lifted her up into the air. "Feel her little fingers," he said eagerly. "Feel her toes. Feel her cheeks. Feel how soft they are. She's beautiful, bro. She's totally perfect." He stood her up on his belly, facing him, and wiggled her back and forth in a little dance. "She loves disco," he said, lifting her arms up in rhythm as Gabbi squealed with laughter. "Most of all she loves this song I made up for her," he said. "It's called 'My Song to Gabs,'" he announced, his voice husky, as if he were a crooner like Frank Sinatra about to perform in front of Carnegie Hall. I could hear her little feet bouncing on his belly as he sang:

It's just a dumb little song
But it's one I have to sing
And it says, "I love you, I love you"

It doesn't even rhyme
And it's really really goofy
But I still sing out loud,
"I love you, I love you."

When he stopped singing, Gabbi reached her hands out toward him, wanting more.

In 2001, Mark, along with my dad and Eddi, were planning to accompany me to base camp on Mount Everest to see me off. We especially thought an adventure would do Mark some good by getting him away from Orlando for a while. He had always partied and lived hard, but the canceled wedding had put him in a funk. Even worse, Gabbi's mom had decided to move away to New York State to be closer to her family. Mark had flown up there for a few weekends, but gradually the visits had trailed off. On the phone, I started noticing Mark's voice changing, growing more faltering, his words coming out a little slurred. The day he was supposed to fly out of Orlando, he got in a big fight with a new girlfriend and left a message that he wasn't sure if he was still going on the trip. I called him and begged him to get on that plane. He showed up in Nepal having forgotten most of his gear. Mark always prided himself on having the best equipment, always bought, of course, down in Orlando, at the most amazing camping store. On one trek, he'd bragadeered the entire time about his pack, named the Highlander, which had all the coolest zippers and special compartments for pulling out candy bars at the perfect moment, or a first-aid kit the second I skinned my knee. "The Highlander carries way more weight than your measly little Cub Scout backpack," he said with absolute pride.

So it was unlike Mark to show up without the Highlander. He had even forgotten his insulated Gore-Tex hiking boots with the coolest lacing system that he'd been talking about for months. Before flying up into the Khumbu region to start our approach to base camp, he had to scour the markets of Kathmandu and finally found a pair of knockoff boots. Within two days of our hike, all the metal eyelets were falling out, and one of the rubber heels came unglued, flapping from the boot. Mark's feet were wrecked, and his toes were covered with blisters. At 14,500 feet in the village of Dingboche, we went into a small Sherpa teahouse, and Mark was delighted to see beer for sale. He grabbed a six-pack off the shelf and went into the kitchen to pay. Mark didn't know I was just around the corner, standing outside the door. When he didn't think anyone was watching, he faced into the corner and sucked back the first can in a matter of seconds. I could hear his throat swallowing. It didn't seem he was even enjoying it, more like the way someone would take medicine, as quickly and efficiently as possible to kill the pain. Back in the common room, he proceeded to knock back the rest. Mark didn't realize how the effects of alcohol were amplified at altitude. He told some loud stories, but he didn't seem like the life of the party anymore. His swagger had always been charming, but now there was an edge of darkness just beneath the surface. The group moved away, feeling slightly uncomfortable, and started up other conversations. Something had tipped within him. We had to put him to bed that night, and in the morning, he had a raging hangover to show for it. I could barely rouse him out of his sleeping bag to start the day's trek toward base camp. I sat in the entranceway of his tent as he slowly shoved clothes into his pack. "You can't be getting hammered," I rebuked him, "especially at altitude. Last night wasn't you. It was . . . well, it was embarrassing."

"You don't think I know that?" he shot back. "Everything embarrassing I've ever done, everything bad that's ever happened to me, I can write off to the love of my life. Her name's Anita . . . Anita Drink. Everything terrible in my life is because of her.

"My first memory," he said, "was sitting beside my dad on his tractor."

Although I never thought about it this way, Mark and I were technically half brothers. My father had been a marine aviator stationed at the naval air base in Pensacola. He had met my mother, a divorcée and full-fledged Southern belle. They had fallen in love and gotten married, and he had adopted her two young children, Suzanne and Mark. Mark's biological father had been a hard-charging, hard-drinking farmer from north Florida. Like Mark, he was the star of his football team. When he was sober, he was the first to open a door for a lady and leap to help her with her groceries. However, when he was drinking, as my grandmother put it, "he wanted to whip the world."

"My dad always had a brown paper bag lying next to him on the seat," Mark added, "and every few minutes, he'd tip it back and take a long drink."

"That was your father, not you," I argued. "Why can't you just quit? Just go cold turkey?"

At first I didn't think he was going to answer, because there was only the shuffle of gear. "It's not a matter of wanting to," he finally said. "It's like you're dying of thirst in the scorching desert, and you haven't had water for days. All you can think about is a cold glass of water. The idea of it consumes you. It doesn't matter how many times people tell you not to take a drink, or how many times you lecture yourself that water's no good for you. You take that drink, because if you don't, you're afraid you're going to die."

Over the next few years, I tried hard to understand what was going on as Mark would try to get sober, succeed for a time, and then fall back into a kind of abyss. My dad, Eddi, and I put our heads together on what to do—how best to help. If Mark went quiet for a time, my dad and his wife, Mariann, would drive the three hours from Jacksonville to his house to find a sink full of dirty dishes, hampers overflowing with dirty laundry, and the house in ruins. Mail would pile up in the mailbox to the point that the mailman stopped delivering it. Bills would go unpaid for months. Sometimes they arrived to see that Mark's water and electricity had been turned off. The meager food in his refrigerator had all gone bad. Dad and Mariann would spend these weekends cleaning up, paying bills, and getting everything turned on again. My dad, being a marine and ex–Wall Street executive, had always conducted his life with discipline, so it was particularly torturous for him to watch Mark's slide. Each weekend would end the same, with a long fatherly lecture, telling Mark to clean up his act, reconnect with his daughter, and start the process of reviving his business. He even offered to get Mark's bookkeeping back in order and help him reconnect with clients he'd let drift away, but Mark replied bluntly, "The last thing I need is for you to come down here looking over my shoulder."

After Mark stopped paying his mortgage, we knew he was in jeopardy of losing his house. Dad, Eddi, and I brainstormed again. This time, we decided to put our money together and purchase his house so he wouldn't be evicted. Eddi would send him regular care packages of canned food. No one could send money, since it would immediately go toward beer.

Countless late nights, I was awakened by phone calls from a Mark who seemed alien to the brother I'd known. There was very little laughter and bravado anymore. His calls were rambling, sometimes slurred tirades, going in circles. "I lie awake all night," he said, his voice flat and monotone. "Listening, just lying there listening for the sound of the AC to kick on, or for the humming buzz of the refrigerator. I look forward to those sounds. They're constants in my life. Something I can count on."

One night, he really scared me. "I saw Jesus," he said. "He came down from the cross. He had bloody holes in his hands and blood coming from his eyes and out of his mouth. He told me I didn't deserve forgiveness. I'm a bad person. I've hurt everyone I know. I've done a lot of terrible things."

"That wasn't real!" I practically yelled over the phone line. "That was in your mind. We've all done bad things."

"I haven't seen Gabbi in two years. I don't deserve forgiveness."

"Mark, you told me once that you can't quit. So you sit there and try to suck it up, to pretend it's not a big deal, like eating those hot peppers that almost killed you. But you need to get some help."

"Quitting ain't the problem," he quickly responded. "I've quit probably fifty times, lying on my couch in withdrawal, shaking, going into convulsions, sweating it all out. It feels like a ton of ants crawling under my skin."

"Mark," I protested. "You should be under a doctor's supervision. They've got drugs to help you through detoxing."

"Ah, I don't need doctors," he replied scornfully. "Once I felt my heart stop, and I rolled off the couch on the floor and pounded it back into beating again."

I wondered if this were even possible. *Down in Orlando,* I thought bitterly, *where the girls are hot and the sun is always shining, and where you catch water off your roof gutters, where you lie alone on the couch with insects crawling beneath your skin, and where your heart stops and you pound it back into beating.*

I could actually relate to Mark, more than I'd care to admit. I'd spent a lot of time shoving people away, not accepting help from anyone. I didn't want people to look down on me. Accepting their help was like a core shot to my dignity. It signified that I was a pathetic weakling. In a way it was easier to shut out the world, rather than being vulnerable. "You're a good person, Mark. You've been a good brother, and you deserve a great life. You deserve to get old. Do you remember when I was going blind? I hated it so much, I refused to learn Braille or use my long white cane. I'd step on them and bend them on purpose. I'd drop them off bridges and down sewer gratings. Mom used to get so upset. There was one day, I was so pissed off, I climbed up on the roof. It wasn't like I was going to jump or anything, but I didn't think anyone understood what I was going through. You climbed up there too and sat next to me. You told me you loved me and that you believed in me, that I'd figure it all out. Then you started swinging my cane around like nunchucks and doing karate tricks with it. You said you wished you could switch places with me, that you'd make a super cool blind guy, that you'd purposely tap your cane into the hottest girls and ask if you could feel their faces. By the end, you had me cracking up."

I heard a muted chuckle on the other end of the line. "I needed help then," I said. "I couldn't do it alone . . . without you. So you need some help now, for Gabbi's sake. You can start by forgiving yourself—that's the only way to heal, so you can be a dad to her. She needs you."

I was positive that getting sober for the sake of Gabbi was what motivated him to agree to a six-week rehab program. However, typical Mark, he had to go down hard. He showed up at the center raging drunk. The nurses and staff had to physically restrain him as he slowly sobered up and began the painful process of detoxing again. The doctor described his hallucinatory episodes as "bipolar disorder brought on by alcoholism."

He said, "For much of Mark's life, he seemed to be able to handle it, but then there's a tipping point when the brain is chemically altered by the consumption of alcohol."

A similar thread had weaved through my mother's life, one minute smiling with her arms wrapped around me, the next lying in bed for two days not moving or even responding when I tried to talk to her. So Mark had been born with the double whammy: bipolarism from his mom and alcoholism from his dad. Like me going blind, he had won the lottery, except just the opposite.

On my next trip to Orlando, Mark was doing better. He was on a dry spell. He was supposed to pick me up at the baggage claim at the airport, but he was late as usual. As I pushed my talking watch and brought it up to my ear to listen, a rude guy pushed by me. "'Scuse me. 'Scuse me," he mumbled as he shoved by. A minute later, the rude guy was coming back the other way. "'Scuse me," he said again, elbowing me even harder. A third time, he pushed past, this time shoving hard enough to make me take a step backward. I was about to say, "Hey, you, what the heck. Quit pushing," when the mumbling guy burst into laughter. Then a giant smile broke over my face, as Mark, who had always outweighed me by thirty pounds and towered over me, lifted me up in a bear hug. "I totally got you, bro." He laughed with joy, taking complete pleasure in getting one over on me. Of course, I thought. I should have known. How else would Mark greet me? Others got a mere handshake, but in Mark's world, you got picked up and swung around until you were dizzy.

Later in my hotel room, Mark and I ordered up a movie. It was *Old School* with Will Ferrell. We ordered dessert through room service and lay on the bed eating ice cream and talking. In one scene, Will Ferrell gets mistakenly shot in the jugular by a horse tranquilizer gun. His voice goes into slo-mo in the middle of his kid's birthday party, and he falls headlong into the pool. Mark and I rolled on our backs, belly laughing, practically going into convulsions. Mark seemed so clear-headed, I decided to share something with him. I blurted out, "Ellie and I have been thinking Emma needs a brother or sister. We're thinking maybe we could look into adopting."

"What's there to think about?" Mark replied. "Being a dad is the best thing in the world."

"We're not sure," I kept going. "We're kind of waffling back and forth. We thought about having another the natural way, but it's like when you look for a new house. I get so irritated when people have to build a brand-new one from the ground up, when there are so many amazing houses to choose from.

I think the same goes for kids. We've already made one, so why not get one who's already out there, somewhere?"

"What if you get a bad one," he said softly, "like me? He'd wind up breaking your heart."

"Do you remember one time when you offered me one of your eyes?" I asked. "You said you'd give me one—when a surgery was possible. You told me that we could walk down the beach together side by side, and I could check out chicks on the left side and you could check them out on the right. And you made sure to say that you had first dibs on the hottest one."

Mark laughed. "Sounds like me," he said.

"So if he turned out like you," I continued, "I'd be okay with that. If we actually do this, I'm expecting you to meet him someday, and I'm also counting on you for that surgery. I'll have one blue eye, just like you, and I'll use it to hypnotize the ladies."

I hoped that Mark could finally say good-bye to those demons, to reinvent his life. He had the support and love of his family. He had the dream of being a good father to Gabbi. When we said good-bye, I gave him a big hug. I only wish I'd held on longer.

7

LEADING THE WAY

After I got home from Florida, there was a lot on my mind. I struggled with
what else to do about my brother Mark. Also, Ellie and I were now seriously
considering the adoption possibilities and were beginning to do research in
earnest.

Then out of the blue, I got a call from a guy who introduced himself as
Dave Shurna. He ran a travel program for teenagers. Teams of kids would
spend a school year learning about an area. They'd study the environment,
the animals, plants, rocks, and trees. They'd study the history and its people,
and then, with all the prep complete, they'd be rewarded by traveling to that
place and embarking on a big adventure. Dave and I met for coffee, and he
told me about his dream to add a program for blind teens to their roster.
"Only problem is we have no experience with blindness. That's where you'd
come in. You're an expert on all the things we want to achieve, and I'm hoping you'll show us the way."

I thought about my experiences with other blind kids; I had spent a whole
summer at blind computer camp in high school and had learned a lot of essential skills, but I also thought about my experiences with sighted friends,
like the kids on my high school wrestling team. Mostly every week, my guide
dog and I would travel on a crowded school bus to away matches around
the state of Connecticut. My dog would follow the pack of teenagers down

the twisting hallways of an unfamiliar school to the locker room. Before my match, my best friend would always lead me out to the inner circle of the wrestling mat and help me line up my feet over the white markers to face off against my opponent. I reflected on my climbing teams—those countless times roped together with sighted teammates, moving over glaciers, and those same sighted people actually trusting me to catch them if they fell. "Dave," I said, "for blind kids to succeed, they don't just need other blind people. They'll need to work with seeing people, to harness those abilities and learn to thrive in the sighted world. What if we brought sighted and blind kids onto one team, ask them to go on an adventure together, and help each other along the way?"

Dave agreed immediately and asked me to help kick-start the program. He also had a new partnership with the National Park Service and was excited to test out a new location, a rafting trip through the Grand Canyon. "We'd just do the first half," he said, "through some of the easier rapids, and then hike out of the canyon after a week."

I was a mountain guy and knew absolutely nothing about rivers. They were mysterious to me, yet intriguing. The Grand Canyon, I learned, is known for over one hundred and fifty named rapids, rated on a scale all its own, from 1 to 10—the 10s being some of the biggest in North America. It was not a typical setting for a blind kids' field trip.

"Grand Canyon," I repeated. "Sign me up."

Over the next six months, we recruited through rehabilitation centers and organizations like the National Federation of the Blind, and kids began signing up from around the country.

When we met up in Flagstaff, Arizona, the recruits impressed me. There was a blind girl from Kansas, the valedictorian of her class; a kid who'd gone blind at six years old from ocular cancer yet had wrestled and been elected to the student council; another who was on course to compete in the Paralympics as part of a crew team. On the other side of the spectrum, there were several who had hardly been off the pavement, let alone hiking canyons or rafting white water. It was a miracle some were even there. The parents of a kid named Chase had been petrified that he'd fall off a cliff or be drowned in the river. It took major persuasion from his blindness counselor who sat down with his folks for an hour convincing them their child would not perish and that this might be good for him. Being sheltered by overprotective parents was a small price to pay, I thought. They were lucky to be born in America.

After returning from our Tibet expedition, I'd spoken at a conference for teachers of the blind. I told them the stories of the blind Tibetans I'd gotten to know, their harsh treatment by the sighted community, and our ultimate accomplishment together. Afterward, a teacher stood up. His voice was strangely agitated as he blurted out, "You went to the other side of the world to find barriers, but we got 'em right here. Blind kids in America may not be tied to beds, but it amounts to the same thing."

His tirade caught me off guard, and I stammered through a lame response, my pride from the trip turning to defensiveness. His assessment seemed stark and exaggerated. How can you compare kids from America to kids whose parents tell them they shouldn't have been born and others who were sold into slavery, cold and hungry on the street, scraping for spare change, and, even more importantly, their dignity? It was a ridiculous comparison. This American team tapped around with shiny new canes; they wore Nikes and listened to iPods, went to school where people accepted them, received recorded books from the Library of Congress free of charge, had full bellies and families who loved and supported them.

The first morning we spent packing the rafts and going over safety training. "These aren't life vests," the trip leader, Marieke, stressed. "They won't save your life. They only help you float. Find the four clips and pull the tabs tight. If you swim, a loose PFD [personal floatation device] could lift up over your face and actually suffocate you."

With that, I heard the zipping sound of many nylon straps being cranked down. I should have been thinking about the safety of the kids, but her comments about the life vests spun my mind to all the help we'd been throwing to Mark: the late-night pep talks, the purchase of his house, the constant care packages, and the many rehab programs. I wanted to believe that our love and support could actually save his life, but I feared Marieke was right. That "life vest" could only keep him afloat until he rekindled the inner resolve to save himself.

The river guides drew me out of my thoughts by calling us over to the rafts that were lying on the beach and showing us our various positions. The teens lined up three on each side of the rafts, air paddling with the guide calling from the back and steering. "Left paddle!" I heard paddles clapping together, even on the right side. I wondered if there were some blind dyslexics on the trip. "Left back" meant for the left side to paddle backward while the right paddled forward. There was more clanging.

"All paddle forward"—and the loudest crashes of all.

"Let's rearrange the order," I suggested. "Let's have the blind kids sit up in front. You'll get the brunt of the waves, and it will be more pressure to get the commands right, but this way, the sighted kids can watch you and paddle on your rhythm."

"Right paddle!" the guide yelled. "Left paddle!" And the banging began to subside a little.

Next they simulated various scenarios, like "high siding," a situation when the raft hits a rock and gets stuck. All the water pouring against that rock will flip the raft in the blink of an eye, so everyone is supposed to dive to the downriver side of the boat and redistribute the weight. "High side!" Marieke yelled repeatedly, and eager bodies pitched across the raft, shoulders colliding and bouncing off each other. It all seemed counterintuitive; it would make more sense to dive away from the rock, not toward it. The river seemed like a foreign land, with a foreign language. Like mountains, I was learning that a river had its own complex lexicon to decipher, and it was mysterious and overwhelming to me.

Finally, we simulated an accidental swim, in case a person got thrown out of the raft. Each kid would stand thirty feet away from the raft while another threw the rope bag their way. For the sighted swimmers, the bag could land nearby and they were supposed to swim toward it, but for the blind kids, the rope would actually need to make contact so they'd know where to grab. For the next thirty minutes, bags soared through the air, clocking blind kids in the chests, heads, and groins in a human target practice.

After we'd finished blind boot camp, it was finally time to push off. The action began revving up almost immediately with rapids like Badger and Soap Creek, considered warm-ups, and the next day one of the biggies, House Rock, rated a 7 on the 10 scale. Marieke said it was named for a giant rock that you needed to avoid. We entered down the tongue as Marieke yelled, "Right paddle . . . and stop! All paddle . . . charge!" and we encountered a terrific energy, like an earthquake. The boat pitched and bucked forward and back, left and right. It was dizzying as we rose up the front side of a colossal wave, everyone paddling like crazy. The blind kids in front were digging in hard, but the angle of the boat was so steep, the front half protruded into the sky, and they only dug at air. Then the boat crested the top, and all two thousand pounds lurched downward.

"Brace! Brace!" Marieke yelled from the back, and everyone hunkered down, lodging their feet even deeper under the rubber tubes. There was a terrific explosion as the bow hit the trough and stopped momentarily. The force was like a car crash, the stiff rubber boat folding and everyone being thrown forward, submerged in massive amounts of water and foam. It was a miracle that everyone stayed in the boat. Riding out the tail waves and safe on the other side, we all cheered, raising our paddles in the air and trying to clap them together. A few of us missed, but after eight tries, we all made impact.

As we paddled through the flat sections, Marieke described to us the thick, silty color of the river, the clouds passing, and the canyon walls with different colors—reds, browns, and blacks, like the layers of a birthday cake— each of the distinct layers representing different geological times throughout history. She said that in the inner gorge, the walls rose up more than a mile high in some places, and at the bottom of the canyon was some of the oldest rock on earth, almost two billion years old. She'd smack her paddle flat against the water so we could hear its rifle crack echoing to the top of the canyon walls. We even pulled the raft over so all of us could run our fingers across this smooth, hard sandstone worn down by the eons.

She also described our entertaining safety kayak guide who also happened to be her little brother, Harlan. He glided around us in a hard-shell kayak. His job was to paddle quickly to the action and assist any swimmers. She described him in his tiny kayak, constantly flipping upside down, staying under for what seemed like an impossible amount of time, and emerging

upright from the dark water with a giant smile across his face. Crazy thing
was that she said he was doing that on purpose—for fun. "I've never seen
someone as comfortable in water as Harlan," she said. "He's been that way
ever since I can remember. It's like he's half human, half dolphin."

At the bottom of each rapid, we'd pull over in our rafts and she'd describe
her brother still upriver, in the middle of the rapid, playing on the biggest,
steepest waves. I learned it was called surfing. Like ocean waves that roll
toward shore, river waves move as well, but some, called "standing waves,"
recirculate over and over, building up and then collapsing on themselves. A
few of the standing waves were giant curlers that were glassy and smooth.
Harlan would ride them like a rodeo cowboy on a bucking bronco and use their
energy to execute superhuman maneuvers like cartwheels and flips. Marieke
tried to teach us the names of each trick: a "blunt," a 180-degree flip where
you land backward; and a "backstab," which was a backflip landing forward. Even from a long way away and in the midst of the roar, I could hear
Harlan whooping with joy as he rode these giant liquid beasts. His kayak was
an extension of his body, working in perfect sync.

That evening, Harlan gave me a tour of his kayak. The smooth plastic felt
like Tupperware, but it was banged up in a few places where he had hit obstacles. It had a blunt point in front and sharp edges on the sides for dipping
in and catching waves. I felt the inside seat and the knee braces he used to steer
and the neoprene skirt that he stretched over the opening of the cockpit to
stop the water from pouring in when he was upside down. Finally, I felt his
paddle, with a straight shaft and wide scooping paddle blades, all impossibly
light and constructed from carbon fiber.

"Try it out if you want," he said. We were beached on the edge of a huge
calm eddy, which I'd recently learned was a section on the side of a river that
recirculated upstream. Sometimes they were flat and calm like this one. I
squeezed into the cockpit. It felt cramped and claustrophobic. Harlan pushed
me out into waist-deep water. I tried to paddle, but the kayak was so squirrely
it kept going back and forth, left and right, like an overly sensitive steering
wheel. I leaned over to take a next paddle and immediately tipped over, slapping face-first into the cold water. I didn't have Harlan's spray skirt around

me and immediately came out of the boat and was swimming. Harlan was right there to grab me and yank me to shore, along with his kayak, now upside down and filled with fifty gallons of water. I shivered.

"It takes a little to get used to," he said gently.

The next morning, Harlan approached me with a question. "We have these inflatable rubber kayaks on the trip. They're called 'duckies.' They're way more forgiving than a hard-shell kayak. They're pretty stable in a rapid. Normally, we let folks paddle them through some of the easy stuff, but I don't have enough experience with blindness to know. Should we let the blind kids paddle them?"

Not being a water person, I didn't have an answer, but I was even more impressed by Harlan. Instead of making a snap judgment one way or the other, he was using this first trip as a laboratory. "Why don't I be the guinea pig?" I said.

I followed his footsteps over to the shore and got a tour of a ducky. It was the same soft, rugged material as a raft and much longer and wider than Harlan's kayak. If his hard-shell was a finely tuned sports car, then this was a tank. We pushed off with Harlan in the water in front of me. He yelled, "How about I blow a whistle and you follow me?"

I paddled furiously and managed to stay behind him, more or less, through the next small riffle. It was exciting to be in my own boat, even if it was a tank versus a Porsche, and it was thrilling and scary being bounced around by the waves that came from all directions and crashed over my boat.

Besides experiencing the exciting white water, each day we'd pull the rafts over and hike up incredible side canyons with pools of water and rushing waterfalls that you could stand under and get a shower. All the blind kids were given adjustable hiking poles, and I showed them how to lengthen and shorten them according to how tall each person was. We showed the sighted teens how to guide their blind partners by ringing a bear bell in front of them and calling out guiding instructions. It was another laboratory experiment at first. "Go left . . . no, not that far. Now a little back right."

"How far right?"

"A little farther."

"How far is a little?"

"Watch that rock."

"I can't watch it."

"I don't mean *watch* it. I mean feel it in front of you with your pole."

On one of our first hikes, up a steep set of jumbled stairs to some ancient ancestral Puebloan granaries, the sighted leaders told me Chase was kind of a spaz. His gangly legs and arms moved independently without much communication between the different parts. With each step, his knees and elbows lifted high and awkwardly into the air. The description seemed remarkably similar to that of Tashi in Tibet, who had also moved with that same uncoordinated style. The end of Chase's poles flailed forward in front of him to find obstacles. Sometimes the carbide tip would happen upon the protruding rock, but as many times as not, he'd miss it entirely, trip, and go flying through the air. Despite his knees trickling blood, we trekked every afternoon, and there was so much to experience: to hear, to touch, even to taste. Many times, Harlan would spot something for us to feel in the Redwall Limestone, like the tracks of prehistoric marine vertebrates that he called "nautiloids." They felt like fossilized clams, long and conical, with rounded ribs. Another time he brought us to some sharp, ridged rock above the river's edge.

"This is part of the Supai Group," he said. "You can feel how it fractures, round on top and flat underneath, like an upside-down ledge." Sometimes, he'd pull up some desert grass and say, "Chew on this; it tastes like peppermint," or, "This leaf was a natural stimulant. The Indians used it to stop their hunger when they were on hunting expeditions."

That night, Marieke sat us in a circle and told us about the first expedition down the Grand Canyon. "It was led by Major Wesley Powell. Like some of you, he had a disability too. He'd lost an arm in the Civil War. His dream of exploring this canyon became an obsession. Some of his special wooden boats bashed into the rocks and sank. Many of their provisions washed down the river, lost. They almost starved to death along the way. Imagine, for Powell and his crew . . . they had no idea whether their journey would end in triumph, or whether they'd drop off the face of a massive waterfall and plunge to their deaths. For you guys, this trip involves some uncertainty too."

On day two, we hiked up to an old tunnel dug into the rock. Marieke said the Grand Canyon was almost lost to a giant dam that was planned for construction there, and it would have drowned the canyon. It was pitch black inside the tunnel, the perfect setting to reverse roles. For the next hour, the blind kids led their sighted partners through the winding passage, and the darkness was pierced by the cries of disoriented teenagers. "Slow down . . . where'd you go? Is that you, Chase? I'm totally turned around."

After the blind tour, we ate lunch on a sandy beach. Marieke, Harlan, and the crew unloaded tables and coolers and set up a buffet. With all the blind kids in line feeling for bread, cheese, turkey meat, and mustard, we started calling it the Braille Buffet. We shared our lunch as the kids sat in an impromptu circle in the sand. They wanted to know everything, and I felt like the designated big brother. They especially wanted to know about girlfriends and boyfriends and were fascinated that I was married to a sighted woman. I told them about Ellie, who drove our car, piloted our tandem bike, guided me down mountains on skis, and had learned Braille to prepare for one of our early dates. The kids then went around the circle sharing their backgrounds. Chase had begun the trip in silence, but he had soon warmed to the group, his words coming out in rapid fire like an old engine sputtering to life. "I'm really into computers," he said. "I'm on mine for hours pretty much every day."

He told us that his parents worked long hours each day. He got a ride home from school on a special bus for handicapped kids. Once inside his house, he hung out alone in his room, doing homework, listening to music, and programming on the computer. "I love the computer. I learned Basic last year. This year I'm learning Java, but it does get kind of lonely sometimes. I'm not really allowed to go outside. I can't even go down my driveway to get the mail in the mailbox. My parents say I'll get lost, or I could get hit by a car. I'm honestly surprised I'm even here."

"Last call for lunch!" Harlan yelled, and I headed back to the table and felt for a couple of oranges in a bowl. Back in the circle, I dropped down next to a shy kid named Joey and offered him an orange. I reached out with it, and we found each other's hands. I was eating my orange when I noticed a lot of silence in his direction.

"You going to eat that?" I asked.

He stammered a little but didn't reply.

"You got to eat and stay hydrated on the river," I said.

"Can you peel it?" he asked.

"Peel it yourself," I joked, but he didn't laugh back.

"I don't know how. I've never done it before," he replied.

"What? Eaten an orange?"

"No. Peeled one."

"You've never peeled an orange?" I said, trying to tamp down the shock in my voice and trying to let the sentence sink in. "Nobody's taught you to peel an orange?" I asked.

The next few minutes I had him feel my hands as I showed him how to use my thumbnail to dig in and peel back the skin, how to try to spiral the skin away in as few pieces as possible, then how to separate the fruit into neat wedges. When it was peeled, he broke off a section and offered it to me.

After lunch, we went for a hike up a beautiful side canyon. Along the trail, Harlan took me aside. "I want to talk with you about Joey. He can't hear us; he's up ahead. I think he needs a little help. He's been peeing on the trail, in plain view, which is kind of a problem for at least half the group. It's a little strange too. He doesn't do it normally." Harlan chuckled sheepishly.

"What do you mean?"

"Well, he puts his hands behind his neck and kind of pushes his hips forward."

I put my hands behind my neck. "Like this?" I asked.

"That's right," Harlan said. "You got it. That's how he does it. It's kind of a weird request," he pushed on. "But I think you're the perfect guy to teach him how it's done."

I had heard about blind boys being taught to pee in a toilet by sitting down. It was easier than orienting yourself with your knees against the bowl and trying to aim for the sound of water. So it made sense that no one had taught him to pee in the outdoors. I tried to remember who had taught me. I honestly couldn't recall. Maybe it was having two older brothers who had pushed me and connected me to the sighted world. I remembered on a trek in the Peruvian Andes when the two of them had seen a sign that read BEWARE OF SNAKES. All three of us had lined up and peed in front of that sign. I still had a photo somewhere.

At the next break, I took Joey aside and asked if he had to take a leak. I had him grab my pack, and I used my trekking poles to navigate away from the trail. I tapped the thorny branches of a mesquite tree, and we worked our way around it. I told him that would block him from the group.

"And last piece of advice," I added. "You can't put your arms behind your head like that. You got to hold it. You got to own it." I laughed. "If there was snow on the ground, you could even write your name."

An hour more up the canyon, we reached a beautiful amphitheater with a large pool of water. Harlan immediately splashed in, swam across, and climbed up the other side. "Come on!" he called back.

Then I jumped in along with most of the kids. Yet Joey held back. A couple of kids tried to persuade him, but he held fast. "I don't like getting my feet wet," he finally said. So half joking, I offered to carry him across. Surprisingly, he took me up on it, and I found myself with Joey on my shoulders wading across the waist-deep water, with Joey lifting his feet up above the water's surface. I could feel the slick rock bottom under my feet and probed beneath the surface with one of my poles; it wouldn't be much of a confidence builder if I pitched over and spilled him into the pool. I deposited Joey on a short wall, and he clambered up into an even narrower canyon, the perfect steepness to scramble on hands and feet up the clean, polished sandstone.

We all followed Joey and Harlan. A couple of hundred feet farther, we stopped against a vertical wall, and we called and whistled, listening to the echo of our voices reverberating. Harlan had brought his guitar, and he played and sang a few songs. My favorite was "If I Had a Boat" by Lyle Lovett: "If I had a boat, I'd go out on the ocean, and if I had a pony, I'd ride him on my boat, and we could all together, go out on the ocean, me upon my pony on my boat." The lyrics cracked the kids up, and by the last chorus, we were all singing along, blown away by the crisp, clear acoustics of the canyon.

That night, I lay on my Paco pad under a sheet that I had soaked in the frigid Colorado River. The temperature was still over ninety degrees. I thought about the surprising day. I had counted on guiding those who had never hiked before, but teaching them how to peel an orange and how to pee behind a tree had honestly floored me. I considered the teens in Tibet who were much worse off. Opportunities were scarce, and they had to scrap for everything they possessed. They'd been spit on, ridiculed, and made to feel subhuman. But in response to that, they'd fought back. Since the expedition, Gyenshen and Tenzin had started up their own massage therapy businesses; Gyenshen wrote me proudly that they had purchased a refrigerator and had expanded into selling cold soft drinks. Sonam Bhumtso, after repeated denials, had finally been accepted to a prestigious sighted school and now was ranked first in her class; she was on track to graduate in the spring. Tashi had fallen in love with one of the sighted den mothers from the center; she was a few years older, but they were madly in love. And Kyila was transitioning into taking over the center. She was going to make a great teacher and was still planning to fulfill her Dream Factory goal of opening a kindergarten. She had also recently been accepted for a scholarship and had studied in England at a special language school.

If the analogy was a boxing match, the Tibetan kids had taken multiple blows to the face, been beaten down and bloodied. They knew they were in the fight of their lives and had come up swinging. It's human nature, I thought. We're better equipped if our backs are against the wall. But what if you don't even know you're in that fight? No one's knocking you down. No one's cursing at you and calling you a blind fool. In fact, just the opposite; the ones you love and trust the most are peeling your oranges for you and teaching you to sit down on the toilet instead of standing. They tell you to stay in your room because it's safe, and you have no idea that the prison bars are slowly closing in front of you. The greatest injustice is that you don't know. You never even know! It's better, I thought, to be punched in the face and knocked flat, to get back up with your broken nose and black eyes and square off against your oppressor. Better that, I decided, than to be doomed to a life of quiet acquiescence.

The next day, we stopped at what had to be one of the natural wonders of the world, at least for the blind. It was called Redwall Cavern, a huge beach the size of a couple of football fields, all covered by a massive rock overhang. You could conduct a concert with a thousand people on the beach. Many of the kids had never sprinted before, so we set up blind races and told the kids there was nothing to trip over but sand dunes. Even the sighted kids were blind-folded. Then I challenged Chase to a race. I showed him how to start in runner's position, crouched down and one hand touching the sand. He bounded out of the gate like a newborn foal. As I ran beside him, I envisioned his gangly arms and legs churning. He kept falling to his hands and knees, each time leaping up again and flailing forward. I beat him by a few feet and was at the finish line to tackle him. We both came up like sand monsters, covered from head to toe with gritty Colorado River clay. For the rest of the day on the raft, he kept poking me excitedly in the shoulder to say, "I'm going to beat you next time. You just got lucky."

Toward the end of the week, the team had now graduated to blind and sighted duos paddling on tandem duckies through the small rapids, then to blind kids paddling solo and following Harlan, and finally to two blind teens paddling together. They'd zigzag through the waves, getting "window shaded," turned sideways, and dumped out of the boat, with Harlan always right there to tow them back to their duckies and help them back aboard. I traded off with the kids as well, and one day after an exhilarating rapid, Harlan said, "You're pretty good. You should learn how to paddle a hard-shell kayak, and someday, I'll guide you down the whole canyon."

I thought about the baby rapids I'd come through in the ducky, which were plenty scary and difficult. We'd all been avoiding even the medium-size ones. And the real monsters were all on the second half of the trip, which we were skipping. I had tried his kayak in flat water and had lasted less than a minute before tipping over. "Sure," was all I was able to offer weakly in reply.

On the last night, we sat in a circle again reviewing the experience. We called the highs and lows "sunshine and clouds." For one of the sighted kids, his highlight was learning to guide his blind partner down the trail. For others it was the thrill of the big rapids. For Joey, I was proud to hear it was being carried across the side-canyon pool and scrambling up the gulley on the other side. And for Chase, it was sprinting through Redwall Cavern.

"What did that feel like?" a kid asked.

"Well, it felt kind of like I was a bird let out of a cage," he replied. "I love running full throttle. I'd never done it before. I have to admit, I don't like falling down, which I do a lot."

He paused for a few seconds and then resumed, "I know it sounds stupid, but I think I've figured something out. I want to run more, but I think I'm going to fall a lot. Falling sucks, but that's just part of it. I've got to get up and keep running. I guess what I mean is that you can't run if you're not willing to fall."

I, along with the entire group, sat back speechless. I wasn't sure if Chase's revelation was foolish or one of the wisest Forrest Gump speeches I'd ever heard. I tended to think the latter. For some reason, what Chase said made me think about Harlan's offer to kayak the Grand Canyon. Mount Everest had been hard enough, I thought, bordering on preposterous. But kayaking down a river like the Grand Canyon, well, that moved into the realm of fool-hardy. I wondered if it were possible.

8

ANITA, MY LOVE

I had only been home from the Grand Canyon a few days when Mark had another relapse, and we pushed him into his third rehab program. This time, he walked out early, saying he had it under control, but the journal Mark kept during the program expressed much more doubt. It was titled "Anita, My Love."

Anita was my first love. Anita Drink was her full name. It was a powerful love. I had my first drink at 13 years old. She made me feel invincible. She took all my fears and inhibitions away. With her, I could do no wrong. I was funnier, stronger, the life of the party. I could have anything I wanted. I charged through my 20's, working hard, playing hard, partying hard. I did some crazy things. Lots of girlfriends. Some I cared for, but they all lost out to Anita.

In my 30's, I tried to settle down. I became a parent to a beautiful amazing little girl, and I felt deep satisfying love, like nothing I'd ever felt before. By experiencing this new kind of love, I knew what I felt for Anita was false. So I tried to split up with her. I'd go for a few months without seeing her, but I'd always find her again, or she'd find me. Finally, I made up my mind to leave her for good. I realized that everything bad in my life, bad decisions, hurting others, shame, self-hatred, pain, regret, was all because of her. But she was having none of that. She wouldn't let me go. If she couldn't have me, no one could. Now I hated her and wanted a divorce. More than that, I wanted her gone for good. I needed to bury her in a coffin with five strong padlocks that could never be broken. I would lower the coffin into a twenty-foot hole and fill it in with concrete. I know this may sound drastic, but Anita has been known to escape like Houdini. To be honest, I hated to see her go, but I knew with every fiber of my body, she deserved to go where I was sending her.

So I told her she was finished, but she changed right before my eyes. She went from a beautiful woman to a heavyweight boxer, and not just any boxer. She was the world champion, and we were in the title fight. She kicked my ass and sent me sprawling and bleeding in the corner, but I keep crawling back for more. I know she's not my love anymore. She's my enemy. I'll probably get my ass kicked again, and I don't know if I can ever win this, but I'll never stop crawling back into the ring to fight her again and again, because I know real love now, and for that, I want to live.

Eddi, my dad, and I got the doctor on the phone, and he spoke bluntly. "Mark is a really tough case. His disease is profound. I've seen it before, and I hate to tell you this, but he is either going to wind up in jail or dead."

After another family huddle, it had finally sunk in; this was becoming life or death. Eddi offered to have Mark come up to live with his family—his wife and four kids. Mark was great the first several days, putting the kids to bed and helping cook and do dishes, even vacuuming and dusting the house. Mark and Eddi spent each evening at the end of Eddi's dock, fishing for catfish and reliving old stories late into the night, cans of iced tea in their hands instead of beers. On the fourth day, however, while Eddi was at work, Mark went to the cash drawer, walked three miles to a convenience store, and got some bottles of wine. When Eddi came home, Mark was floundering around the living room, incoherent and belligerent. "You can't do this here," Eddi said, angry and disappointed. "I've got four little kids now, and I've got to keep them safe." So with tears pouring down his face, Eddi drove Mark to the bus station and gave him sixty bucks for a bus ticket. "There should be fifteen left over for food," he said. Mark didn't use the money for a ticket. He hung out on a bench in the station for two more days, drinking the money away with a few bums. One of the attendants finally called Eddi. He drove back and this time bought the ticket for Mark and put it in his hand.

A few weeks later, I flew to Orlando and met my dad. Together, we drove to Mark's house, and when we arrived, his door was locked, and the electricity had been turned off again. We pounded on his door, but he didn't answer, so we went around the back and knocked on the windows. Finally, after a long time, he came shuffling to the door. He was in bad shape. I hugged him, and he shuddered a little. His face and hands were crusted with dried blood, and I felt a homemade sling around one arm, from a wrapped ACE bandage. He was a frightened and withdrawn shell of his former gregarious self.

"What happened, Mark?" I asked.

He'd been in a car accident. A couple of nights before, he'd been driving and had seen shadowy people on the road. He swerved to miss them and crashed his truck into some trees. On the side of the road, he looked again, and they weren't there anymore. It was just an empty road. "I think they were spirits coming to get me," he said. "But there's no way they were going to catch me. I took off running through the woods."

Mark climbed over chain-link fences and concrete walls and found a strip mall. He stole a bike from a rack outside a restaurant and rode it all the way home. As he pedaled, he looked up and saw hooded demons reaching down from the trees with long arms to grab him and pull him up. He weaved and dodged their shadowy hands. "It was the most terrifying ride of my life," he said. "But I was flying, going so fast, they couldn't catch me."

That night, the ghosts had come for him again. "I saw them sneaking up in the backyard," he said, "and I ran out and smashed them with a baseball bat."

Outside the window were the fractured remnants of these nightmares. I walked around his backyard crunching over the decorative ceramic statues, fountains, and garden gnomes, now all shattered to pieces. Finding his abandoned truck, the police had come to his house. "They banged on the door, but I hid, and they eventually went away."

We didn't know what to do, but he hadn't eaten since the accident, so we took him out to dinner to what had been his favorite restaurant, Steak and

Ale. In happier days, he had said, "It's the best salad bar you'll ever eat, with giant plates that are prechilled, shredded cheese, cloves of garlic, and real bacon bits."

Mark had loved being in charge of making my salad. He'd bring the plate back to the table and slap it down, heaping tall with all the fixings. "How's that for a salad?" he'd say proudly, but this dinner was somber, with none of the past chatter. The only words spoken were my father's as he laid out the plan to get Mark's electricity turned back on.

I sat there desperately trying to think of solutions. Maybe I could drop my upcoming climbs and move down there. I could keep his house clean and make sure he wasn't drinking. We could take taxis to the grocery store to get food. I bet sometimes his friends could drive us too. But almost as soon as these thoughts crossed my mind, the plan disintegrated as I recalled all the previous failed attempts at help: the multiple drives back and forth to Orlando my dad had made, the dozens of late-night phone calls, all the rehab treatments from which he'd left early. Eddi had even tried having Mark live with his family. All had failed. If I moved in with him, it wouldn't be a week before I was trying to wrestle the beer cans out of his hands and being abruptly booted out the door. Mark Weihenmayer would not be taking orders from his little bro, I realized with a heavy heart.

After dinner, we drove him home. Mark got out of the car, and I gave him a hug. He didn't hug back. His one arm lay in a sling; the other hung limply at his side. I just couldn't stand it anymore. "Mark, man, you know I love you," I said, "but I think you're going to kill yourself."

He took a few steps up his driveway toward his house and then turned around. When he did, he was crying. I was crying too. "I never gave up on you," he yelled with anger and pain, "so don't you give up on me! Don't you ever give up on me!"

Just two weeks later, I sat with my family squeezed into couches and chairs at Eddi's house near Pensacola, watching old Super 8 videos of our family adventures around the world. One was of my Denali summit back in 1995. As I listened, I allowed myself to relive the experience, filled with crushing exhaustion and suffering, mixed with steep pinnacles of elation. Denali is the tallest peak in North America, my first of the Seven Summits and one of the hardest. At 4:30, after nineteen backbreaking days in the Alaska Range, we'd reached the summit. I hadn't known at the time, but it turned out it was Helen Keller's birthday. And the best part of that thirty-below-zero summit was getting to share it with my family who were there with me, in a way. As we took our last plodding steps, circling above us was an Otter plane containing my father, Ellie, Eddi, and Mark. As we heard the plane engine approaching, my team and I cheered and waved our ski poles. We had timed it perfectly by radioing down to base camp operator Annie, who radioed out to the four Weihenmayers waiting in Talkeetna on a dirt runway. They'd been hanging out for four days while we sat through a storm up high. The video is priceless. Ellie, who was on the couch watching beside me, described the cloudy image, the lens pointing downward through a dirty cabin window, toward seven little red dots on a lump of snow in space, with a sea of white all around.

Behind the camera was Mark, narrating as always. His voice ramped with energy as he yelled against the roar of the engine, "There they are! Unbelievable! There they are! Ellie, you see 'em down there?"

The camera turned toward Ellie, all bundled up, with a furry fleece hat, headset over her ears, and oxygen mask covering her face. Her eyes were wide with awe and amazement.

Mark continued to shout, "You see 'em, Ed Boy? Do you guys see 'em? I think they're waving. That's my little brother down there. He did it. He's on the summit. That's my bro. Taught him everything he knows."

His voice continued through a string of commentary and on-the-spot interviews with the family. As our grandmother always said, his jaw never stopped flapping in the breeze. "How about a cheer?" he yelled. "You guys ready?"

The four all erupted into a hip-hip-hurray, and Mark then let out a loud roar of pleasure, pure joy, pure emotion. Not to say my oldest brother was innocent in most ways, but at that moment, his voice had a childlike love and, yes, even innocence that I'll always associate with Mark. We rewound the DVD player and listened again and again to Mark's voice shouting down on me from the window of the plane. He was right. Mark had never given up on me, and that made the pain a thousand times worse, like a knife stabbing into my heart. I had gotten a team of Tibetan blind kids to twenty-one thousand feet on Mount Everest and another team of blind kids safely down the Grand Canyon; I'd carried a paraplegic on my back for over a mile, and I'd climbed to over twenty thousand feet on Denali with my family looking down, but in the end, I couldn't save my big brother. A neighbor had found Mark lying peacefully on his couch. This time, Mark hadn't been able to pound his heart back into beating.

A plate lay on the coffee table next to him. An empty package of ground beef lay on his counter next to a spatula and a dirty skillet on the stove. It looked like he'd just eaten lunch, then settled onto the couch to take a nap. There wasn't any beer in the refrigerator either; he must have been on another dry spell. He was forty-six years old. I reviewed the evidence like a detective: the dirty skillet, the spatula, the empty plate, all seemed trivial on the surface, but somehow felt like clues. Maybe it was because they symbolized that he hadn't planned to die that day, that he was still hoping to beat this thing and return to being a father again. Despite his yearning, he hadn't been able to break through the brick wall, but, instead, had beaten his head against it, over and over, until his body had failed him. But the burger in his belly was the indisputable proof that he was still fighting. It was the fuel he planned to carry him forward into his future.

Nobody ever expects to bury their own brother, but my dad, Eddi, and I stood together in the cemetery on a steaming July day in Jay, Florida. We passed the shovel around and dug a hole. Mark had been cremated, and I held the heavy bag, having trouble comprehending Mark being reduced to ashes and bits of bone. I placed him in the hole. Gabbi, now a tall, beautiful nine-year-old with wavy brown hair, had written a note for her dad. It simply read, "Remember me." She placed it in the hole next to the ashes. We threw dirt on top and packed it down. He was resting right next to our mother, who'd also died at the same age of forty-six.

After the funeral, we returned home to Colorado, and I tried to move forward. Checking her e-mail, Ellie rushed over to me. I was on the living room floor playing with Emma, who was six now. "We got a picture today from the agency. They've connected with an orphanage in Kathmandu. There's a little boy."

"Well, describe him," I said, bursting with anticipation.

"His name is Arjun Lama, and he's four years old. He's wearing an orange winter parka that looks way too big for him. He's barefoot, and his feet are a little dirty, and they must be so cold. His face is kind of round, and his eyes are not looking straight ahead, but off to the side. He's not smiling. I think he looks like a poet, about to tell us a secret, something so profound that it may change our whole world."

As I listened, my daughter, Emma, and I were playing Polly Pockets. My job was to dress the little plastic people. I was attempting to put the little shoes and plastic pants onto Polly, which required immense patience and dexterity. As I tried to get a pair of groovy bell-bottom pants onto Polly's rubber legs, I split the seams. Emma reached for it. "No, Daddy," she squealed. "Not like that. You broke it."

I must have been channeling Mark, because I laughed and said, "Ripped jeans are the rage these days, Emma. Don't worry. Polly will love them."

"No, she won't," Emma protested, about to cry.

Ellie, looking down at the chaos, said, "I think you need someone you can climb with, wrestle with, someone you can have burping contests with. Maybe a little boy, as active as Mark."

A few days later, my friend and Mount Everest teammate Eric Alexander called and asked to take me on a climb. He knew I was grieving, and he had the perfect mountain picked out—Mount of the Holy Cross, a fourteen thousand–foot peak in Colorado's Sawatch Range. It was named for the distinctive cross-shaped snowfield on the northeast face. Our route would be straight up the cross to the summit.

As we started up the couloir, it was frigid and an icy wind blew down the gulley into our faces. I lowered my numb, stinging face against the wind. Finally, the sun began creeping up behind us. It's a curious thing, that when the first rays of the sun lift over the horizon, it actually gets colder for a time. Mountaineers know this as the coldest part of the day, a window of endurance as you look forward to the warmth of the day still to come. As I plunged my axe into the deep snow time and time again, I panted hard and my calves burned. I was also feeling drained, not from altitude, but from the lingering effects of the previous week. As we reached the intersection of the cross, we stopped, drove our axes into the snow, and anchored our packs to them. We sat on a protruding rock, sharing some cheese and an energy bar between us.

Eric is my friend of faith. He's the best kind of Christian, never beating you over the head with his beliefs and never once in our friendship exhibiting any kind of dogma. But as we sat, I broached the subject. "How does a life get taken away?" I said. "Mark had so much to live for, and now it's all gone, leaving his daughter to grow up without him—without a dad."

Eric was quiet for a long time until it became an uncomfortable silence, like the void of oxygen in the mountain air. "None of it is fair," he finally said. Then more silence. Finally, he resumed, "Did you know that historically it was the custom for people in times of mourning to actually lie in ashes? Isaiah 61 says God is going to take your mourning and give you beauty, to pick you up out of the ashes and make something new. The Hebrew word for ash is *epher*, and the word for joy is *pheer*. Move one letter and *ashes* becomes *joy*. I'm not sure what that beauty looks like for you, but perhaps it's out there."

As we started up again, the sun climbed higher in the sky, as if it were tracking us on our ascent. It shone down and finally warmed my back, and I admitted Eric had a point: Even in the midst of pain and struggle, there was a touch of beauty.

On the summit, Eric stepped away and let me have a minute alone. I squeezed into a cleft in the boulders and tried to pray for Mark, but I didn't seem to have much to say. I gave up, listening to the sky and the wind howling and feeling the snowflakes stinging my face. For some reason, I thought about my old friend Sabriye, standing on a cold beach on the North Sea and feeling the unfairness and sadness bubbling up from within and merging with the stormy ocean and sky. That fury had led her to Tibet. So I decided to do the same and let the rage out of the box.

"You asshole!" I yelled. "What the hell is your problem? We were supposed to get old together and watch our kids grow up. When I went blind, it totally sucked, and you were there to help me, but you never let me help you back. You closed yourself off. You didn't let anyone in. You left us. You didn't have to leave us. It was your own fault. I never gave up on you!"

Then I sat silent for a while, spent, as the wind spiraled the snow around me like mini tornados. I didn't want this to be the cold, bitter ending. I wanted to believe that Eric was right, that the wisdom of the Bible was right: that out of ashes could come something else, a new beginning.

But there was no denying it or changing it; Mark was now only ashes. Once, long ago, however, his future had been like an open road, all possibilities and potential, no sickness, no dependence, no disappointment. One of my father's favorite stories recalled when Dad was a young marine driving across country with my mom and his newly adopted children. They'd been stationed at Kingsville airbase in Texas and had been reassigned to the Marine Corps air base in El Toro, California. They were all packed between suitcases in his red-and-white Plymouth Sport Fury convertible, he and my mom in the front and five-year-old Mark and six-year-old Suzanne in the back. The two kids sat up on the body of the car with their feet on the backseat. On training missions, my dad had touched down at El Toro a few times in his F-9, and he started singing, "California, here we come, right back where we started from. California here we come, California, here we come."

Everyone joined in, and the whole family sang at the top of their lungs as they rolled across the Arizona desert, the hot wind rushing at their faces. The scene had always seemed rife with new beginnings, and I desperately wanted that now.

When I'd brought up the idea of adoption with friends, even close ones, some had said, "You have such a great life—why would you want to bring a wildcard into your family?"

I imagined a little boy pulling Emma's ponytail and cheating at Monopoly, or maybe Buckets. It would definitely disrupt the order of our lives, I thought. I imagined Emma and her little brother dressing up for Halloween, and afterward, furiously trading for their favorite candy, or arguing over who would get the window seat. There would certainly be some tears. I wondered what Mark would do. Surely not the normal thing, the predictable thing, the boring thing. Maybe that wildcard was just what we needed, someone to draw us in, to lift us off our feet, spin us around until our lives were dizzy with chaos and joy. So I forced myself up. I was through wallowing in the ashes. I needed to follow my heart toward new beginnings.

"Arjun Lama," I said silently. "Arjun Lama Weihenmayer." It had kind of a ring to it.

9

A GRAIN OF SAND

In the fall of 2006, I found myself bouncing down the narrow streets of Kathmandu in a taxi. Outside the window, acrid fumes of burning trash seared my eyes and nose. Throngs of kids clamored and laughed as they chased our vehicle, and packs of dogs snarled and barked. The engine revved and the car shot forward, then lurched to a stop. My head swung forward as the driver laid on the horn. I felt small hands protrude through the open window and poke my shoulder. "Namaste. Namaste. You buy, mister."

The little hands retreated instantly as the driver shot forward, yanked hard left, whipped hard right, and accelerated again, tires squealing. The voice of a high-pitched woman warbled Bollywood-style on the radio in rhythm with the start and stop of the car, and the bumpy road thumped like a drum. Kami Tenzing Sherpa, the *sirdar* (manager) from my Mount Everest and Tibet expeditions, sat in the front passenger seat. Next to me, in the backseat, was my good friend Rob Raker. I was charged up with anticipation. "Maybe I'll change his name to Kami," I said. Kami laughed.

"I hope this all works out," I said. "I'm a little nervous."

"This is a big day for you," Rob said.

We were minutes away from the Helpless Children Protection Home in Kathmandu where I was about to meet Arjun. I repeated the words in my head, "My son . . . This is my son . . . I have a son . . ." It didn't seem real.

. . .

A week earlier, Nina, the head of our adoption agency, had gone over to Nepal to try to set up more adoptions and to establish more in-country partners who could help her. While there, she'd stopped in at the Helpless Children Protection Home to visit four-year-old Arjun. Ellie excitedly read me her e-mail from Kathmandu, fresh after her visit.

Dear Erik, Ellie, and Emma,

Arjun appears healthy. He was shy with me at first but slowly warmed up as we explored the gifts you sent. He seemed very curious. When we looked at the little book together, he touched the English script and kept running his hands over it. The director told him "that is English words." He said, "English is pretty."

He especially liked the two stuffed animals. He examined them carefully. He understood that I don't speak Nepali and tried to communicate with me through miming. He touched the eyes of the stuffed animal, then touched his eyes and then mine and said the Nepali word for eye, "kaan," like he was trying to teach me and also show me that he recognized that the toy had eyes.

I got a good smile out of him when I made the toys sniff him and check him out. Then he took over playing, making them dance and talk. But he really showed he is all boy when he made one of the animals sniff the butt of the other, then had the animal pretend to pass out in disgust.

When the orphanage director was sending him back out to play, she tried to convince him to store the stuffed animals in the gift bag so they would stay clean. Arjun wheeled off a big string of emphatic words in Nepali, which made her laugh out loud, and then she sent him out with the toys. When she stopped laughing, she translated what he said as, "You told me that my new mother sent these toys. I think she wants ME to have them. They belong to me, so I can decide if they get dirty or stay clean, and I have decided to keep them with me."

The director said, 'There is no sense arguing with him. He will persist until you give in. He is not going to scream or be loud. He just will do and do and do or say and say and say until he has what he wants. He never gives up!'

So in conclusion, sounds like he'll fit right in as a Weihenmayer.

P.S. Don't think you can count on Emma having a little servant—he knows his mind too well!

"If I didn't know any better, I'd think he was the reincarnation of Mark." I laughed and continued packing. This would be my second trip, I thought, that began with a letter. Nepalese adoption regulations required two separate visits, the first to meet the child and officially agree, and the second to complete a slew of paperwork and medical records. I also had a secondary purpose, to climb one of the hidden gems of the Himalayas, and I'd asked my climbing partner, Rob, to join me. Rob was an expert ice climber and alpinist.

When our taxi pulled up to the orphanage and we got out, more kids surrounded us, calling out, "Namaste," in singsong voices, and they escorted us into the home. Just like at Sabriye's school, Braille Without Borders in Tibet, I could hear that I was in a noisy courtyard full of kids. Children were shouting and kicking balls around. There was the sound of construction somewhere in the distance, and more yipping dogs. I could hear a Ping-Pong ball bouncing back and forth. I reached out and touched the table. It was made of concrete, with bricks lined across the center serving as a net.

The procession of kids ushered us inside. More children's voices echoed throughout what sounded like a large bare room. The escort then led us into an office, and Sabitri, the director, said, "Namaste," and presented us with ceremonial scarves called *khatas*. In return, I gave her a gift, also a scarf, from Colorado. "From my family," I said. "I like your home—lots of noise, lots of laughter."

"Big E, you've got someone standing a couple of feet in front of you," Rob said.

Sabitri spoke in Nepali, and I heard tiny feet and pants shuffling closer, yet not speaking.

"He's shy," I said to the room.

Kami then spoke to him, and he inched even closer. I knelt down and could hear his soft breathing just a foot away. I could sense he was staring at me. I reached out tentatively and felt his short cropped hair and stroked his shoulder. He was wearing the same puffy jacket as in the first photo Ellie had described to me.

"He's a little guy," I said.

"He's a lucky guy," Kami added.

"And I'm a lucky dad," I replied.

Then I handed Arjun my long white cane. He took it and handed it back. I had just bought a new cane for the trip. It was a new kind: Instead of folding like most canes, this one telescoped down, so you could place it in a bag. I pushed down on the top, and the cane began collapsing and didn't stop until it was less than a foot long.

"He likes that," Rob said.

I handed the cane back, and Arjun carefully extended it again to full height, which was more than twice as tall as he was. Then he tried to shrink it, but couldn't reach the top. I helped, and it disappeared again.

"It's magic," I said.

Then I pushed my talking watch, and it spoke the time.

"Another big smile," Rob called.

Arjun sat down on the couch next to me and spent the next five minutes pushing all the buttons on the watch, hearing the time, the date, the year. Then I let him hear the list of menu options for the alarm. Little tunes like "London Bridge Is Falling Down" played. Arjun pushed through the menu, and when he got to the last option, it was a rooster crowing, and I heard him giggle for the first time.

Sitting on the couch in the orphanage, I pulled out the treasures Ellie and Emma had tucked away in my suitcase. I showed him the photo gallery Ellie and Emma had made of our family. I'd memorized the order of the photos.

"That's Emma, your big sister, *Didi*," I said, "and that's Willa, our dog, *kukur*. That's your mama, *Ama*. *Romro cha*—good boy," I said, and I realized I'd just exhausted most of the Nepali words I knew. I then reached into my backpack and handed him a sweatshirt that said COLORADO, then a coloring book, a big carton of crayons, and a little penguin with a yellow nose. He poured the crayons out on the couch, picked them up, and clutched them in his hands. "You color with them," I said, taking one and pretending to color the book. But Arjun had another idea. He began to color over the penguin's nose. That got the second laugh of the day.

"His nose is turning green," Rob said.

Then Arjun shifted gears.

"This is very interesting," Rob narrated. "He's organizing his crayons according to their colors . . . Now he's placing them one by one back in the box. The tips are all pointing up, and he's being very meticulous."

"Maybe he'll take after you, Rob," I said.

As I sat with Arjun next to me, I thought how miraculous it was that I was even here. It wasn't legal for Americans to deal directly with foreign orphanages, so after careful research, Ellie had chosen a well-reviewed adoption agency out of Boulder, just twenty miles north of Golden. They would act as our liaison for the tricky process ahead. In our first meeting, we'd inquired about Nepal, and Nina, the head of the agency, had cautioned us against it. "It's almost impossible," she'd told us. "If I were you, I'd give up that idea."

We learned the restrictions were vast and seemed senseless from a Western point of view. For instance, regulations stated that prospective parents couldn't adopt siblings of the same gender; if you already had a girl, then you couldn't adopt another girl; if you had a boy, you couldn't adopt another boy; if you already had two children, then you no longer qualified—no exceptions. The policy didn't offer an explanation either, but I thought it had something to do with the fact that one boy and one girl met the definition of a perfect Hindu family.

We had written Kami about our desire, and he'd soon written back, telling us he'd found a little girl in a small Sherpa village whose parents were so impoverished, they welcomed their child being given to a well-off American family. He wrote, "Though it is hard for any parents to give their child away, still they are very much concerned about her future! So, they feel very happy and lucky about having you to adopt their daughter! She is very healthy! And she had indeed all the vaccinations which any child is supposed to have!" Kami added that there were ways around all the regulations too; Nepal was one of those places where you could circumvent the law with the right connections and enough money. But after reading his note, Ellie and I both knew, immediately, we couldn't proceed. It sounded too much like adopting a puppy at the kennel. We couldn't take a child away from her parents, even with all the right vaccinations. We instead sent Kami a check so the family could stay together.

In order to shift our desire from Nepal, the agency showed us pictures and descriptions of children from countries like Guatemala that produced over four thousand adoptions a year. However, Nepal had remained our top choice. I had grown to love this country and felt a deep connection. The mountains and people had helped to transform my life. I thought about the Sherpas who had risen above their superstitions about blindness and supported our climb to the top of the world. I remembered kneeling at the South Summit of Everest at over twenty-eight thousand feet and asking Ang Pasang to read the dial on my oxygen mask.

"It's good," he assured me.

"Is the weather holding out?" I asked, waving up at the sky.

"It's good," he repeated.

"So we have enough time," I asked, "to cross the knife-edge ridge up the Hillary Step to the summit, and back again?"

"It's good. We go up," he urged. And even at extreme altitude with barely enough oxygen to function, it occurred to me what a remarkable statement this was. Ang Pasang had been up Mount Everest twice before, and he knew the Sherpa code well. Up higher, if I fell down in the snow and couldn't get back up, his options were severely limited. He'd most likely die in an effort to drag me down the mountain. I knew Ang Pasang had a wife and two young children, so his simple statement had just linked his fate to mine, to that of a blind man. It was one of the most profound offerings of trust and belief I'd ever experienced. Nepal had plenty of problems: pollution, overcrowding, corruption, and desperate poverty. But I loved this country, not for its shortfalls, but for its aspirations, its hopefulness. It made me feel more optimistic about the world and the future, that humanity had the potential to elevate itself, to become the best version of itself.

So sitting in Nina's office, leafing through adoption brochures from Guatemala, I leaned back in my chair and thought hard. "I think we'll stick to Nepal," I said.

Judging by all the children in Emma's first-grade class, from Korea to China to Vietnam, international adoption seemed like a common practice, but with the endless paperwork required, we couldn't believe how anyone got to the finish line. It included multiple visits from social workers, bank statements, U.S. federal tax returns listing net worth, autobiographical summaries, police clearances, physical and mental health letters from doctors, fingerprints for the Colorado Bureau of Investigations and the FBI, proof of health insurance forms, original copies of marriage and birth certificates, copies of passports, a current vaccination report for our dog and cat, five letters of recommendations, commitment statements, motivational statements, adoption guarantee letter, list of properties statement, ten passport-size photographs of each parent, and two sets of ten photos taken of our house, including bedrooms, yard, and kitchen. As careful as we were, Ellie was constantly discovering outdated notary stamps, stamps pressed upside down, or seals not raised enough. If everything wasn't completed with 100 percent accuracy, two all-important forms would be denied: the Central Registry Form sent to the State of Colorado Department of Human Services and, the granddaddy of them all, the USCIS I-600: Application for Advance Processing of Orphan Petition.

Almost a year into the adoption process, all this work hadn't gotten us anywhere. Emma's T-shirt imprinted with the words BIG SISTER didn't even fit her anymore.

In the fall of 2006, Nepal was reeling with internal unrest. The Maoist civil war, simmering for the last ten years, mostly throughout the rural areas of Nepal, had now spilled into the streets of Kathmandu. The country was paralyzed by massive strikes. The protesters were attempting to force the monarchy to reinstate the parliament and instill democracy. In November, there was a breakthrough when the government signed a peace accord with the Maoists, curtailing the power of the monarchy and ending the long insurgency.

I had previously felt this conflict firsthand, when it exploded on the heels of my Mount Everest expedition in 2001. Sitting at thirteen thousand feet at the airstrip in Syangboche, Kami and the other Sherpas had begun wailing. They had just heard over their shortwave radio that ten members of the Nepali royal family had been assassinated. The prince had walked into dinner, pulled out an arsenal of guns, and shot everyone at the table. He'd then killed himself. The king's brother, not in the room at the time, was to be ordained as the new king. He was a hated figure and suspected to be behind the murders. He was a strict monarchist, and it was predicted his first act as king would be to suspend parliament and roll back hard-earned reforms. So we sat on the airstrip drinking a homemade rice wine called *chang* from old fuel containers while the Sherpas mourned and talked about the future of Nepal, which was now in jeopardy.

We had finally flown Russian helicopters into an abandoned Kathmandu airport. Our taxi couldn't get us very far through the city, so we had walked through the main part of town toward our hotel. A cacophony of sirens, loudspeakers, and angry chanting assaulted my ears as thousands of people rioted around us. Police behind barricades pointed AK-47s at the crowd. People were burning everything they could get their hands on, including vehicles. We were choking on the smoke. I was walking with Charley Mace from my team when his hand suddenly shoved me down so hard, I almost dropped to my knees, and a flaming brick soared just over my head. *How ironic*, I thought, *to survive the Khumbu Icefall only to die on the streets of Kathmandu.*

Our hotel was under curfew the rest of our time there. Nepali TV aired the funerals, a procession of bodies being paraded through the streets on a national day of mourning. We were all relieved when our flight finally took off, lifting up out of a cloud of chaos.

So now a period of tranquility contributed to our adoption agency feeling comfortable enough to establish contact with some key partners on the ground in Kathmandu. One of these was the Helpless Children Protection Home. The agency even hired a local liaison to start laying all the groundwork.

"We still don't recommend this," Nina said. "It's going to be a rollercoaster ride, but you've talked about Nepal so much, and the door is now open."

We had told Nina we were looking for a little boy, closer to Emma's age, perhaps four or five. Most people were looking to adopt babies, so once a child was out of diapers, his chances of being adopted dropped dramatically. The agency had followed with a photo. It was in low resolution, taken on a cheap phone. Ellie had stared at it for a long time, and she was immediately drawn to the boy inside. There was no test or a trial period to ensure the child would fit into your family. There was not a stack of pictures to choose from. It was just one grainy photo of a dirty-faced, barefoot little boy not quite staring at the camera. He was wearing baggy pants that were way too big for him and a pumpkin-colored puffy jacket. He looked like one of the pickpocket children in *Oliver Twist*. But Ellie knew, almost instantaneously, she was looking at her son. She had fallen in love. Then she described it to me, and as if through osmosis, I fell in love too. Most decisions are best made logically, with hours of careful deliberation, but this one was the opposite. It was like plucking up a grain of sand on a wide beach, or picking a star in the vast universe, and deciding, on the spot, it was the right one.

"How will he feel," Ellie asked, "when he learns someday he was chosen based on a photo?"

"I guess the same as Emma will feel," I answered, "when she learns someday she's the result of a million sperm racing toward an egg. If another sperm had won out, she wouldn't be here either. There's a randomness to everything in life."

"Maybe it's not random," Ellie countered.

After that, there was no other direction, no other option. I was on the phone booking a flight to Kathmandu, while Ellie was driving up the highway toward the agency to sign the next set of papers. On the way, she was pulled over for speeding. How could she explain to the officer that she was in such a hurry because we were having a baby? Later that day, Ellie said, "I feel guilty about not going with you for this first visit, but Emma's big art project is due, and her winter pageant is coming up. She's been practicing for a month and her class is counting on her. Besides, this has already been a test of resiliency, and my heart is already aching. So if it falls through, if it doesn't happen, I think you may be able to confront it better."

Our next days in Nepal were busy. Kami, Rob, and I needed to run around to complete all the initial paperwork. It was a tangled process. Apparently, the intent to adopt needed to be signed by a panel of governmental bureaucrats comprised of different ministries like the Ministry of Women, Children and Social Welfare, the Children's Federation, and the Ministry of Foreign

Affairs. We met with a procession of officials who assessed all our paperwork. We had to now wait for the files to be sent to another ministry and finally on to one more legal department before the orphanage would be notified that the adoption process was official. Since we had a few days to wait, Sabitri said it would be okay for us to visit Arjun at his school.

When we walked into his classroom, Rob described Arjun looking a little sheepish, hunched down in the back row in his navy-blue uniform. When he saw us, he hunkered down even farther—most likely embarrassed by the two "long noses," one with a camera around his neck and the other with a white stick, standing at the doorway smiling and waving. Typical Nepali schools were much about memorization and had a strict code of discipline. Incorrect answers often received a whack on the back of your hand with a ruler.

When we introduced ourselves, the entire class responded in unison, "Hello, sir. How are you, sir?"

"We're doing great," Rob said back. "How about you all?"

"Thank you, sir. We are fine, sir."

"So what are you learning today?" I asked.

In unison, they responded, "Hello, sir. How are you, sir?"

"I'm good," I said.

"Thank you, sir. We are fine, sir."

"Do you like school?" I tried again.

In unison again, "Hello, sir. How are you, sir?"

Rob and I chuckled and excused ourselves, saying good-bye as we departed.

As the door swung shut behind us, we heard their faint voices chiming still, "Thank you, sir. We are fine, sir . . ."

Sabitri also gave the okay for Arjun to spend the days at our hotel. So despite it not being official yet, and the fact Arjun didn't speak any English, Sabitri dropped him off the next morning and waved good-bye, saying, "Be back at 6:00 P.M.!"

Kathmandu didn't have much open space, but one of the old-English-style hotels, Hotel Yak & Yeti, had a beautiful quiet backyard with gardens, pruned hedgerows, statues, and fountains. So we decided to head there with Arjun for the day.

We started with an early lunch. On our first day at the orphanage, we'd witnessed the lunch routine. Each child was handed a small tin bowl filled with rice and lentils. There were no tables or silverware. Instead the kids sat on the ground in the courtyard scooping up food with their hands. So when Rob, Arjun, and I sat down at an outside table, I said, "What do ya say we fatten this guy up?"

"You know me, Big E," Rob said excitedly. "I never turn down food."

"And he might as well get used to American food," I added as I ordered Arjun a pizza and french fries and Rob and me club sandwiches. While we waited, Arjun sat swallowed up by his chair, his feet dangling. He beat on the table with his fork and spoon. At the next table over sat a young European couple with a little Nepali girl. Rob said quietly, "Guess you're not the only one adopting around here."

Rob made eye contact, and the mom approached our table to introduce herself.

"We're adopting as well. How wonderful you two are adding to your family!"

My face creased into an awkward grin, and Rob said sheepishly, "Actually, I'm just helping with Erik's family." And then he said a little more softly, "He has a wife back in Colorado."

"Oh. Well," she continued, "I hope it all goes smoothly."

"So far so good," I said as Arjun sat sawing at the table with his steak knife.

As she turned back toward her table, Rob added, "His wife is coming on the next trip. I'm actually married too."

When the food arrived, Arjun devoured his pizza and fries astonishingly fast. My belly was a little upset, a feeling you came to expect in Nepal. The typical joke was:

"How was your meal?"

"Don't know yet. Tell you in six hours."

So the second half of my sandwich still sat on my plate. Arjun dropped off his chair, climbed onto my lap, and began eating the other half. I felt a little guilty, because I knew this was probably Arjun's first taste of meat. I recalled the police report, which stated that he was found on the street crying, so malnourished he couldn't walk. The orphanage had nursed him back to health on an all-vegetable Hindu diet.

After finishing the rest of my plate, Arjun moved around the table and polished off a chunk of bread still left on Rob's plate. Then he saw a dish full of ketchup that the waiter had brought for the fries. He grabbed it and began drinking it down.

"Whoa," Rob said, pulling him back. "That's going to make you sick."

Apparently, Arjun got the message not to guzzle the ketchup, so like I'd seen before at the orphanage, he switched gears and began pouring water, then Fanta, and then salt and pepper into the ketchup dish and mixing it all together in a potion. As he mixed, he chattered energetically to himself.

"He's a mad scientist," Rob said, chuckling.

After lunch, I took Arjun's hand, and we walked through the hotel grounds. We dipped our hands in the fountains and felt the two stone lions that guarded the entrance to the garden. Then I put Arjun on my shoulders. He seemed to like it as I began veering around pretending to careen into trees and bushes.

"I'm a crazy taxi driver," I said, swaying from side to side. Arjun began squealing and howling with laughter. Then I spun a 360, and he squealed more, shouting out in Nepali words I thought meant, "More! Again!" I was about to do it even faster when a waiter rushing by with a tray called out, "He is saying *stop*."

"I've gotta learn Nepali," I said. "He almost threw up on my head."

During our walk, Rob found a Nerf ball and handed it to Arjun, who immediately proceeded to reach into his deep pocket, find the fork he apparently saved from lunch, and jab it into the ball and laugh.

"No, no," I said, pulling the fork from his hand.

Changing tack again, Rob said, "How about a game of catch?"

He backed away and threw Arjun the ball. Arjun chased after it like a puppy and stood contentedly with the ball in his mouth.

"Throw it back now." Rob clapped his hands, and Arjun chucked the ball.

"Wow. He's got quite an arm on him," Rob said. "Now let's test your soccer skills." He kicked Arjun the ball. Arjun adeptly kicked it right back. "Wow, he's got great coordination."

Then Arjun dropped to his knees and began batting the ball back with his hands.

"Now he's a goalie," Rob called out.

On the next kick, Arjun picked up the ball with one hand, and with the other, he reached into a nearby planter. Suddenly, he came up with a pinecone and hurled it at Rob.

Laughing, Rob called out to me, "Whoa! He just whipped a pinecone right by my head."

Arjun reached into the planter, and more pinecones flew toward Rob as he laughed mischievously.

"Sneaky little guy," I said. "I think the shy boy from the orphanage has been replaced."

"Maybe we should try another game," Rob said as pinecones whizzed by his head and Arjun continue to call out, "Ball . . . ball."

We took a break and sat at our table, figuring out what to do next. Arjun took the lead and came up with the next game. He grabbed a two-liter water bottle, flattened one side on the table, and began to swing it.

"He's making a bat," Rob said excitedly.

"Makes sense," I replied. "Where does an orphan get a bat in Nepal, so you get innovative and make one out of a plastic bottle."

Rob ran out onto the lawn and pitched Arjun the ball. The bottle crunched as Arjun whacked the ball thirty feet past his head. "Nice line drive," Rob said, and with the next, "Home run. Out of the park."

Whether with two arms in baseball style or creating his own one arm cricket style, Arjun was batting nearly a thousand. "You've got quite an athlete here," Rob called as Arjun slapped his hand against the bottle, eager for the next pitch.

That afternoon, Arjun and I headed up to my room for a rest. As soon as he entered, he spotted something that grabbed his attention. I listened as he paced around, attempting to surmount some kind of challenge. Then he used a chair to climb up onto the desk and leap across to the dresser. From there, he monkeyed his way up the large TV. Then I understood. He was going for the basket of fruit placed at the top. He was so tiny. It was like King Kong climbing the Empire State Building. Retrieving the basket, he amazingly shimmied back down, jumped off the desk, and sat on the bed, eating every piece of fruit, from bananas and oranges to mango and half a pineapple. I wondered when I should make him stop. Maybe he was like one of those dogs that didn't know to stop eating and would fill its belly until it literally exploded. I took the fruit basket away and put it back on the TV. As he finished off his last banana, he grabbed the remote control off the side table and, as natural as can be, clicked on the tube and began flipping through the channels until he got to a *Power Rangers* cartoon. How the heck, I wondered, did he know how to use a remote? The orphanage did have one small TV, but it was shared between fifty kids, so it wasn't like he was getting a lot of practice. Maybe it was programmed into the DNA of children everywhere. I laughed.

After an hour, Arjun slid off the bed and walked around the room, clearly restless. I had a suspicion what the problem was and showed him into the bathroom. I was right. He climbed up on the toilet, but instead of sitting down, he stood up on the seat. I realized he'd never sat on a toilet before and was used to doing his business Nepali style, which was to squat over a hole between two-foot platforms. He didn't know what to do with the toilet paper I kept handing him either. Despite my effort to teach him, even performing a little skit of wiping my backside, he just stood holding the clump of toilet paper. Again, I realized Nepali style was to use your left hand to wipe and then wash in a small bowl of water. *That's the last time I'll shake a Nepali left-handed*, I thought. After a few more awkward minutes, I knew this was my first big test of fatherhood. So I fortified my resolve, took the paper out of his hand, and rolled up my sleeves.

"Here's to many big adventures," I said as I dove in.

On our last day in Kathmandu, we went on a tour of the city. I bought Arjun a new set of clothes to replace his shabby ones. His favorite was a sweatshirt that he immediately put on and proudly wore the rest of the day. It was emblazoned with the words POWER RANGERS.

Next, we visited the Boudhanath Monastery, a sacred destination for Buddhist pilgrims. In the '50s, many refugees had escaped over the mountains from Tibet and had settled around Boudhanath, which was now a center of Tibetan culture. People were telling me that judging by Arjun's facial features, he was possibly Tamang, one of the tribes that had descended from Tibet. So as we followed the throngs of worshipers circumnavigating the stupa, Arjun must have fit right in. However, the tall white guy holding his hand and tapping a long white cane in front of him probably drew some attention. To our right, I could hear and sense the temple, 120 feet tall and surrounded by a sixteen-sided wall, with paintings in the niches. The base of the stupa symbolized Earth. The next section narrowed to a tower, capped with a gilded canopy representing air. The final piece was an even narrower spire, symbolizing ether. The whole temple was meant to represent man's ascension toward enlightenment.

As we walked, Arjun had more earthly problems. By his pull on my hand, I suspected something was urgent, and I figured he had to pee. Rob had raced ahead snapping photos, so it was left to me to find a bathroom. Public restrooms were nonexistent in Kathmandu. I couldn't speak much Nepalese and couldn't make eye contact with the passing crowd. I was at a loss.

Finally, in desperation, I awkwardly interrupted a group of women speaking in Nepalese. "Bathroom?" I asked, and I pointed to Arjun who was now squirming and holding his crotch. One of the ladies said something I couldn't understand. I stood confused as she kept talking. Finally, she grabbed my hand and pulled me ten feet over to the left. My foot stumbled over a foot-wide gutter in the pathway. Then it dawned on me what she'd been trying to tell me. She'd probably been pointing too. Arjun unbuttoned his fly and began peeing right there in the gutter, and I assumed it was common practice for children.

Crisis averted, we resumed our stroll, but I couldn't stop thinking about all the reasons I shouldn't be adopting this little boy. Emma had been challenging enough to raise, but she had pretty much followed the rules. This guy was already turning out to be even more active and demanding. I hadn't even been able to find a place for him to pee. So how would I teach him to ride a bike or to read? I couldn't play a game of catch with him or shoot hoops with him. I couldn't teach him to drive his first car. The list kept compounding in my mind. Far above, I could hear the prayer flags draped over the temple, flapping in the wind, bearing prayers toward the heavens. So I put in my own silent prayer.

"Please," I whispered, "let me be a good father to this little boy."

As hard as I listened, there was no answer from Buddha or from God, but the flags fluttering in the breeze and the ravens squawking from the trees sounded a little like Mark laughing. "What the hell?" he said, amused. "You gonna puss out? You got this, bro. I taught you everything I know. Now suck it up."

That night, Rob, Arjun, and I had pizza together, and on the taxi ride back to the orphanage, Arjun must have been amped up on carbohydrates, because he raced back and forth over our laps trying to look out the windows. On his next lap, I grabbed him and tried to wrestle him into his seat belt, but it was obvious he'd seldom been pinned down. I finally got him sandwiched between Rob and me with the belt buckled around him, and soon, his small frame went limp. He tipped over and fell asleep with his head on my lap. I stroked his short hair, his full cheeks, and his tiny round nose, just the opposite of my long prominent one. He was a boy I barely knew. There were wide expanses separating us. We didn't look alike or speak the same language. I didn't know many of the facts that comprised his life. Yet this boy softly snoring on my lap was my son.

10

THE ADVENTURE GLUTTON

The next day, after taking Arjun back to the orphanage and while we continued to wait on official adoption paperwork, Rob, Kami, and I flew toward the second half of our Nepali adventure. Six years before, while trekking into the Mount Everest base camp, my team and I had passed by a mammoth ice climb across a deep valley from Namche Bazaar, the capital village of the Khumbu. Pasquale described it as a line of bluish-white ice snaking up three thousand feet through deep clefts in a vertical cliff face. Kami told us its name was Losar. Although I had 99 percent of my brain focused on Mount Everest, 1 percent was left to dream about this incredible line of ice. *Someday*, I thought, *I'd love to come back to climb it.*

So now, Rob and I were on our way, flying over the Khumbu Valley in an A-Star 350 helicopter, the cabin vibrating and rattling my teeth. The *thwop thwop thwop* of the rotors whirred at high speed. Kami pointed my gloved finger out the window and yelled in my ear, describing the huge river drainages below and the massive white-capped mountains rising above. We passed over steep rocky ridges, dramatically contrasted on each side: flinty, brown, and treeless on the southern exposures, and dense green forests sloping steeply downward on the north. We took a swooping right, and Kami and Rob began shouting as Losar came into view out the left window. It was a thin strip of white shooting straight down a gorge and disappearing into the mist. From a distance, Rob said it appeared like a moving, flowing waterfall.

Kami said its name, Losar, was Tibetan, *Lo* meaning *year* and *Sar* meaning *new*. The Tibetan New Year was one of the most festive celebrations in Sherpa culture, spanning over a couple of weeks, with ceremonial offerings to the gods, dancing, feasting, and drinking a substantial amount of *chang*. "On the Tibetan New Year," Kami yelled, "the Sherpani women will wait until the first rays of the sun and then run out to fill their buckets in the streams."

He said that was the most sacred and pure water of the year, and to drink it signified good luck. The timing was perfect, I thought. Tibetan New Year started in about a month, just as the ice of Losar would begin to melt. So perhaps we'd be touching the same water that would be filling Sherpa buckets in the coming year.

Then our helicopter banked again, and we shot across the gorge to the steep slopes rising up the other side. Rob pointed out a succession of terraced agricultural fields perched along the ridges. Then Kami shouted, "Namche Bazaar!" He described the narrow rooftops of sky blue, sea green, and coral red, all crowded together, ascending up the hillside. I knew from my past trips that Namche Bazaar was a stunning sanctuary, the gateway to climbing in this region, but it was also one of the most unlikely places for civilization— so severe and inhospitable.

Above Namche, we landed on a flat expanse of pasture, carved out of an impossibly steep mountainside. Sir Edmund Hillary had landed in this same spot. His greatest contribution to this area was the school he built in the village of Khumjung with the help of the Sherpa community. There was a statue of Hillary standing proudly in the playground. In the Khumbu, he was revered as much for his outreach in the years after his ascent of Mount Everest as for the climb itself. Tragically, his wife and daughter landed here as well. They were meeting him to help with one of his many development projects, but the pilot got disoriented, and the plane slammed into the mountain, killing everyone on board. So as I stepped out, feeling the brilliant sunshine, and the sky that felt open and clean, I knew these mountains were equal parts joy and heartbreak. I contemplated that dichotomy as we piled our bags in a heap. Then we hiked down to the bottom of the airstrip where the ground plunged away, and Rob used the telephoto lens of his camera to look a mile across the deep valley at Losar.

"It's one of the strangest things I've ever seen," he said. "Only in Nepal can you see a frozen waterfall surrounded by semitropical vegetation like rhododendron and bamboo growing out of the cliff bands."

Losar had only been climbed a few times, and, unlike most Himalayan classics that ended at the top of a mountain, the frozen waterfall topped out on a rolling grassy terrace. Beyond, the mountain of Kongde Ri continued ascending, muscular and jumbled, like knuckled fists. Human conquests could sometimes feel arbitrary and false, like the case I'd heard recently of a climber being dropped off via helicopter near the top of a peak. The person had only climbed the final ridge and descended back to the helicopter before being whisked back to the city. I had also heard stories of Mount Everest climbers taking breaks from their expedition by flying from basecamp to Kathmandu for a few days of R&R poolside at the five-star Yak & Yeti hotel. Afterward, they were flown back to the mountain to resume their expedition. At best, it was a blurry line between achievement that felt substantive and achievement that felt more about appearance.

Conversely, the trip I'd led in Tibet had felt like a potent discovery. Even though we hadn't actually reached the high point of Lhakpa Ri, I'd come home with gifts that I'd carried with me that had helped guide the map of my life. So it felt good to sever the ties to external summits. Perhaps this would unburden me in a way to simply climb for its own sake, for the sake of those other kinds of summits that felt less tangible, obscured by mist and buried deep beneath the surface. I was just beginning to comprehend the meaning of these kinds of summits, and I was finding they took patience and devotion, like waiting for the ice to melt in order to taste the sacred water locked inside.

Losar was a climb that ended in a yak pasture, on the flanks of an even higher peak. It was a climb to nowhere, yet what a spectacular climb it was. As Rob looked south across the valley, he described the line of ice narrowing down like an hourglass in the middle. "I'm not even sure if there's enough ice for us to climb," he confessed.

He looked through his telephoto lens again and described the crux near the top, giant protruding columns of ice that hung in space like prehistoric mushrooms.

"I'm honestly not sure if there's a way through them," he reiterated.

The next day, Rob and I hiked up and down the many stone steps, snaking through the narrow alleyways of Namche Bazaar and exploring the markets. Tibetan traders herded yaks over high mountain passes, the animals burdened with all kinds of trinkets to be sold: intricate gilded yak bells hanging from thick leather collars, sheep wool blankets, sacred singing bowls and prayer wheels, and jewelry inlaid with amethyst, turquoise, and coral.

That afternoon, we relaxed on soft Tibetan rugs in our teahouse, drinking milk tea. Namche Bazaar was over eleven thousand feet in elevation, so Rob and I needed to rest and acclimatize. But it was hard because Rob could never sit idle. In fact, his friends had nicknamed him the Hammerhead because of his hardheaded desire to always be doing some sport or activity. For example, when he had moved from his home in Santa Barbara, California, to Colorado, he had honored his time there with a multi-activity adventure weekend, completing thirty different distinct events from rollerblading the steepest road in the city to rock climbing, kayaking, and scuba diving to the bottom of an old oil rig outside the harbor.

Even though we both lived outside of Denver, it had taken a chance meeting in Antarctica to bring us together. We were on separate expeditions to climb Vinson Massif, the tallest peak in Antarctica. I was continuing my Seven Summits quest, while Rob was part of a production crew filming an episode of the *Nova* science series. His team, including notables Conrad Anker and Jon Krakauer, were studying the dramatic effects of climate change on Antarctica, as well as trying to complete a new route up Vinson. Our teams were both waiting out bad weather at the communal camp called Patriot Hills, next to the blue ice runway scoured by constant, fierce crosswinds. We were bundled in down suits, sitting around a folding table, when Rob and I realized our houses were ten miles apart from one another. "Howdy, neighbor," Rob had said, cheerfully patting me on the back. We'd made plans to get together, but once back home again, I'd been busy training for Primal Quest, a nine-day adventure race through the Sierra Nevada. Rob had also been busy sprinting around the world as an adventure filmmaker, so we failed to connect again.

Three years later—in the fall of 2003—my team and I were in our fifth day of Primal Quest, about mile 300 out of 537. We'd already kayaked fifteen miles across Lake Tahoe, tandem mountain biked over a sixty-mile mountain pass, ran thirty miles, crawled through caves, ascended a thousand-foot rock dome, and paddled inflatable kayaks down the American River. We'd just gotten out of our boats and were running over loose river stones, my wet feet grinding against the inside of my boots and my ankles twisting and turning at irregular angles, when I heard a chipper voice behind me say, "Howdy, neighbor."

Turns out, Rob was one of the film crew. He'd followed the winning teams to the finish line and then was assigned to follow the slower teams. For the next few days, he ran behind us filming, joking, and laughing with our team. When I struggled to tie a bowline knot, I heard Rob's voice over my shoulder say, "You want to trail the rope the other direction, around to the right." And then, "Sorry. I'm actually not supposed to give advice." And later when I was trying to find the right-size wrench to raise my bike seat, he said, "It's the next size up." And then, "Oh, sorry, sorry. I shouldn't be helping."

When he left to follow another team, we were sad to see him go. Rob's even-keel disposition, his sunny optimism, and even his inexhaustible advice had been motivating.

Near the end of the race, we only had one more hurdle left: another boating leg, this one a midnight paddle across Lake Tahoe to the finish line. I hadn't slept in thirty hours and was so exhausted I'd begun to hallucinate, seeing students from my former middle school cheering me on from the sidelines. As I pulled my clothes from my backpack and laid them out in front of me, I tried to clear my head and stay focused. Then I heard a familiar voice coming from over my shoulder. Rob was there again, clearly noticing my inadequate layering.

"It's going to get pretty cold out there," he said quietly. "Do you have anything else to put on?"

"That's it," I admitted. "As they say in adventure racing, 'Fast and light.'"

"As you well know, mountains can be cold," he continued, "but when you're wet, it's a whole other story."

I heard him reach into his backpack and rustle around. "I'm really not supposed to lend any help during the race," he said, "but I think you're going to need this," and he slipped me a fleece top. I put it on and, for the next four hours, paddled furiously across the lake. I was in the front of our four-person kayak and took the brunt of whitecaps constantly slapping me in the face. When we dragged our boat onto the beach at 4:00 in the morning and trotted up to the finish line, I was soaking wet and shivering uncontrollably. For the next hour, I had to sit in front of a big heater before I could stop my body from shaking. Without Rob's extra layer, I would have definitely gone hypothermic, and from that moment on, I loved the guy.

For dinner back in Namche Bazaar, Nepal, Rob and I started with a big plate of *momos*—boiled dumplings filled with potatoes and spices. When it came to Nepali food, I was a little leery. I'd had episodes that had laid me out for days, one time in particular after a meal of poorly cooked yak steak. At the Mount Everest base camp, we'd often referred to breakfast as "salmonella and eggs" and "E. coli and toast."

Rob, however, was just the opposite. He had no inhibitions when it came to food, and he seemed to have an ironclad constitution. The only one who could come close to competing with him was Arjun, and I'd witnessed meal after meal with the two of them going elbow-to-elbow as the plates piled up on the table. Together, they were spectacular to behold. Once I'd invited Rob to Taiwan, where I was speaking to a Chinese company. Afterward, our host had treated us to the local cuisine with an endless stream of delicacies. It was as though they had gathered up the most exotic, and in my opinion, most disgusting collection of animal parts in the world. The first offering was what the waiter called a "century egg," and after inquiring, I'd learned it was a pigeon egg, aged for several months. Hearing that, I pretty much gave up and spent the rest of the night shaking my head and politely declining, while Rob treated it like the chance of a lifetime.

"Jellyfish salad?" the waiter asked.

"Sure. Why not?" Rob replied.

"Braised duck tongue?"

"Sounds delicious!"

"Raw sea urchin?"

"Most definitely!"

"Stinky tofu?"

"Wouldn't miss it!" Rob exclaimed.

When the waiter approached with the stinky tofu, I could smell it from five feet away.

Wincing, I said, "Rob, it smells like dirty socks."

"It's the national dish of Taiwan," Rob retorted. "And it has to be fermented a really long time to obtain that special bouquet."

When a lump of coagulated pig's blood was placed in front of us, I almost gagged. "Big E," he said, "you're such a lightweight," and he happily chewed away. "A texture like Jell-O, and surprisingly delicate!" he declared, waving a piece under my nose as I quietly dry-heaved and hoped the other patrons didn't notice.

So sitting with Rob in our teahouse in Namche, I smelled the next course arriving, a very pungent nak cheese pizza. I slowly let out a breath and willed my stomach to stop grumbling. At the best of times, nak cheese had a gamy scent; at the worst, it resembled stinky tofu, and it was now bringing up nauseating memories of my dinner with Rob in Taiwan. After a few bites, I said, "You want the rest?"

"Big E," he replied eagerly, "when it comes to food, you never have to ask."

I smiled as I recalled Rob's other nicknames, "You Gonna Eat That" and "the Food Raker," earned through his reputation of hovering over everyone's leftovers at the end of a meal. My plate scraped across the table, and the sound was immediately followed by vigorous chomping. He attacked the rest of my pizza with the same ardor as he attacked an ice face. I pictured him leaning over the plate, elbows spread, eyes half-closed, lips smacking, savoring each bite like he was gazing upon the Sistine Chapel.

As we whiled away the hours, Rob's palate was a point of curiosity to me. When a moment of boredom set in, I could always reinvigorate the conversation by firing questions at him, trying to find a weak spot in his defenses.

"I know you love food," I said, "but what's your favorite thing to eat?"

"I like everything," he replied.

"But if you could just choose one thing," I pushed. "Your absolute favorite."

"I have no preference," he pushed back. "I like it all."

"But nobody likes everything," I insisted. "You must have something you don't like, or maybe something you like, say just a little bit more than you like something else."

"Nope," Rob proclaimed. "I love it all."

"So you'd eat cardboard?"

"Of course not, Big E. It has to be something edible."

"It's edible to termites," I argued.

"Edible to a human being's digestive system," he clarified.

"So would you eat chicken feet? Or snake?"

"Of course. Actually, I've eaten both of them. With the right seasoning, snake can be quite tasty."

"Aha!" I said. "So without the right spices you would find them *less* tasty?"

"You're confused, Big E. I never said I didn't prefer food that is well prepared to food that is poorly prepared. What I'm saying is that I like every variety of well-prepared food: fried grubs, roasted porcupine, squid sautéed in its own ink, cane rat. Shall I continue?"

"No," I said, feeling defeated.

Even though I teased Rob for being a glutton, I knew his love for food really reflected a broader approach to life. Some climbers were known for mastering incredibly difficult rock climbs. To ascend a face rated 5.13, the very best climbers in the world might prepare and rehearse for an entire year or more, working out each painstaking movement until they'd connected the dots to the top. But Rob never had the patience to spend the time required to work a route over and over again. Rob yearned to know what was around the next corner. He wanted to breathe in, feel, experience, and taste everything new, and that included food. I guess you could say he was the ultimate adventure glutton.

Thirty sports in one weekend? "Sure. Why not?"

Another helping of coagulated pig's blood? "Most definitely."

Lead a blind guy up a three thousand–foot ice climb? "Wouldn't miss it."

The next day, we weaved down the trail switchbacking out of Namche, which grew progressively steeper and narrower. Some places we had to down-climb boulders and exposed roots. The trail was primarily used by wood-cutters searching for firewood. At the bottom, the Sun Kosi River churned down the valley. I crabbed across the two wet, icy logs that comprised the bridge, with cold spray surging up and enveloping me. Rob and Kami spotted me from front and back, and I knew a slip would most likely result in death.

On the far side of the river, there was a small, flat clearing where we set up camp, and afterward, we slogged up the thick, forested hillside to scout the climb. After two hours of thrashing through vegetation, we arrived at the base of Losar. Rob looked up the steep, freestanding pillar of ice that made up the first part of the climb, and conditions were far from ideal. We decided to climb a couple of rope lengths to get a better sense, and the ice felt rotten and mushy by sun exposure. In some sections, the ice was melting into slush that gave no purchase to our ice tools. Icicles and stones were raining from somewhere above. Standing on a little ledge at the top of the first rope pitch, a big chunk of ice screamed right by me and exploded below. A hit from a piece of ice that size would break your shoulder, or, even worse, your spine.

At 3:00 A.M., the rooster alarm on my watch began crowing, and we lay in silence for a few minutes. Rob checked the thermometer he'd hung on the tent. "Not good," he said, shaking his head. "Twenty-nine degrees Fahrenheit, and this is the coldest part of the day. That means the high may reach fifty degrees. Ice and sun—they're not really a good mix."

"Do you think there's a way to do this relatively safely," I asked, "like are there some ice caves where we could hide to escape from the falling ice and debris? Are there ways we can traverse off to the side if the day heats up too much?"

"Remember the chunk of ice that flew by you yesterday? That was the size of a suitcase, but hovering near the top of this thing are truck-size daggers of ice. We'd be climbing straight up a gun barrel, and if one of them cut loose, we'd be in the direct line of fire. There'd be no way to escape."

As we debated, I remembered the story of Rob climbing the Cassin Ridge on Alaska's Denali. The Cassin consisted of steep, technical alpine ice rising straight to the summit at 20,300 feet. He and his partner had struggled upward through a battery of storms that scoured the mountain. It had ultimately taken them thirteen days, with only an eight-day supply of food. The team in front of them had tried to traverse off the ridge to get to a safer spot; their broken bodies were found a week later. Rob and his partner had hunkered down inside an open crevasse with avalanches hammering over the lip above them.

So sitting in our tent at the base of Losar, I knew Rob wasn't overplaying or underplaying the situation. He was presenting the facts and allowing me to make the right call.

"Let's say we climb this thing," I proposed. "There's a 90 percent chance we reach the top, and there's a 10 percent chance we get taken out by ice. That about right?"

"That's about the size of it," he said. "How are those odds for you?"

"Not so good," I said glumly.

"Before we left," Rob continued, "Ellie put in a direct request for me to bring you back alive. If I brought back a dead blind guy, I don't think she'd ever forgive me."

I smiled and said, "I'd never forgive you either."

"You wouldn't be much of a factor," Rob replied, "because you'd be the dead blind guy."

"You've got a point there," I replied.

"Losar will always be here," he finally said, "but I have a prerogative to bring you home for the sake of your family, for Arjun. He's gonna need his dad."

After that, it was an easy call. We packed up our camp and began trudging back up toward Namche. Following the bell jingling from Rob's trekking pole, I posed, "So say I did die, and you're trapped next to me. There's no escape. Would you eat me?"

"Big E!" Rob said exasperatedly.

"Human beings are edible," I added, "if you're a cannibal."

"You're definitely fattening up in your old age," he quipped, "so yeah. I'd probably try a couple of bites."

11

ARJUN'S PLAYGROUND

Just a month after returning from meeting Arjun, we got crushing news. Nepal's turmoil had erupted again, with dozens of local skirmishes between the rebels and government forces. There were many casualties and a few incidents of foreigners being kidnapped, beaten, and even killed. Bombs had been detonated around the city, killing scores of people, all attributed to domestic terrorism. The upheaval had been ruining tourism, their country's primary industry, so in order to appease the rebels, the government invited some Maoist leaders to head a few nonessential governmental ministries. One of these was the Ministry of Women, Children, and Social Welfare. The new Maoist minister had suspended all intercountry adoptions.

The reason behind the shutdown was to stop the child trafficking so prevalent in Nepal. Throughout the upheaval, thousands of rebels were arrested and sent to jail, leaving their children to fend for themselves. Other rebels were killed. Families flooded Kathmandu to escape the violence or to find work. The country faced an epidemic: one of the highest densities of abandoned children in the world.

To respond to the crisis, many homes and orphanages began to spring up, but some were covert trafficking centers. They sold children through criminal networks to countries like India to become domestic servants or, even worse, sex workers. It was just another way to work the corrupt system, to profit from impoverished, desperate families. A few bribes to the right officials squelched any action or debate. Representatives from these orphanages would show up at the jails, telling the parents that they'd feed and educate their child while they served out their time. However, when the parents got out, they'd find their child vanished, sold away to another country.

The problem went even deeper, however. Nepal was a country made up of numerous ethnicities, all with distinct cultures, customs, languages, and most importantly, religions. This could already be a volatile mix, but then it was further combined with a rigid caste system, in large part enforced by the Brahmans who held much of the power and influence. It wasn't part of accepted practice for a Brahman to adopt a Gurung, a Tamang, or a Sherpa. Conversely, a Tamang, Gurung, or Sherpa wouldn't adopt a Brahman, so the result was thousands of children on the streets, running around in ragged gangs. The lucky ones might sell pencils, chewing gum, or trinkets in the markets. Or they might sell hashish. Most of the street children sniffed glue to reduce their hunger, and they walked around in a fog. Many were arrested. The less fortunate were sold as prostitutes.

As I read the report, I fumed. I had toured the official governmentally sanctioned orphanage, Bal Mandir, while there on an earlier expedition. When we walked in, the smell of sewage was overpowering, and my climbing partner described the squalid, overpacked room. Many of the kids had "thousand-yard stares," most likely from a lack of human contact. There were just too many kids and not enough caretakers. I'd read that if children didn't get love and affection in their formative years, they were damaged goods. They'd have attachment disorders the rest of their lives. Rumors spoke to even more brutal conditions: twenty or more children packed into one small room, infrequent meals, and savage beatings. Caretakers were accused of rape and torture. I'd even read that one guardian was seen dripping hot candle wax onto a little girl as a punishment for wetting her pants.

Born with the right opportunities, a child could fulfill her wildest dreams; but born onto the streets of Kathmandu, or ending up in Bal Mandir, she'd be lucky to make it out alive. Those who survived came into adulthood with glassy eyes and numbed hearts; any light they may have once had was now extinguished. They were a generation of soul-destroyed children, and it didn't bode well for Nepal's future.

Outwardly, the new minister looked like he was taking decisive action, but in reality, it was only to save face, and there was almost zero effort to attack the real problems that festered beneath the surface. Now, children like Arjun sat in dirty junkyards waiting for their new mothers and fathers to bring them home. I knew other families had small babies aching to be held, while loving families waited across the ocean, desperate to receive their children. It seemed like everything pure was tainted by politics, self-interest, and human depravity. How long would Arjun, and all the other children, wait? As I finished the article, I slammed my fist down on my desk and yelled, "You're holding my child hostage!"

While Ellie and I waited for eight torturous months, I had plenty to keep me busy. I guided our second Leading the Way expedition with twenty blind and sighted teenagers through the Peruvian Andes. In the high village of Chilipaua, we painted a schoolhouse for the locals, and even though we'd partially painted over the blackboard, the locals were thrilled.

We also held another No Barriers Festival, this time in Squaw Valley, California. It was our first in the United States. Major Dave Roselle spoke to our community about losing his leg in Iraq. After being carried off the battlefield, he assumed his military career was over. But after being fitted with a prosthetic leg, he became the first U.S. Army officer with an amputation to lead a platoon in combat since the Civil War. He told a story of his prosthetic breaking off in the midst of a firefight, and, with bullets flying overhead, hiding behind a waist-high wall, taking out his tool kit, and screwing on a new foot.

I met a woman who, after being paralyzed, sit-skied across the Greenland Ice Sheet, and a quadriplegic athlete who learned to surf sitting down with a specialized seat and backrest. Besides the tales of valor and athleticism, there were more down-to-earth stories that seemed just as heroic. A mom from North Carolina, diagnosed with multiple sclerosis, still wanted to ride bikes with her kids. One of our engineers fit an electric motor to her bike, and she zoomed around smiling from ear to ear. A veteran who was tired of taking the narcotics prescribed by the VA was searching for alternative ways to manage his chronic pain. Exploring acupuncture and an adaptive yoga class, he found he was more flexible and mobile than he'd been in years. I shook hands with a lady who told me she hadn't left her house much in the last five years, increasingly consumed by fear and anxiety. Then I listened while she rock climbed on Mark Wellman's climbing wall and scuba dived in a tank we set up in the plaza. Another guy told us he hadn't walked down a flight of stairs since his injury. We set him up with special trekking poles, and we trained him to slowly descend without assistance. At the bottom of the stairs, he broke into tears and said, "Today is my Everest."

Even though we'd done very little marketing, people were showing up from all over the world. They were united by their will to push forward and to find solutions to the barriers that held them back. Our festival was starting to feel less like an event and more like the inkling of a movement.

Throughout the summer, I found myself deep in thought. If a soldier could lead his platoon into battle with a prosthetic leg, if a quadriplegic could learn to surf, if blind kids could paint a schoolhouse, then why couldn't we figure out a way to bring this little boy home? It sounded crazy, but I wished our situation with Arjun were as concrete as hauling my way across the Greenland Ice Sheet on a sit-ski. Wind, snow, crevasses, sore muscles, and exhaustion—those could all be overcome with preparation and skill, but the obstacles we faced were inscrutable. I felt paralyzed by forces beyond my grasp. Outwardly, I forced myself to stay positive, but I honestly wondered if our dream of a growing family was ending.

Sometimes, though, I'd come in from a day of training to hear Ellie in front of the television watching the four hours of video Rob had shot of my first visits with Arjun: Arjun collapsing my cane, pushing my talking watch, giggling and whipping a pinecone at Uncle Rob's head, and cracking the ball with his flattened bat. She hadn't met Arjun in person, yet she'd fallen in love with this little guy. She yearned to buy him clothes, fix up his room, and prepare for his arrival. Like any mother waiting upon the arrival of her child, she held herself in check. What if he never came home? What then? To keep her mind positive, she took an active role by seeking out other families involved in their own waiting game. The Internet chat rooms on Yahoo were filled with stories of hope and of despair. She wrote letters to each of the congressional delegates from Colorado as well as our state senators.

In November, the Yahoo site announced a glimmer of hope. Four hundred adopting families from around the world had completed all their paperwork from the Nepali side and were just waiting for a signature from the minister. Arjun was number 237. The site exploded with chatter as word went around that Nepal might allow these 400 to squeak through. However, with the good news, we discovered our entire file was outdated. Everything from home studies and FBI checks to fingerprints and immigration forms had to be redone.

I didn't know how long we would have to wait. The progress was still only hearsay and speculation. I'd been contemplating another trip to Nepal to give Losar a second try. "Ellie," I said, "this is an opportunity for me to go visit Arjun again. I want him to know we're still here, that we're not ever going away, that we still love him no matter what."

So Ellie and Emma packed a suitcase full of presents, and in January 2008, Rob Raker and I were once again pulling up to the Helpless Children Protection Home. It now felt like a familiar place. We got out of our taxi to the sound of exotic chanting. All the children were packed together in the courtyard singing Hindu prayer songs, their sweet, high voices lofting over the narrow street. Then I heard little footsteps pattering toward me.

"There he is," Rob said. I bent my knees and spread my arms. Maybe, I thought, he'd be so excited, he'd leap into my arms. I readied myself for the catch. But then he stopped just shy of me and backed away laughing. I was confused.

"Dude," Rob mumbled, "he just took the pile of cash out of your pocket."

As adeptly as he'd batted the plastic bottle on our first trip, Arjun had just reached into my pocket and pulled out my pile of rupees. He danced around me, just out of reach, holding the money up with a huge grin.

"That's Daddy's little pickpocket," I said.

We spent the next several days together: more baseball behind the Yak & Yeti, hikes in the foothills outside the city, a tour of the famous Swayambhunath Monkey Temple, where Arjun got to feed the monkeys. We visited Bhaktapur, an ancient town and World Heritage Site, where Rob and Arjun dove into a plate of the local specialty, *Ju Ju Dhau*, a smelly custard-like yogurt, while I only nibbled. We visited a palace painted with dozens of Hindu deities. There we learned the origins of Arjun's name: Arjuna, who rode on the war chariot next to Krishna. He was an expert archer, known for his loyalty and valor. "Just like you," I said to Arjun. "Like a Power Ranger," I added. Arjun beamed.

One day, we joined Kami and his family for a picnic at the Pharping monastery, just outside the Kathmandu Valley. It was famous for a tall wooden structure with hundreds of *khatas* hanging from it. The custom was to pay one of the many Nepali kids, who crowded around the base, to climb it and place your scarf. I bought a couple for me and Arjun, leaned my white cane against the structure, and, to the surprise and horror of the locals, climbed twenty-five feet to the top where I hung ours over the pile. When Arjun would get tired, I carried him on my shoulders. We'd play a silly game in which he'd take off his cap and shove it over my eyes. I'd pretend to stumble all around, bending forward and back, left and right, taking him on a wild ride. I'd stomp my feet, snorting and bucking, as he clutched the collar of my shirt and howled with laughter. When it was time to say good-bye, we dropped Arjun off at the orphanage and took turns giving him hugs. Rob and Kami had now become Uncle Rob and Uncle Kami. As he turned away and silently melted into the throngs of children, I wondered what he was thinking, whether he had any idea what an impact he had already made on my life.

After our days together, I found it hard to refocus on the challenge ahead, our second Losar attempt. This time, we added a third climber, Ian Osteyee, a good friend of mine and expert ice specialist. The three of us warmed up by trekking to an isolated valley above the village of Phortse and climbing several frozen waterfalls. As I hung from one of the pillars, I could feel its chill on my face. Solid ice rose up above me and dropped away below me. It was such an improbable medium; to make it possible, humans actually attached daggers to their hands and feet. For me, I had the added bonus of not knowing exactly where to swing my ice tools. Sighted climbers looked up and aimed at the blue healthy ice. They could visually assess whether it was a good stick or whether cracks were spidering outward and the ice was about to splinter. If I were to swing at the wrong section, I could dislodge massive blocks of ice that could crush me or, even worse, my partner below.

But through a lot of patience and struggle, I had found another way forward by sweeping the tip of my ice axe across the surface, searching for the stable sections, for small divots, for the concave dishes above the bulges. When I felt like it was a good place, I'd lightly tap my tool against the ice, listening for the sound and feeling the vibration through the metal pick. When my tool bit in deep, it was a glorious, satisfying *thunk*, and it was a satisfying rhythm: kick feet, stand up, scan tools, breathe, then *thunk, thunk.*

Not so long ago, this realm of ice had felt precarious and forbidding, but the all-consuming process of discovering a way upward had given me a glimpse of freedom. As I pulled over the top, hearing the wide valley below me, I realized that my fear had transformed into awareness, beauty, and wonder. The world could feel like a prison, I thought, but could also feel like your own private ice palace.

Standing on top together, Ian said, "You know, Kami says no one's climbed in this valley before, so I think this is a first ascent. What are you going to name it, Big E?"

The name formed instantly. "Arjun's Playground," I said.

A few days later, we were at the base of Losar, precisely where we'd camped one year before. Thankfully, the weather was colder, and the ice conditions were much improved. That night, we lay in our tent when Rob asked, "Big E, why did you want to adopt Arjun? I mean, you don't see many blind guys bringing a kid home from Nepal."

"Well, Emma wanted a little brother," I said, "and Ellie's also adopted, so she knows what a powerful experience it can be. Ellie also thought it would be good for me to have a little boy, someone to watch *Rocky* movies with. Emma has no interest." I paused, trying to organize my thoughts. "But I guess there's one more thing," I said. "This may sound cheesy, but you know that scripture from the Old Testament? The one that says an eye for an eye—a tooth for a tooth? It's sort of like that, but kind of the opposite."

"I'm not quite following you." Rob laughed.

"There are a lot of things you can't do anything about," I said. "You can't control getting old or getting cancer. You can't control being abandoned as a little kid or going blind. But then there are things you *can* do something about. A life gets taken, and you can't do a damn thing, but you can decide to do something else, to take on another life."

"Are you talking about Mark?" Rob asked.

"Yes and no," I answered. "I think it goes way beyond the death of my brother. I think pushing forward can feel like moving through a war zone. There are so many things that want to knock you down and kill hope. There's a lot of wreckage and pain along the way. So why not take those burned-out craters and grow love in their place? It winds up being a kind of draw. Maybe, in fact, you come out a little ahead. Maybe your life, and other lives, are even richer for that choice. Does that make any sense?" I asked.

"Strangely, I think it does," he said.

At 4:00 A.M., we started up Losar and climbed vertical ice for the next thirteen hours. Exhausted and uncertain of what lay ahead, we found a ledge to rest for the night, just to the side of the ice runnel. A large boulder pinned me to the wall. I curled around it, knowing it lay between me and the bottom of the gorge. The night was freezing cold, with a harsh wind blowing down the cliff. Crammed into my thin sleeping bag, I barely slept. All night long, I had strange half dreams. In one of them, I'd fallen asleep on my living room floor. The front door had swung open, and a raging blizzard was blowing snow on top of me. Somehow, miraculously, Arjun had made it to Colorado. He and Emma were standing together above me. *He's home!* I thought. *He's home!* Tears rolled down my face.

"Daddy, wake up. You're dreaming," they were saying, shaking me. "Go back to bed." In my frozen, half-dream state, I could hear Rob's and Ian's voices too, mixing with Arjun's and Emma's; apparently, my gibberish was keeping them awake.

"All right," I said, racked by cold. Every so often I'd wake up and realize grimly where I was: in a fetal position high up on an ice face with the wind roaring down and frost collecting on the outside of my sleeping bag.

By the next morning, I couldn't stop shivering as I fought to get my boots and crampons on and get geared up. Above me remained the last five hundred feet and the steepest section of the climb. Near the top, I found myself climbing out of an ice cave and swinging my tools into overhanging globs of ice. As I strained and grunted, trying to make the tips of my tools bite into the irregular ice, I knew that between my back and the Sun Kosi River, raging below through the bottom of the canyon, was over three thousand feet of air.

By noon, the vertical face leveled off, and I slowly crabbed over the top, entering the sun for the first time in three days. I just stood there for a moment, allowing a deep satisfaction to wash over me as the brilliant sun touched my face.

"Happy Tibetan New Year," Rob said as the three of us hugged.

I knew that in front of me were more forests and high pastures before the dramatic mass of Kongde Ri rose far above. As if to remind me, the warmth of the sun quickly shrank away, retreating behind spiny ridges. Where the sun had been there was now a void, and I thought about Arjun. The journey had already been formidable, and I knew there was still a long way to go. "Somehow we'll bring you home," I said to myself. I clipped my ice tools to the back of my pack and prepared for the twelve-hour rappel back to camp.

In Namche Bazaar again, I called Ellie from a satellite phone from our teahouse. Through the broken connection, I heard Ellie's distant voice yelling all the way from Colorado: "We're only five numbers away from being approved. Don't ask me how or why, but the minister has been flying through applications, and I think it'll be very soon."

"Then what are you waiting for?" I shouted with joy. "Get over here as quick as you can."

"We've already got tickets!" she yelled back.

Like a mother entering her last weeks of pregnancy, Ellie raced around frantically, buying Arjun new clothes, toothbrushes, and a bedspread with baseballs and basketballs on it. She ordered a huge Nepali flag to hang on the wall. She told the neighbors the news, and they started painting Emma and Arjun's room blue. Emma got to keep her pink curtains!

What she didn't tell me was the very important fact that she wasn't supposed to travel until she had all the appropriate documents, including an immigration form signed by a bureaucrat at the U.S. Citizenship and Immigration Services in Denver. Despite her best efforts, she hadn't been able to get an appointment. Online, she'd learned the office was backed up and wasn't taking appointments. Finally, she got through to a receptionist who told her the next opening wasn't for another ten days. The flight she'd just booked took off in three.

I don't fully understand how Ellie managed to get on that plane with an impossible-to-acquire document signed. She showed up at the immigration office as soon as it opened, determined to do what it took to get that form. She told me later it involved a half dozen governmental officials, each listening intently to her story about a little boy in Nepal. It was like a scavenger hunt; one after another, the person behind the desk would report, "I can't help you"—and then more softly—"but I may know somebody who can."

Their clues led her down a trail of bread crumbs to small offices buried in obscure, poorly marked buildings. The final man stated, "I can't help you. The information officer who signs off on this is booked all week with interviews." But then he glanced again at the picture of Arjun wearing his overgrown pumpkin jacket and said softly, "What's your e-mail address?" When Ellie got home, the document was approved and waiting for her in her inbox.

When Ellie called the head of our Boulder agency to tell her what had happened, Nina was furious. "It's not done like this. You should have gone through the Adoption Alliance, which then faxes our office, and then we send it on to the U.S. Citizenship and Immigration Services. You bypassed the system. The ministry in Nepal still needs two more documents, the police approval, and a letter of concern from the orphanage, so you're still not officially approved. You can't fly over there until this is all done properly. I'm strongly recommending you cancel that flight."

Ellie called me that night and told me Nina's advice.

"You're getting in position," I said. "It's one of the first rules of mountaineering. Remember my first climb of Aconcagua? We weren't at high camp when the good weather happened. So we missed the window and didn't summit. But my next try, we pushed as hard and fast as we could, got to high camp, and waited. There were two clear days that season, and we stood on top during one of them—all because we got in position."

Ellie, along with Emma—who was just seven years old—flew out the next evening. After their long flight, I met them at the airport with Kami, and we rushed to the orphanage. When Arjun emerged chameleonlike from the crowd of children, Ellie stared at his face, flooded by a mix of complex emotions. While pregnant with Emma, the stages were clearly defined: celebration, healthy eating, wearing those horrible maternity clothes with expanding waistbands. Then there were all the hours spent reading pregnancy books and setting up the crib. Finally, came the labor, filled with screaming, pushing, and electrifying pain. But when she looked at Emma and held her, a wave of love washed over all the blood and agony. The bond was instantaneous.

Seeing Arjun for the first time, the feeling was the same, but the timing was all off-kilter. She had thought about him constantly for the last year, and the uncertainty and shattering setbacks had felt like the physical pain of labor. She looked at his hands covered in dirt, the dark circles under his eyes, his runny nose, his shabby clothes, his untied shoes, and knew he was as vulnerable as a newborn. She reached out and hugged him, but he stared back at her as a stranger. He'd survived without her for five long years, and there was so much history and personality already formed. What was it that made him laugh, that brought him joy? What secrets were inside him waiting to be revealed? There was so much lost time, so much to make up for—numbers, colors, alphabet, and nursery rhymes. Each day ahead would be an uncharted journey to comingle their worlds until their memories were shared. She was ready.

After that, we went to work. There was an amazingly long list of reports, documents, and authorizations to be completed, translated, and distributed to the various ministries, as well as the U.S. Embassy in Kathmandu. Ellie wrote out the long list of steps on a sheet of paper in her notebook and began checking them off one by one. At night, we'd regroup and strategize for the day ahead. The process was so convoluted it made me feel stupid. I couldn't decipher how the steps and materials all fit together.

"So wait," I said to Ellie, "the 1600 and the I-600A get sent from the USCAS to the NVC, and that turns into an I171F?"

"That's correct," Ellie replied.

"And the Application for Advance Processing of an Orphan Petition—is that the same thing as the DS-230 Forms Part I & II?"

"No," Ellie replied. "They're completely separate."

"And does the NVC also send the I-797C?"

"No, the I-797C is sent by the Department of Homeland Security. Remember? That was the one they sent to Nebraska and got lost for a few weeks?"

"So the NVC sends all this material to the U.S. Embassy? And how does it turn into a cable 37?"

"I have no idea," Ellie replied with a sigh.

"Makes me wish I was back shivering on Losar," I said.

As we sorted it all out, one thing was for sure. The illusive cable 37 hadn't arrived yet. It was supposed to be sent from the immigration office in Denver to the National Visa Center somewhere in New Hampshire. I pictured a vaulted fortress, like Fort Knox, protected by electric fences and attack dogs hidden in the north woods of New England.

It was against some regulation to send the document first-class mail, so there was no way to track it. Its ultimate destination was the U.S. Embassy in Kathmandu, but when we stopped by, an official told us it hadn't arrived. Without it, there'd be no visa authorization for Arjun to enter the United States. The National Visa Center website had an 800 number that we'd tried dozens of times from our mobile phones, but it rang and rang. Ellie wrote an e-mail to Nina, with growing panic, but Nina's note seemed more a lecture than help.

"I advised you not to go to Nepal until everything was approved," she wrote. "I fear you're juggling chain saws here and I only hope you don't get hurt."

Nina's words made little sense. Yes, Ellie had left for Nepal before we were officially approved. However, hundreds of adopting families had been here for months waiting for their numbers to be called. Besides, at this point, we needed to be in-country anyway in order to meet the embassy senior officer, and Nina had assured us for several weeks that our file was totally complete and en route to Nepal. The close of Nina's note was the strangest part: "Do you know what you are doing to me?" It seemed oddly self-absorbed, especially in the midst of our problem.

With no help coming from Nina, we wrote my dad a frantic e-mail asking him to step in. He was finally able to get through to the National Visa Center, and although the receptionist was friendly, even getting a manager involved, they had no record of our file. Apparently, it had completely vanished.

Each night, Ellie laid all the compiling documents over the bed and scrutinized them meticulously. She was finding plenty of mistakes, like Arjun's police report that had said he was abandoned on the street. This was an essential document, but after having it translated into English, Ellie noticed that the report had described Arjun as a girl, and they'd gotten his age wrong.

So she made an urgent appointment at the central police station. When we arrived, the building was dark. Kathmandu experienced regular blackouts. The power supply couldn't keep up with the skyrocketing population. Many people still burned wood, or even garbage, which accounted for the thick gray smog that blocked the sun. Some Western hotels had generators that kicked in, but the government offices were often left dark. When we entered the cinder block building, we walked right past the jail cell, about the size of a shed with one small window. Ellie could barely make them out, but a half dozen sets of eyeballs were staring silently at us. The office was bare—just a desk, a chair, and one old 1970s typewriter that an officer used to retype the report. Standing in the dark, spare room with the sound of the typewriter plunking away, listening to a clerk rewriting Arjun's documents, I almost laughed. It was preposterous, yet it accentuated the way business got done in Nepal.

The next day, Sabitri set up an appointment with a doctor. Arjun tested positive to a variety of parasites and worms. He also took the test for tuberculosis. The doctor pricked his arm, and if he was clear, his skin wasn't supposed to react. But a large purple lump formed on Arjun's arm. Kami spoke Nepali with the doctor and the one nurse. I knew 50 percent of the world had latent TB. It could lay dormant under the surface for a lifetime, not ever affecting the person, but there was a chance of it manifesting and leading to a life-threatening illness. To kill it totally, it required six months of an intensive cocktail of antibiotics. We waited and worried what the doctor would do, but an hour later, the clean health certificate was signed, and we left scratching our heads.

"Okay." I turned to Ellie in the taxi. "I thought the police visit was weird, but that just beat it."

"From all I've read, that test isn't even reliable," Ellie explained, checking

My guide, Harlan Taney, and I test our Neptune Communication system above Lava Falls in the Grand Canyon. *Courtesy of James Q Martin*

Harlan holds his broken paddle as I grasp for my kayak, just below the "Cheese Grater" rock on Lava Falls. Rob Raker looks on. *Courtesy of James Q Martin*

Washed up on the shore and shattered after my first attempt of Lava Falls. *Courtesy of Michael Brown*

With my teammates Jeff Evans (L) and Eric Alexander (R) on the summit of Mount Everest in 2001. *Courtesy of Luis Benitez*

Our team leader, Pasquale "PV" Scaturro, outside his tent at Camp III on Mount Everest. *Permission by PV Scaturro*

Winning my first high school wrestling tournament at New Milford, CT. *Permission by Weihenmayer Family Collection*

Ellie and I share wedding vows on the Shira Plateau at 12,622 feet on Kilimanjaro. *Courtesy of Jeff Hauser*

After my mother's death, trekking the world's mountains helps my family to heal. (L to R) Eddi, me, Mark, Ed. *Permission by Weihenmayer Family Collection*

Terry Fox on his historic Marathon of Hope across Canada. Terry passes away before he finishes the run, but the movement he began has raised almost seven-hundred-million dollars for cancer research. *Permission by CP Images*

Sabriye Tenberken and her partner, Paul Kronenberg, proudly stand before their training center, Braille Without Borders, in Lhasa, Tibet. *Permission by Paul Kronenberg*

As soon as I arrive in Lhasa, the kids challenge me to a wrestling match. I'm moments away from being "yak-tied" with our climbing rope. *Courtesy of Didrik Johnck*

(L to R) Best friends Kyila and Sonam Bhumtso excitedly embark on our Himalayan trek. The girls constantly entertain us with renditions of American 60's pop songs, like Sonny and Cher's "I Got You Babe." *Courtesy of Didrik Johnck*

Concentrating on the boulders in front of our feet as we trek up the Rongbuk Glacier toward Lhakpa Ri, we are also acutely aware of the massive peaks, including Mount Everest, that surround us. *Courtesy of Didrik Johnck*

I try to comfort Tashi as he prepares to descend. *Permission by Blindsight*

Gyenshen and Dachung in the Ice Palace. Dachung rides atop his "ice camel" to do battle with the lake serpent. *Permission by Blindsight*

I struggle to carry Mark Wellman to the base of "Ancient Art" on the Fisher Tower in Castle Valley, UT. Mark's a little nervous, since he's never been carried by a blind guy before. *Courtesy of Eric Perlman*

Hugh Herr leads the final pitch of Ancient Art, about to confront the corkscrew that leads to the summit. *Courtesy of Eric Perlman*

Mark Wellman, the first paraplegic to climb El Capitan, uses his innovative system on our ascent of Ancient Art. *Courtesy of Eric Perlman*

Andy Parkin rests in his "high altitude studio" in the Langtang Valley, Nepal. After his devastating climbing accident, Andy says painting saved his life. *Permission by Andy Parkin*

Mark Wellman rides his "One-Off," a hand-pedaled mountain bike, at our first No Barriers Summit in Cortina, Italy, 2004. *Courtesy of Wayne Hanson*

My brother, Mark Weihenmayer, with Little Miss Gabrielle, his pride and joy. *Courtesy of Julie Pacatte*

I'm blown away by Harlan Taney, our kayak safety guide, as he surfs the waves of the Grand Canyon like a rodeo cowboy. As his sister, Marieke, describes, "It's like he's half human, half dolphin." *Courtesy of James Q Martin*

I help one of our Leading the Way teens keep his feet dry on a hike up North Canyon. *Permission by No Barriers USA*

At camp, we play a round of "paco pad" Sumo wrestling. *Permission by No Barriers USA*

My brother, Mark, cradles seven-year-old Gabbi, their last time together. *Courtesy of Julie Pacatte*

Our first photo of Arjun. Ellie says he looks like a poet, about to tell us a secret so profound that it may change our whole world. *Permission by Weihenmayer Family Collection*

After a few rounds of cricket, Arjun and I get ready to play "crazy taxi driver" outside the Hotel Yak and Yeti in Kathmandu. *Courtesy of Rob Raker*

Rob Raker (L) on one of his many ascents in Yosemite Valley. *Courtesy of Kevin Steele*

I join the adventure glutton in a desperate attempt to polish off a pan of spaghetti on one of our many adventures. *Courtesy of Kevin Steele*

Climbing the thrilling vertical ice face of Losar in the Khumbu region of Nepal. *Courtesy of Rob Raker*

We find an uncomfortable bivy ledge below the last 500 feet of Losar, where the steepest climbing begins. *Courtesy of Rob Raker*

After two attempts, I finally reach the top of Losar and feel a brief moment of sun on my face before the last rays pass behind Kongde Ri. *Courtesy of Rob Raker*

Playing "mechanical bull" with Arjun and Emma. The goal is to hang on for a full minute. They never make it to the end, always winding up in a pile, with the mechanical bull snorting over the tangle of bodies. *Courtesy of Ellen Weihenmayer*

Arjun's first birthday party in America with his two best friends, Ryan (L) and Gabe (R). *Courtesy of Ellen Weihenmayer*

We embark on our San Juan River journey. Those early trips give my kids the chance to express their imaginations. Sticks and deer antlers become swords, and raven feathers their warrior headdresses. *Courtesy of Kathleen Moffett*

The sound of the river echoes off canyon walls during my first kayaking adventure on the Green River's Gates of Lodore. *Courtesy of Rob Raker*

Rob guides me through Split Mountain, a succession of six rapids that mark the end of the Gates of Lodore. *Courtesy of Greg Winstonn*

With the help of the BrainPort, I play tic-tac-toe with Emma. *Courtesy of Michael Brown*

Utilizing his first hiking system of bath towels and packing tape, Kyle Maynard crabs to the top of a 12,000-foot peak above Winter Park, CO, during our 2011 No Barriers Summit. *Courtesy of Clyde Soles*

"Robo-Kyle" Maynard ascends Mount Kilimanjaro in 2012, becoming the first quadruple amputee to reach the summit. *Permission by Kyle Maynard and K2 Adventures Foundation*

it off her list. "It often gives a false positive. The kids in Nepal all have had inoculations against the worst kinds of TB, and Arjun has a scar on his arm to prove it. Just be happy he signed the form."

Next, Sabitri accompanied us to the passport office. As always, a long line snaked out the door. However, Sabitri walked right through the line, parting the sea of people, and pushed directly to the front. Within minutes, Arjun's passport was completed. It was all such a murky process, I thought. You could wait in line for an entire day only to hear the official say, "Not possible today," but with the right influence, you marched right to the front, and the passport simply appeared. Walking out of the building, I said quietly, "We couldn't make this stuff up."

"Yes," Ellie agreed, "but let's just get through this." Stepping into the small taxi, she pulled Arjun onto her lap and wiped his nose with a Kleenex. Turning to me, she whispered, "We'll fix the system later."

For the next document, the required official had recently left on a vacation, and no one knew when he'd be returning. So instead of waiting around for him, I convinced Ellie and Emma to fly up into the Khumbu. I wanted them to see the Himalayas and maybe catch a glimpse of Mount Everest. Kami joined us, and we flew a helicopter out of the city, over the foothills, and into the high mountains that dwarfed our tiny flying bubble. We passed near the jagged ridges of Kongde Ri, with Losar dropping away into the clouds. In the past, I'd always flown on clear days, but, on this one, menacing black storm clouds surrounded the peaks like angry deities. Our helicopter swooped and veered to avoid the storm. Several times, we hit thunder cells like walls, and our helicopter was buffeted left or right or dropped what felt like a hundred feet.

"Is it always like this?" Ellie asked, grabbing my hand.

"Totally. No problem," I lied, sweating and squeezing her hand just as hard. Emma fell asleep, her fear turning into a self-induced coma.

This time, we landed right outside of Namche Bazaar, in a little clearing near the school, and we got out to the sound of kids playing. It was cold and snowing, with a ferocious howling wind, so we hung out playing board games at the same teahouse where I'd called Ellie after Losar. That night, we visited the home of Mingma Sherpa, a kitchen boy on my Mount Everest climb. In the Tibetan tradition, his mother had two husbands who both greeted us at the door with gracious hugs. Mingma told me that his situation was nothing compared to a family he'd known from Tibet in which one woman had seven husbands—all brothers.

"One for each day of the week," I replied, laughing.

Kami, Ellie, Emma, and I ate dal bhat, a spicy lentil and rice dish, and Mingma's parents waited on us, continually filling our cups with slightly rancid nak butter tea. As soon as we'd choked them down an inch, our hosts would be right there to fill our cups to the top again. Their Tibet-style house had two floors, with the living quarters at the top and heated by a yak-dung fire. When Ellie asked where the bathroom was, they pointed toward the poorly lit stairway. I escorted her down, but at the bottom, there was no bathroom. There was, however, a door into a dark room, the floor covered with hay.

"They mean for you to go in the hay," I said.

"I'm not going in there," Ellie protested, laughing nervously.

"It's the custom," I insisted, holding the door open.

As she squatted in the darkness, however, she screamed and leaped forward as a large wet nose nuzzled her neck, followed by a snort and grunt.

"I forgot to tell you," I said, "you're sharing the facilities with Mingma's yaks."

By January 18, we were finally approved by the Nepali Ministry of Women, Children, and Social Welfare, but there was still plenty to do. There were appointments with the Ministry of Foreign Affairs, more doctors' approvals, and more documents to be translated. Arjun's pending adoption also needed to be posted in a local newspaper to give his natural parents a chance to reclaim him. Lastly, there were several meetings at the U.S. Embassy—culminating with the all-important interview with an embassy senior officer to review every step, every document, and give the final thumbs-up or thumbs-down.

It crushed me, but the next week, I had to leave. A year earlier, before we'd anticipated any delays in the adoption process, I'd committed to leading another No Barriers expedition. I deeply regretted it now. It was tragic and unfair leaving Ellie and Emma to fend for themselves, but I didn't feel like I had a choice. I'd made a commitment, and as painful as it was, I had to stand by my promise to a group of blind kids who had trained for a year to trek in the Blue Mountains outside of Sydney, Australia. I took solace in the fact that I knew Ellie could handle it. Although I wouldn't have wished the hardship on anyone, I felt like Ellie was actually in her element. She had taken this process that felt amorphous and overwhelming, had broken it down, and attacked each impediment with clarity and purpose. The results were starting to show. I also took solace in the fact that Ellie and Emma were in good hands with Kami. I knew he would be right by their side.

The day after my departure, Ellie had an important appointment at the foreign ministry. She was in the lobby ready to leave when Kami rushed in.

"The government raised the price of oil yesterday, and there are now big protests on the streets."

Kathmandu was always crazy with congested narrow streets with no sidewalks. Tuk-tuk drivers and mopeds flew through the tight alleys, honking and bumping people out of their way. I once had my leg burned by a hot engine. Little Emma was at first shocked by the visceral sights and strong smells, like a hog's head lying on a market shelf with eyes staring dully and a halo of flies swarming. Walking the day before, she bumped into someone and politely said, "Excuse me." When she looked up, she was staring into the eyes of a goat. In fact, it was a herd of goats blocking the road.

But this day was even crazier. She glanced at the Kathmandu newspaper, and the headlines read: PETROL PRICE HIKE FUELS NATIONWIDE STRIKES. TRANSPORT FARES INCREASED BY 25%. LIFE IN CITY PARALYZED. PROTESTERS INJURED IN CLASH WITH POLICE.

Ellie then looked at the U.S. Embassy website, and it read,

Travel Warning: Nepal continues to experience sporadic incidents of terrorism and politically-motivated violence in major urban areas. Given the nature, intensity and unpredictability of disturbances, American citizens are urged to exercise special caution during times when demonstrations are announced, avoid areas where demonstrations are occurring or crowds are forming. Avoid road travel, and maintain a low profile.

"Do you think we have to cancel?" Ellie asked, disappointed.

"It is impossible to get a taxi," Kami said. "But it is no problem. We will walk to the office—only one hour."

So Ellie found herself walking with Emma through throngs of people, elbows jabbing, sweaty bodies pushing, with Kami leading the way. The mobs marched, yelling and chanting slogans. Tires flamed and smoldered in the streets. Thick plumes of poisonous black smoke rose into the air as the three weaved and maneuvered toward their appointment.

It was like an episode of *The Amazing Race*, except it was a spin-off called *The Torturous Race*, and the grand prize was a little Nepali boy instead of a million bucks. "Get through this mob and these burning tires, and this boy can be yours!" the announcer in her head proclaimed.

Ellie made it through the flaming gauntlet to the initial meeting that day, but her amazing race was just getting started. The next two weeks were a flurry of activity. Ellie's journal was smattered with notes, some showing that her communication with Arjun remained largely nonverbal:

Breakfast today, Emma and Arjun drew pictures of houses. Emma's house contained a dog, a cat, windows and a door. Arjun's Nepal-style house—a thatched roof and a stone entranceway. So much to learn and share.

Dinner at the hotel buffet and Arjun ate and ate until he had tears in his eyes. Had to make him stop before he threw up.

First time-out today. Arjun wouldn't stop sawing on the table with his knife.

Took his first bath tonight. Emma got in first and encouraged him by splashing around. He eventually got in and played for an hour. When he came out, Emma cried, "Mom, look. He's three shades lighter."

Slept over tonight. Wet the bed–Talked in his sleep and twisted around like he was living through a nightmare.

Broke lampshade tonight. Even though I saw through bathroom mirror, he denied it. Pointed at Emma. Emma cried. They fought over remote control. Arjun wanted to watch Power Rangers. Emma wanted to watch Dora the Explorer.

I'm feeling nauseous. Think I have Giardia. Emma's scratching a lot. Think Arjun gave us lice.

Kids had extra energy tonight. Held races down the hallways. Other adopted kids joined in. I said 'Ready, set, go!' Arjun kept repeating 'Ready, settee, go.' Emma and I cracked up.

Emma and Arjun wild tonight-jumping and screaming on couch outside elevators. Elevator door opened with Japanese tourists gazing in shock. I looked away and pretended they weren't mine.

Gave Arjun a handkerchief for his runny nose but he keeps losing it. After dinner, I gestured with my hands, 'Where's your handkerchief.' Arjun shrugged his shoulders, so I went to go find it, but Emma shouted, 'look.' I turned around and he was holding out his baseball cap with the hand-kerchief slyly tucked inside. Arjun was smiling and dancing.

Ellie and the kids were now stopping by the U.S. Embassy every day. The administrators were getting familiar with the Weihenmayer family. "No cable 37 yet," the secretary would repeat. Ellie knew her final meeting was fast approaching. The secretary called the visa office in New Hampshire and got the same story, as my father had—no record of it ever arriving.

Ellie wrote another note to Nina.

We walked over an hour to the ministry the other day because the streets were all on fire due to a strike. It was worth it. We are officially approved, but I am pleading for your help. The embassy has been kind to give me an appointment. However, they do not have my file from the National Visa Center. I told them, according to you, it should have arrived.

Nina's note back read as follows:

The paperwork went to the NVC and will be forwarded, which is what the embassy needs to complete the process. NVC has stated they will update them next week. According to you, I guess the embassy is getting

a different story. I realize you are used to people asking how high when
you say jump, and that you expect everyone to change their normal
processes to fit your schedule. You are leaving a scorched trail. It is the
clients' lack of patience and inability to respect personal boundaries that
has led us to the decision to close the agency.

Ellie was crushed. Nina had hosted our family for dinner. Ellie and Nina had even gone to lunch a couple of times, so where was all this anger coming from? However, as Ellie perused the Yahoo site that night, the big picture became shockingly clear. The site read, "It's likely that Nina Rosen, founder of Claar Foundation, will be indicted in the next month for defrauding families." Ellie read further, and the accusation was that she was using money from one adoption to pay for another, like a Ponzi scheme. She had a tangle of nonprofit and for-profit organizations and was shifting money around from one to another in a desperate effort to stay ahead, but the game had finally caught up to her when she didn't have the funds to complete an adoption. The family had pressed charges. Nina was in the midst of going bankrupt, most likely losing her law license if convicted of a felony and looking at jail time. Nepal had been an incomprehensible place, and it was easy to write it off as a corrupt system, but now Ellie felt off balance. She had chosen Nina's agency through careful research, and it gave every appearance of being a highly rated and professional organization. America was supposed to be a place of clear rules and intentions, but now Ellie didn't know what to think. She had just learned our U.S.-based adoption agency was the sketchiest of them all. Our biggest advocate had turned out to be the biggest crook.

Ellie's next journal read:

Kami took us to Boudhanath Monastery to have us blessed by the lama.
Another day of protests and burning tires. After the blessing, we looked up
into the smog and saw a large jetliner. I'll take it as a sign.

Ellie could now sense the finish line. She was finally done with all the paperwork from the Nepal side and now awaited her exit appointment at the U.S. Embassy scheduled in two days. For the fifth time, she stopped by to inquire about the paperwork and got the same response. This time the secretary said there was a chance the files may be lost permanently. Ellie watched her through the glass window typing on her computer in a last-ditch effort to track the file, when Ellie noticed another woman standing in the background, making frantic hand gestures. She was smiling. In one of her hands was a package. "Your cable 37 just arrived this morning," she said, slapping it on the desk.

The day of Ellie's appointment, however, she learned that all interviews were canceled due to the unexpected death of an American citizen. The next night, Ellie wrote in her journal:

> *Got our interview rescheduled. 10:00 AM interview—4:00 PM flight. Going to be tight. Kami spoke to Arjun in Nepalese. Told him he was getting on an airplane tomorrow and asked if he had any questions. Arjun only wanted to know if there was a place to pee. But later, out of nowhere, he broke into an inconsolable wail. It was mournful and seemed to come from a deep place. This boy has a story.*

On the big day, Ellie, Arjun, and Emma sat in the waiting room with a number of other families. As she was called into the office, Emma and Arjun began arguing over a ball.

"It's mine!" Emma cried.

"My ball!" Arjun yelled back.

"Give it to me!" Emma screamed and reached out for the ball. Arjun danced away. The embassy representative sat silently, witnessing the ruckus in the cramped room.

"How's your day going?" the lady asked.

Before Ellie could answer, Emma yelled, "Mom, he's got it in his pocket, and it's my ball!"

Arjun stuffed the ball down in his deep pockets and yelled even louder, "My ball!"

Ellie glared sideways at the two of them and screamed silently, "Don't you want to go home?"

Arjun patted the ball tucked down in his deep pockets, repeating, "My ball."

"He's lying!" Emma screamed.

This is it, Ellie thought. It had all come down to this interview. After a hundred excruciating steps, after lice and giardia, after fighting through burning streets, riots, and documents lost and miraculously appearing, now the lady was about to give the final verdict: whether Ellie was a fit mother or not, whether we were a happy, loving family, and whether we could leave this country together. So close, and it was all about to fall apart. Emma began crying. Arjun sat on his chair, clutching the ball through his pocket with an angry scowl.

"How is your day going?" the representative repeated.

Ellie forced her gentlest smile. "Fine," she replied. "Everything is going well."

And after a short conversation, they were approved. Just like that, Ellie and the kids were racing back to the hotel, running around thanking all the people who had been so helpful along the way, especially Kami Sherpa. Nina had been right. It had been a roller coaster, but Kami had stuck by her every step of the way. He had been a faithful guide for me on Mount Everest, and now he had navigated Ellie through another, even trickier challenge. Then they were fighting through traffic and blaring horns, arriving at the airport five minutes before the cutoff. As Ellie and the kids sprinted in, some other adopting parents cheered.

On the plane, Ellie was so exhausted she fell asleep before the flight even took off, but she had a fuzzy recollection of her eyes briefly opening as the plane taxied down the runway and seeing Arjun out of his seat, standing way down the aisle, pulling magazines out of a magazine rack. When her eyes blinked open again, Arjun was back in his seat smiling and insistently pushing the flight attendant call button with Emma explaining, "Sorry. He's never been on a plane before."

When she woke up the third time, Arjun was watching the movie *Toy Story*.

"He's watched it four times now," Emma said.

When she finally woke up for good, Arjun was watching the TV screen. Instead of *Toy Story*, he was examining their plane, a tiny glowing dot against a world map, the dot almost imperceptibly creeping over the vast Pacific Ocean.

A half an hour before touch down in L.A., Ellie nervously reviewed all the documents one last time. She had an official, sealed envelope from the U.S. Embassy and Arjun's newly acquired passport stamped with his entry visa. Gazing down on the stamp, Ellie's eyes bulged. She read it a few more times, not believing what she was seeing. The stamp was correctly dated January, but not 2008. Instead, it read, "2009." Technically, Arjun couldn't enter the country for another whole year. But by now, Ellie was an old pro. She could hear the announcers voice revving up in another episode of *The Torturous Race*: "Figure out how to get this boy through U.S. customs without a valid passport, and he could be yours."

Ellie shoved back the flash of panic collecting in the pit of her stomach and began formulating a plan. In the seats in front of her sat another family who Ellie had gotten to know over the last month. They had a son, and they were bringing home a little Nepali girl. Ellie brought them into the plan, and they whispered together as fellow conspirators.

Near customs, Ellie and the other family were brought over to a special line, and instead of approaching the officer separately, they all bunched in together, beginning to pile passports on the desk in one stack.

"Hold on now," the officer cautioned. "Whose are whose?"

"Where's Cooper's?" the other mom said. "I just had it a second ago."

The ladies started separating and handing passports back and forth. "That's yours. Whose is this? I think that's mine there."

"Do you know if there's a bathroom nearby?" Ellie asked as the officer sorted through the stacks. "My son is looking pretty uncomfortable, hopping up and down like he has to go."

"Right around the corner." He pointed with his thumb. "This should just take a minute."

As he opened each passport and checked them against a computer screen, the ladies pleasantly chatted.

"Mohini loved that *LEGO* movie," said the other mom.

"Arjun watched *Toy Story* four times," Ellie said as the officer stamped a passport. "And when I woke up during takeoff, he was up front checking out the magazine display. So much for the FASTEN SEAT BELT sign."

The officer chuckled as he stamped another.

"During dinner, Mohini must not have liked her butter," the other mom said, "considering she chucked it at the people sitting across the aisle."

Another chuckle—another *stamp, stamp.*

"Is this Arjun?" the officer asked.

"Yes," Ellie answered. "Arjun Lama Weihenmayer," she said. "Has quite a ring to it. Don't you think?"

The officer looked at Ellie and then down at Arjun for an uncomfortable amount of time. Then he stamped his passport. Ellie quickly gathered up the stack of documents and took a step toward the exit.

"Ma'am," the officer called out.

Oh God, Ellie thought, her heart feeling like it was about to explode. She should have known this amateur game of smoke and mirrors could never work. She swallowed, looked back at the officer, and waited for the axe to drop.

"Welcome to America," he said, smiling.

12

"NOT MY YAK!"

Home for just a week, Arjun and Ellie sat on his bed, leafing through a stack of picture books. When they'd finish one, Arjun would pop off the bed and stand in front of the nearby bookshelf stuffed with more children's books, selecting the next one. He pulled one out with a picture of the solar system on the cover and brought it back to the bed. Very interested now, his eyes darted from planet to planet. He pointed to all the rings of Saturn, and Ellie named the planet. His finger pointed to another planet, and another. Ellie named them all. When he pointed to Earth, she said, "Our planet. Earth!" She pointed to Arjun and then to herself. "That's where we live."

"Nepal?" he stated, pointing to one of the other planets.

"No." She laughed. "Here," Ellie said, pointing to Earth again.

"Nepal," Arjun pointed to yet another planet.

Ellie was confused, but then it dawned on her. Arjun had somehow surmised he lived on a round ball, but he had traveled so far on the airplane, he thought he had arrived on another planet. When Ellie shared her observation with me, I said, "Probably feels just as alien as another planet."

Ellie retrieved our globe and placed it in Arjun's lap. "This is Earth," she said.

Spinning it around, she showed him Colorado. Another spin and she pointed to Nepal.

"This is where you used to live," she said. "Then you flew in an airplane all the way over to Colorado." She made her finger take off from Nepal and buzz over the route. Arjun touched the globe and spun it round and round a few times, but soon he lost interest and grabbed another book.

As Emma and I sat listening, I tried to imagine what Arjun must have been thinking. He'd never seen a globe. He had never flown before. He didn't really know where he was living before and had no sense about where Colorado was. He was lost. Then Ellie separated one of the WELCOME HOME helium balloons the neighbors had given us. She led Arjun out to our back deck, which faced west toward the Rocky Mountains. In the previous days, Ellie had sat out here with Arjun, watching the sun set below the hills and disappearing for the night. In the mornings, she'd shown him the sun again, rising to the east. "There it is again!" she'd exclaim.

Now, handing Arjun the balloon, she pointed to the mountains and said, "Nepal—this way." She gently took the string and let it go. "Nepal is a long way away," she said, "but that balloon could fly all the way there. Namaste, Nepal!" she shouted with a grin.

"There it goes," Emma said. We all waved good-bye as the balloon rose into the sky, turned into a tiny dot, and disappeared.

"Same planet," I said, "just far away."

Emma was so excited to have a little brother, before leaving for Nepal, she'd insisted they share a room together. On the dresser that separated the two twin beds, she shoved all her little toys, books, pictures, and jewelry to the right side, near her bed. Then she paused and shoved her possessions over even more. "He can have more than half," she said exuberantly.

Arjun took full advantage. He didn't understand his side versus Emma's side. Emma watched in horror as he instantly dove into her prized collection of stuffed piglet dolls and flung them around, performing kung fu kicks to their heads.

At first, it was hard to tell what Arjun needed. We were divided by a language barrier, but we got by with a lot of pointing and hand gesturing. We also had a friend, Lhakpa Sherpa, who owned the local Nepali restaurant, come over and speak with Arjun in Nepalese. However, Arjun's responses were brief and didn't reveal much.

But there were deeper barriers that made the one of language seem easy. While Emma had cried over the years, letting us know her needs, Arjun was stoic and silent. It was like his time in the orphanage had forced him to suppress his emotions, making it tricky to assess if he was hungry, tired, or cold. Whether he was getting stuck by vaccinations at the doctor's office or falling down and skinning his knee, he never cried. That made sense, I thought. You learn to cry as a way to let your protector know you're upset or in pain, but if no one is there to hear you, to soothe you, then it loses its purpose. We couldn't even trust Arjun to nod yes or shake his head no. Instead, he'd do a head bobble, common in Nepal, tipping his head left and right. It often indicated a noncommittal response as if to say, "Either way," or "As you wish," or "I have no idea."

Arjun, however, couldn't hide his feelings forever. At a point, they'd bubble up into fits of frustration. While Emma attended school, Ellie and Arjun went on field trips around the Denver area. The Colorado Railroad Museum was near our home. It seemed to us like the kind of place a boy would love. One time, at a neighbor's house, we'd observed him playing with a small electric train set; Ellie had noticed that he loved moving the little lever that caused the trains to switch directions on the tracks. He seemed utterly transfixed by the mechanical movement of the train and by his ability to control its direction with the lever, so we figured he'd love real steam engines and locomotives, but after climbing aboard his third train, Arjun said, "No trains!" Just like that, he was done.

Halfway home, as Arjun sat silently scowling, Ellie figured it out. These were relics from the past. They didn't move or do anything. They didn't actually work! When Ellie told me the story, I laughed, picturing his mind bubbling over and the words dying to spill out: "Stupid, no-good, broken trains!"

Soon, Arjun was speaking basic words of necessity, like *rice*, *bike*, or *train*. He then added a *yes* or *no* to the item, and it was often a *no*. "No white!" when he'd point at a stick of butter or bowl of sugar, both things he'd never tasted in Nepal. "No! No! No!" We heard the word a lot.

If Arjun was going to enter kindergarten, he had a lot of catching up to do, and Ellie threw herself into the task with the same fervor she'd had in bringing him home. She read him nursery rhymes and books that taught alphabet and numbers, all the things she did with Emma when she was just a baby. We all jumped in as well. I had a pile of books with illustrations and the text, both in print and in Braille, so I could read to him as well. He especially liked a series about Froggy embarking on different adventures, like *Froggy Goes to School* and *Froggy Gets Dressed*. Similar to Arjun, Froggy was constantly putting his boots on the wrong feet, putting his shirt on backward, or forgetting a glove. When Arjun learned that Froggy got all ready to play in the snow but had forgotten to put on his underwear, his laughter couldn't be contained in one room. He fell off the bed in fits of joy over Froggy's mishap.

Often, I'd walk into the kids' room to hear Emma and Arjun together on one bed, Emma reading him stories, with Arjun staring at the pictures, mesmerized. He caught on so fast. He was forming sentences in English in just a month.

There was no stopping Arjun in his inexhaustible effort to learn everything. When he spotted the little bike in the garage, he demanded to try it. Once Emma's bike, we had painted over the pink with shiny gold and removed the sparkle streamers. We attached some training wheels and figured the snowbanks would soften his falls. Ellie strapped on his helmet, and he rode out of the garage on his maiden voyage. He'd weave up and down the sidewalk, with one of us right behind him. He'd tip over into the left snowbank, and then into the right, while I yelled out, "Watch out for the crazy taxi driver!" Within an hour, Arjun was riding solo, with no intervention. On the third day, he pointed to the training wheels and said, "No!" He was a quick learner for sure.

By the fifth day, Arjun pushed his bike up the steep hill above our house, insisting on riding back down again. We'd given him plenty of lessons on how to brake by pressing his foot down on the pedal and skidding to a stop. Ellie reinforced it one more time by tapping his feet and saying, "Remember, never let your feet leave those pedals." But at the top of the hill, instead of coasting, Arjun started pedaling, shooting off in Kathmandu taxi-driver style. I heard Ellie running down the hill after him and yelling, "Stop! Stop!" and then he flew by me, with Ellie breathing hard close behind him. I heard one of our neighbors standing in his driveway say, "Oh! That's not going to end well."

I followed behind, and when I reached Ellie, she gave me the play-by-play.

It had started by Arjun's feet flying off the pedals and flailing out to the sides, while the pedals whipped around faster and faster. He veered around a parked car, avoided a mailbox by an inch, ran up another driveway, and crashed into a big hedge. Getting up out of the sticks and leaves, he stood silently next to his downed bike, his hands hanging limply by his sides and his face expressionless. He seemed a little in shock. Ellie took a deep breath, hugged him tightly, and then immediately had him go a short way back up the hill and coast down again. This time, however, she kept a firm hand on his bike seat, with his feet squarely on the pedals.

Speaking English and riding his bike had come so quickly, it was puzzling how difficult other adjustments were, especially rituals most families took for granted. Ellie showed him how to brush his teeth, using toothpaste, and they practiced together, but when she'd send him into the bathroom on his own, she'd check afterward to find the toothbrush dry and the toothpaste clearly unused. From then on, we had to implement the "fresh breath test," with Arjun blowing in my face. There were a lot of angry moments when I'd have to send him back into the bathroom for another go.

He was also still peeing in his bed, a problem we knew about from Sabitri and from our experience with him in Nepal. It wasn't a big deal and common for a lot of little boys, but we thought with the right tools and structure, we could make some progress. One of our first rules became no drinking water just before bedtime, but Ellie immediately caught him filling the water glass on his bathroom counter and drinking it to the bottom. "We're smart people," I said. "Just take the cup away." But the next night, Ellie caught him guzzling water straight from the faucet, and not just a little bit. It was as though he was dying of thirst in the desert.

We also made sure he was peeing before bed. When Ellie would stand next to him, he'd have no problem going, and he soon began making it through the night. We then began sending him into the bathroom independently. I'd stand outside and hear the toilet flushing, but we couldn't figure out why the problem was resurfacing. It was all explained when Ellie secretly observed Arjun's nightly ritual. He'd enter the bathroom, wait beside the bowl for ten full seconds, flush the toilet, and come out to wash his hands—all without actually peeing.

The dinner table became another ongoing battle. Arjun would inhale his food, bypassing the chewing phase. That, combined with the fact we still hadn't fully eradicated the parasites from his belly, was causing him to be sick after most meals. Ellie wanted to slow him down, trying different approaches like showing him a mirror of his face, with food plastered from his eyelids to his ears, or even pulling his plate away for one-minute breaks. At one point, she turned away for just a moment, and Arjun downed his entire glass of juice, then proceeded to throw up all over the table.

She also discovered him gouging marks on the underside of our kitchen table with a pen. Ellie put him in a time-out and made him sit on his bed.

After ten minutes, she went to retrieve him, but he refused to move. He sat there for the next hour as if to say, "Oh yeah? You wanna put me in a time-out? I'll show you. I can sit here all day."

After a while, I heard things crashing and ripping. Ellie had given Arjun a bunch of posters from her classroom when she was a teacher, and as I rushed into his room, he was tearing those posters off the wall and throwing them onto the ground in a rage. When I entered, he tried to slip past me toward the door. Now that he knew a balloon could get all the way to Nepal, perhaps he was going to try to walk there, but I caught him and swept him up into my arms.

He fought me with all his strength, pinching, kicking, and screaming. I sat down on his bed and held him tight against my chest, trying to calm him down as he flailed around, trying to escape. The harder I held him, the harder he fought. His teeth clamped down on my arm, and I pulled his head away. "It's okay, buddy," I said. "It's gonna be okay."

The struggle lasted a full thirty minutes, and when he finally gave up, his body went limp, and he fell into a kind of muttering slumber in my arms. "This is your home, and it's gonna be okay," I whispered as I tucked him in under his covers.

After a nap, Arjun woke up more calm, and we sat with him on his bed.

"What's wrong?" Ellie asked, stroking his hair.

We were met with silence.

"Are you sad?" she asked.

Arjun did the head bobble.

"Are you missing Nepal?" she asked.

Arjun gave a slight nod.

"Your friends?" she asked.

He nodded again.

Finally, Ellie said, in her quiet way, "Do you miss anyone else? Your mother?"

Arjun nodded.

Ellie wondered if Arjun was remembering Sabitri, the head of the orphanage, but she had a strong feeling that wasn't the case. Being adopted herself, she knew the search for your parents never ended. The loss was always there.

"Tall or short?" Ellie pressed on.

"Tall," he answered.

"Long hair or short hair?"

"Long," he said. "Black hair."

"She's pretty, isn't she?"

Arjun nodded.

"Arjun, where are your parents?" I asked, afraid of the answer.

"Ja," he answered.

"Is that her name?" Ellie asked. "Ja?"

Arjun didn't answer.

Ellie had him repeat it several times, and it came out the next time as "Jai" and "Jaya," but neither of us understood the word, even after Ellie looked it up in a Nepali dictionary. It remained a mystery.

In March, Ellie started taking him to kindergarten and would stay with him for the half day. Arjun was intensely curious and loved being around kids his age. Even though he still spoke with broken English, it didn't stop him from trying to answer every question, whether he knew the answer or not. He loved being first and would wolf down his lunch and sprint out onto the playground to make sure he was the first to the swings. Whenever his teacher would say, "Line up," he would shove kids out of the way to be in front. At home, we practiced what an organized line looked like. Ellie, Emma, and I would form a line and show him how to calmly take his place, but in school, he'd just push to the front again. I thought about Sabitri's words describing Arjun in one of our original letters: "He just will do and do and do or say and say and say until he has what he wants."

A couple of days later, we were walking as a family down a narrow sidewalk. It was single file, but Arjun kept darting in front of us and sprinting way ahead. Most worrisome was that he was crossing driveways and small streets without looking left or right. When we finally caught up to him, Ellie ordered him to walk behind her, but every chance he got, he'd shoot by, with Ellie calling him back again. Finally, it was a showdown. The next time Arjun tried to push by, Ellie shuffled right and blocked him. He made a quick cut to the left, and she matched him. After that, he took it as a personal challenge, waiting for a gap to form, before rocketing through the gauntlet, but Ellie would nimbly cut him off. By the end, he was walking directly behind her, feet shuffling, head hanging, like a wild stallion that had just been broken.

As Arjun resigned himself to all the rules and structure of our life, we left plenty of time for play. I loved listening to him on the playground running around with other kids. With little boys especially, there wasn't much language required, defined rules, or deep connections. The physical play itself seemed to be its own language, with its own underlying rhythms.

Home from school, in the afternoon, he kept right on playing. Our basement had a thick wrestling mat across an open room, and we'd wrestle and battle for hours. Our favorite game was called Force Field, in which Arjun could choose from a host of magic tools and weapons like the club of destruction (a pool noodle), or the ball of disaster (an inflatable exercise ball). He'd shield himself with an impenetrable force field (a gymnastics mat), while I'd pound his defenses with the ball of disaster and the club of destruction, trying to break through. Arjun, wrapped in his force field, would be flung around the room as I reached through the gaps in the shield, his little feet and hands scurrying away like a turtle into his shell.

Often Emma would join in, and we'd play our second favorite game, Mechanical Bull. They'd both get on my back and slide the imaginary quarter into the slot, which was my ear. Then the mechanical bull would begin bucking and kicking, while they clutched the hood of my sweatshirt. The goal was to hang on for a full minute. They never made it to the end, always winding up in a pile, with the mechanical bull snorting over the tangle of bodies.

Ellie had been attending kindergarten with Arjun for a month, and he was adapting and adjusting pretty well. He'd even written the following poem, which Ellie and I loved and displayed on the refrigerator:

> I love books
> I love school
> I love outside
> I love blocks
> I love inside
> I love swings
> I love upstairs
> I love my backpack
> —By Arjun

Then one morning, I was surprised when Ellie came home from the school alone. She explained they'd been sitting in a circle with all the other kids and the teacher, when Arjun turned to her and said, "Go home, Mommy. Go home."

I laughed. "In other words, he told you to beat it." Part of me marveled at his independent streak, but another part of me worried he didn't yet have the maturity to back it up. Unfortunately, that was proven right a couple of weeks later.

Ellie and I were picking Arjun up from school, and the teacher said that she needed to talk to us.

"What happened?" Ellie asked, concerned.

"A fighting incident in Foothills Forest," she said. "You know that little stand of trees near the playground that the kids go to during recess? They build a fort in there with planks and branches and bark. We encourage cooperation, and once recess is over, the next group of kids come out, and they sometimes dismantle the fort and start their own or build on it more."

I could imagine where this was heading, but I kept quiet and listened.

"Well," she went on, "Arjun had built a fort all recess, and when it was time for him to come in, and the next group arrived . . ."

"What did he do?" asked Ellie.

"He used a stick to defend his fort," the teacher said. "A few of the older boys ran back into the school, crying. They were afraid of him."

I pictured Arjun squatting down, crouched in the pounce position, then leaping up and going into full-on Nepalese-Ninja street-fighting mode, calling out "Hi-yah!" and cracking a pack of fifth graders in the kneecaps. I didn't know whether to be proud or mortified.

"We'll talk to him, of course," Ellie said. He was banned from Foothills Forest for the next few months.

What was most puzzling to me was that one minute, Arjun might be fighting off a pack of kids twice his age, and the next, he seemed paralyzed by simple scenarios. It came when he accidently spilled a glass of milk and stood motionless above the puddle watching it spread. It also came in more serious situations, like when a vicious neighborhood dog lunged out toward Arjun. He didn't react as the dog snapped at the end of its leash, an inch away from Arjun's face. Ellie grabbed his shirt and hauled him back. The near-miss gave me a flashback to Arjun standing as if frozen by his little bike, his resolute face masking any emotion after crashing into the hedge.

As Arjun's English improved, so did his storytelling, which took on such elaborate fantasy that it was difficult to distinguish fact from fiction or figure out where the tales began or ended. He still had vivid recollections of Nepal, but they were mixed up with his new life. We were at a neighbor's house having dinner one night, and they had ordered lobsters from Maine. When they showed Arjun the lobsters crawling around, Arjun said in a direct deadpan voice, "Oh yeah. I ate lobsters all the time in Nepal."

We all laughed.

"Yeah, they catch them right out of the Kathmandu River," I added.

"What else did you have in Nepal?" our neighbor asked.

"Many things," Arjun replied. "We had sharks too. I fight one off once." Then he swung his fists to reenact the battle.

That night, we were lying down together reading a book before bed, and I said, "Tell me about the orphanage. What was it like?"

"It was loud and cold, and I was hungry all the time," he answered.

"That must have been hard," I replied.

"I was in a room with many boys," he said. "I had two other boys in my bed."

"What were their names?" Ellie asked, but he didn't know.

"But they were loud, and they kept me wake," he revealed. "They elbow me, and snore, and they fart a lot." With that, he let out a laugh.

We laughed with him.

"I would tell them, '*Shut up!*'"

And we laughed even harder.

"Then I turn into superhero," he continued. "And I fly up over Nepal, and I fly all around Kathmandu and get away." As we thought about him crammed into a small bed with two other smelly boys, it made sense. You blur the line between reality and imagination as an instrument of survival. I suppose that's what he had to do to simultaneously remember and forget.

It had to be confusing for him, all the old memories and new ones, bleeding together as he tried to make sense of the jumbled images and recollections.

"Do you have memories of your family?" Ellie asked. "You told me once that your Nepali mom was beautiful and tall with long dark hair."

"Yes," he said. "I can remember her face."

"Do you know where she is?" Ellie asked. We were always careful with this line of questioning. Unless he was ready, it wasn't smart to pry about his past.

Arjun answered with the same word he'd used months before. "Jaya," and again, Ellie asked him to repeat it. This time, the word began to form more clearly.

I whispered to Ellie, "I think he may be saying *jail*."

Emma had been very patient with Arjun his first six months, but he tested that patience daily. In the orphanage, he had competed for everything, without enough resources to go around, so now, he was suspicious of Emma getting more food, more attention, more love. His appetite for all three of these things was insatiable. When eating, he would scope out her plate to see if it was piled a little higher. When Ellie poured milk, he'd carefully examine the two glasses side by side. He was so obsessed, Ellie eventually broke down and started pouring the milk and telling Arjun to choose whichever glass he wanted.

So a little sibling rivalry started. We had just moved the kids downstairs into their own rooms with separate bathrooms. One morning we heard Emma yelling from her shower.

"The water!" she screamed. "It's going from scalding hot to freezing cold!"

After this went on for a few more mornings, Ellie got suspicious and tip-toed down to the other bathroom. She peeked in on Arjun, who was stand-ing in his own shower, gleefully turning the knob from cold to hot and back again. He'd figured out if he spun the knob back and forth super fast, it would affect Emma's shower temperatures as well. There he was, behind the curtain, like the Wizard of Oz, making Emma squeal by alternately burning and freez-ing her. It was like the spirit of Mark Weihenmayer had come back to wreak chaos upon our family. Although Arjun tried to deny it, he had been caught in the act of sabotage.

During our first summer, Sabriye and Paul came to visit. They were trav-eling around the States, and we invited them to come stay with us. I was so happy to reunite with them after our experience together in Tibet, and I was excited to welcome them into our family.

When they arrived, they gave the kids each a toy yak, covered in actual fluffy yak hair. The next morning the kids retrieved the yaks from their rooms and showed us. Immediately, we noticed Arjun's was already broken; its head bobbled and was about to fall off. Ellie and I felt terrible, because the kids had just received the gifts. So many of Arjun's toys ended up maimed in some way or another. We immediately cornered Arjun, holding the yak out in front of him.

"How did this happen? You just got this."

"Emma broke!" he yelled back.

I called Emma over and said, "Emma, he's saying you broke his yak."

"Dad, what are you talking about? Who is the liar in the family? Arjun is always the one lying. I don't lie. You know me."

Now pretty frustrated, I said, "Okay, Arjun, quit lying. You're going to be in big trouble."

"Not my yak!" he yelled in an angry, defiant voice. "Emma's yak!"

I just shook my head. "I can't believe you're just standing there lying to my face."

Later that evening we were having a glass of wine with Sabriye and Paul, and Paul said, "I wanted to let you know that during our travels, one of the little toy yaks we brought was damaged in the baggage. I know that Arjun is new to the family, and younger, so we decided to give Emma the damaged one; we thought it wouldn't bother her."

I couldn't believe it. She'd gone into his room and swapped them out. Good little Miss Emma had pulled the old yak switcheroo on Arjun.

We went into her room, holding the nearly headless yak. "Emma, you're lying to us."

She just broke down in tears. She'd been an only child for almost seven years, and now there was this new kid getting everything, even the milk glass. She'd been so kind and generous, sharing her room, and she was being rewarded with scalding showers. She was over it. "I really wanted the good yak!" she cried.

I held her, and when her sobs subsided to a sniffle, she said imploringly, in her sweetest voice, "Dad?" She started hemming and hawing.

"What is it, girl?"

"I was wondering . . . is there any way that maybe . . . when you adopt a kid and maybe it doesn't . . . I dunno, work out . . . is there a way to make it . . . not happen? Like, is there a way to make things go back to before, when Arjun wasn't here?"

"No, angel," I said, holding her close. "I know it's sometimes hard, but there's no return policy. There's no going back. This is forever."

13

THE GATES OF LODORE

Anytime Rob Raker stopped by the house, Arjun and Emma would grin excitedly, shout out, "Uncle Rob!" and run up to greet him. Rob would take Arjun out in the yard to kick the soccer ball around or play catch. Once he showed up with a Red Raptor Osprey Sport kite, and we all went to the top of a nearby mesa where the wind was gusting hard. He taught Arjun how to play out the kite strings as he ran into the wind, and how to make the kite perform acrobatic moves, climbing and diving and inverting. Often, he'd arrive with little gifts in hand like a feather from a prairie falcon, a chunk of fool's gold, or the vertebrae he'd found of a small animal. He'd have the kids explore the skeleton and make conjectures based on their observations. "Exactly," he'd say when they were onto something.

He would also show the kids his various cameras and latest photos of coyote cubs or a family of beavers. Arjun was fascinated with the different buttons, and especially liked to take pictures of himself making funny faces and then viewing them on the monitor. Rob had been an environmental scientist in an earlier career, and in addition to eating and adventuring, he had two loves: nature and science. He was unable to merely skim the surface of any subject. He had to know, to understand. He had the patience, intellect, and curiosity to pursue thoughts and ideas to their absolute end point. When he was showing one of his treasures or explaining something technical to Arjun, he reminded me of Phineas J. Whoopee from a cartoon I loved as a kid. Tennessee Tuxedo and his walrus buddy were constantly being faced with problems they had no idea how to confront. So to get started, they'd consult with "the man with all the answers," Mr. Whoopee, who would give a joyous lesson on his "fantastic, fantabulous, three-dimensional blackboard," or "3DBB."

"Ha ha ha ha, my boy!" I could almost hear Rob saying giddily to Arjun, his bushy eyebrows lifting and falling as he showed him all his different camera lenses. "A telephoto lens is like a telescope, allowing you to look at something from far away. It makes the object appear closer. The focal length of a lens determines how 'magnified' the photograph is. The higher the number, the more magnified the image becomes. To take pictures of animals, it's not always easy to get up close or you will scare them away, so it's best to have a really big telephoto like this one. It's 500 mm. Look down there at that magpie. Look at it with the 500 mm lens. See the difference? Ooooh, that's a black-billed juvenile. His tail will grow even longer."

While on the Losar ice face in Nepal, Rob and I had spent hours in the tent discussing all the different sports we were looking forward to doing when we were back home in Colorado. Rock climbing, skiing, and hiking in the foothills were Rob's favorites, but whitewater kayaking was also on the list. I'd told him that kayaking intrigued me and that I'd taken a class in a pool to learn to roll, but I'd never quite gotten it.

"I can teach you to roll in two hours," Rob declared.

I privately wondered how that would work, but I had learned by now not to doubt Mr. Whoopee. When you flip a hard-shell kayak—either by getting hit by a wave, ramming into a rock, or just by tipping over—you are still sitting in the boat, but now upside down underwater. The "roll," simply stated, involves going from being upside down to right-side up. But being blind, learning how to pull off the move was complex, nuanced, and turned out to be really difficult. I couldn't just watch a video, memorize the moves, and emulate them. It was really hard to visualize the big picture. While underwater, I was disoriented, and everything was confused and backward.

"I think this will be an interesting challenge for both of us," Rob said.

We settled on going to a pond near our cabin at eight thousand feet above sea level, an hour west of Golden. Rob and I pulled the boat from the back of his truck and carried it to the edge of the water. We reviewed the pre-paddling routine, including how to slide into the neoprene spray skirt that would keep water from filling the kayak cockpit once I was upside down. I'd done some paddling in an inflatable kayak during the Grand Canyon trip and also during the Primal Quest Expedition Race, so I understood the basic strokes. I also remembered Harlan Taney on the Grand Canyon, and his sister, Marieke, describing his roll to me, but the move had seemed foreign and incomprehensible.

"I've been thinking about why you might have struggled to learn to roll before," Rob said as he waded waist deep into the water beside me, holding the edge of my boat. "Since you can't see to visualize the moves, you need to learn them kinesthetically, by feeling them and actually going through the motions. And we are going to keep it simple. The kayak roll can be reduced to three steps once you are upside down: paddle to surface, hip snap, head out last. The head is the last thing to come out of the water."

A breeze blew through the trees and rippled the water. Rob shivered despite his dry top. He started out at the bow end of my kayak, his hands placed on both sides, as I rocked the boat side to side, from one edge to the other.

"That's right, even more than that," Rob encouraged me. "It's clear that you don't disco! You're very stiff, Big E. Loosen up."

It felt very tippy, but I noticed I could rock the boat pretty far: right edge, left edge, right edge, left edge. Next, Rob went around and held the side while I leaned over in the opposite direction, until the kayak was tipped perpendicular and my head was actually resting in the water. From this position, he told me to "snap" my hips hard and return to the sitting position with the boat bottom flat against the water. After I repeated a bunch of these, Rob had me flip the boat completely over, and I used his steady hands at the surface of the water to grab on to and hip snap back upright.

"Okay," Rob said, finally handing me my paddle. "It's time to put all the steps together. At first, getting two out of the three will be a victory. Say them to me again."

"Paddle to surface, hip snap, head out last," I repeated, feeling the apprehension building inside me.

"Exactly!" said Rob, slapping me on the back.

He guided my paddle to the setup position, so that my torso was turned to the left and my paddle ran alongside the boat edge. "Good setup," he said. "Now, this is going to feel disorienting and a bit suffocating, but relax. I'm right here to flip you upright if something goes wrong . . . now, ease over and flip upside down."

Blip. Blurp. I was underwater. It was so icy cold my brain hurt, and, despite inhaling before going over, I felt instantly out of breath. The water pressure crushed in around my face. My eyes bulged. Water hammered up my nostrils. My spray skirt and dry top squeezed tight around my chest and neck, compressing the little oxygen that remained in my lungs. I could hear bubbles floating up toward the surface, and I tried to imagine the orientation of my body and the boat bobbing above me, but it was all inverted and topsy-turvy. I felt Rob's hands guiding my paddle to the surface and tried to snap my hips as my head lifted out of the water, desperately floundering for air. Taking a gasp of air, I heard Rob's voice saying, "Head last," as I plunked back over. Then Rob grabbed the boat and turned me right side up. I gasped, shook my head, and blew water out of my nose.

"Let's try it again," Rob said. "Remember, the average human head weighs about ten pounds—it's really heavy, and it acts like an anchor trying to sink back into the water. And Big E, your head is way bigger." He cracked up at his own joke.

We practiced over and over, with Rob helping me up. Each time, the motion made a little more sense to me as Rob peppered me with helpful tips. "Your paddle needs to be at a right angle to your boat as you sweep," and "Your paddle blade needs to be flat against the surface. Otherwise, it'll slice through the water. When you're under, bend your wrists from side to side and see if you can feel when the blade's flat," and "Your hips are a lot more powerful than your arms, so use your core. Don't just muscle it with those biceps."

After a few times, he said excitedly, "That was 90 percent you, Big E."

On my next try, I forced my paddle up, snapped my hips, drove my knees, tucked my head down, and found my kayak slowly tipping up out of the water. The motion then stalled out as the boat hovered on its edge. I thought it was going to flop back over. I dropped my head even more and strained with my hips and abs. The boat inched over a little more and then plunked down. I was sitting upright, happily breathing air, honestly surprised it had worked. By the end, I'd performed four successful, yet very shaky, rolls.

In the spring, our neighbors told us that they were going on a rafting trip down the Green River, and they asked if my family and I would like to come along. I immediately called Rob.

"Hey, Rob, we're doing a family raft trip down the Green River over Fourth of July. Want to come?"

"Most definitely!"

"You want to kayak?" I asked.

"Absolutely!" he fired back.

"I was thinking, I might like to kayak too."

"One hundred percent."

"Would you have any interest in guiding me?"

"Sure, why not!"

After we hung up, the idea of kayaking jolted me back to Harlan Taney's offer when we'd finished that Grand Canyon trip: "You should come back someday and kayak the Grand Canyon." Harlan's offhand remark had struck me as so preposterous at the time, and it still did. But now, I thought, maybe it would be worth just dipping my toes into the kayaking waters, just to see what it might be like. The Grand Canyon featured some of the biggest rapids in North America, with thirty-foot waves crashing over you. Rapids range from I to VI, with I being "easy" and VI being "extreme risk of life," but this section of the Green River was intermediate. It had numerous rapids going up to Class III+.

Many of my mountain expeditions took me away from my family for great lengths of time, sometimes months. I had missed so much with my family. I was on Mount Everest when Emma had taken her first steps. I'd had to learn about it via a crackling, distant-sounding satellite phone. With Arjun new to the family, I especially wanted to be there to navigate all these new family dynamics.

When I'd considered a bunch of different family adventures, backpacking came to mind, but slogging up and down steep mountain trails could feel more like work than play, and you had to carry all your own food and provisions on your back. I wanted the kids, now six and seven years old, and Ellie, to really have fun together. I remembered a line that PV (Pasquale), the leader of my Mount Everest team, once said when we were coming down off a big mountain after an epic fifteen-hour death march: "The worst day on the river still beats the best day in the mountains." It sounded good—exciting rapids, short scenic hikes, fun beach camping, river baths, and all the great food and beer you wanted. What a perfect way to show the family the beauty of the natural world, while still enjoying some creature comforts.

To prepare, Rob and I went to Bear Creek Lake, just fifteen minutes from my house. We paddled around for a while, and Rob suggested I try to paddle in a straight line, keeping the boat going in one direction. The wind pushed against my bow, and I felt the boat turning. I tried to adjust by paddling harder on one side or the other.

"Big E, you're turned around backwards now," Rob shouted, "and paddling in the opposite direction!"

A bit later, "Ah, now you're heading sideways towards the shore . . ." And I felt my hull scraping against gravel and rocks.

"Now, you've veered right . . . and now you've done a 180 and you're heading back to shore." More rocks scraping under my boat.

Next, we decided to have me follow Rob as he paddled just ahead, blowing a whistle he had tethered to his neck. I'd experimented with following Harlan's whistle on the Grand Canyon and in other sports like skiing and trekking, I was accustomed to following sound. But even the flat water of Bear Creek Lake proved difficult, as the kayak turned sharply with each hard paddle stroke, and once it began veering, it was difficult to get it to track in a straight line. We zigzagged around the lake, and I was constantly making adjustments and recalibrating to try to follow Rob, still unable to tell exactly which way I was going.

"We'll continue to hone our system," Rob said, "but the most important skill for whitewater kayaking is having a bomber roll."

"Can we settle for decent?" I asked.

At the put-in to the Gates of Lodore—a forty-four-mile stretch of the

Green River—we stood cooling off in knee-deep water and splashing ourselves. It was a hot July and the temperature had broken one hundred degrees. The river guides went through a pre-trip safety talk and showed everyone how to properly put on their PFDs. I remembered Marieke Taney's words from the Grand Canyon: "These aren't life vests. They won't save your life. They only help you float." I helped Ellie make sure that hers, Emma's, and Arjun's were cinched down tight.

We had a pretty big gang—my dad, my brother Eddi, and his two oldest children, Edwin and Brooklyn, who conveniently matched the ages of my two kids, plus Rob and another family. Rob and I would descend in hard-shell whitewater kayaks, while the rest of the group would ride in rafts. We'd also brought a couple of inflatable kayaks—duckies—just like the ones I'd tried out on the Grand Canyon.

As everyone loaded into the rafts, Rob guided me over to the kayaks on the shore, their bows just touching the river's edge.

"You ready?" Rob asked.

My mind conjured all the life-threatening river hazards I'd learned about on the Grand Canyon: boulders you can ram into or get pinned between; undercut ledges you can get sucked beneath; fallen trees and floating logs; churning hydraulic features called "holes" that can submerge you and hold you under.

"I'm good," I said. Sweat was pouring down my temples, and I splashed some cold river water on my face, trying to convince myself that it was from the scorching heat and not my active imagination.

The rafts cast off downstream. I could hear the kids' happy voices chattering excitedly, bouncing off the river's surface. "Bon voyage, brave, strong kayakers!" Ellie yelled. I stood next to my boat, kicked as much sand off my feet as I could, and slid inside. I stretched my neoprene spray skirt down tight over the lip of the cockpit, tightened the strap on my paddling helmet, and followed Rob's voice and the screech of the whistle out into the easy current. The river felt languid as a lake, just a mellow flow drifting the boat downstream. Staying close to Rob, I flipped intentionally a few times to practice my roll, popping back up like a cork each time. We cruised along comfortably for a while, with me working to follow Rob as best I could. Sometimes the bow of the boat wouldn't track properly, or I overpaddled—and once it started going in a direction it just kept going, and Rob would correct me, saying, "Right, right! You're not actually turning right . . . more right!" and eventually I'd straggle back on course. Our boats collided a few times, the hard hollow hulls making a loud, drumlike thump. I slammed into a rock, bounced off, flipped over, and managed to roll up on my second attempt. As I floundered around trying to stay on course, I heard one of the guides say, "I don't like the looks of this."

I got back on course and followed the whistle. Rob reminded me of the T-rescue, which I could use if I failed to make my roll. From upside down, I was to beat my hands on the hull and then run my hands back and forth along the sides to give him a target. He'd then ease the nose of his boat into the side of mine, and I'd grab his bow and use it to leverage upright. If this failed, I knew to pull my spray skirt, slide out of the boat, and swim. But swimming was a last resort. Your kayak partner then had to fish you out of the water and get you to shore, and then chase down your boat, which would be filled with a hundred gallons of water that had to be drained. It was a debacle that was unsafe and best to avoid.

I could feel and hear the terrain ahead narrowing, constricting as sound began to patter off rimrock walls. Also, I felt a cooling temperature change as a shadow slid across me, and I sensed we'd tucked in next to a rock wall.

"We're heading down into the canyon now, with towering walls of red and beige sandstone rising from the river," Rob said. "Oh, and that's Winnie's Rapid up ahead. The first real rapid. There's a big boulder in the middle of the run that we need to stay right of. Try to lock on to the sound of the whistle."

My boat picked up speed. The whistle blasts bounced around—ricocheting off the walls as the water rushed and rumbled under my boat. I paddled hard forward, but the whistling had vanished. Waves poured over the bow and hit me in the chest and face. Water splashed me from the left, then the right. My upper body bobbled as something seemed to grab me from below. I almost went over, but somehow recovered. Which way was I pointing? Maybe to the left? Maybe upriver? I felt alone. Bolts of panic seized me, but I tried to stay focused and keep paddling. I swung my head around to listen and heard the bleat of a distant whistle behind my right shoulder. I cranked my paddle and began to turn, but the rumble of the rapid was subsiding, and I drifted into calm water. Rob paddled up beside me.

"I lost you!" I yelled. "The whistle was bouncing all over, and then it just got washed out by all the river noise," I said through short breaths.

"Yeah, we got quite separated," Rob called back. "By the time I turned around, I tried yelling, but you couldn't hear me because you'd gotten pulled over into an eddy and spun around. Nice job staying upright."

We floated next to each other, our hulls knocking together.

"Definitely a wake-up call," Rob went on. "You gave your family and the guides a good show. But ahead we've got three pretty straightforward miles of small wave trains, where we can work to improve our system."

"Yeah, let's not play 'drown the blind guy' in front of my whole family."

I was still a little rattled as Rob yelled, "Follow me!"

The wave trains he'd described were continuous gentle rollers, and it was fun bobbing along behind him. I could hear his voice better than the whistle—his voice didn't seem to reflect off the rock walls as much. The water felt solid beneath me, and I craned forward to interpret the rising, cresting, and falling of the waves. There was almost a discernible pattern to them, but they went by so fast that I was merely reacting to the feel and sounds without comprehension.

That evening at Kolb campsite, the guides prepared dinner, and my family played and hung out at the river's edge. Rob and I sat in folding chairs talking about the day. I couldn't believe how exhausted I felt. I was mentally spent from concentrating and trying to follow directions. My brain actually hurt, and the tension worked through the back of my neck, shoulders, and arms. We both agreed that our current guiding system needed some tweaking.

"It's really difficult to turn around and look back upstream to see where you are," Rob said, "and what direction you are facing."

"Maybe you need a rearview mirror," I joked.

"Actually, that's a sound idea, in theory," said Rob. "They make small rearview mirrors for bike helmets, but it would never really work, as I'm too jumpy to be able to watch carefully. And it's also really tricky doing the reverse-image calculations.

"Another flaw with our system," he continued, "is that when I detour around a rock or hole, I can't just blow the whistle. That will draw you right into the obstacle, precisely what we need to avoid."

That made sense, since I couldn't see the danger that lay between us, and, in the moment, there was no time for detailed explanations.

"Also," I added, "when you did manage to stay right in front of me so I could hear, our boats rammed into each other a few times, and I almost flipped."

"It's a conundrum," said Rob. "There must be a better way for me to convey the necessary information to get you safely and confidently down these rapids. Let me think on it."

Rob headed out to photograph birds, and I went over to check out what the family was up to. Eddi had challenged the kids to a rock-skipping competition, and he was waxing philosophical about the perfect skipping stone, showing one to Arjun.

"Not too big," he was saying. "And smooth, round edges like this, that won't catch on the water. Now throw it sidearm, like this." I heard the whirr, and *pop pop pop* of a sweetly skipped stone.

"No, Arjun. Not toward shore!" Eddi reprimanded. "Only in the water, and away from people. Yes, like that."

Eddi whispered to me, "He's thrown a couple at the girls, but dang, he's got a really good arm."

The kids abandoned rock skipping to build a fort on the sand with rocks and driftwood. I sat in the warm sand and listened to their construction project. Dressed just in swim suits, their bodies became caked with sand and river mud as they played for hours. It was great to be away from electronic entertainment, instead using only their imaginations and these objects provided by nature; sticks and deer antlers became swords, and raven feathers their warrior headdresses. But the activity wasn't totally free from conflict. Arjun wanted to name the fort "the Tower of Doom," and Emma wanted to name it "Fort Yippy-Ki-Yay." They argued back and forth, and the boys finally stormed away to build their own exclusive clubhouse.

Ellie came up and sat down next to me. "Arjun's as dirty as when we gave him that first bath." She laughed.

Rob returned from his sojourn around sunset. I could hear him snapping pictures around camp, then he took a seat in one of the folding chairs.

"Arjun, come check out my notebook," he said.

Arjun sat down next to Uncle Rob. I hung over to the side, listening.

"I photographed five different bird species on that walk," Rob said, "including a spotted towhee, formerly called the rufous-sided towhee. Check him out." Rob handed Arjun his camera.

"He's got red eyes," Arjun said.

"There are 914 wild bird species in North America. I've spotted about 750 of them. Arjun, do you know what the fastest animal in the world is?"

Arjun paused for a minute and then said, "Cheetah?"

"How about you, Big E?"

"Yes, I think it's the rufous-sided Raker as he sprints for the buffet table," I said, very pleased with myself.

"Actually, you're both incorrect," Rob said, not acknowledging my insult. "It's the peregrine falcon. During its high-speed dive—called a stoop—the peregrine reaches two hundred miles per hour. It is by far the fastest. So keep your eyes open. We might spot one."

As our flotilla left camp the next morning, I could hear Ellie talking to Arjun in the raft in front of me. "This is the third time you've forgotten something on the beach," she said. "You were playing instead of packing."

Emma and Brooklyn called out, "Bye-bye, flip-flops." Uncle Rob was nice enough to paddle upriver and snag them, adding them to the list of caps, sunglasses, water bottles, and sunscreen he'd already rescued. Arjun had to sit next to Ellie for the next hour instead of playing with the other kids.

On the flat water, I floated along between the lead raft and a caboose raft. Rob and I ducked beneath the water fights that broke out between the different factions. Eddi had brought along an arsenal of high-powered water guns—a Stream Machine, an Aqua Blaster, and his secret weapon, the dreaded Hydro Stick.

Arjun, finally released from his time-out, would lead the charge, followed by Eddi and Edwin. They would paddle their inflatable duckie quietly into position and ambush the girls relaxing on the raft. I loved hearing Emma and

Brooklyn shriek as they were drenched with water. That would always begin the water-war games that lasted for hours. As our flotilla moved easily down-river in the rising heat of the day, I practiced my roll and would have the kids count how long I could stay under. Upside down, time tends to speed up as your instincts scream to get upright again. My goal was to reach five seconds, but on my first try, I popped up and proclaimed, "I did it. Five seconds," and lifted my paddle in the air. Everyone was laughing.

"Dad, try two seconds," Arjun said, smiling. I couldn't help laughing along with them. They were having so much fun at my expense as I stressed out underwater.

"This time, I'm definitely making five seconds," I vowed. I flipped again. This time, I made a couple attempts to roll up but, for some reason, couldn't pull it off. Each time my head came partway out of the water, I could hear the kids on the rafts counting, "One, two, three, four, five . . ." but I missed my third attempt and started worrying about my air. I reached my hands out of the water to get a T-rescue from Rob, but I missed his boat as I groped around, and I panicked, quickly reaching for the grab loop and releasing my spray skirt with a hard yank. I swam to the surface, hyperventilating as the kids cracked up even harder than before.

Above Harp Falls, the day's first rapid, Rob slid up next to me. "I have a new plan," he said. "I'll paddle slightly behind and to your side and call out signals 'Left' or 'Right' as needed. When you are headed in the correct direction, I'll say, 'Hold that line.' And I'll make adjustments as the waves and swirling eddies alter your course. How does that sound?"

The idea ran counter to my standard following technique in most other sports, but as there was no manual for blind kayaking—and we were figuring it out on the fly—I agreed to try it.

Nerves clenched my arms and chest as I thought about heading into a jumble of obstacles with no lead sound in front of me to paddle toward, but I could hear Rob right next to me. He seemed to be able to stay close, and that was a comfort.

"Okay, there are just two main rocks to run between," Rob called out.

Responding to his calls, I paddled hard into the rapid, feeling spray in my face as my bow plunged and rose on the waves. Even with the rushing noise of the rapid, I heard Rob's commands, and his voice at the end, "You threaded those rocks!"

For the rest of the day, we continued to tweak the new technique, and I was feeling slightly more confident. Whitewater kayaking was beginning to shift from "terrifying" to "almost fun."

After a couple of rapids, Rob suggested he reduce the frequency of his voice commands. For one thing—he was losing his voice yelling constant instructions; but he also thought I should be listening to the river sounds and trying to understand and process the information those sounds provided. It felt like learning a new language, and I strained to notice subtleties: the far-off hush-roar that signaled an upcoming rapid; the slurping sound of eddies pooling above a rock; how the narrowing and widening of canyon walls altered sound and signaled the opening or constricting of the river flow. We settled on Rob only giving me information when needed, allowing me to relax some and navigate on my own.

Rob also tested my awareness of body positioning. "Which way are you pointing?" he asked. "Since it's the afternoon, the sun is to the west. So where do you feel it on your face?"

"On my right cheek," I said, "so I must be traveling south."

"And how far are you from shore?" he asked, and I tried to use the echo off the rock walls or trees to gauge my distance. Sometimes he'd say, "The wind is moving directly up-canyon, so paddle into it. If you feel it trailing to your left or right, you'll know you're off course."

Our system improved steadily. We scouted Triplet Falls, a Class III+, and despite Rob telling me about two huge boulders I needed to avoid (known as "the birth canal") and another nasty rock section called "the sieve," I decided to go for it. With Rob's precise commands, we snaked right through the entire rapid.

At eighteen miles into the Gates of Lodore, the river widened and the skies opened overhead. Near a big buttress called Steamboat Rock, the Yampa River joined the Green, adding considerable flow and creating bigger, toilet-bowl swirling currents that tried to tip me over. I had to fight hard to keep the nose of my boat going where I wanted it to. But after that, it was mostly easy water, and Rob added a few new commands. "Charge!" called for short, powerful strokes to gain quick speed and was needed to accelerate through small holes. "Stop!" required me to back-paddle with a quick burst of two to three strokes to cease forward progress downstream, an important skill for getting properly set up above a rapid. And "Stop paddling!" meant to let my paddle blade trail in the water and coast along, awaiting instructions.

Rob also started yelling out, "Eddy line!" to alert me to upcoming eddies, and on easier flat water, we experimented with him yelling, "Follow me!" and then transitioning back to me in the lead as we entered the next rapid. As Rob tucked in behind me, it felt like we were race cars jockeying for position. In this way, we were starting to perform our own fluid river dance, choreographed by Rob's voice and our combined actions.

By midafternoon, we made the Jones Hole campsite, where we hiked up a creek to check out pictographs and petroglyphs left by the Fremont people a thousand years ago. Some designs appeared humanlike. Others were antlered animals and lizards, and the kids loved them. But in the intense July heat, our favorite was a section of Jones Hole Creek called Butt Dam Falls. We took turns standing in the cascading waterfall. Directly above our heads was a perfect butt-size depression in the narrow channel in which you could sit and temporarily block the water flow. Arjun couldn't get enough. He'd sit above us, butt-blocking the stream, tempting his victims to stand below. He'd, of course, promise to hold back the flow, but as soon as we'd take the bait, he'd yell, "Cowabunga!" and lift his cheeks, and the cold water would come pouring down over our heads.

After the hike, Rob disappeared on another bird-watching adventure but returned with an excited voice. "I found something you may be interested in, but we have to be quiet and walk softly." Rob refused to reveal anything further.

We all followed him up the beach and through the brush, Emma hushing Arjun several times when his voice got loud. Then Rob stopped and pointed up at the cliff. One at a time, he let the kids look through his binoculars. Seventy-five feet up, in a cleft in the rock, was a nest. Emma described three grayish-white fledgling birds.

"Peregrines," Rob said proudly. "The nests are called eyries."

Then the kids gasped as one of the birds leaped from the nest, flapping its wings awkwardly. The bird plummeted downward, but thirty feet off the ground, it caught a draft of air, leveled off, and then lifted up into the sky.

"How beautiful," Ellie said.

"*Ki bu la*," I said, remembering the Tibetan phrase for *how beautiful*.

"He might be flying for the very first time," Rob whispered with awe in his voice.

With Uncle Rob, a rare sighting of juvenile peregrines was just the start. He next took all the kids on a bouldering adventure. He found a rock about twelve feet high, and he carefully spotted each in turn as they climbed it. Arjun was like a little spider monkey, but while Rob was trying to give all the kids a chance, he refused to wait his turn; he kept cutting in front of Emma and Brooklyn, saying, "My turn! Emma's always first!"

As I pulled him back, I noticed he was going into one of his sullen moods. I put my arm around his shoulder and steered him away from the bouldering rocks and down to the river's edge.

"Emma's not always first," I said. "That's not true, and you know it." We stood with our toes in the river. "What's the matter?" I asked. "What's really wrong?"

As he sat next to me, he was breathing hard, and I could tell he was angry.

"You like Emma better," he finally said.

"What? No, I don't, Arjun." Inside I felt terrible, knowing he could think that. But given where he'd come from, he had plenty of reasons to be suspicious. There'd been a lot of disruption in his short life. The trust he was beginning to build with his new family was still fragile, and, I imagined, didn't yet feel real.

"I'm not really like you," he said. "I don't even look like you."

I knelt down to him, and the hot sand burned my knees, but I hugged him tightly. "What do you mean you don't look like me? We both have brown eyes," I said. A year earlier, I'd had my prosthetic eyes replaced. Even though I'd had green eyes as a teenager, the ocularist had painted new eyes that had a tinge of brown to them. At first, I'd been annoyed, but then over the dinner table, I blurted out, "We're now a perfect family. The girls have blue eyes, and the boys have brown." It had wound up being one of those mistakes Hugh Herr referred to in his speech at a past summit—a wonderful, glorious mistake that you wouldn't change for anything.

Arjun plucked up a rock and tossed it into the river and said, "It's not really true. You used to have green eyes."

"In my mind, we look exactly alike," I said. "But even if we don't, you're still mine."

Arjun didn't say anything, and I felt like I wasn't getting through to him, so I changed tack, remembering a children's book I had read to him in Braille. The book had been entitled *Guess How Much I Love You*. In it, a dad (Big Nutbrown Hare) was talking to his son (Little Nutbrown Hare), trying to describe the magnitude of his love. "Guess how much I love you?" he asked. "Right up to the moon . . . and back," he said.

I thought for a moment and said, "Guess how much I love you? If a mountain lion attacked right now, I'd block you with my body and let it gnaw me right down to the bone. That's how much I love you."

Arjun was now listening, so I went on, "If we were walking across a street and a Mack truck was barreling toward us, I'd throw you out of the way and get squished myself. That's how much I love you."

"No, you wouldn't," he said quietly.

"Yes, I would," I replied. "If we were in a burning building, I'd tie sheets into a rope and lower you out the window while the flames burned me to a cinder. That's how much I love you."

"Really?" he asked.

"Really," I answered, now on a roll. "If a giant pterodactyl pooped on us right now, I'd lift you up so you could breathe, while I suffocated."

"Pterodactyls are extinct, Dad!" he said and giggled. The fact that I'd be chewed up, squashed under a tire, burned alive, and drowned in poop—all for him—seemed to make an impression on him. I rubbed his back one last time, and he scurried off to play with Edwin.

That night, we sat around the fire. My dad had brought a book that traced the Green River's descent from the Wind River Range in Wyoming, south into Utah, then curving over into Colorado. Eventually, it plunged into Canyonlands National Park, then joined the Colorado River, and eventually raced down through the Grand Canyon. He told the kids that in 1869, on this very river, Major John Wesley Powell and his ragtag band of nine mountain men embarked on their journey into the unknown. He said we were retracing history. "That makes us explorers too," Arjun said.

My dad continued, "Powell named this section the Gates of Lodore, after a poem called 'The Cataract of Lodore' by English poet Robert Southey," and he read a portion:

> The cataract strong
> then plunges along,
> striking and raging
> As if a war raging
> Its caverns and rocks among;
> Rising and leaping,
> Sinking and creeping,
> Swelling and sweeping,
> Showering and springing,
> Flying and flinging,
> Writhing and ringing,
> Eddying and whisking,
> Spouting and frisking,
> Turning and twisting,
> Around and around
> With endless rebound:
> Smiting and fighting,
> A sight to delight in;
> Confounding, astounding,
> Dizzying and deafening the ear with its sound.

As we sat around the fire, I found myself a little sad the trip was ending the next day. It had been such a blast doing a family adventure that everyone could enjoy together and challenge themselves in their own way. The whole family had tried their hands at paddling the inflatable duckies. At sixty-nine years old, my dad had paddled through one of the rapids and gotten sucked against an overhanging wall. He'd ducked in the nick of time, squeaked under the rock lip, and narrowly avoided a nasty swim. Arjun had especially loved riding through the rapids, with Edwin in the middle and Eddi at the helm. A couple of times, the waves had lifted up the front of the duckie, catapulting little Arjun up and over Eddi's head. In the midst of the rodeo action, Eddi would reach out, grab him by the PFD, and toss him back into the boat. While paddling together, both Emma and Ellie had also gone airborne. Emma had swum frantically to the nearest ducky but found herself atop Arjun and Edwin as they dropped and exploded through another series of waves in a tangle of bodies.

The big mountains had kept me away for long stretches of time, but on a river, each night, after the gifts of the day were earned, I got to come home. I'd sit back, surrounded by my loved ones, listening to the stories of waves and whirlpools, tosses and near misses, and the sense of connection felt as deep as the river itself.

Rob and I had just gotten through sharing our highlight of the day, when I'd gotten knocked over in a hole and failed my first two rolls. I was about to pull my skirt when Rob had saved me from swimming with a T-rescue. Throughout the trip, I'd been absorbed in learning to kayak and, in my remaining free moments, was focused on Arjun, but now, I noticed how quiet Ellie was. We took a walk down the beach together, and I said, "I really like having you here."

"I like being here too," she replied. "But when you're upside down like that and struggling to get up, it's hard to watch. I want to help you, but I can't. It was like watching Arjun barrel down that hill for the first time on his bike. I have to look away."

"Now, I'm the crazy taxi driver." I laughed.

"But I want you to know how proud I am of you," she said. "Today, I watched you just above a rapid. You took a deep breath, then another, and you paddled forward, right into it. I told myself to remember that face, because that's what courage looks like. That's what I want for Emma and Arjun. That's what I want for myself."

"It's a full circle," I said, "because knowing you're nearby, it makes me feel a little braver."

. . .

On the last morning, Rob said we needed to up our game. Ahead, near a place called Split Mountain—where the erosion forces of the Green River had literally cut the mountain in two—we'd encounter a series of six Class III rapids in succession. It was going to be a wild ride, but Rob stayed right next to me. I could hear him well, and I could even hear the hoots and hollers of our flotilla cheering us on. It felt incredible to end on such a high note, nailing all six without a hitch. At the take-out, I high-fived Rob, thanked him, and said, "We gotta keep doing this."

Before we loaded up into the shuttle vans to head out, I took Arjun aside and down to the river's edge. The poem my father had read the night before had given me an idea.

"You know how Uncle Rob has been helping me, teaching me how to kayak?" I asked.

"Uh-huh," he said.

"Well, that's so I can have fun, but it's also so I can be safe. He's teaching me to avoid the big rocks and other dangerous places in the river. He's helping me find my way downstream. I can't see what's ahead of me, so I have to trust him."

I let that sink in, then I grabbed a little piece of driftwood from the shore and knelt down into the wet sand right at the water's edge.

"A river flows from the mountains down to the sea, Arjun. It's a long journey—with lots of twists and turns. Like you coming to America. It's a journey, and you are just at the beginning. Like me, with kayaking, you can't always see what's ahead, and there will be lots of boulders and rapids along the way," I said, taking his hand. I guided his hand to the piece of driftwood, and I threw it out into the water.

"That piece of wood will float downstream, and there is no telling exactly where it's going to go. There is no one there to help it along the way, to be there if it runs into trouble, or starts to sink."

"Okay," Arjun said. He seemed to be watching the driftwood intently, half listening to me.

"But on your new journey here in America," I said, "Mom and I *are* here for you. We will be here to help you if you flip over or when you run through the rapids. I promise we will be here, always." I reached out and touched Arjun's hair. Then I turned his face toward mine. "Always," I repeated.

Arjun started giggling. I'd hoped he'd take my analogy more seriously.

"Do you think this is funny?" I asked.

"It's stuck," he said, pointing to the edge of the water.

Apparently, the driftwood had hung up on a gravel bar in the shallow, slow-moving eddy.

"Here," I said. "Help me nudge it along. We'll knock it free."

Holding my hand, he led me a step or two into the river, and we bent down together and jarred the driftwood piece loose.

"Is it going downstream?" I asked.

"Yes," Arjun said. "It's floating away."

We turned our backs to the river and headed up the steep bank toward the vans, toward home.

14

BATH TOWELS AND PACKING TAPE

If I was going to become a better kayaker, we needed to push it further and attempt some more technical rivers. In kayaking, *technical* refers to rapids with more rocks and holes to avoid, and a more complicated series of moves to navigate through, all with serious consequences if you didn't hit the line. Fortunately for us, the upper Colorado River was a short drive away, and a section called Shoshone was a perfect training ground.

Because Shoshone had more complex maneuvering, it was going to be really hard for Rob to guide me, while also trying to pick the best line through all the rocks and holes. So we decided to add another kayaker to the group. We'd enlist different friends to be our "line picker," to paddle out in front and choose the ideal way through. That would enable Rob to concentrate on guiding me, while he simply followed the lead boater. In case I had problems and swam, another kayaker could also be there to retrieve my boat, while Rob towed me back to shore.

The rapids in Shoshone were accurately named and spoke straight to my fears: Pinball Alley, Tombstone, and Man-Eater, to name a few. Listening to the full-throated roar of water pounding relentlessly over rocks, my muscles felt weak and mushy. I forced myself to breathe oxygen into my body, but I still felt like I could suffocate.

As we carried our boats down to the river, I had to consciously will my muscles to fire. Climbing mountains was supposed to prepare me in some way for all kinds of challenges, but I didn't feel prepared for this. At forty-one years old, I felt as vulnerable as a child, like I was starting over. My teeth chattered. My hands shook, and I was a little dizzy. My mouth was so dry I could hardly swallow. Rob patted me on the shoulder, assuring me that it was going to be okay.

Pinball Alley was a series of waves between a scattering of exposed rocks you had to zigzag through, with openings only a little wider than the width of a kayak. Despite Rob doing his best to call commands, my kayak would often bounce off one of those rocks, my knuckles scraping and paddle clacking. That would send me careening and ricocheting downriver, desperately bracing to stay upright. In that crazy spin, it was hard to tell which way I was facing, and I'd get totally disoriented. On one run, I slammed into a rock sideways that shook me up and flipped me. I swam out of my boat, and as Rob hauled me to the bank, he shouted, "You blind guys are sure unpredictable! You don't always go in the direction I'm expecting you to!"

Rob was joking, but the underlying point was accurate. Every run, even down the same rapid, felt totally different. If I entered angled ten degrees too far left, or Rob was a second late on a command, or I slightly over-turned, it would begin a cascading chain of circumstances that would make the run go from bad to worse. The river had its own energy that surged and ebbed unpredictably, so sometimes Rob would yell, "Small left!" I'd make what I thought was the turn, without knowing the river was actually pulling me farther right. "Left! Hard left!" Rob would shout with increasing urgency as I swept toward one of the many hazards.

Tombstone was another rapid that made me sweat, especially under all my layers of clothing. It featured a sharp, pointed rock in the middle of the river, with a large hole and a bunch of rocks just to its right. The line through there was narrow, requiring you to squeak to the left of the rocks, drop down into the meat of the rapid, and just before smacking into the Tombstone, make a hard right to whoosh by.

The flow down a wild river didn't move at one consistent pace; so with Rob right behind me, trying to kayak in symmetry with me, it was tricky to begin with. But at Tombstone, I hit the line a little to the right, bounced over a rock, and hit the hole sideways. It stopped me flat and flipped me instantly. I rolled up with just enough time to miss the Tombstone, brushing it with my elbow, but at the next eddy, Rob told me he'd almost T-boned me—or, to put it less colloquially, almost hammered me with the pointed bow of his boat! That could easily break ribs, or worse. So to avoid me, Rob had purposely flipped his own boat, which stopped him in the very same hole. I envisioned the famous dolphin Flipper ramming a shark with his bottlenose, and Flipper had always killed the shark.

"No T-boning," I said.

Floating in an eddy above the last rapid, Man-Eater, Rob said, "Don't be intimidated by the name. As long as we stay center or right, it's pretty straightforward."

"What if I don't?" I asked tentatively.

Rob looked downriver and said, "That's where the name 'Man-Eater' comes in. So just make sure to angle right and you won't have to worry about it."

As we entered the rapid, however, I got pulled too far left and into a circulating eddy. Rob shot by and, within a few seconds, was somewhere downriver. I was stuck, spinning around, totally disoriented. A moment later, I felt myself dropping backward out of the bottom of the eddy and directly into the Man-Eater. Fortunately for me, the river flow was lower than normal, and the Man-Eater turned out to be a jumble of boulders, some just under the surface and others protruding. I scraped and bounced through them, somehow managing to stay upright. My adrenaline surged, and I was hyperventilating as I finally slammed into a boulder that flipped me instantly. I'd had enough. I pulled my skirt and swam.

As Rob towed me to the shore, he said, "That was impressive, Big E. You managed to ride it through . . . until that very last rock." And later, sitting on the beach together, he said, "This speaks loudly to the fact that we need radios. As the rapids get bigger, it's going to be impossible for me to stay next to you. It's going to get harder to hear. We may be separated by a wall of white water, or, you might get pulled into an eddy."

He was right. I was trying to ride an avalanche of water that roared in my ears and blocked out everything else. In the midst of all that, Rob was trying to stay right behind me, yelling at the top of his lungs, and I could only barely hear him. Those commands had to be dead-on, delivered with perfect timing and accuracy, and the other part of the equation: I had to execute his commands flawlessly. Being a foot too far left or right meant the difference between getting hammered or squeaking through, and it would only be getting bigger and louder. So with the memory of Man-Eater lingering in my restless dreams, the search for a radio communication system began.

After a lot of online research, the array of radio choices was dizzying: VHF versus digital, walkie-talkies versus ham radios, simplex versus duplex, push-to-talk versus voice activation. The different headsets were just as confusing. Surprisingly, few of the systems were actually waterproof; the radios, cables, microphones, and earpieces needed to be completely submersible. We tried all kinds of ideas like simply putting our cell phones in waterproof cases, but a lot of canyons had no cell reception. We spoke to companies that made systems for motorcycle racing, skiing, and sailing to see if they could be modified. We tested microphone systems that conducted sound through the bone behind your ear. We talked to the leading provider of military combat radios, who insisted we'd have to settle for a push-to-talk system, but Rob was pretty busy holding his paddle and trying not to get knocked over, so the system had to be hands-free.

We finally found some that were advertised as marine radios, but the first time we tested them, it turned out that although the headsets and microphones were waterproof, the radios themselves were not. Water was entering the battery compartment, which was disastrous for electronics. We tried to put them inside waterproof bags but we had to cut small holes for the cable to run through. The holes had to be sealed again, and despite our best efforts, the seals kept leaking and the units stopped transmitting. Testing them on Shoshone, I bounced and dipped through a rapid, straining to comprehend Rob's directions. Halfway down, they began sending unintelligible gobbledygook, like Charlie Brown's teacher talking in my ear. I could hear that Rob was yelling a direction, but had no idea whether it was a left or a right. I had a fifty-fifty shot. I turned left and slammed hard into a rock, flipping and swimming. I was under for ten seconds, and when my head popped out of the water, sputtering and gasping for air, I expected to hear Rob's voice, but instead was met with a cacophony of voices. "Woohoo!" they cried. "What a show!" And then clapping. It was then I realized I'd emerged right in front of a raft full of tourists. As they cheered, I cursed angrily under my breath.

The next spring, I organized another family trip, this one down Desolation and Gray Canyons on the Green River, an eighty-four-mile section below the Gates of Lodore in Utah. This would give us a chance to test a new radio setup. The river was normally a Class III section, but when we arrived, we found the water was flowing at flood stage—forty-two thousand cubic feet per second (cfs). It was a thirty-five-year high, and Rob said, "Get ready for a wild ride."

At the put-in, I pulled the new radio setup from the rigid Pelican Cases and slid the walkie-talkie box into a pocket in my PFD. I attached the cables that trailed up to my headset, which wrapped around my forehead with Velcro straps. I adjusted the dangling mike against my mouth and finally pulled my helmet over it all.

As I began paddling, I noticed that this new technology added another layer on top of a sport that, with a tight spray skirt, dry top, and PFD, already felt cumbersome and claustrophobic. Now, I had a bulky box jammed into my chest pocket and a series of cables protruding from my PFD, wrapping around my shoulder straps, and connected to an earbud plugging my ear. With my left ear no longer hearing the ambient sound around me, I was now listening to the world in mono, no longer in stereo. Being reduced to one ear made it harder to assess space and distance and respond to the sound cues I was so used to. I felt less connected to the river. But with Rob's voice immediately in my ear, I was now more connected to him, my lifeline, and it gave me confidence.

Rob began his commands as we entered our first rapid. Crammed into my tiny craft, layered in protective gear, and with the new earpiece and microphone covering my face, I felt kind of like an astronaut blasting off into space, with Rob as my mission control: "Okay, Big E. You're now entering the green tongue. At the bottom, there are some laterals we need to break through . . . now hard left. Fight the spin. Hold that line." His voice was now fast and adrenalized through the earpiece. "Hard right . . . charge, charge, charge!"

Rob could now hang back farther from my boat, without as high a threat of T-boning me. Once I got stuck in an eddy, and Rob shot past me, but unlike Shoshone, he pulled over in an eddy a hundred feet down and talked me through. "Small left, small left . . . Now paddle hard . . . You're through the eddy line. Hard left and hold that line."

Despite the advantages, with technology came a higher chance of catastrophic failure. Water could seep into the control panel; a cable could disconnect; a microphone could be clogged with water, and a battery could die. I had to trust that the radio would work reliably. The pre-radio days had been more black and white; I could either hear Rob or I couldn't. But with radios, the worst scenario would be for me to be hurtling down a rapid thinking everything was fine, when, in actuality, Rob was yelling desperate commands that I wasn't following. So using the radios presented a trust issue; they had to work well all the time.

To build that trust, on the flat water, I practiced my roll a lot. Radio waves don't work underwater, so I couldn't hear Rob when I was upside down, but as I rolled up, Rob would begin to speak. Most of the time, I'd hear him, but now and then, with no explanation we could determine, I wouldn't hear a thing. When we checked, we'd find the radio had mysteriously shut itself off.

Our new system was a waterproof, voice-activated system, but we continued discovering some problems. First, the wind gusts and water splashes constantly triggered the voice activation. Since it was often activated, I couldn't talk back to Rob. The big waves also knocked our mics out of place, so Rob's commands became a distant whisper. But worse than that, Rob's first word would kick on the voice activation, and, because of that, it would often miss his first syllable. "Small left," became "—ll left" and "hard right" became "—rd right."

I was always second-guessing his commands, and it began throwing off my rhythm and filling me with anxiety. We also noticed the voice activation had a half-second delay from the time Rob said something to the time it was received in my ear. Half a second seemed minuscule, but in a rapid, when the timing of Rob's directions was everything, it felt like an eternity. A few times I was late on a call and found myself bouncing over a submerged rock and flipping in the circulating hole beneath it. My roll was still shaky, and I was still getting panicky underwater. I really wanted to take Rob's advice to keep trying two, three, even four times. But when I was under, I'd try once, maybe twice, and pull my skirt. I was finding it almost impossible to break my brain's fight-or-flight mechanism, built up over thousands years of human evolution. Instinct took over, and I was no longer consciously making decisions.

The one rapid we were concerned about was called Joe Hutch Canyon Rapid, which came at mile fifty-five. When we arrived a couple of hundred yards above, we pulled over river right and went ashore to scout. With the river running this high, it was the loudest white water I'd ever stood next to, and Rob and I had to yell pretty loud to hear each other over the roar. Rob grabbed my hand and pointed my finger at the river. "Definitely big water. Gotta be Class IV. There's a strainer river right, *a big* hole river center, and *a huge* wave train river left. We'll want to enter the center tongue, then make a hard right as soon as we pass the big hole to miss the giant wave train. After the wave train there's a large rock wall river left we'll want to stay well clear of . . ."

My ears heard the words, but my brain was shutting off. All of a sudden, this didn't seem like a very good idea. I imagined flipping and getting slammed into the rock wall at the bottom.

I half mumbled to Rob that I might want to skip this one, that this was a family trip, and Ellie probably wouldn't want me to try it, but Rob was already off discussing the safety plan with the raft guides.

A little while later, a hollow pit lodged in my stomach as we floated down toward the overwhelming noise. "Are you ready for this, Big E?" Rob asked over the radio.

"I guess so," I replied, fighting down nausea.

"Okay," his voice crackled, "here we go."

Then I heard silence—utter and complete radio silence. For a moment, I worried something had happened to Rob. My boat started bobbing and rolling in massive entry waves, and I heard Rob's voice from at least a hundred feet behind me, completely unintelligible, but unmistakably back there somewhere. As I rode the back of a slippery liquid serpent, I tried to rotate my body and raised my paddle over my head in the sign of distress. "Rob, no radios!" I yelled, and it came out guttural like an animal's dying scream. "No radios!"

There was nothing to do but try to point into the massive waves that were crashing over my head. I braced and tried to stay upright, lifting skyward and riding down the other sides. Water exploded all around me, and the pulse of the river drew me forward. I wondered if I were about to crash into the canyon wall or be pulled into a hole.

After what felt like a lifetime, but was probably only a minute, I finally heard his call behind me, and I was relieved. The radio was dead, and Rob had figured it out and hurried down to me, now hollering, "Plan B!"

In kayaking, your first plan often doesn't happen, so Rob always insisted on a plan B. In this instance, it was to shout at the top of his lungs, like the old days.

"Left, hard left! Charge! Charge!" A huge wave pummeled me from the side, and I went over, but I kept it together and popped back up on my second try.

As the waves diminished and the roaring subsided, Rob yelled, "Nice combat roll! You nailed it, Big E!"

I panted hard and collapsed over the front of my boat. Finally, I said, "I'm done with those fucking radios."

I hadn't been home long and was still thinking about kayaking and how to solve our radio problem when I got a call from Richard Hogle of Wicab, Inc., the head of product development of a company I'd been working with for a few years. They'd loaned me the newest version of their BrainPort device, and Hogle wanted to know how my testing was going. Although it wouldn't help me with my radio search, the BrainPort was a remarkable piece of technology that had far-reaching implications well beyond kayaking. In fact, it seemed more like science fiction than reality. The device, comprised of a digital camera, microprocessor, and tongue display, was allowing me, and other blind people, to "see,"—but not with our eyes . . . with our tongues.

I'd been testing the BrainPort for a number of years and even had the privilege of meeting Dr. Bach-y-Rita, the pioneer responsible for this groundbreaking concept. In 2003, my dad had read an article in a science magazine about Dr. Bach-y-Rita's work, and he reached out to see whether I might be a good candidate to help test the device. A few months later, I met Dr. Bach-y-Rita at the Tactile Communication and Neurorehabilitation Laboratory at the University of Wisconsin–Madison.

Dr. Bach-y-Rita seemed younger than his sixty-nine years, with a firm yet friendly handshake and a voice that rose and danced with a kind of perpetual optimism. As we toured his lab, he and one of the researchers began setting up the BrainPort while Dr. Bach-y-Rita told me about his journey to the current work he was doing.

"The brain has the capacity to change," he started. "If one part, or a number of parts, fail, then other parts can adapt and take over. This is called neuroplasticity. I discovered this in a rather unconventional but very personal way, though the theory had been around for over a hundred years."

In 1959, his father, Pedro, a poet and a scholar, suffered a stroke that left him mostly paralyzed and unable to speak. "At that time," he went on, "stroke rehabilitation programs were quite limited, essentially because of the widely held scientific belief that the brain lacked the ability to truly recover. Conventional thinking viewed the brain as a compartmentalized group of highly specialized processing modules. It was believed that these modules had been genetically hardwired to do very specific tasks, and only those. If one of the modules became damaged, that was it; it could not be repaired or replaced.

"My brother, George, refused to give up on our father, despite being told he would never recover and should be institutionalized. George had no ingrained preconceptions about rehabilitation technique, so he created his own. Instead of trying to go straight to walking, he first taught our father to crawl. After months of crawling, he began walking on his knees, then standing, and finally he was walking.

"George also got our father to do simple household chores as motor training exercises. He'd scrub kitchen pots for fifteen minutes at a time, repeating circular motions over and over, then doing another fifteen minutes in the opposite direction. After only a year, our father had regained his speech, learned how to walk again, and eventually returned to teaching. Until his death from a heart attack hiking at nine thousand feet at the age of seventy-two, he lived a full and vigorous life."

After his father's death, Dr. Bach-y-Rita had a neuropathologist at Stanford University examine his father's brain, and what he found was shocking: His brain was visibly severely devastated, and yet he'd experienced a full recovery. His conclusion was that the exercises his brother had done with his father had somehow reorganized the brain. If the damaged parts had no longer controlled language and motor function, what had? Bach-y-Rita landed on a hunch: The brain was an organ of remarkable plasticity; if one part of it became damaged, another part could serve the same function. In other words, the parts were interchangeable. The idea was revolutionary and eventually changed the way people fundamentally thought about the human brain.

To test his theory, he quit the job he'd taken right out of medical school and enrolled in a residency at Stanford's Santa Clara Valley Medical Center. He wanted to study more people like his father, to work with stroke victims, and to potentially re-create that miraculous recovery. By the late 1960s, he was testing his theories of neuroplasticity with blind subjects.

"It's the brain that sees, not the eyes," he said. "If one sense, such as vision, is damaged, we wondered if another sense could take over. Our theory was that we could find another portal to send input to the brain. We called this 'sensory substitution.'"

Bach-y-Rita rigged a dentist's chair with panels holding four hundred small touch sensors that were connected to a camera. What the camera was seeing was translated to electrical signals that vibrated the chair's sensors. When blind subjects sat in the chair, they were able to translate the vibrating patterns they were feeling on their backs into triangles and squares, letters, and then words.

"When you were a child," the doctor asked excitedly, "did anyone draw on your back? Well, that's what was happening. These subjects were reading with their skin."

Eventually, they were able to detect furniture, telephones, even faces. The visual cortex in the brain was designed to receive information through the eyes, but he'd discovered that another sense, the sense of touch, could substitute. He had created a new connection, one that was thought to be broken permanently, showing that the brain could change and adapt to new sensory input.

"The BrainPort device you'll be testing today has come a long way from a dentist's chair, but the concept is essentially the same, except now, you'll feel the vibrations on your tongue. We discovered the tongue is excellent for sensory stimulation. Its many receptors make it very sensitive, and because it's coated with saliva, it takes well to electrical contact. In normal vision, light hitting the retina provokes electric impulses that the brain translates into images. What the BrainPort does is convert light into electrical impulses that stimulate the tongue instead of the retina."

The researcher handed me a "tongue display unit," a square grid of four hundred tiny electrodes, the whole unit only slightly larger than a postage stamp. The tongue display was connected to a computer monitor on a rolling cart, which in turn was connected to a camera. The assistant attached the camera to my forehead with an elastic headband, similar to a headlamp. I put the tongue display in my mouth and directed the camera on the table in front of me. Instantly, little electric shocks tickled my tongue, like when I had touched my tongue to a battery as a kid.

"Investigate the table," the researcher urged.

At first the sensations felt random, but then something began to emerge. It vibrated in a round shape. I reached out and felt a tennis ball sitting on the table.

"This time," she continued, "I'm going to roll you the ball. See if you can feel it moving."

A moment later, I felt a little circular vibration starting at the back of my tongue and moving toward the front. As it moved, the circle got progressively larger. I reached out my hand and actually stopped the ball that was rolling toward the edge of the table. Saying I was blown away would have been an understatement. As a blind person, it had been twenty-five years since I had experienced hand-to-eye coordination. There were ways of compensating, but nothing was as beautiful and fluid as reaching out and plucking an object out of space. In five minutes, the BrainPort had just reestablished that connection, although I guess this was tongue-to-hand coordination.

The BrainPort I was now testing at home after the Desolation Canyon river trip was much smaller and more portable. I put on the sport sunglasses that housed a small video camera on the nose bridge, acting as the "eyes" to gather visual information. The images got transmitted to a small handheld computer about the size of a cell phone, which translated those visual signals to the tongue display. I sat on my couch, moving my hand around in front of my face, holding one finger up, then two, then all my fingers, and finally moving my hand close up against my face and farther away. When Emma was a baby, Ellie described her doing the same: wiggling her fingers and toes and using those familiar appendages as a starting place from which to branch out into the world. I felt like a child as I walked around the house, trying to interpret all the images I was feeling.

"What's that, Dad?" Emma asked as I fiddled with the controller and zoomed the camera out wide. The sensations on my tongue were only in two dimensions, like a line drawing on a piece of paper. As I concentrated, I thought I felt a body and some protruding sticks that might be legs. "Is that Willa?" I asked, popping out the tongue display and kneeling down to touch the furry coat of my guide dog. Emma and Arjun brought me around the house in a game of "Stump Blind Daddy."

One of the objects really confused me. It started with a stick pointing straight up. On top was a tiny blob with a sharp point that danced around in a crazy way. I was reaching out to investigate further when Emma yelled, "Stop! That's the flame of a candle."

"I remember those days when I used to tell you not to reach out toward the hot stove," I said. "Guess now it's my turn."

I next moved into the kitchen and looked down at the counter. The tingling on my tongue became a small circle connected to a rectangular peg. The circle was more defined around the edges.

"Coffee cup?" I asked.

"That's too easy," Emma said. "Now try to grab it." It was hard enough to interpret my surroundings, but it was even harder for my brain to translate the tactile information on my tongue into perspective and dimension. It all took time and practice, like learning a new language, and it was mentally exhausting as I stretched to put the pieces together.

Using the hand controller, I zoomed in and out on the mug, and matched how big it was on my tongue versus where it was in space. I put my hand out until it enveloped the cup. Then I eased my hand down. It landed lightly on top of the handle. I lifted it up and, with a smile, took a drink of Ellie's coffee.

I had taken the BrainPort to the climbing gym to see if I could find holds on the wall. It was a fun exercise, and afterward, I started getting a bunch of media inquiries asking me to use the device to test it in skiing, kayaking, or rock climbing. But I thought they were missing the point. I didn't need the BrainPort for extreme pursuits. The ways it lent meaning in my life were subtler. When I became blind, two barriers had arisen. Not being able to see anymore had been difficult, but the true deficit was that I'd lost a vital connection to those I loved. I couldn't play a game of rock-paper-scissors with the kids or praise a beautiful picture they'd drawn in school. I couldn't tell Ellie how beautiful she looked in her new outfit or catch a knowing glance from her across the room. Without those connections, my life could sometimes feel lonely and isolating.

So it felt like magic when I could use the BrainPort to share a moment or play a game. One day, Emma challenged me to tic-tac-toe. She'd drawn the crisscrossing lines on a large drawing easel, and I could clearly recognize the nine boxes. It was tricky watching the tip of my pen in hand, as I shakily drew my circles. The first few missed closing the loop, and wound up looking more like apples with stems. Emma was sitting on my lap, laughing at my apples, as we traded turns.

"I think I beat you," I said.

"Nuh-uh," she replied happily. "I won!"

It would have been easy for me to miss something, so I strained again at each box, one at a time: "Don't I have one on top, one in the middle, and one at the bottom?" I asked, moving my Sharpie down the paper.

"Nope!" she emphatically denied. "I won! I won!" she squealed, bouncing on my lap. Out of the corner of my tongue, I think I caught some surging movement, and I was pretty sure it was her hands lifting up in a victory arm pump. I turned and studied the boxes—trying to see what I'd missed.

"Emma, are you sure?"

"Oh yeah," she reexamined, sounding a little deflated. "Maybe we both won."

I studied the easel one last time and said, "You little stinker!" and tickled her until she squealed. "I bet you've been cheating me for years."

I also used the BrainPort to teach Arjun how to read. I could decipher letters on Arjun's cue cards, and we'd sound out the words together. When he
got tired, we'd go downstairs to the wrestling mat to play games. One day, I
used the device to look down and noticed a ball rolling across my tongue, like
the first time at the laboratory, but this time, it was Arjun kicking me his soccer ball. I knelt on the wrestling matt like a goalie, and I'd stop the ball and
throw it back. In Nepal, when we were trying to bring Arjun home, I'd held
a deep fear that I'd never be able to play catch with my son, yet here I was,
throwing him the soccer ball.

Later, it was back to reading, but as usual, Arjun started horsing around,
telling me jokes the other boys had told him at school. "Knock, knock," he
said.

"Who's there?"

"Banana."

"Banana who?"

"Knock, knock."

"Who's there?"

"Banana."

"Banana who?"

"Knock, knock."

"Who's there?"

"Orange."

"Orange who?"

"Orange you glad I didn't say banana?"

Arjun cracked up, and his laugh was contagious. I pointed the camera at
his head and zoomed in as he told another joke, and then another. His face
filled the frame of the camera, and I studied his lips moving, shimmering
in wavy pulses. I lost track of what he was saying, transfixed by the electrical
impulses that were my son's eyes squinting and twinkling, his round cheeks
lifting, what I thought were his teeth, and, most remarkable, his curling smile.
With each new joke, his head would tilt back. His mouth would spread out,
and his entire face would transform. I had forgotten the details of how a laugh
seemed to engulf the face as it erupted with joy. I couldn't help but smile too,

and the tongue display flopped out of my mouth. Spit flew everywhere and trailed out in long tendrils of drool. Soon we were both bursting with laughter until tears were rolling down my face.

That summer, Rob Raker and I were taking frequent trips to our local creek to paddle and test different radio systems. As we sat on our boats gearing up, I gave him an update on the BrainPort and how excited I was with the prospects. I also told him how intrigued I'd become by the concept of brain plasticity, by the brain's ability to rewire itself and create new neural pathways.

"But I have to admit," I said, "it's pretty exhausting."

"I totally agree," Rob said. "And I probably wouldn't be here guiding you right now, if the brain weren't so adaptable."

I wasn't sure what to say to that, so I blurted out, "What the heck are you talking about?"

"I never told you about my accident, Big E?" he asked.

"I think I'd remember that," I replied.

"It was about fifteen years ago, just a couple of years before I met you, I was skiing with Annette and a friend of mine. He was a really good skier, and I was kind of . . . well, testosterone got the best of me, and I was showing off."

"You?" I said, "Showing off? I can't imagine it!"

"The guy was ripping really fast, and I wanted to keep up with him. Annette was in front of me. I went to pass her, but she turned, and sort of cut me off. I swerved and lost control and went flying off into the trees."

"Tell me you were wearing a helmet."

"Ah, no. This was before everyone had the good sense to wear one. I was pretty busted up. I can't remember much, but my elbow and knee really hurt; I could hardly use them. Apparently, I skied down on one ski. Annette later told me I kept saying, 'Where am I? What's going on?' And they would tell me, and a couple of minutes later I'd ask again, 'Where am I? What's going on?' I didn't know who anyone was. Turned out, I'd broken my elbow and torn the top of my tibia off where the ACL connects to it. Oh, and I'd suffered a traumatic brain injury, although back then, they didn't call it that."

"What did they call it?"

"They usually just said something like, 'You got your bell rung!' But they actually called them 'closed head injuries.'"

As I slid into my boat, it was shocking to think that Rob's brain was damaged. He was one of the smartest people I knew. He had an engineering mind and was known as a problem solver, but if someone were to look at his brain, it might look very similar to Dr. Bach-y-Rita's father's. Rob had been in rehab for nearly a year and on disability for nine months. He tried all kinds of progressive brain treatments, one using biofeedback in which he was connected to an electroencephalograph (EEG) through electrodes placed on his scalp.

"There are four primary kinds of brain waves," Rob explained. "Alpha, beta, theta, and delta. They're all based on the brain's electrical activity, and each is associated with different cognitive functions. Some are more prevalent when you're deep in sleep, others when you're daydreaming, and others when you're alert and concentrating. With TBIs, those waves fall out of balance, or get scrambled. So they'd put me in a quiet, darkened room with my eyes closed. The technician would look at a computer monitor that displayed my brain activity and set the system up to produce an audible tone when I was able to achieve the proper balance: more alpha and beta waves, which are associated with conscious thought. It was all about refocusing and reshaping the waves and creating new neural pathways, a similar process as a toddler learning to walk, or Arjun learning to ride a bike."

"Or a blind guy learning to kayak," I added.

"That's right," he affirmed. "It was really hard, but with practice, I could sustain that state of mind for short periods of time."

However, ten months later, he was still suffering problems characteristic of TBIs: excessive sleeping, memory loss, and challenges with decision-making, analyzing ideas, and multitasking. "I was working as an environmental scientist, managing projects in hazardous-waste and air-quality compliance, but after the accident," he said, "I wasn't really able to do the job anymore, not at the same level at least. During all that time, through three knee surgeries and rehab, I was laid up, and I did a lot of reflecting. I'd always burned the candle at both ends: working sixty-hour weeks, climbing, training. Until the accident, there was never really time to think about my life, but lying on my back, I thought about how lucky I was to be alive, and I asked myself, 'On my deathbed, will I be psyched to be the guy who completed 653 environmental impact statements?' It was like I woke up. The brain injury had caused a lot of pain and confusion, but in a way, it also gave me clarity, because I knew I wasn't satisfied."

"That's a scary place to be," I said. "You're derailed, and you know you can't go back, but you have no idea how to go forward. You're kind of paralyzed."

"Yeah. It was a little scary," he admitted.

"So what got you to move forward?" I asked.

There was a pause as Rob put one of the radios together and handed me the headset.

"It was a peacock flounder," he answered.

I smiled and said the only thing I could: "Of course it was."

"A friend invited me to go to the Cayman Islands to do some rock climbing. I was just off crutches and couldn't climb much, but I went along to do some diving, a passion of mine. I'd been shooting still photography for a while, but a guy had sold me an underwater housing for a video camera, and I wanted to experiment with it. One day, diving off Cayman Brac, I was cruising along the bottom, filming. I looked down and spotted these two tiny nodules protruding from the sand. Then the nodules moved just slightly, and I realized they were eyeballs looking up at me. As I came closer, it lifted up out of the sand, and I could tell it was a flounder. They're really cool creatures, flat bodies that undulate when they swim, like an underwater magic carpet. The crazy part is that they're born with eyes on both sides of their bodies, but as they mature, one eye migrates so that both eyes wind up on the same side. That's much better for hiding in the sand and spotting prey. As I followed behind, the flounder was a drab brownish color that matched the bottom, but it reached a colorful reef, and I watched through the camera as its body began to change. It became purple, and paisley shapes formed all over its sides and fins. It wasn't just any flounder. It was a peacock flounder, a marine master of disguise. I watched it come to rest on the reef, close its eyes, and disappear. It was perfectly camouflaged again. You see, a still photo only captures a tiny slice of time, but with video, the entire story of animal behavior could be revealed, the story that nature often hides unless you are paying careful attention.

"That week," Rob went on, "I shot eight hours of video: sea turtles waving their flippers like wings and soaring through the water, octopus, squid, and cuttlefish. Each night, I showed my friends the footage and narrated why the animals were behaving in certain ways. That experience solidified the two things I love—"

"Let me guess," I interjected. "Breakfast and dinner."

"Actually," he clarified, "the two I was referring to were the natural world and sharing those discoveries with others, to open their eyes to all that wonder."

It was hard to picture Rob lying broken and derailed, unable to see ahead or behind. That was a perilous point that many didn't recover from, but that moment underwater had become the energy to shift his lens just enough to envision a future and nudge him in a new direction. Thousands of years of evolution and millions of mutations had enabled the peacock flounder to camouflage itself. It was hard work. Nothing came easily. Rob had feared his brain was broken, but watching the flounder go from brown to purple in an instant, he knew his brain could change and adapt to new possibilities.

"After that, it was easy," he went on. "It's all curiosity from there. I had a dozen questions. How to edit? How to get the best sound? How to frame shots? Turns out, I didn't have to go back to the office. That spring, I signed up for film classes at a community college, and in the fall, I'd landed my first job as an adventure filmmaker."

"And two years later," I added, "we met in Antarctica when you were doing that *Nova* show. So if you didn't crack your noggin, we would have never met."

"Exactly!" he said. "Let's call it a happy accident."

"I've been experiencing a lot of those lately," I said.

"And now, here we are on this creek," he said, "trying to figure out how a blind guy can whitewater kayak," and he slid his boat into the water.

That July, it was time for another No Barriers Summit, this one just an hour from my home, in Winter Park, Colorado. It was our fifth No Barriers Summit, and we featured all kinds of new technologies: a vehicle with tanklike tracks for paraplegics to access the deep backcountry; a kayak that enabled quadriplegics to paddle; and a power-controlled wheelchair that a person with severely limited mobility could operate with his or her tongue. I showed the newest version of BrainPort, and Hugh Herr updated us with a new feature that enabled him to control the resistance of his prosthetic joints with his iPhone.

There were plenty of new people joining our community, showing up from all walks of life. On the first day, I was introduced to a twenty-five-year-old guy in a wheelchair, Kyle Maynard. I reached out to shake his hand and felt a callused stump at the end of a short, powerful arm that was as hard as a baseball bat. Kyle told me he was born with a rare condition called amniotic band syndrome (ABS). He was a quadruple amputee, his legs ending above the knees and his arms ending above the elbows. Kyle had recently heard about me and No Barriers and wanted to push himself and test his boundaries. "I'd especially like to join your hike in the morning," he said.

For a moment, I was speechless. The hike was up a nearby twelve thousand–foot peak. We had all kinds of folks signed up—blind people using trekking poles and amputees using high-tech hiking crutches—but I wondered bluntly how a guy without arms and legs was going to hike a mountain. Countless times, people had asked a similar question of me, so I pushed that doubt away.

"That sounds great," I finally replied.

Besides, we are No Barriers, I thought. If this idea was real, we had to find a way, and we didn't have much time. That evening, I assembled a team to figure out how we were going to help him pull this off. Kyle seemed incredibly strong. His buddy Dan told me he was a champion weight lifter, pulling off twenty-three repetitions of 240 pounds to win the GNC's World's Strongest Teen competition. But climbing mountains required moving up steep, jumbled trails, through mud and snow, over giant piles of boulders, and across loose scree slopes. Kyle would essentially have to crawl, moving over the landscape like a crab. We scratched our heads, brainstormed, and schemed. Finally, we went to our hotel rooms and snagged a bunch of bath towels of different sizes. I knew it was dicey and improper to be jacking bath towels from a hotel, but we figured they lived boring daily lives, and we wanted to give them some real adventure. We went to the front desk and sweet-talked the clerk into letting us have a few rolls of clear packing tape used for mailing Lost & Found items. Last, we found a number of plastic grocery store bags. It wasn't Hugh Herr's $60 million prosthetics, but at least it was a start, and we hoped it would work.

The next morning, we took turns pushing Kyle up the steep dirt road in his wheelchair. When the road ended, we wrapped all four of his stumps with bath towels to provide a thick padding. Knowing it was going to be wet and muddy, we covered the bath towels with the plastic grocery bags and then taped everything down tightly, wrap after wrap, until it created a strong armor around his stumps. He hopped down and started crawling. Kyle had been moving through the world for twenty-five years on his arm and leg stumps, and he was surprisingly fast.

For the next eight hours, I hiked right behind Kyle as he scurried upward. Sometimes, he had to drag himself through deep snow with his jeans and shirt getting drenched and cold. When he got to a wall of boulders, he performed a cool acrobatic cartwheel over the jumble, landing on the other side. At rest stops, I peppered him with questions, and the more I asked, the more I was intrigued by his life.

From the outset, his parents decided to treat Kyle, their firstborn, as a typical child. Instead of carrying him around, they put him on the ground and encouraged him to crawl.

His father, Scott, was worried Kyle would need to be hand-fed the rest of his life, so he determined that he would need to learn to eat on his own. Kyle learned to clamp his short arms together like pincers and hold food like fruit or drumsticks. He also learned to drink from a cup and pour a pitcher of juice. His parents got Kyle a special prosthetic spoon that cupped onto his stump, but as he got older, he gave up the prosthetic spoon and replaced it with regular silverware, inventing an ingenious way to feed himself with an innovative move. He would tightly pinch the very end of the spoon between his stumps, then reach down to the bowl and snag the food. Then, raising his arms upward, he'd use one stump as a lever to press down on the end of the handle resting on his other stump and swivel the silverware so the food landed precisely in his mouth.

Kyle got strong support from his parents and his three sisters, even though one day in the sandbox, he discovered how to squeeze the plastic shovel between his stumps, dig into the pit, and come up with a shovelful of sand to dump over his sisters' heads. In school, he was mainstreamed. His freshman year, he joined the football and wrestling teams, despite only weighing seventy-five pounds. Kyle went on to receive a scholarship to wrestle at the Division I level for the University of Georgia, his home state. Beyond his sporting exploits, I was impressed to learn that he had also figured out how to drive a car and could type fifty words per minute.

I related pretty strongly to Kyle's story. My family had also encouraged me to reach. My brother Eddi had pushed me to join the wrestling team, and just like Kyle, I lost a whole season's worth of matches before I finally experienced victory. My family had taken me camping, and my dad had been my primary guide through a half dozen family trekking adventures around the world. At first we had no idea what we were doing. He'd hike behind me, grabbing the elastic waistband of my shorts and steering me through the chaos. We had some pretty big spills together, and he never let go, even when we found ourselves bouncing and tumbling off the side of the trail. That technique had eventually progressed to me holding the straps of a guide's backpack, then navigating with two long white canes, and finally using sturdy trekking poles and a bear bell ringing in front of me.

About an hour from the summit, Kyle asked me more about No Barriers, and I shared my goal to grow this idea into a powerful movement. "So many people get shoved to the sidelines and never recover, but imagine," I said, "thousands, maybe millions of people, all coming together to break through their barriers, to get stronger as a community, and contribute to the world."

"I know you'll do it," Kyle said. After a long pause, he said, "I have a No Barriers goal too."

"Tell me," I urged.

"Well, maybe I should wait until the summit. I don't want to jinx it." With that, Kyle started crawling upward again, and I took his cue and strode out.

About an hour later we were standing together on the high, broad expanse that marked the top. Kyle said his jeans were wet and caked with mud and grass. "But it was worth it," he said, his voice beaming. The shopping bags were now ripped, the packing tape shredded. I knelt down and put my arm over his shoulders for a few summit photos. Then we both sat silently, catching our breaths. For Kyle, the view was visual, but for me, I could hear and feel the ground giving way to air and space that seemed to swallow me, spreading out into a massive expanse of sky. It seemed limitless.

Kyle began, "The goal I wanted to share with you, well, it needs a little explanation. My dad was in the military, and I always felt guilty I couldn't serve my country. I was feeling kind of depressed sitting in the airport on a layover when these two servicemen came over and introduced themselves to me. They were MPs who'd both suffered severe burns in Iraq. They told me that as they lay in their hospital beds after being ambushed, they made a suicide pact with each other. But on the day they made that decision, they happened to see me on a TV show. After watching, they decided not to go through with it. I managed to keep it together while I was talking to them, but when I got to my hotel that night, I broke down and cried for hours. I think about those guys almost every day. So the reason I came to No Barriers was to see if my dream was crazy, or whether it might actually be possible."

I waited for him to continue.

"I want to climb Kilimanjaro, the tallest peak in Africa," he said. "I want to send a message to those guys in the airport, to all our vets, and to kids with disabilities, that regardless of our challenges, no obstacle is too great."

I'd climbed Kilimanjaro twice. It was a long ascent, over many miles and tough terrain, and seven thousand feet higher than where we now stood.

"We'd want to get a solid team around you," I said, "and you'll want to replace those bath towels with something a little better . . . but I know you'll do it."

I remembered Rob Raker's experience underwater. In a strange way, I thought, those soldiers had become Kyle's peacock flounder—a chance meeting that created the energy to propel him toward this moment. And No Barriers, I hoped, had taken his dream and begun to make it real.

After the summit, I connected Kyle to an old friend of mine, Kevin Cherilla, who'd been my base camp manager on Mount Everest. Kevin now ran a guide company, K2 Adventures, regularly leading Kilimanjaro climbs. With

Kevin's support, Kyle's plans took shape and his hiking technology began evolving. Through dozens of iterations and hundreds of hours of testing, bath towels and packing tape had become oven mitts and potholders, and then welder's sleeves. Those had eventually given way to mountain bike tire treads, secured to his body with black gaffer tape. Finally, Kyle had connected with a Phoenix-based orthotics designer who developed the technology that transformed him into Robo-Kyle. His denim jeans became abrasion- and water-resistant nylon pants. Welder's sleeves and tire treads became carbon fiber arm and leg sockets, held in place by a modified climbing harness. At the tips of the prosthetics, he attached flanged feet, shaped like elephant's hooves and made from sticky Vibram rubber. To power up steep snow and ice, the Vibram soles could be replaced by steel-pointed crampons when needed.

Similarly, Dr. Bach-y-Rita's idea of neuroplasticity had given birth to a dentist chair and eventually to a tiny camera on a pair of sunglasses and a microprocessor that enabled a blind person to see the world through his tongue.

Ideas like these were born in a burst of mental energy, but they usually languished and died as "impractical." However, on rare occasions, people like Kyle struggled forward, painfully, awkwardly, to explore their world and push the parameters. There was a lot of flailing, even bleeding, along the way. Yet with enough time, they stumbled upon the tools that gave the idea substance. And that, in turn, fed the light of the human spirit and caused it to blaze. It was nothing but bath towels and packing tape, but combine it with that light, and you could go to amazing places.

Everything that lived and breathed had a life cycle, and dreams were not so different, starting unformed and indistinct and eventually taking on shape and clarity. I could hear Harlan Taney's voice in my head, inviting me to paddle the Grand Canyon—277 miles and some of the biggest rapids in North America. Those rapids dwarfed anything I had ever experienced so far. I could remember vividly all the rocks I'd slammed into, the desperate swimming, the inaudible radios. I thought about the panic of being upside down, the fear that seemed to melt my will like wax, and the feeling of being massively overwhelmed by forces more powerful than me.

There was a moment when I had made a silent commitment to climb Mount Everest. At first I didn't tell anyone. I was too scared to say it out loud. Now a new dream seemed to be beginning again and spinning me off in a new direction. Just as Kyle's dream must have begun, my secret still hid tenuously in the deepest recesses of my mind. I could easily kill it and tamp down the feelings of regret and disappointment. But Kyle had reached the summit above Winter Park and decided to let his dream live and grow. I had to do the same. As daunting as it sounded, despite my many questions without answers, I would commit and then find a way. My dream to kayak the Grand Canyon was now real.

15

SOLDIERS TO SUMMITS

Back home, I was elated after achieving my summit with Kyle Maynard, and I shared some of the photos with Arjun. He was fascinated by all the things Kyle could do, immediately picking up Kyle's memoir and reading it cover to cover. Over dinner, we talked about what compelled people like Kyle to believe they could do something, so bold and so seemingly unattainable, that most would dismiss it outright as impossible.

The question made me think of an experience I'd had on a family trip down the San Juan River earlier that summer. The San Juan, running through Utah into Lake Powell, was known for its massive sandy beach camps. We were stopped at one of them thinking up games we could play as a family, when Ellie suggested we all race across the sand and to the top of a steep fifty-foot dune that served as the finish line. She said it was wide open in front of us, with nothing to stumble over. I knew my big brother Mark would have loved this game, so I channeled his spirit and started gunning for the summit. I'm not known for being quick—more like a steady, reliable mule—and Arjun was light and fit from a season of soccer. Across the flats, I could hear his feet slapping the sand ahead of me, but when we got to the steeper sand dune, my uphill climbing talents kicked in, and we were soon neck and neck. However, I was huffing pretty hard, and Arjun was barely breathing.

"Come on, buddy!" I shouted between gasps. "You're about to beat your old dad!" I heard his pace slacken a little. I slowed down too, giving him a chance. "You got it, AJ," but as I came over the top, Ellie told me that he had stopped halfway up the hill and just stood there watching me cross the make-shift finish line.

I tried not to ride him too much, but I thought about it a lot and was convinced he could have beaten me. I had to admit, I was irritated. I had always tried to push my averagely talented body and brain further than they deserved to go by working hard. Arjun, however, was blessed with natural talent. He had speed, coordination, and an incredible sense of balance, so it seemed foreign to me why that talent wasn't realized. It was almost as if we were speaking from two different places, planets with two different languages, assumptions, and beliefs. I'd encouraged him to speed up, yet he had slowed down. Arjun and I watched all six *Rocky* movies, and in all of them, Rocky had risen above himself to knock out rival after rival. So Arjun was supposed to glance sidelong at me, see that he could actually pull this off, and with a final burst of energy and willpower, edge me out to win the race. Instead, at the exact moment he'd seen me to his left, the exact moment when he should have poured it on, he had given up. How could I learn to speak and understand the language inside his mind that would motivate him and not bring forth the opposite effect? I honestly didn't know.

I did have some clues, however. When I was going through my master's degree program to become a middle school teacher, I'd come across a puzzling study. It was about kids with self-doubt and others with high self-esteem. The odd part was that the researcher had equally encouraged both the kids with high self-esteem and those with low self-esteem, even saying the same words. However, the conclusions were unexpected. The kids with self-confidence used the encouragement as motivation and performed better on tests, but the kids with self-doubt performed worse. The thinking was that the kids that performed better believed they had what it took to improve, but the other kids couldn't relate to the encouragement. They felt like frauds and were terrified of even trying. It was easier on their psyche to quit early, to not risk almost winning and almost succeeding, and then fall short. Why subject yourself to the hell of trying and then have your worst fears realized? That would crush the spirit entirely. So the signals to the brain scream, "Retreat! Stay safe! Protect yourself, and don't ever dare to hope or dream! That's dangerous!" I couldn't help but think of our race up the sand dune. Why bother to pour on the speed if you were convinced you were going to lose anyway? It hurt me deeply to think about Arjun being caught in that never-ending, ever-perpetuating cycle, like spinning in a hole beneath the surface of the river.

I'd also been thinking about the deeper meaning behind Kyle's Kilimanjaro climb in honor of those two servicemen he had met at the airport. That story had struck a chord with me. In a few weeks, I was about to leave for our second expedition traveling with injured veterans and my Mount Everest team. I remembered back in 2009, sitting around my kitchen table drinking coffee with Jeff Evans and Charley Mace, both Everest teammates and also on the Tibet expedition with Sabriye and her students. We debated how to celebrate the tenth anniversary of our climb together, considering all kinds of options. As we brainstormed, I thought about the countless times I'd put my life in these guys' hands. Once, I was inching across a narrow ledge with my heels hanging over four thousand feet of air, with Charley sitting in the safe zone reeling in rope. I yelled, "Hey, Charley, get a photo! This is cool!"

His response was, "I can't. My hands are kind of busy right now, making sure you don't die."

It was blunt, but it perfectly expressed the bonds that would become strong enough for a lifetime, more like those between a family than a team.

"Maybe a Disney cruise," I said sheepishly and laughed, picturing a bunch of rugged mountaineers in Mickey Mouse hats and Hawaiian shirts.

"Dude," scoffed Jeff. "What about a first ascent in Nepal?"

"You know," I said, "it's pretty remarkable what the people on our team have done since Everest."

Pasquale "PV" Scaturro, our team leader, had subsequently rafted the Blue Nile from its source in the Ethiopian highlands to its terminus in the Mediterranean Sea. The unprecedented 3,500-mile epic journey took 114 days, during which PV fought off hungry and aggressive crocs and hippos, Sudanese rebels who took potshots at him and his team, and intermittent bouts of malaria that left him weak and delirious. Luis Benitez had gone back to guide and summit Mount Everest another six times. Charley had been with me on almost every expedition since, from Mount Kenya to Carstensz Pyramid in west Papua, New Guinea. I had completed the Seven Summits, and together Jeff and I had been part of a TV adventure reality race called *Expedition Impossible* in which we ran, rafted, and galloped Arabian stallions and camels across the northern Sahara. We'd placed second out of a field of thirteen fully sighted teams, including a team of professional football players. Kevin Cherilla, our Everest base camp manager, had gone back to summit Mount Everest himself, and now he'd been handpicked to guide Kyle Maynard up Kilimanjaro. None of us had exactly been idle.

"It needs to be something big, something as transformative as what happened to us," I said.

Charley agreed. "That celebration on Everest, below the Khumbu Icefall, was one of the greatest feelings I've ever had."

"What if it were repeatable?" Jeff asked. "I wonder if we could do something similar for others? Or at least try?"

We were all quiet for a bit as we pondered the weight of this idea. I thought about my father. He was a marine who'd served in Vietnam, flying A-4 Skyhawks in 118 combat missions. He had been part of the generation who had come home from an unpopular war to protesters shouting and holding signs that read BABY KILLERS.

Jeff, Charley, and I talked about the different barriers people faced. There were way too many people who had been pushed to the sidelines, their potential all but lost. We wondered how they might be drawn back into the world. At the top of our list were U.S. veterans. The wars in Afghanistan and Iraq were still raging, and the evening news was filled with stories of young men and women coming home burned, disfigured, missing limbs, and emotionally broken. At our last No Barriers Summit, we'd provided scholarships for a group of injured soldiers who'd recently returned home and were working hard to transition back into civilian life.

"But what can a bunch of dirtbag climbers do?" I asked.

"I think there are a lot of connections between military missions and climbing expeditions," Charley replied. "They both require serious preparation, physical challenges, and a reliance on your team."

"These vets, they've served and led and sacrificed a lot," Jeff said. "They need a little help right now. Maybe we can do something."

I went out on the road to obtain funding, doing a number of my talks to garner corporate sponsorships, as well as meeting with individual donors interested in supporting our cause. The reception was positive, and once we had enough sponsorship for our first trip, we moved into the next phase: finding the team.

So with the help of the VA, we'd recruited a team of veterans. People signed up so quickly our team was filled in a matter of months. Luis Benitez helped us come up with the perfect peak: Lobuche, 20,075 feet and right on the way to the Mount Everest base camp. Soldiers to the Summit would be comprised of eleven U.S. veterans, each dealing with different injuries and issues and all looking for ways to reclaim their lives. The team was an eclectic mix: some who had survived land mine and underwater mine explosions, improvised explosive devices, and helicopter crashes. With injuries ranging from amputations to hearing and vision loss to brain injuries, I quickly learned that merely describing their disabilities wasn't so simple. One team member named Steve Baskis was blind, having been blown up by an IED in his armored vehicle, but blindness was only one of the many injuries that plagued him. He was also deaf in one ear and was burned and disfigured, with scars all over his body, pits and divots where pieces of superheated shrapnel had struck him. The burn mark on the back of his neck was shaped like lips, which he referred to as the "kiss of death." He'd almost lost his left hand; it was weak, barely able to grip a trekking pole, and got cold very easily. He'd also suffered a traumatic brain injury from the shrapnel that had sliced through his temple, combined with the concussive blast of the explosion. His brain had been shaken, bouncing violently off the inside of his skull wall. Worst of all, Steve's partner to his right, a friend named Victor, who had two kids back home, took the brunt of the blast and had been killed right next to him. Steve felt certain that Victor's body had shielded him from the blast, absorbing the bulk of the explosion and enabling him to live. The survival guilt became a psychological trauma embedded in his mind.

I fully understood physical deficits like blindness, but I struggled to understand this disease that was invisible yet possibly more profound. What we discovered with Steve and nearly all the other vets was that PTSD was the worst and most mysterious injury of these modern wars, with a devastating effect on these soldiers' lives and futures. Post-traumatic stress disorder was defined as a condition that develops in some people who'd experienced a traumatizing or dangerous event so overwhelming the mind didn't know how to respond or move forward, like it was somehow stuck. In wars past it was called different things, like "shell shock" or "combat fatigue," but the condition had been largely ignored. Now, it was becoming known as the "soldier's disease." Depression, suicidal thoughts, anxiety, memory loss, and extreme personality changes were all symptoms that could become chronic and debilitating. During one of our trainings, a tough marine sergeant named Dan Sidles told the group that when his tour ended, after so many near-death experiences, he wondered why he wasn't thrilled to be alive. Instead, all he felt was numb inside, like his tank was empty. He said that although he was only twenty-eight years old, he felt like an eighty-year-old man.

"Home," he said, "that's where the real war begins." With a physical injury like a missing leg, you could be fitted with a prosthetic and live a relatively normal life, but there was no prosthetic device for the brain.

Along the trail to Lobuche, we'd stop each afternoon at teahouses and talk about our progress, our fears, and our futures. As we got closer, the mountain loomed larger, and the journey began to take on a metaphorical meaning—as if the mountain had a mystical power to lay people bare. Kate Ragazzino, an ex-marine nicknamed Rizzo, admitted, "I'm kind of in a hole right now." As she spoke, I could hear her obsessively picking at her fingernails. "I don't have any foundation. Sometimes I feel . . . just so lost. I don't even know what goes through my head. But the pain is there, and it's sad because people still don't get it—that not all pain is physical."

Aaron Isaacson, an army captain, said he'd watched a video filmed by the Taliban. It was the horrific deaths of friends in his platoon. Since then, he'd experienced regular nightmares in which his dead comrades reached out to him with a slip of paper. When he opened the note, it bore his name. "It should have been you," the note said.

Steve Baskis told us that blindness was like a deep, dark, black abyss that he stared into. "It's never-ending," he said. "It feels like a dream, and I'm gonna wake up someday, and someone has just shut off the TV . . . and hopefully someone will turn it back on. I wish I could see everything around us.

I wish I could see the sunset and the sunrise. But I can't. So it doesn't matter how much pain and suffering, blood, sweat, whatever. I'll push as hard as I can."

A few days later, we stood at our high camp at midnight, bundled in down jackets, hoods, and goggles. As everyone assembled outside the tents, Charley said a few departing words: "We're all about to head off on an epic physical challenge. I know many of you are hyperfocused on getting to the top, ready to charge up there and hold your flags, and by doing that, you think your life will change—just like that." He snapped his fingers. "But this journey we're on together, it's not all physical. In fact, that may be the easy part." He then read his favorite quote, from the author C. Day-Lewis: " 'Those Himalayas of the mind are not so easily possessed. There's more than precipice and storm between you and your Everest.' The most important summits," he continued, "they don't happen up there. They happen right here." I didn't need to see to know that Charley was pointing to his head, layered protectively under a fleece hat, helmet, and down hoods.

Eight grueling hours later, Steve Baskis, weak and wobbly, stood atop Lobuche, with most of the team surrounding him. Charley led him up the final pitch, and at the top, I yelled in triumph, "Steve, you're at 20,075 feet!" We all hugged, with tears streaming down our faces.

After descending Lobuche, everyone was on a major high. We celebrated in the greatest way: by passing around different sweaty, unwashed prosthetic legs and drinking a few toasts out of them. When we debriefed the next day, Dan Sidles drew a connection between military missions and mountaineering expeditions. "Nobody is shooting at us, but we are on a mission with a clear goal. There's a chance we might not come back. You put your life in another's hands, and you are looking up and down the trail, ahead of you and behind you, to see if everyone is okay. It's like this expedition is halfway between the battlefield and home."

As I listened, I thought about the soldiers' new lives as they tried to heal their wounds. It was going to take a lot of time and hard work, I thought, but I believed it was possible. One day earlier in the trip, when we were all trying to cross a raging mountain creek, Steve Baskis didn't think he could make the jump. It was just too wide. So Luis took a bunch of large, flat boulders and began piling them into the stream. Ultimately, rocks were spaced evenly like steps across the water. One of the soldiers plunged in and stood knee deep in the river and gave Steve a little support as he tentatively stepped from one rock pile to the next until he was safely across. As I listened to the team yelling directions to Steve, it suddenly clicked what we were doing here. The river between their old lives and the new ones they were trying to build was simply too wide to leap, but by making the steps more manageable and throwing in a little help, it would become possible to cross over. I hoped this expedition could be that bridge, the stepping-stones for these wounded soldiers to find their way forward.

For my Mount Everest teammates, our climb had reproduced the same feelings we'd had ten years before. And for the veterans, many told us that being part of this team, trekking in the high valleys of Nepal and standing on top of Lobuche together, had been more therapeutic than five years of counseling through the VA. We had thought our Mount Everest reunion climb would be a one-off, but now we all agreed this project was deeply ingrained in our No Barriers mission. We knew it was something worth repeating, but sometimes duplicating a recipe is almost impossible, especially when you're not exactly sure what the original ingredients were. We were clear on one thing, however. Charley explained, "I think we got the name of the project wrong. 'Soldiers to the Summit' implies that you reach the top and you're healed, that you're good to go, but it's not one-and-done. These summits are physical, mental, and psychological, and they're never-ending." We all immediately concurred, and the new name became "Soldiers to Summits."

Next, we chose another stunning peak called Cotopaxi, a 19,347-foot active volcano in the Andes of Ecuador. This time, the team possessed even fewer visible disabilities like amputations or blindness. Many of the members had been injured but had been pieced back together through multiple surgeries and reconstructions. However, this time, there were more brain injuries and PTSD patients.

Once we had the team assembled, we headed up to Leadville, Colorado, to the Outward Bound training facility at ten thousand feet to do some basic training like team building and learning some essential mountaineering skills. Even fundamentals like how to wear your backpack revealed gaps between military and civilian life. On a mountaineering team, we always clipped the waist belt on our packs, since it took a lot of weight off the shoulders and redistributed it around the hips. Over time, this could save huge amounts of energy and mean the difference between summiting or not. Yet, in combat missions, soldiers didn't wear waist buckles, since they had to whip off their packs at a moment's notice to be ready to fire their weapons. As leaders, we had to reinforce that this was a new kind of team with some overlaps but with some clear differences from their former training. For some reason, these changes began causing friction from the start.

One morning, we left in the predawn darkness to hike nearby Mount Sherman, a fourteen thousand–foot peak. We all piled into a bunch of different cars. As guides, we thought we were fairly well organized; there were guides driving our four cars, each assigned to a group of soldiers. We had no formal roll call but felt confident everyone was accounted for. Yet when we unloaded from the vehicles, one army ranger was livid with our casual approach. He informed us that by leaving in the dark and taking no formal roll call, we had endangered lives. "What if one of us had slipped on the side of the road, fallen and hit his head on a rock, and lay there bleeding in a ditch? We could have lost one of our own." From his military training, you had to know where every one of your team was at all times. You operated with a strict manifest—a document specifying the plan, objectives, the passenger list, and all the gear carried for the destination. It was extremely important to the success and safety of the mission, and in our more relaxed, more flexible civilian approach, we'd totally overlooked it. We'd need to figure out how to get those two distinct mind-sets to align.

Hiking up the mountain, I found myself behind a vet named Matt Burgess. He had a deep, raspy voice, a cross between the character in *Sling Blade* who loved biscuits and "french-fried potaters" and one of those synthesizers people use after losing their voice boxes from smoking. And Matt smoked a lot. Jeff described him as rail thin, almost delicate. He had a lengthy laundry list of medical conditions. He'd been deployed twice in the military spanning eight years, including tours in Bosnia and Iraq, and suffered not one brain injury but an astonishing five. The first three events took place during the U.S. "peacekeeping mission" in Bosnia, resulting from land mine and IED explosions while out on patrols. At the time, Matt began to notice a host of symptoms: memory loss; difficulty recalling words, facts, and ideas; increased headaches; and trouble staying engaged in conversations and tasks. But he remained deployed.

As we ascended, he told me, "I don't think the words *traumatic brain injury* were even officially recognized by the military at that time; or if they were, nobody was really using them or talking about them. I was still in the infantry, and the mind-set was pretty much 'Suck it up. You're fine. Complete the mission.' Complaining about a chronic headache back then would have seemed weak." Matt had also been reduced to only 50 percent of his normal lung capacity as a result of the gases, smoke, and exploded depleted uranium he'd inhaled while in Iraq.

"Depleted uranium?" I repeated.

"Yes, sir," he answered. "Our ammunition was coated with depleted uranium. It makes the shells twice as dense as lead and slices through tanks like a knife through butter, but they leave behind radioactive dust that you constantly breathe in."

Stopping for a quick break, I suggested that Matt should try to eat and drink, and that launched him into his third medical condition. "I can't eat most nutrition bars," he said. During his Iraq deployment, he'd been given the anthrax vaccination and had had a terrible allergic reaction that had caused all sorts of other problems. After getting home, the VA had prescribed him twenty-one different medications to take daily. He was exhausted, unable to get out of bed, and failing college, so he had finally made a decision to go off all the meds because of their side effects, including horrible gastrointestinal problems that made it very difficult for him to stomach solid foods. He had shifted to a homeopathic diet, eating only fruits and vegetables, in powder form that he mixed in a shaker bottle, or nutritional powders that he put into capsules. He said these had given him much more energy and a better quality of life, but he still worried that he was going to hold the team up, that he wouldn't be able to make it. "I'm worried, though, that they won't let me take my capsules through customs," he said.

"We'll figure it all out," I said, "step by step," but he lit up another cigarette, and I could tell he was pretty overwhelmed. They were very different, but something in Matt reminded me of Tashi from our Tibet trip. Tashi had struggled mightily and had consistently straggled into camp behind the other children. He'd been the outcast with a painful backstory: beaten up and thrown out on the street to beg, and the worst part, dozens of cigarette burn scars pitting his skin. Sadly, every trip I'd ever led had a Tashi, and on this one, I already knew it would be Matt.

As we approached the tree line, Matt fell far behind the rest of the team. He kept stopping for smoke breaks, which irritated some of the others. At the next rest stop, we waited for him, and when he finally arrived, he slung his pack down grumpily and said, "You all didn't give us enough time to get ready," as he struggled to find his water bottle and gloves buried somewhere deep in his backpack. Even worse, some had been waiting there for a half an hour, so on his arrival, Charley gave the two-minute warning, and everyone got up to head out. Matt, panting and covered in sweat, grumbled, "That's not much of a rest stop," shoving gear back into his pack.

With a lot of patience, we managed to make the summit of Sherman. I used the time to get to know the team members and map their voices by asking them to walk in front of me, ringing the bear bell and describing the terrain.

That afternoon, back at the Outward Bound headquarters, we debriefed, discussing and assessing the first two days and our initial training climb. As I'd feared, some of the team complained about the slow pace, and it was obvious they were referring to Matt.

"I'm not a professional mountain climber," Matt said defensively. "I was moving as fast as I could."

One of the guides said matter-of-factly, "Matt, we're going to a much higher altitude than today. You should use this as an opportunity to quit smoking. On Cotopaxi, you'll be part of a rope team, and you'll all need to move at the same pace."

A couple of soldiers then piped in, "You won't make it up Cotopaxi if you keep smoking."

"And the team can't wait while you sit on the side of the mountain puffing away."

At that, Matt grabbed his pack and stormed away from the circle. "I'm out of here," he said. "I'm done."

For this program, several vets from the first trip were back to serve as mentors. We asked one of them, Dan Sidles, if he'd go speak to Matt and reason with him. Dan found him packing his bags in his cabin. He looked up and said angrily, "I know I should quit smoking. I don't need anyone to tell me that. I picked it up in basic training. They said, 'If you don't stay busy, you die,' so smoking became a way to stay busy, to distract me, to cope with the anxiety. And with my TBIs, it allows me to step away and process the situation, to take a break when things are moving too fast—like they are now." He was panting and stopped talking long enough to light a cigarette. "I can't do this. I'm not in shape. I've got all these medical conditions. You guys are expert mountain climbers. I'm not. I don't want to embarrass myself, and I don't want to let myself, and everyone else, down."

Dan listened, and instead of debating, he simply said, "I know what you mean." The two sat quietly together on Matt's bunk, and then Dan continued, "You should have seen me the first day. It was my caseworker at the VA who recommended this program to me. I was so bored, so numb inside, I said, 'Climb a mountain? Sure. What do I have to lose?' So I showed up, but on the first day—the first hour, actually—sitting in the circle, they asked me to introduce myself, and I froze. I broke out in a sweat. I started shaking. I had to leave the room. That day, I was thirty seconds away from turning around, getting back on the plane, and going home."

"Why didn't you?" Matt asked.

"I'm not really sure. Maybe it was wanting to be a part of a team again, or just being fucking bored sitting in my house eating ramen noodles, or maybe I was tired of blowing everything up in my life. Whatever it was, it was telling me I wasn't done yet. Matt, I'm not that different from you. We need you on this team, because if you leave, then I'm asking myself, 'Why shouldn't I go too?'"

Matt thought for a couple of minutes as smoke rose toward the ceiling. "Okay," he said. "I'll try a few more days."

Matt showed up at dinner that night, and afterward we both volunteered for KP duty. As we scrubbed dishes, he admitted he still had plenty of doubts. I must admit that I did too. The plethora of medical conditions he cited seemed almost hard to believe. Back home again, I Googled his name, and it didn't take long to find an article from the *Washington Post* in 2004 confirming Matt's claims. The story shocked me to the core.

In April of 2004, after being discharged from the army, Matt had participated in a study at Walter Reed Army Medical Center to determine whether his migraines, fatigue, nausea, and chronic diarrhea were connected to the anthrax vaccine he'd received when he was deployed to Iraq. During the study, the medical technician gave Matt a sedative, asked him to strip to his shorts, connected him by wires to monitoring equipment, and had him lie down. Then, as Matt lay unconscious and helpless, a surveillance camera captured the technician fondling his groin. The technician ultimately pleaded guilty to second-degree sexual abuse, but it was learned later he'd already been accused in two different incidents, and the cameras revealed two more victims. For Matt, it was an unforgiveable betrayal of his trust.

The article read:

"I had already lost my health because of the anthrax vaccine, and this on top of it," said Burgess, whose illness was ultimately determined by the Army to have been caused by the vaccine, medical records show. "The Army always tells you all the way from basic training that we're a family, and if you do the right thing, we'll take care of you."

Matt wasn't reluctant to have his name used in the article, despite how demeaning and embarrassing it must have been for him. He said he wanted his story out there in the public to illustrate the army's neglect of Iraq war veterans and to raise questions about Walter Reed's practices and oversight. As my voice synthesizer finished reading, I felt deep empathy for Matt. If anyone had a right to mistrust the world, to crawl into a hole and cower, it was Matt. Everything he'd counted on had let him down in the most egregious way possible. I promised myself to pay careful attention to him on the upcoming expedition.

16

THE OPEN-HEART POLICY

When we arrived in Quito, Ecuador, we had a couple of days of training and acclimatizing scheduled before we started trekking. Jeff Evans rounded up the team at the hotel for what he called his "pregame locker room talk."

"It's all about hormones," he said. Some of the more cynical guys chuckled, but Jeff knew well enough to just keep rolling.

"Whether on the battlefield or high up in the mountains, part of what our bodies and brains are responding to is trauma. There are five basic hormones that are the most important: endorphins, dopamine, serotonin, oxytocin, and cortisol. Some of them overlap, but essentially each has a function, a reason for being produced: to be able to keep us alive or incentivize us to do things that we normally wouldn't do, or to help us rebound from emotional or physical pain. Since you'll be experiencing some or all of these heading up Cotopaxi, I want to talk a little about each."

Everyone was listening intently now.

"First are endorphins. They're designed to do one thing, and that's mask pain. Endorphins are the main reason why every species has been able to perpetuate. Because when a woman gives birth, she's flooded with endorphins. If she wasn't, the woman would be like, 'Hell no, I'm never having sex again. Because sex makes babies, and having babies hurts like a motherfucker!'"

Everyone laughed.

"Endorphins also mask pain for endurance. To track animals for days, we had to have endorphins. To mask the pain of climbing Cotopaxi, we will need them. When a soldier in action gets his leg blown off and can still reach over, grab his morphine, stab himself in the leg and keep shooting to protect his platoon, that's endorphins at work."

Everyone in the room knew exactly what Jeff was talking about.

"Then, there's dopamine. We get a dose of it when we achieve something, when we hit the target. Dopamine makes you feel good. We make a post on Facebook and get fifty-five likes immediately, we get a shot of dopamine. But it also has a dark side, because it's highly addictive. We get shots of dopamine from Facebook, from drugs, from drinking; so we need to learn to seek out the shots of dopamine in healthy and organic ways, like finishing a 10K or summiting a mountain, as opposed to the artificial, contrived ones.

"Serotonin is more or less the leadership chemical. It's based on our pride and status within a group. You get a shot of serotonin from being a part of something that's positive and powerful and bigger than you, so that's critical for us as human beings. And it's especially important for the veteran community to reflect on, because you get flooded with serotonin being a part of something. Same thing with the rope team you'll be on.

"Then there's oxytocin," Jeff went on, "which is like unicorn farts and rainbows and love and trust and friendship and 'I've got your back.'" Everyone cracked up. "It feels good, and everybody loves everybody. You get oxytocin from giving of yourself. It's the servant hormone. You feel really, really good and connected—flooded with emotional connection to another human being. We have to have it, and to lose it sends us down into an ugly little rabbit hole of despair."

I was still pondering the concept of unicorn farts when Jeff said, "The last one is cortisol, the fight-or-flight hormone. We need it to protect ourselves. We get shots of cortisol when we don't feel safe. It's great, and it can save your life, but it can also kill you, because with extended trauma, we get long, sustained hits of cortisol, when through evolution, it was meant to come in short bursts, quick hits. Sustained injections cause high blood pressure, diabetes, and heart attacks. When we live in fear-based environments, when we're just scared all the time, we've got this steady state, low-dose cortisol just surging through our bodies, and it creates a condition of continued stress and fear. And I think that's honestly what a lot of us, and vets especially, are experiencing. Stress and fear. So what we need to do is put ourselves in positions to manage our landscapes, and therefore manage the way our bodies respond to assaults. And that's what we'll try to do as we head up the mountain. And hopefully, as we move forward in our lives."

It was a lot to take in, but Jeff wrapped it up with a tight summary. "On this expedition, hopefully, we'll create an atmosphere of camaraderie and fellowship: that's serotonin and oxytocin. We'll teach and use the skills we've learned to manage personal challenge and mitigate threats like crevasses and avalanches—that's cortisol. We will journey toward the summit, which will provide us with a reward—there's your dopamine. It all hinges on managing the stressors and assaulters and nurturing a healthy reward cycle. I think that being outdoors provides us the environment to develop this balance. So let's see how it goes."

"What about endorphins?" Matt Burgess asked. "You forgot about them."

"Oh, they're gonna kick in the minute you walk out of the Refugio door and start up the mountain. And hopefully, sustain you all the way to the top."

My roommate in Quito was a medical corpsman named Max, who had yet another heartbreaking background. As we organized our gear in the room and got to know each other better, I learned he was taken from his family by child protective services when he was ten. Most of his family had been convicted felons, mixed up in guns and drugs. In high school, he'd get calls from his father in jail, but he wouldn't answer the phone. Max even said that once, he'd been watching *America's Most Wanted* when he turned to his friend and said, "That guy on the screen—that's my brother." Max was a huge, muscular guy, swaggering and confident, at least on the outside. He'd joined our program because, as he put it, for years after coming home from the war, he'd been in "self-medicating and self-destruct mode" and wanted to try to do something better with his life.

But sitting on our beds after the first long day, he said, "Erik, I listened to all that stuff you said today about No Barriers, about change and transformation, but you gotta understand, I'm not you. I can't be like you."

His words caught me by surprise. "Why would I expect you to be like me?" I stammered.

"Look, I'm here," he replied, "and I hope to get something from this experience. I've managed to stay out of trouble recently, but I don't have the ability to affect anyone or anything. About the only thing I'm really good at is kicking people's asses."

"But, Max," I argued, "you've already led and served your country. You can contribute again. You're capable of more than you think."

"Nah," he responded. "My problems began way before I joined the military. Marching fifty miles with a giant pack? Summiting a mountain? Those are easy, but taking this experience and using it to change somehow, that's bullshit. I don't even know what that means. Maybe, someday, I'll be able to look in the mirror and be okay with who I see, with what I've done, with the things that have happened to me, but right now I don't know."

I felt the deep pain behind his words, like, thirty years later, he was still peering out at an uncaring, intractable world through the eyes of a ten-year-old child, terrified and panicked, as social services dragged him away from his family. I didn't push back, given everything he'd just shared. The day had obviously stirred up some debris and restlessness in him, and that was enough for now. I was already learning that there was a blurry and shifting line between challenging the team toward something bigger and driving them over an abyss, and part of me wondered if the two were almost the same thing. Once they felt exposed, backed up against the edge, you needed to be ready because you were awakening a tempest, one that, until that point, had lain largely dormant.

The balancing act began soon enough as we started our acclimatizing trek toward Cotopaxi. On the team we had some soldiers who'd been in combat and some who hadn't, and that became a point of contention as the two factions began to have friction and divide. Dan said that Jamie, who had lost his leg in a motorcycle accident in peacetime, was inflating his PTSD symptoms just to get attention. Some murmured that those who hadn't seen combat didn't belong on the trip. Max accused one guy of downright faking his symptoms and lying about his combat record.

"I can take one look at you and tell you're a poser," Max said. I impulsively stepped between them and, for a moment, thought Max was so riled up he was going to swing at me. He towered over me and put his huge hand on my shoulder as he yelled, "Get out of my way, E! This is none of your business!"

But I stood my ground. "You could take me out with one punch," I said, trying to sound relaxed, "but you'll have to live the rest of your life with the fact that you knocked out a blind guy . . . that's bad karma," I added. That seemed to edge down the mood and end the immediate crisis, but the bad blood persisted.

The next few days, we ascended into the rolling plateaus of the *páramo* grasslands, undulating expanses of tall, spiny tussock grasses, giant rosette plants, and dense shrubbery. Since none of the gringo leaders had done this trek before, we relied on the local guides, which turned out to be a mistake. However, our biggest blunder was following the route description relayed to us by the locals. After receiving instructions, Charley announced with seeming confidence that it would be an easy day, just a few miles over rolling terrain, but the purported three-hour tour wound up taking nine hours.

On typical expeditions, this happened quite a bit. I remember on Aconcagua asking Chris, our leader, how far to the summit. He replied, "I could throw a rock to it."

Two hours later and still climbing, I said grumpily, "You have one hell of an arm." Chris just laughed, but this was different. Part of building trust as leaders was presenting accurate information, especially for soldiers who were used to the structure of military life, with all its manifests and mission briefings. And this group was still fragile, only tenuously ascending back into the world. Jamie, an amputee, was fighting through the high grasses, the sharp plants tearing at his face and pack. His prosthetic leg kept getting caught in deep hidden ruts between the tussocks, wrenching against his stump. It was causing blisters, and I could hear him nearby, groaning and letting out deep, exasperated breaths.

"Easy terrain, my ass," he said as he yanked his prosthetic out of another hole and turned around. "You guys screwed me," he said angrily. "I'm going back to camp." He trudged off, not speaking to anyone. Charley followed him back and miraculously arranged a bus to carry him around the entire mountain range to get to our next Refugio. I felt terrible, realizing our lack of planning had only furthered his mistrust. Adventure could quickly turn into a nightmare that retriggered the brain into a state of fight or flight. And once there, you were no longer learning or growing but in total shutdown. As they left, I thought of Jeff's hormone talk. I turned to him. "Cortisol," I said.

"Yeah," is all Jeff replied, with worry in his voice.

Later, I came across Matt Burgess sitting on the side of the trail, taking off his running shoes. "I went cold turkey on the cigarettes back in Quito," he said. "I'm having a pretty rough day of withdrawals. Plus, Charley told us the terrain wouldn't be too severe, so I didn't wear my heavier boots. I think I just reinjured the ankle I broke back in Macedonia. It's swelling, and my shoe is cutting into my skin."

To my astonishment, Matt shoved his shoes in his pack and began tromping through the prickly grasses in his socks. The terrain began dropping away so steeply, he was falling down, tumbling over fallen trees, and thrashing through the thick vegetation. Eventually, he was so exhausted, he just sat on his backside and began sliding downward, sending piles of leaves, rocks, and deadfall tumbling down onto his teammates below. He hadn't brought enough food or water, and even though the guides shared theirs, he went silent, not saying a word for the next three hours. I imagined him fuming inside, hating Charley, Jeff, and me for talking him into this hideous expedition. I wondered how much more he could take and secretly feared this was the beginning of the end for Matt. As leaders, we had blown it. This debacle of a day had given the team just the chance they needed to lash out, blame, retreat, and quit.

At the Jose Ribas Refugio at 15,840 feet, it really started to fall apart. The high Refugio was the staging point for our summit bid. For most of the vets, this was the highest elevation they'd ever been to, but Jeff described the glorious snowcapped dome of Cotopaxi hovering nearly four thousand feet above us. The Refugio was pretty spacious, holding about eighty-five people, but we weren't the only group readying to summit. It was crowded as we piled in. The trek from the trailhead up to the hut had been cold, sleeting, and windy, and folks were tired. Some had headaches, and fuses were short.

Dan and Jamie had been riding each other since Quito, and it escalated again as Jamie demanded a lower bunk and started aggressively clearing a stranger's gear off the bed. Dan called him on it, and the two were soon in each other's faces in a full-blown shouting match.

"I could kick your ass right now," said Dan, "but you're not worth it."

Jamie grabbed his gear and left. I followed and caught up with him a hundred yards down the trail.

"I'm fuckin' outta here!" he yelled. "I can't handle these people, any of this. You are all a bunch of hypocrites; you call this a team? Nobody is true to each other. And don't let me get started on the guides. You get us lost on the mountain. You say the hike will be an easy three hours, and it's a death march. The whole thing is flawed. I'm going home."

Some of what he'd said was true. There were a few on the team who had been immature, even bullies. Instead of lifting everyone up, they had pulled people down. And we, as guides, had been working hard yet had failed to understand the support Jamie had needed to continue. The truth ingrained in his words made it sting all the more. I didn't know how to respond.

"You know I'm right," he said, his voice catching.

I knew that Jamie had tried a couple of other veterans' programs and left in a similar way. I didn't want it to happen again. "Even if you're a thousand percent right," I said, "it's still a terrible mistake to leave. You've got to see this through."

"I can't," he replied. "I've tried, and it's not worth it anymore."

I stepped forward and squared up with him, touching his arms with my palms. He was crying now.

"How do I tell you," I yelled over the wind rushing down the hillside, "that your brain is betraying you? It makes sense to blame, to blame the team, the guides, to blame your folks, to blame the alcohol, or even blame the motorcycle that took your leg. Everything you know tells you to turn outward and mistrust the world for all the shit it's piled on you. But that's only the path of least resistance, and it's dead wrong. This is the time to do the exact opposite of what your brain is telling you to do. You've got to turn inward. If you blow it all up right now, it will confirm all your suspicions, but then you'll never know what's inside you."

"I'm sorry," he said so softly I could barely hear him. Then he turned downhill and began walking away. Like the first time, Charley hiked down and found him at the road. He arranged a car for him, but this time it was taking Jamie to Quito, from where he'd be flying home.

I was devastated and sank down on the nearest rock. As I thought about this disastrous trip, the sleet turned to snow. The irony wasn't lost on me either. We were on the flanks of an active volcano. It seemed quiet up there now, but over the last three hundred years, Cotopaxi had erupted fifty times, sending lava and ash a hundred kilometers in every direction—to the Pacific Ocean to the west and on to the Amazon Basin to the east. Our trip so far had been nothing short of volcanic. We had only wanted to help, but all we'd done was exposed their wounds and confirmed their fears. I remembered Dr. Bach-y-Rita's story about rehabilitating his father after his stroke. Walking was out of the question, so his brother had first taught him to crawl, then shuffle on his knees, and finally to walk again. The wounds of the mind had to be similar, I thought, except nobody fully understood the steps to resume walking again. How could you teach someone to turn inward when his brain had no idea how to start the process? Then I heard Jeff's voice beside me and felt his hand on my shoulder.

"You should come inside. We have a big day tomorrow."

When I got back up to the Refugio, Jeff went inside and left me with Matt Burgess, who was standing in the courtyard. I thought he'd probably broken down and gone out for a smoke because of all the stress. "Having a cig?" I asked.

"No, sir," he said. "I told you I went cold turkey, and I'm sticking to it. The withdrawals are giving me the cold sweats and making me shaky, but being up here in this fresh air actually helps. I realized the nicotine was only a mask. All the anxiety, all the pain, it was still there."

I was preoccupied by Jamie's abrupt departure. It was crushing to lose one of our team in this way, and I worried how this was going to impact the others and the rest of the trip, especially with tomorrow's long summit.

"Jamie's gone," I said bluntly. "He's not coming back."

Matt didn't respond at first, and when he spoke, it seemed like he was changing the subject. "Erik, there's a book that means a lot to me. I've been reading it every night throughout this trip—that is, when I haven't been too

exhausted to lift my head up. Can I read you a quote from it? It's by Mari-
anne Williamson, and I think it may explain why Jamie left." He pulled the
book out of his backpack and, with his gruff, *Sling Blade* voice, read to me as
high mountain winds whined over the hut roof.

> Our deepest fear is not that we are inadequate.
> Our deepest fear is that we are powerful beyond measure.
> It is our light, not our darkness, that most frightens us.
> We ask ourselves,
> Who am I to be brilliant, gorgeous, talented, fabulous?
> Actually, who are you *not* to be?

Matt stopped reading and said, "I graduated second out of 110 other soldiers from Military Police School. I was being fast-tracked. I was supposed
to be promoted, but when I came back from Iraq, I lost everything. Erik, that
passage, it's me. I'm terrified of that light. I fear success more than I do failure. See, failure's easy. It's familiar, like an old friend, but the idea of success
is overwhelming. So I make excuses, mistrust everyone, and overdramatize
things—all to avoid success. That's Jamie. That's Max. It's easier to sabotage
yourself than it is to build something."

"What is that light?" I asked.

Matt was deep in thought for a minute and then said, "I think of it as being centered, full of assurance that no matter what happens, we will be okay.
For me, that means loving myself, which is sometimes hard to do. We often
spend our lives disconnected from our potential, from ourselves. It would have
been so much easier to stay home, to not even apply to this program, to stay
in the darkness I was living in. The light was terrifying. Although I know the
light will propel me forward, I know it's also a path with the most resistance."

I thought of Terry Fox, of Hugh Herr and Mark Wellman. All of them
were just broken-winged birds with no business to ever fly again. Yet that
light had transcended. I thought of Arjun then, how he sometimes walled
himself off from his own possibilities. Then I felt my own wall crumbling, and
I saw myself sitting at a table alone in the lunchroom just after I'd gone blind,
those same thoughts of isolation, of helplessness, of crippling self-doubt

flooding to the surface. In those early days of blindness, when I dared to dream about bigger things, other, darker voices stepped in, like hecklers in a theater, like squatters crowding into an abandoned building: "Who are you to think that you deserve something more?" But like Matt, I knew somehow the only way forward was to keep my heart open, if only a sliver, so that the light could begin to grow.

"We're a lot more alike than you might think," I said. "I spend a lot of time wondering if I'm an imposter, like some kind of Walter Mitty character whose dreams outweigh his means."

"Well, a lot of your dreams seem to have come true," Matt said as the temperature dropped and the sun crept behind the mountains. "I know that tomorrow is going to be the hardest thing I've done in my life, but I know I have to do it. There's an inner voice telling me that if I don't try, I'm going to stay stagnant and keep struggling; if I don't do this, I'll never move forward."

I patted Matt on the shoulder. "One step at a time," I said. I had no idea whether he would summit Cotopaxi the next day; in fact, I had serious doubts. Physically, he was another broken-winged bird, but weren't we all?

We left the Refugio just after midnight and reached the glacier around 2:30 A.M. The plan was for about an eight- to ten-hour ascent and a six- to eight-hour descent. Charley, Jeff, and the other guides each led a rope team. Matt joined Charley's team, and we all crept upward. The day began with some excitement, when one of the soldier's crampons failed to penetrate into the ice, and he took a big fall. I was impressed by his three rope-mates who reacted in textbook fashion, diving to the ground and arresting his fall with their ice axes.

Global warming had over time severed the glacier, searing it with huge crevasses that were wider than normal. There was even a section where an entire portion of the mountainside had collapsed, and someone said it looked like tufts of giant white popcorn. We weaved and scrambled through these broken chunks of ice for hours. Jeff Evans said it reminded him of the Khumbu Icefall on Mount Everest, and he nicknamed it the "Khumbu-Paxi Icefall."

Well up on the mountain, my rope team was lagging far behind. Our team had a soldier who'd had nineteen surgeries to repair his foot. He'd almost lost it, and it was still not fully healed. We had an above-the-knee amputee, and all day his prosthetic had been giving him trouble. Another soldier was afraid of heights, and she was just happy to be at her altitude record. When it became obvious that we weren't moving fast enough, we decided to turn back. There would be no Coto summit for us. As the day warmed, avalanches and dangerous icefall became more likely. A second rope team had gone past the turnaround time and made the heartbreaking decision to descend, just a half hour from the summit.

Through it all, there was Matt, plodding, picking, weaving, and wheezing his way up the mountain. Numerous times it appeared that he would quit, clinging to his rope ascender and staring up with tears in his eyes at the few thousand feet of forty-degree slope between him and the summit. Charley noted that he was shivering, shaking, and extremely weak, and he seriously questioned the wisdom of bringing him any higher. But he knew how badly Matt wanted it, so he went against his better judgment and urged him on. As they moved up through giant, overhanging seracs, Matt could barely breathe. He was wobbling, sometimes buckling to his knees, hardly able to stand. But after twelve arduous hours, Matt Burgess stood on top of Mount Cotopaxi, at 19,347 feet.

Charley hugged him and whispered in his ear, "*Poco a poco, se va lejos.*"

Matt, his voice raspy to nearly inaudible, said, "Huh? What's that mean?"

"Little by little, you go far," answered Charley.

As it turned out, only Charley's and Jeff's teams made the summit. Nine veterans, including Matt Burgess, stood on top of that conical volcano. Matt was so broken down from his efforts he was coughing and gagging incessantly on the descent, and his legs jellied; he was stumbling and falling, becoming a danger to his rope team. Through a few sections, Charley had to shoulder him and carry him fireman-style as Matt babbled, going in and out of consciousness. At one point, Charley heard him whisper, "On the way up, Charley Mace, I hated you. But now I love you."

When we finally all got back to the Refugio, Matt had been moving continuously for nineteen hours, and it became obvious he needed medical attention. We worried that he wouldn't be able to get on the plane to fly home. He spent two days in his hotel room, wrecked, barely able to rise from bed, and coughing so raggedly it sounded like he might break a rib. Matt was prone to pneumonia from his medical challenges, and Jeff listened to his lungs gurgling and thought he might have it again. Outside his room in the hallway, I whispered to Charley, "I'm not worried whether the trip was a success anymore. I'll just be happy if no one sues us."

When I asked Jeff's opinion, all he said was, "Maybe we've been looking at this all wrong. Maybe growth happens more like the way Cotopaxi spews lava and smoke. It explodes from deep inside the earth and lays a fresh coat of skin over the old terrain. That's how the earth constantly redefines itself. Growth is not pain-free, and it ain't for sissies."

I stepped back into Matt's room. It smelled like sweat and dirty socks as I leaned over his bed, touched his hand, and asked, "Matt, can I get you anything?"

"I'm good," he said, almost imperceptibly. Then he squeezed my hand, pulled me in close, and croaked, "Thank you." The next day, he rose zombie-like, shuffled silently through the airport, and managed to get on board.

I also got on the flight, and when I arrived home, my mind was still consumed by questions and second-guesses, but everyday life quickly took over. There were soccer games, teacher conferences, and school plays to attend. There were other struggles to contend with, much more immediate than a faraway expedition.

While I was away, Ellie was having some ongoing troubles with Arjun. She was a dedicated mom and loved playing games with the kids, taking them on outings, playing sports with them. But she'd try to play soccer with Arjun, a game she'd played for years. "I'll kick the ball to you," she'd say, "and you kick it back to me." Arjun would purposely kick it in the wrong direction and make a game out of having Ellie run for it. The family would play Monopoly, and Arjun, sensing he was losing, would "accidently" kick the board, sending the figures, buildings, and cards scattering everywhere. The worst was when the family was setting up the Christmas tree. Ellie carefully showed Arjun her favorite ornament that she'd loved and cherished since she was a young girl. It was a delicate, hollowed-out egg with a blue ribbon wrapped around it; there was a tiny plastic window through which you could see this little toy soldier inside. Arjun asked to hold it. Ellie hesitated but reluctantly handed it to him. As soon as she turned her head, she heard a sickening crunch. She tried not to react, to raise her voice or show anger, but inwardly, she was heartbroken and fought back tears.

The act seemed, at the surface, defiant, but Ellie knew it was actually more of a question, as if he were asking, "You say you love me, so let's test that theory. Will you still love me if I do this?" *Crack!* "'Cause if this isn't real, I'd like to know sooner than later, before my heart is shattered, just like that egg."

I was only home for a day when Arjun came down with severe flu-like symptoms. As it got worse, we took him straight to Urgent Care. While there, Ellie left the room for just a minute, and when she came back in, she saw the nurses trying to insert a tube up Arjun's nose. Apparently, they were trying to tell what kind of flu strain he might have. I sat in a nearby chair, completely unaware, because Arjun was totally silent, just taking it as they hovered over him, wrestling the rubber tube up his nostril. Unlike how Emma would have reacted, unlike other children, he wasn't crying. He wasn't fighting. This had been the case in the orphanage too, when Sabitri told us Arjun had been chased by a vicious stray dog. He'd fallen and busted open his chin. He hadn't cried then, or when the doctor in Kathmandu stabbed him repeatedly with needles, checking for tuberculosis. He hadn't even cried when he crashed into a hedge on his maiden bike ride down the hill in front of our house.

As Ellie saw what was happening, she was irate. The nurses hadn't bothered to try to explain to Arjun what they were doing. They'd treated him like some kind of automaton. Ellie rushed over to the bed, got in front of them, and held him close. She explained what they were doing, and why it needed to be done. When the nurses finally withdrew the tube, he remained stoic. Ellie turned his face to hers and said, "Arjun, it's okay to cry. That was a terrible thing to go through." A few tears came then, but not many.

At this same time, my energetic guide dog of eight years, Willa, was also sick, and, tragically, it wasn't just a flu. She was listless and didn't want to eat or drink. We all loved Willa despite her quirks, like the times we'd leave the house for an hour and return to a collection of Emma's stuffed animals, Arjun's dirty socks, and my underwear all heaped in the middle of the living room floor. Willa would stand drooling over the slobbery pile, and I think it was her way to show us how much she missed us. She was sneaky too. Once when Ellie and I were at a movie theater, we were blissfully unaware as Willa army-crawled under five rows of chairs and was sitting in the front sharing a bucket of popcorn with a total stranger. But by five years old, she was a seasoned pro. She could step off the airport train, immediately find the escalator, and then cruise right to the moving sidewalk toward my gate; she could also locate my exact hotel room, pointing her nose to the door handle, and the next morning find the revolving front door of the hotel lobby. She was a star, but now she was sick. A large tumor appeared from under her tail, and the veterinarian diagnosed it as cancer.

There was nothing to do, and in her last days, we fed her all the treats she could never eat as a working dog: bacon, cheese—all mixed with peanut butter. When she could barely lift her head, we called a vet who came to our home so Willa could pass in a familiar place, surrounded by her family. We placed her on her blanket near the railing in the living room, where she'd spent hundreds of hours as the kids drew artwork and did their puzzles. Emma and Arjun had made the courageous decision to be there at the end during the euthanizing procedure. I thought it was important for them to witness this inevitable part of life that sometimes came much too soon. They kissed her, then gently held her paws and told her how much they loved her. They said good-bye as Willa's eyes closed.

The strange part was, Emma, always the avowed and devoted animal lover, cried a little bit as you'd expect, then sniffled, and seemed okay. Arjun, who on the other hand never had an especially close bond with Willa, broke into a deep, mournful wail that didn't end. We'd heard that soulful cry before. It was the night before he'd left Nepal for America. Ellie said he lay on the bed in the hotel room and sobbed, and it seemed to come from as deep a place as pain could come. Now he cried in that same way, plaintive and inconsolable. We all held him for a long time until there was nothing left inside him.

I'm not a psychologist, but if Jeff's analogy was right that change didn't come as a soft summer breeze but in an erupting volcano—or in a torrent of burning tears—then saying good-bye to Willa may have been part of Arjun's own process of letting go. Of what, I wasn't exactly sure, but there had been a lot of disruption in his young life. He'd been separated from everything he'd known and asked to trust and love new parents and a new big sister. The transition was staggering. I think Willa's death represented other long-ago memories for him, fuzzy and dreamlike, yet piercing his consciousness like the tip of a spear thrust up from the depths. After the tears dried, I prayed Jeff was right—that this was a chance to deposit over the wound a fresh layer of hope and possibilities.

Emma, now beginning seventh grade, was struggling with her own turbulence. She'd applied for the honors program earlier in the summer and had been turned down. But now, two weeks after school had begun, a student had dropped out and one spot had opened up. The teachers had offered the spot to Emma and given her just twenty-four hours to make her decision. "I'm fine," she first said. "I'm pretty settled now."

Ellie and I encouraged her to think it through and give it a little more time.

"What would you do?" Emma asked me.

"I'm not sure," I said, "but on my last trip, I met this soldier. He was pretty fragile, with a dozen different medical conditions. Each one of them should have been enough to take him out. He almost didn't apply. When he was accepted, he said he was actually shocked. Then, on the second day, he almost quit."

"What made him stay?" Emma asked.

"I'm not sure how to describe it," I answered, "but I guess you could say he had a kind of open-heart policy. Every time something happened on the trip that should have made him close his heart, he opened it more. Sometimes, you need to trust and just give it a whirl."

The next day, Emma came to Ellie and me to weigh her options. "Well, I'm in classes now with some of my friends. The courses seem okay, and I've got all my books already. The honors classes are in a totally different wing, so I'd have to change my locker, and I'd be way behind the other honors students . . . I think I've made my decision: I'll give it a whirl."

17

WHIRLPOOLS

The BrainPort device I'd been testing at home was going to get a trial run in the field. I'd taken it to the local climbing gym, and its helpfulness intrigued me. Normally, I hung from a hold, stepped up as high as I could, and with one arm bent and locked off, I'd scan my free hand across the surface, searching for the next hold. It was a slow process and a race against time, since I only had so much stamina to hang on as I scanned. With the BrainPort, however, I found I could locate handholds on the wall a few feet above me. It was disconcerting at first to spot a hold on my tongue, step up, and reach for it in space. I was actually surprised how hard it was to rewire my visual connection with the world, which had been extinguished long ago. It took a lot of focus, but with practice, I was beginning to speed up and save energy. So when a producer from the BBC called me to ask if I was willing to try the BrainPort on a climb up Castleton Tower, near Moab, Utah, I agreed, interested to test the unit in natural light conditions on a real rock face. Because of Rob Raker's experience working on climbing productions, I was thrilled when the BBC hired him to film.

In early spring, I stood on a ledge in the morning chill of the Moab desert in the Canyonlands region, feeling the sun creeping up the cliff and warming me. Looming above was the four hundred–foot vertical sandstone face of Castleton Tower, considered one of the fifty classic climbs in North America. We had already ascended to the base, a steep cone that jutted dramatically out of the valley floor, and I geared up, which now included putting on the BrainPort glasses and tucking the control panel into my pocket. As I started to climb, I noticed I could actually detect ledges, pockets, and cracks zigzagging up the smooth rock. In front of the face, I could feel on my tongue display the sharp line of the rope running up to my partner above. As I got higher and rounded a corner, I reached for the crack but only palmed the smooth surface of the rock. Scanning around with my hand, I noticed the crack was actually a foot farther to the right. I climbed on, wondering if the BrainPort had been damaged. But then I noticed the morning sun on my right shoulder. I had a vague memory of playing all day in the forest as a kid, when I could see, and watching the trees cast shadows that lengthened and shortened with the angle of the sun. I realized then that I was reaching into the shadow of the crack. As the sun rose and came around behind me, I could see the shadows shorten and merge with the features on the face.

At the next belay ledge, I pointed the camera at the rock and felt an oblong blob on my tongue. But when I touched it, there was nothing but blank rock. As I swayed my head side to side, the shape moved along with me. *How the heck can an object move like that?* I again thought the device was playing tricks on me. Now the sun was directly behind me, and I laughed at myself, as it became obvious that I was watching the shadow of my own head. The last time I'd seen myself, I'd been almost thirty years younger, and it was sort of trippy as I bounced up and down, back and forth, and watched my shadow partner stay perfectly in step. I was completely absorbed by this entertainment, when I heard my climbing partner yell from far above, "If you're finished with your dance routine, you can climb anytime!"

I got to lead the last pitch to the top. The afternoon sun had gone behind the tower, eliminating the deceiving shadows and glare that made objects shimmer and disappear. In this perfect light, the face came alive, and the features popped out on my tongue. I could see the metal gear I used for protection as my hand slid them into the cracks. I could see the carabiners as I clipped them onto my rope. As a blind person, I'd almost forgotten about these nuances of vision, but the BrainPort had reintroduced me to this language of sun and light and shadow. Even though I was only glimpsing a tiny portion of what real eyeballs could see, it was still so beautiful.

The top of the tower was a flat plateau surrounded by sky, windy and exposed on all sides. After getting all the film shots he needed, Rob grabbed my hand and pointed in a sweeping panorama for 360 degrees, describing features as my arm swung clockwise. "Adobe Mesa, a fresh dusting of snow on the La Sal Mountains way in the distance, the Colorado River to the west, cutting a wide swath to my right," he said.

I'd loved this area from my first visit, and I asked Rob, "Where are the Fisher Towers and Ancient Art? Can you see them?"

Rob took a minute to get his bearings, looking through the telephoto lens on his camera. Then he grabbed my hand again and pointed to my two o'clock. "Right there. About, oh, six miles to the northeast. The towers are casting long shadows in the evening light. Ancient Art is the most distinctive, with its narrow, corkscrew summit. It looks like the swirly tip of a soft-serve ice cream cone."

I thought of Hugh Herr and Mark Wellman, and that amazing "all-gimp climb" Mark had organized. It dawned on me that much of the present journey I was on—testing new technologies, reaching into the unknown, and trying to find new ways to break through my barriers—had been born across the desert on those very spires ten years before. I thought of how far I'd come, but the uncertainty of what lay ahead on the Colorado River loomed even larger. I heard the *thwop thwop thwop* of the production helicopter that had been filming, and as it neared and circled, I tried to locate it on my tongue and follow it through the air, like a little buzzing insect pasted against the wide-open skyline. Feeling for the chopper's image on my tongue, I knew that Hugh and Mark would approve.

The next morning, we awoke in our motel to gale-force winds scouring the Canyonlands. The weather window that had allowed us a brilliant climb on Castleton had slammed shut, replaced with a violent spring squall, armed with percussive wind gusts and lashing rain. Rob and I had planned to do some climbing before heading back to Colorado, but hammering rains on slick vertical sandstone created a bad combination, so we drank coffee and waited it out. We were tired and sore from the previous long day of climbing and filming, and Rob had scouted out a pool and hot tub in the back that looked inviting.

"Gate's locked on it, though; I checked," he said. "Also, the sign says it's closed due to weather."

"How high is the fence?" I asked.

"Big E, no fence is too high for you and me," Rob replied, his voice rising with mischief. "I see steam rising from the hot tub, and I think it's calling our name. And with the weather out there, trust me, no one will expect anyone to be getting in the water."

We threw on our suits, slung towels over our shoulders, and slunk down a cement path leading to the pool area. Something sharp scraped against my leg as it bounced along the ground. "Tumbleweed," Rob said. "Fence is only about six feet high!" he yelled over the wind buffeting us. I could hear the grating feet of the patio furniture scraping along the cement, pushed by the gusts.

"One pull up and over, right here." He placed my hand near the gate. "Right foot in the crossbar there, and you can sling yourself straight over."

Rob bounded over after me and grabbed my shoulder. "Duck!" he yelled. I heard the *wumpth* of something flying over my head and then bouncing off the chain-link fence beyond. "Foam pool noodle." Rob laughed.

The rain hammered down so hard it hit the patio and splashed back up against my ankles and shins. We were drenched by the time we slid into the hot tub, but the water was just hot enough, a perfect remedy for the plunging spring temperatures. I heard a loud pop, like a firecracker going off. I hoped it wasn't a lightning strike, but before I could even ask, Rob said, "Huge umbrella just blew inside out."

"Are we gonna die out here?" I asked, only half joking. "Should we be wearing our climbing helmets?"

"Good news is, all the patio furniture has blown across and is slammed against the fence, pinned there. No more deck grenades. Looks like we're safe—unless the wind changes direction . . ."

We soaked neck-deep in the warm water as the wind continued its high-pitched whistle across the valley's badlands.

"We've had a lot of great adventures together," Rob said after a time, sounding lost in memories.

"And many more to come," I said. "We've got to kick the kayaking into high gear if I have any hopes of making it down the Grand Canyon," I said.

Summer was coming up, and we had a bunch of local trips planned. Plus, we'd tentatively started scheming some big waters outside the U.S. that we could paddle during our winters.

"Erik," Rob said finally, "I am going to be sidelined for a little while, at least."

Rob was in great shape, and he hadn't mentioned any injuries on the climb the day before. For a moment I wondered whether it could have anything to do with his brain injury from long ago.

"What's going on, Rob?"

"I have prostate cancer, Big E."

The words buckled me like a gut punch. I had not been prepared for them. Not Uncle Rob. Not the Adventure Glutton. At first, I was too floored to say anything.

"I got diagnosed last month. I've been waiting for the right time to tell you."

I stammered for a minute, still thinking of the right thing to say. Was there a right thing to say? I thought of my dad, who'd been diagnosed two years before. He was in his seventies, and with treatment, his prognosis was good.

"You know Ed's been getting treatment," I said finally. "Prostate cancer is slow growing, right? And you caught it early, right?" I was grasping for positives based on the little I knew about the disease.

"Well, yes and no," Rob clarified. "It can be slow growing. I had a biopsy done, and prostate cancer is classified by what's called a Gleason score, which rates its aggressiveness, from a low of 2 to a maximum of 10."

"So, like golf scores, sort of." I tried keeping it light. "Low is good, high is bad."

"Exactly. Unfortunately, the biopsy took six samples from each side of my prostate, and all the samples from the left side were positive for cancer. I had a Gleason score of 9, with nearly all cells cancerous. Cases like mine are termed 'high-grade cancer,' and they were concerned that it had spread from the prostate."

The wind died down a little, and Rob hopped out of the water to turn the bubble jets on. My mind was racing, and I didn't really know what to say. But

I knew that Rob would by now have weighed all his options carefully, consulted the best medical experts in the field, and would have constructed a detailed, meticulous, and thorough plan of attack.

"What's next?" I asked.

"Having surgery next month to remove my prostate and pelvic lymph nodes. In New York, at Memorial Sloan Kettering Cancer Center. Then we'll see. Radiation. Possibly chemotherapy. But one step at a time. At any rate, as I said, I'll be sidelined for at least a little while, dealing with this and recovering. You might want to consider some other kayaking guides."

My mind was whirling with his words and the whine of the wind. Radiation, chemotherapy. Cancer. I shouldn't even think about paddling a kayak with those words floating in the air, and yet here was Rob, thinking beyond his own predicament to what it might mean for my damn kayak training. I slid beneath the water, listening to the low hum of the Jacuzzi jets surging, slow and rhythmically, blowing hot water into the tub. I felt the soothing warm water envelop me, and I held my breath as long as I could, practicing as if I were upside down in my kayak, waiting to get spit out of a keeper hole, readying to stick my roll. Rob had worked with me on how to remain calm below the surface, to relax, to forget about the chaos all around me and just be in the moment.

I surfaced finally and took a huge gasp of air. Rain came down heavily again, pelting my face and cheeks. I licked my lips, and the raindrops tasted salty, like tears.

"Whatever you need," I said to Rob, reaching out my hand and waiting to find his. "You know I'm there for ya."

Our hands clenched into one fist.

"I know it, buddy," he said. "I know."

Rob approached his cancer just like he did our climb up the three thousand–foot face of Losar, or a kayaking trip down the Green River: armed with research, information, opinions and second opinions, a plan A and a plan B. And in true Rob fashion, he spent the weeks right before his surgery in New York climbing with his wife, Annette, in the Shawangunks. He even climbed the fabled Skytop, the very section on which Hugh Herr once snapped off a prosthetic foot and named the route "Footloose and Fancy-Free."

In May of 2010, Rob had his prostate and eighteen surrounding lymph nodes in his pelvis removed. Yet nine hours after landing home in Colorado post-surgery, he called me to announce with pride that he was going climbing. Rob pushed his recovery, maintaining incredibly high activity levels. But as the pathology began to come back from his surgery and tests, the news was grim. Of the eighteen lymph nodes removed, four were positive for cancer, which meant metastasized cancer cells had spread beyond his prostate, into his body, making his cancer Stage IV. When I asked him what the implications were, Rob tried to stay positive.

"Annette says my cancer is an overachiever, just like me!" He laughed. "My high Gleason scores of 9 make it the most aggressive kind. Also, in the prostate cancer world, the time that it takes for your PSA, your prostate specific antigen, to double is one of the factors used to estimate the progress of the disease and how long you are likely to live. Mine is actually doubling every fifty-three days. That's very fast, and not so good."

I was a bit overwhelmed by the numbers and by him bringing up his own mortality. "What's your next move?" I asked.

"Still working out the program and the different points of view on it, but because of the fast-growing cancer, I'm going to start with an aggressive type of androgen deprivation therapy—or ADT—called a double-blockade; it eliminates testosterone from my body, because cancer cell growth is promoted by testosterone."

"Are there side effects?" I asked.

"Well, they don't call it 'chemical castration' for nothing!" Rob said, now serious. "Loss of libido, general 'shrinkage' where guys don't want shrinkage, hot flashes, mood swings, and what was worse for me, muscle loss. Within a few months, all my women friends will have more testosterone than me."

"Ellie and Annette already do," I said, slapping him on the arm.

"If the predictions I'm reading are correct, I'm going to get fat, grow boobs, and lose a lot of stamina. But taking the ADT, followed by an eight-week course of pelvic radiation, potentially followed by chemotherapy, might just keep me around for a while!"

A little over a year after being diagnosed, in the fall of 2011, Rob was over at the house discussing a possible whitewater guide he'd found through his research. Rob was really excited, though he was a diminished version of the old Rob. His voice had become hoarse and tired sounding, and his normally sinewy and muscular upper body was soft and pudgy. The Hammerhead now needed a two-hour nap each day. Still, we'd managed to keep paddling and training intermittently throughout his cancer treatment, which had been an amazing process to witness. He'd endured three rounds of the ADT, the "chemical castration," and that, combined with some apprehension and anxiety, made him more emotional; sometimes we'd be getting our boats ready and he'd go unexpectedly quiet. It was the third time before I realized these were episodes of silent tears. He'd also gone through multiple rounds with a state-of-the-art radiation machine he described as "the Varian Clinac iX linear accelerator," that delivered high-dose beams of radiation to his entire pelvic region, aimed at killing any residual prostate cancer cells. The radiation also ravaged bowel and bladder function, so he'd had to deal with that as well, and he had even been forced to wear diapers under his paddling pants in his kayak.

But now here he was, giddy with excitement about a potential training trip. Just recently, he'd decided to quit taking the ADT and had altered his diet to eliminate all dairy products and animal fat, which he learned could slow the progression of prostate cancer. For Rob, who ate anything and everything in his path like a swarm of locusts, this was particularly challenging and impressive.

"The guy's name is Rocky Contos," Rob said, "and he's probably the most experienced river explorer in all of the Americas. He runs a river conservation organization called SierraRios, created to conserve wild and free-flowing Mexican rivers. And he guides trips down the big, warm-water rivers in Mexico, Guatemala, Peru. These are effectively the Grand Canyons of Central and South America and perfect winter training for you. The absolute best way to replicate what you'll encounter paddling the Grand Canyon: big water and long, loud rapids with imposing hydraulic features."

"Sounds like everything I've ever dreamed of," I said. "But how about you? Will you be okay?"

"Just what the doctor ordered," Rob followed. "A river trip is nonprescription medicine with no side effects."

By early January 2012, I was standing next to Rocky Contos on the sodden banks of the raging Usumacinta River, the "Sacred Monkey River," a name with some controversy and blending of Aztec and Maya origins.

"Sacred Monkey," Rocky said in his distinctively high-pitched, tightly nasal twang, "refers to the howler monkey's sacred status in Mayan culture. And also to this jungle area, with the greatest density of primates in all of Central America."

"Actually, there's a howler in the tree right above your head!" Rob added.

I could hear its raspy growl and the thrashing branches and leaves as the monkey leaped around. I could also hear the rapid-fire motor drive on Rob's camera zinging as he clicked away.

Rocky had agreed to take us down through the heart of the Mayan region, in the Mexican state of Chiapas, a densely jungled and vast rain forest wilderness featuring numerous Class II–III rapids, gigantic waves, sprawling beaches, and major archeological sites. The Usumacinta, or Usu for short, had earned a reputation as one of the best river trips in the world but also one of the most dangerous. In the 1970s, the Usu had been a favorite winter destination for Grand Canyon guides and river aficionados, but then in the 1980s and '90s, spurred by a simmering Guatemalan civil war and the Zapatista movement in southern Mexico, the banks of the river teemed with armed militants who routinely robbed boaters. Word of the dangers got out, and rather than be held up by machine gun or machete point, tourists stayed away.

But Rocky tried to explain that the eighty-eight-mile stretch we intended to run, paralleling and partly forming the Mexico-Guatemala border, wasn't nearly as dangerous as it used to be.

"When I ran it solo two years ago, I was, to my knowledge, the first person to paddle it in a decade," he said. "I did end up getting pulled over by armed men," Rocky laughed, "but they were Guatemalan army, not banditos. Guatemalan soldiers actually police the region and help serve as caretakers of all the Mayan ruins along the river."

Rocky represented a peculiar mix of talents. He possessed a Ph.D. in neuroscience but was clearly more at home on a big, wild, remote river than in a laboratory. In the last decade he'd logged more than two hundred first descents down five thousand miles of Mexican rivers. Some of these were through Mexico's rugged and dangerous Copper Canyon region, a notorious haven for drug cartels growing marijuana and trading in opium. But for Rocky, the risk was worth it. He was a true crusader, bent on saving these beautiful free-flowing rivers and keeping them from being dammed for hydroelectric power. Rocky spoke fluent Spanish, had an easy and trustworthy manner with strangers, and a demeanor that deflected contentious situations. He never seemed to get rattled, and he never seemed to rattle others. There was no one more experienced to guide us safely into the jungle.

The group I'd organized for this training adventure was not exactly conventional. With us were three guys in their late twenties named Taylor Filasky, Eric Bach, and John Post. They were the team (they called themselves the Modern Gypsies) that Jeff and I had placed second to in that wild TV adventure race across Morocco, and we'd really developed a strong bond with them. I was impressed because they were passionate about international projects for social good. They'd taken their winnings from the show and put it toward projects raising awareness about the needs of people in developing countries, like a clean water project in Ecuador and a partnership with a company creating cleaner-burning stoves to reduce wood consumption and deforestation. I liked their spirit and their hipster style. After *Expedition Impossible*, they made me an honorary Gypsy by dressing me in black skinny jeans so tight I had to lie on the floor to wriggle them on. They added a gray T-shirt strategically tucked in only one spot, and with a soul patch and appropriate surrounding facial stubble, I could have passed for their older brother.

The Gypsies loved adventure but had never been on a big whitewater river expedition. So I invited them along, as well as my brother Eddi and another skilled paddler named Chris Weigand to serve as a second guide. And then there was Rob, low energy, beaten down, overweight, and suffering from osteoporosis and lung-capacity issues from the various drugs, but poised with paddle in hand, ready to help guide me.

At the Frontera put-in, Rob snapped last-minute photos of toucans and scarlet macaws, and he described Mexico's largest river. From the beginning, we knew the Usu was going to be big water. It normally ran about forty thousand cfs, larger and faster than anything I had ever encountered. But on our arrival, torrential rains had swelled it to almost three times its normal flow. The Usu was now running at over one hundred thousand cfs, and almost eight times the normal flow of the Colorado River through the Grand Canyon. I had flashing memories of our Green River trip when a similar thing had happened. We seemed to have an uncanny knack for arriving at rivers right when they were at record flood levels!

From the moment we got on the river, it was different from any experience I had ever had, like paddling through a real-world Jurassic Park. As we raced along, the slurp and gulp of the enormous hydraulic features sounded alive, like riding the back of a gargantuan, slithering snake disappearing into an endless jungle. The shoreline teemed with the lionlike roars of howler monkeys, the piercing calls of macaws, and the guttural, lengthy drum-croak of giant toads.

The first couple of days were devoid of big rapids, but the immense volume of water coursing downstream created challenging river features even Rob hadn't experienced before. Giant phantom boils would surge up randomly and explode a couple of feet higher than the river's surface. The way Rocky described them, the massive energy of the river moving downward wasn't consistent. The water flowing far beneath the surface would get slowed down by boulders or sped up by drop-offs, and it would create different currents that rose up, sometimes colliding with other currents and erupting at the surface like lava from a volcano. It was disconcerting to be paddling downriver and suddenly realize the bow of my boat was pointing uphill in a boiling upheaval. Even more frightening were the enormous, unpredictable whirlpools—or, as Rocky called them, vortexes.

Like the boils, the vortexes materialized out of nowhere and moved across the water, but instead of pushing up, these sucked you down. Rob could spot them for me, calling out, "Whirlpool on the left! Hard right! Hard right!" But they arose and then vanished, reappearing some arbitrary distance away. It was impossible for Rob to call out all the appearing, shifting, and reappearing features that gave the river a crazy chaotic energy, like tendrils of angry fingers shoving, lifting, spinning, and pulling my boat under. I was suddenly aware of a story one of the soldiers told me about trying to navigate through a field of land mines, the uncertainty of what was beneath his feet, almost as real and shattering as the bombs themselves.

To increase my stress level, the new radios we were trying out provided no improvement. They were muffled and inconsistent, and often I had to guess what Rob was yelling at me to do. I flipped a bunch of times on the upper section, all the while getting hypertense about what lay ahead. Sometimes, the pitching and bucking would get so overwhelming, I'd ask Chris or Rob to link up in a flotilla. I'd grab their boats and desperately latch on. It was strange that even though I couldn't see, squeezing my eyelids tight somehow helped fight the sense of dizziness.

That afternoon, I got flipped upside down by a boil that rose up right in front of my boat. I tried to hit my roll, but the boil bumped me into a massive whirlpool that spun me around and sucked at my helmet. I worked to get my paddle to the surface, but the vortex yanked the paddle blade downward. After a couple of feeble attempts, I ran out of air, pulled, and exited. As the vortex drew me around and around, tugging at my legs, Rob dropped in beside me, and I grabbed the stern of his boat.

"Hang on!" Rob yelled as the spin accelerated in a tightening circle. As we flushed down the world's largest toilet bowl, the whirlpool vanished as quickly as it had appeared. Rob paddled me toward shore. "I thought I'd seen it all," he said, "but being sucked down a ten-foot whirlpool is definitely a new experience. It was so deep, I couldn't see the horizon."

The first night at camp, against the chirping backdrop of cicadas, I lay in the sand, trying to calm myself down and recover from the forces of the river. I was just glad to be on stable ground. We built a fire, told stories, and got to know each other. Everyone especially wanted to hear some stories from Rocky, and he told us the improbable way he'd gotten started.

"I bought my first kayak," he said, "after a UC–Davis outdoors program trip on the American River. It was before I even had a car. I caught a ride from college to Lake Natoma, bought the boat, a paddle, and a spray skirt, and paddled home to Sacramento—about 120 miles down the American River. I hadn't brought food, but figs and blackberries were in season, so that's all I ate for four days."

"Wow, that's quite a solo journey," Rob said. "How experienced were you at the time?"

Rocky mused for a moment. "It was only my third time in a hard-shell kayak, but I was hooked."

That had been the start of two decades of wild and crazy solo adventures, the last fifteen years of which had been devoted to Mexico and Central America.

"For me," Rocky said, his high voice lilting and gentle against the snap and sputter of the fire, "paddling has always been about adventure. Lots of people love the thrill of the rapids, or going over waterfalls, and sure, I like that aspect too. But even more, I like being in a kayak on the water because it's the most natural way to travel through a river landscape. Gliding along on the river, at its pace, on its level, and on the river's terms."

I really liked what Rocky was saying. Although scary and intense, the rapids themselves comprised quite a small portion of a river trip. There was much more that made them memorable. Spending time with good friends you trust, experiencing amazing places, pushing the boundaries of your abilities, facing down fears. River trips had it all. I also really liked Rocky's meticulous and inquisitive approach. Rob had told me that Rocky was constantly charting and mapping every drainage, access point, and location where springs flowed for freshwater. In 2010, he had compiled a guidebook of Copper Canyon and the Sierra Madre del Norte, and now he was working on one for the Chiapas region. We'd pass an intriguing side canyon, and he'd remark, "I haven't hiked up that one yet; maybe next trip," and he'd scribble notes on his map. It felt really impressive to be in the presence of a modern-day explorer, not simply a river rat or a thrill seeker. Rocky was an anachronism, like he would have been perfectly suited for Powell's first descent of the Grand Canyon.

When it was time to turn in, I rolled out my pad in my tent and stretched out. We'd camped on a wide beach, halfway between the surging river and the dense, thrumming jungle. It was a warm night, and I could still feel the sand's heat radiating upward.

Rocky, I noticed, had rolled out a pad nearby but was sleeping right out on the sand, and pretty near the water.

"Aren't you worried about bugs and critters?" I asked him through the jungle night.

"No, I like sleeping out. I mean, there are crocodiles and jaguars around, but they usually don't bother you."

I edged over to the tent doorway and fumbled for the zipper.

"And there are also vampire bats," Rocky said calmly.

"What the hell? Really?" I asked.

"Yes. They are nocturnal and feed exclusively on blood. They navigate by sonar but also have super heightened vision, with huge, wide eyes. They fly out at night to feed and drink about half their body weight in blood. When they reach their prey, which are usually sleeping, they use their razor-sharp incisor teeth to impale the skin. They have an anticlotting agent in their saliva to keep the wound flowing. Most people think they suck blood, but they really lap it up as it oozes out."

I found the zipper and closed the tent door a little quicker than I usually would.

"They have plenty of other mammals around to feed on, so they rarely bother humans," he added as I checked all the inside corners for holes and settled in for a fitful sleep, filled with images of silent, furry, fanged creatures with huge, wide eyes winging silently through the jet-black night.

At breakfast, Rob's first words were, "That's incredible." I sidled up to him, feeling my neck and face for vampire bat incisions as he described Rocky's strange breakfast ritual. He was squatting in the sand with a pile of orange peels in front of him, engorging himself on the fruit in rapid succession. "He's on his seventh orange," Rob said quietly. Rocky was in his forties yet was still super lean and fit. He told us he fasted a day each week and one full week a year. He did everything at warp speed, but in a comforting, casual way, and

I pictured him sucking oranges like a hummingbird drinking sugar water from a bowl. Perhaps his hyperactivity had to do with these megadoses of sugar. Rocky then washed his hands and pulpy face in the river and started breaking down camp in fast motion.

"Makes me hungry for a breakfast burrito," I said to Rob.

The next day, we stopped along the river and explored the pre-Columbian Mayan ruins of Yaxchilan and Piedras Negras, which sat on the banks of the Usu and had been inhabited in the seventh century B.C. Yaxchilan had been fairly well excavated, but Piedras Negras was like walking into an *Indiana Jones* adventure. The plazas, temples, and palaces, all constructed of limestone, had only been partially exposed by archeologists, while most of this ancient ruin remained choked with thick jungle vines and vegetation. Rocky pointed out, with concern, that a proposed series of dams threatened to flood this incredible ruin and others throughout this entire region.

We climbed the steep rock stairs to the tops of sacred pyramids once used for human ritual sacrifice and touched the carved depictions of ancient rulers. We found a sundial, still faintly visible despite the ravages of time. It was unnerving and exhilarating to explore the remains of this ancient world, shadowed by giant ceiba trees, crumbling back into the jungle, forgotten by the modern world. In the Mayan culture, nothing was born and nothing ever died. Life and death were cyclical, like the seasons of the year or the rotation of the earth around the sun. In the afterlife, you embarked on a dangerous voyage through nine levels of the underworld, then thirteen levels of the higher world, and ultimately to a paradise—a mystical mountain of eternal happiness. Your journey began, however, in a dark kingdom called Xibalba, translated as "Place of Fear." As you ascended, you passed through a gauntlet of gods who would just as soon destroy your soul as they would help you: a hunched skeleton with protruding ribs and an owl's head, a crocodile with a long knobby bill and snapping teeth, and a paddler god in a dugout canoe with a snarling jaguar face. I shuddered as I envisioned that menacing journey, much of it below the surface of the earth and water, beneath our awareness, and even beyond what we perceived as real and unreal.

As Rob ran around snapping photos of the structures and recording the sound of shrieking spider monkeys, he said, "Be happy you weren't alive then, Big E. I think blind people would have been the first to be sacrificed." He laughed and slapped me on the back.

Not far downstream, we came to an amazing natural wonder called Cascada Busilja. Here, a tributary entered the Usumacinta and announced its arrival with a spectacular fifty-five-foot waterfall.

The force of this cascade shoved us back as we tried paddling over to the bottom. The sound of a thousand showerheads engulfed my ears and hammered me in the face. Rob noticed that there were actually two waterfalls, one on top of the other, with a big pool between them.

"From a ways off," he said, "they look like big knuckles, with foamy white spray cascading down over them."

Rocky said the knuckles were a typical feature found in this area called travertine, a buildup of soft minerals deposited in layers by the water and hardened over time. "I don't think anyone has ever kayaked over them," he said, "but I've heard of people jumping off the highest one."

That was all the Gypsies needed to pull their boats out and begin clambering up to try it out. They took turns flinging themselves into the foaming wash more than fifty feet below.

"That looks too fun." Rob turned to me. "The old guys can't get left out."

But when I scrambled out onto the launching point, I found slippery, wet, and exposed roots hung from space. I questioned the sanity of the leap. The landing zone wasn't that forgiving either. In fact, Rob said I needed to leap out about eight feet to clear some protruding rocks and nail the window of water that spanned about twenty feet. I pointed my trekking pole exactly where I needed to hit, once, twice, and then a third time. I stood for a minute, listening to the crashing waterfall and the open expanse below me. As I jumped, the thought that this might be a really stupid idea flashed through my mind, like those redneck jokes I'd heard: "What's the last thing a redneck says before dying?"

"Hold my beer."

Then I was soaring through the air, longer than I would have expected or intended, my stomach flip-flopping, my arms flailing in windmills, and then my body slapping hard into the roiling pool. As my head emerged, I heard

whoops and hollering from the onlookers, but I immediately knew something was wrong. Like a bonehead, I'd left on my helmet, and upon entry, the
visor snapped my head back. My neck felt rubbery, with the tendons firing,
like I had been whiplashed.

As I clung to a rock on the side of the pool trying to stretch my neck, Rob
leaped. Eddi and the gang described his jump; he got leaning backward too
far in the air and hit the water at a bad angle, like he was reclining too far in
a chair. The impact lurched his upper body abruptly forward, and when he
reemerged, he flailed and groaned, barely able to swim to shore. The boys immediately swam in and pulled him out, but as he lay on his back in the sun,
Rob continued to grimace in pain. Immediately he knew he'd made a big
mistake. The ADT treatment had stripped Rob of his testosterone, the body's
primary mechanism of rebuilding and repairing. His bones were weakened
from osteoporosis, and he feared he'd ruptured a disc or caused a compression fracture in one of his vertebrae. For the rest of the day, Rob couldn't get
comfortable. He couldn't rotate to look from side to side without excruciating pain; sitting in a kayak was out of the question. He took some muscle re-
laxants and a dose of anti-inflammatory meds, and to his chagrin and
disappointment, he was reduced to lying on his back on one of the rafts for
the rest of the day. The Hammerhead never liked being sidelined.

He did manage to sit up to report, as we pulled in to camp that evening,
that a ten-foot-long crocodile was entering the water, slithering away from the
exact spot we intended to set up camp. "That should make you want to hit
your roll, Big E," he said weakly.

I liked hearing him joke around, but it was torture to see Rob so reduced.
He had been hands down the toughest guy I knew, unbreakable, indestructible,
like a superhero. He'd led me up many spectacular rock and ice climbs, patiently taught me to kayak, and rescued me in rivers and dragged me to
shore countless times, and here he was, now as fallible as the rest of us, like
Superman having just encountered kryptonite.

That night at camp, while Rob nursed his ailing back with cervezas and
pain meds, we ate chorizo and a Chiapas favorite called *chayote*, a cross between a cucumber and a squash. As we crammed the food in, everyone pushed

Rocky for more stories. The Gypsies, who were on their first big river trip and new to white water, wanted to know if he'd ever had any close calls.

"Well, I've lost my boat while kayaking a couple of times, and I don't recommend that," he said.

Their interest piqued, they waited, and he went on.

"On a remote river in Peru, it was getting late in the day when we entered a narrow gorge section. At sunset, we weren't finding any good camp spots, so we just kept going. The river was running high, and I drifted into a very big hole. It was river-wide and no way really to avoid it. I tried to charge hard and bust through, but I didn't make it and got tossed back and thrashed around for . . . oh, maybe two minutes. I was popping up long enough to get air a few times, but eventually I had no choice but to exit. It was just about dark at that point, and my dry suit had filled with water, and I was so out of oxygen I was about to black out. My paddling partner had been behind me about ten yards and got through the hole. He towed me to some rocks, but by the time he'd gotten me there, my boat was long gone downstream. I'd been carrying a lot of important things in the boat like my laptop, my GPS, my river notes, and all the maps of where we had been, plus my food, camping gear, and all my warm clothes. I slept on the side of the river that night and then climbed out of the canyon the next morning. I had to cross a really dangerous cable bridge hand over hand because the wooden slats were all rotted, then hike about six miles or so. It was about one hundred degrees out. Meanwhile, my buddy went looking for my boat downstream. Miraculously, he found it. It was pretty mangled, but amazingly the laptop still worked, and most important, I recovered my river notes!"

Rob, who'd done his homework on Rocky and had read a bunch of articles about him in paddling magazines, chimed in from his prone position in the sand, "Tell them about the Kern, Rocky."

Rocky was normally understated, more about action than words, but he perked up at this recollection.

"Ah, the Kern. In California. There's a nasty rapid called Royal Flush, which is a legit class V/VI. About 99 percent of paddlers portage around it. It's narrow and bouldery and has a monster hole and a dangerous left wall undercut. I had run it a few times before, but this one day I got sideways, off-line, and after the main drop, my boat drifted far left and into the large wall there. I flipped and couldn't roll back up. Underwater, I could feel the boat moving down and underneath the ledge wall, and after waiting about five seconds, I pulled my skirt and exited."

I heard John, one of the Gypsies, crack a beer. "Damn good story," he said.

Rob laughed. "You gotta wait for it! That's just the beginning!"

Rocky continued, "I got pushed into an underwater alcove, and I hoped I'd be flushed out, but ten more seconds went by, then twenty at least, and I realized I was stuck. Powerful water was pushing me against a rock wall. It was dark; I had no bearings, and I was running out of air. Surprisingly, I could actually think rationally, and I speculated my PFD was holding me in the pocket where I couldn't flush out, so I frantically started removing it over my head. Luckily, a few of my tightening straps were broken, so it came off pretty easily and floated away. Within a few seconds I felt myself moving with the current, banging around on the rocks of the final drops, slamming my head. Still submerged, I was being rag-dolled downriver, and was so oxygen deprived that I was about to pass out when my head finally popped out of the water after about ninety seconds under. My friends fished me out after I'd swam about a third of a mile and deposited me on shore. I'd lost my paddle, my PFD, and one of my Teva sandals. I lay on a warm rock like a dead lizard for at least a half an hour, reviving and reliving my experience. I realized it was the closest I've ever come to dying."

Everyone was quiet as they contemplated themselves shoved against that undercut. I knew I didn't have the wherewithal to think my way out after thirty seconds of near drowning. Thankfully, Rob broke the dead silence.

"Big E," he said, "as I keep saying, you can hold your breath a lot longer than you think."

"Hope I never have to learn," I said softly.

"I also had a brush with death on the Upper Kern," Rob kicked in. "It was very early on the learning curve of my kayaking, and I really had no business even being there. It was running at about seven thousand cfs, definitely flood stage, even higher than experienced kayakers would consider. I was with just one other guy, and we were both confident and cocky because each of us had learned really quickly. But we were too stupid and filled with testosterone to carefully consider the consequences. Or to care."

"I'm glad you've grown up so much since then," I interjected, recalling Rob's less-than-wise jump off the cliff.

Rob paused for a second, most likely smirking, and then continued, "My friend in front of me got through this big rapid called Fender Bender, a Class V, but he swam at the end. On my run, I hit a boulder at the top, got flipped, yanked out of the boat, and was getting worked in this massive turbulent hole. I thought I'd pop out, but I wasn't coming to the surface; I was being held down, thrashed, and washing-machined. Somehow, right as I was thinking this might be it—like, the end—I remembered some advice I'd been given early on: If you get stuck and can't get out, try swimming down. So I did. I swam for my life straight down and got below the powerful recirculation of the hole. In the rocks below, I got the hell banged out of me, but, gasping and floundering, I managed to make it to shore. I had a massive hematoma on my femur and was on crutches for a few weeks."

"Yes," Rocky reminisced in his typical mild-mannered voice. "Good to be able to hold your breath. Where we're going tomorrow, we may need that skill. We're heading into the Gran Cañon de San José. It's about twenty miles through a constricted gorge. It possesses, by far, the largest rapids we've seen, but with this unusual water flow, it will have some serious hydraulic features, including haystacks—big standing waves that break on their upstream face, back on themselves; powerful and shifting eddy lines; and of course, phantom whirlpools, some so big they may hold you under for more than a minute. I won't tell each of you what to do. It's your choice, but if you kayak, some of you will flip and probably swim, and a swim through this canyon will mean a very long one. The vertical walls make it impossible to get to shore, and there's so much water coursing through the gorge, the waves crash against the sidewalls and push you back into the middle of the river."

Rocky's words were followed by an even longer silence than before. Not one Gypsy cracked a beer. I tried to stretch my neck that screamed back at me. And I thought of Rob with a possible fractured spine. This time, I broke the pause: "Rocky, with that lovely description, I think I'm out!"

And as if the tension couldn't get any thicker, a piercing whine-whistle cracked through the night and shrieked over our heads, exploding in the jungle behind our camp. I instinctively dropped to my belly in the sand. "That's an RPG," Rocky said as nonchalantly as announcing that dinner was served.

"Should we extinguish our fire? Hide in the jungle?" one of the Gypsies said urgently.

Rocky just laughed. "No. It's only the bored Guatemalan army doing some random target practice," he said as another whistled over our heads and exploded even closer.

I woke up the next morning groggy and unsettled after a fitful night. Between Rocky's and Rob's near-death river stories and the evening fireworks, I felt raw and exposed. The good news was, the day started with some really fun paddling over the waterfalls of the Rio Chocolja, a tributary of the Usu. Rob described deep, turquoise-colored water, with tiers of small waterfalls as far as he could see up the canyon. We hiked our boats upstream and ran five of the drops, including one about eight feet high. Rocky offered to guide me, and he'd call commands, yelling, "Paddle hard!" as I hit the edge, hearing the rush of the water ahead, the open chasm below, and the churning slosh at the bottom. I'd go momentarily airborne, then land nose first, slapping down flat. Sometimes, I flipped, but more often I stayed upright. It was momentarily frightening, then exhilarating, then a relief.

Taylor of the Gypsies had a little mishap when he went over the big waterfall at too steep an angle and too far to the right. He bashed the nose of his kayak against an underwater rock, got stuck, and swam out. Afterward, the snout of his boat was totally dented inward. Eddi in his inflatable duckie was the comic relief. His massive, muscular, 230-pound frame barely fit in his boat, and he came in sideways, hung up on the lip of the drop. He then tottered dubiously and toppled over sideways with his arms flailing, kerplunking into the pool below. When he popped back up to the surface, the yellow duckie came down after him, bonking him on the head.

In the afternoon, we entered the main gorge, and I could hear the limestone walls closing in and soaring thousands of feet straight out of the river. Rob surprised me when he decided to run it in his kayak, even though he had to remain rigid, unable to twist his torso. He wriggled into his kayak slowly and carefully like a ninety-year-old man. It was no surprise that the Gypsies decided to run it too. I hopped into the front of a double inflatable duckie with Eddi, not ready to kayak, but still unwilling to miss the action. Rocky was correct: The power of the water roiling through this constricted canyon sped up the current, intensified the rapids, and magnified the boils, vortexes, and eddy lines. And instead of separated rapids, broken up by calm pools, this stretch seemed to surge and compound into one long, violent maelstrom.

The group carnage began immediately. Taylor of the Gypsies flipped a record of nine times in the first rapid, La Linea, which Rocky had warned would feel "very Grand Canyon–like: big and fast and hard to stay on line." John fared much worse, however, flipping at the top of La Linea and swimming, emerging, and disappearing as he was carried downriver. As his head appeared, Rob had somehow gotten over to him and yelled, "Grab on!" and the two roared down the turbulent gauntlet together, with Rob paddling furiously, looking for any escape to shore.

There was so much volume, however, the waves rose up the sides of the canyon walls, like a half-pipe, and each time he'd get near the side, the massive waves would collapse over him and shove him back toward the center of the river. The power of the water was so strong, at one point Rob had to yell for John to let go. He was about to flip himself and, with his injury, didn't want to have two swimmers in jeopardy. As John let go, a massive haystack hit Rob sideways, and he had to test his theory. It knocked him over, but after three tries, he was up again, looking for John's head bobbing somewhere below. It was a shock when he saw John appear, resurfacing some two hundred feet down the canyon, a very long time to be underwater. Rob raced downstream and got to John again, and the two rode the furious energy, Rob using all he had to avoid the huge whirlpools that were materializing all around him. Out of breath and totally spent, John yelled desperately, "Don't leave me, Rob! I don't have much left! I'm done!" He was gurgling, his mouth getting filled with water. After another two miles, the canyon finally widened a bit, and Rob found some rocks where he deposited John, who lay on his belly, gasping, moaning, and spitting out great gobs of brown water.

Finally, John pulled himself up to his knees, then his feet. He wrapped his arms around Rob.

"Not so tight." Rob winced with pain.

"You saved my life," John said, and he sank down again, hanging his head in exhaustion.

While all of this was going on, Eddi and I were having plenty of drama of our own in the double duckie inflatable. As hard as we paddled, the energy of the river was taking us where it wanted us to go. Several times we rode up one of those crashing waves against the canyon walls, got upended, and spilled into the river with whirlpools forming right below me. A ducky has a lot of buoyancy, so I latched on to the upside-down handle, while the monstrous spin cycle grabbed my feet. If my shoes hadn't been tied tightly, they would have been sucked right off, and if I hadn't been holding on with all my strength, my body would have been pulled down with them. When there was finally a break in the action, we took a rest at shore, and I approached Rob, who was sitting quietly on his kayak, taking a drink from his water bottle. "I heard you finally got some exercise on this trip," I said.

"Exactly, Big E. It was the beginning of my new Gypsy fitness plan. A Gypsy a day keeps the doctor away."

"Even with a little kryptonite," I said, putting my hand gently on his shoulder. "I want you to know, you're still pretty awesome."

"Not exactly sure what that means," he replied quizzically, "but I'll take it as a compliment."

The next morning, I did force myself back into my kayak. Rocky said that three of the largest rapids still lay ahead, and from the moment I started downriver, I felt so nervous, it translated into a sluggishness. I couldn't get my muscles to fire, and I felt like I was about to vomit. The first rapid I encountered was appropriately named Whirlpool, and it took every ounce of skill and fitness I possessed to stay upright in the chaos. Rob was doing his best to call out shifting river features, but he shot past me as I caught the edge of a big vortex. It spun me around as I managed to escape, and I wound up paddling upriver. I had no clue where Rob was through the muffled radios. I swept my hand across the earpiece, shoving it away from my ear. Then I heard Rob faintly calling from far behind me and far to my left. I turned but caught a boil that lifted up my bow and spun me again. Where was Rob? I heard his distant call from my right, and turned around again, trying to paddle through the submerged fingers grabbing at my boat.

Suddenly, I felt an enormous whirlpool gurgle up just behind me. Rob was about a hundred feet in front of me, calling, "Paddle, E! Harder! Harder!" I could feel the whirlpool as it reeled me backward. I cranked it up, paddling as hard as I ever had. I could actually feel my consciousness beginning to slip away into some kind of primeval instinct for survival. I was hyperventilating, oxygen no longer absorbing into my lungs and blood vessels. I was going anaerobic. My thinking mind was reduced to a sliver, only enough room for the sound of my ragged breathing, my muscles that felt on fire, and the roar and suck of the swirling cauldron behind me as it hauled me into its mouth. I could feel the stern of my boat hovering over the hole as I dug and churned with my paddle blades, but to no avail. I honestly couldn't remember whether the vortex simply vanished, or whether I was able to paddle away, but I somehow broke free, made it through more tempest, and busted through a fierce eddy fence, sinking over my boat, safe for a time in the semi-calm pool.

I heaved myself out of my boat and flopped onto a rock, weak and dizzy. I could barely lift my head as I poured sweat and tried to slow my labored breathing. My arms and hands shook uncontrollably. It felt like my nervous system had broken, like a wire that had been frayed and exposed to the elements. I leaned over. Waves of nausea sent me into a series of convulsive dry heaves, and I could taste bitter acid rising in my throat. Rob sat beside me and tried to convince me to get back in and give it another go, but even if I'd wanted to, I knew I couldn't. No pep talk or motivational speech could get me back in the water. I felt like my brother Mark must have felt going into the ring with Anita. I had gone toe-to-toe with the river, and it had kicked my ass, sending me sprawling into the corner battered and bloody. Yet, unlike me, Mark had been willing to go back in, again and again. Then I thought of Jamie, who had left the S2S expedition. I had pleaded with him not to quit, but he had closed his heart and ridden away down the bumpy mountain road. Like him, I was done!

I rode in a raft for the next day and a half until the take-out and tried not to bring everyone else down, but emotionally, I was shattered.

Then when we got to the airport in Villahermosa and back to the world of e-mail, I got the news that Kyle Maynard had made it to the summit of Kilimanjaro, the tallest peak in Africa. The report didn't say a lot, only that Kyle had become the first quadruple amputee to climb Kili, crawling to the 19,341-foot summit in ten days.

Outwardly, I was happy for Kyle. His No Barriers dream that had solidified on a mountaintop in Colorado had become real. It was an amazing accomplishment, and I understood the pain, suffering, and bloody stumps he must have gone through to get there. But although I could envision him at the summit, my own dream had become nebulous, like the wispy jungle haze evaporating over the Usumacinta.

Once I got home, I tried to put on a tough façade for Ellie and the kids, but inside I felt flat and damaged somehow. My only strong emotion seemed to be fear and a vague dread. I often found myself lost in thought, fighting the boils, or lying on that rock trying to convince myself to get back in my boat. The doubt and questioning began to eat at me like roiling tentacles reaching out for me from the dark water. In my typical dreams, I could see the way I did before I went blind, with rudimentary shapes and images. It was pleasant to revisit wonderful places from my childhood like the forest behind my house, the trees blazing with vibrant fall colors. But in my new dreams, I was totally blind. In fact, more than blind. Everything was thick, suffocating blackness with the overwhelming roar of the rapids engulfing all sound. Rob was nowhere to be found. I was totally on my own as I rushed headlong downriver, twisting and turning, into a raging tumult that I knew would drag me under and consume me.

18

EIGHTEEN CLICKS

I wasn't even home from the Usumacinta before Rob had already begun enthusiastically going over future battle plans. Sitting on the plane flying toward Colorado, with Rob squeezed into the seat next to me, I was feeling exhausted and beaten down from the previous week. All I'd wanted to do was to relax. I had my soundproof headphones around my ears, an indication I was off limits for a while. But no social cues could stop Rob. I could hear him talking toward me, right through the headphones. I reminded myself to get a refund; they weren't actually soundproof, I thought as I pulled them off and began listening.

"I've been thinking," he started. "I've watched you ski over the years, and you like to do the same run over and over. It's like you're learning the slope and its parameters each time you go down. I've seen the same in the rock gym. You seem to get better the more times you climb the same route. Blind guys seem to like familiarity and repetition. If I were blind, I'd like that too. It makes sense. The problem with natural rivers is that you can only do each rapid once. Well, there's a place called the U.S. National Whitewater Center. It's in North Carolina, and it may be a very good solution."

I'd learned about the Whitewater Center from a speaking engagement I'd done in Charlotte several years before. After the presentation, the founder, Jeff Wise, had toured me through the property, still just woods and pastures, laying out his unrealized vision of an elaborate series of man-made channels burrowed through the Carolina clay, replete with pools, flat water, and big, exciting rapids. His dream had taken shape, and now it was where the U.S. National Paddling Team trained for the Olympics.

"We can do it over and over," Rob explained. "We can get a ton of mileage. You can map it in your mind. Then you won't be thinking as much about the course and can focus on building your skills."

I'd heard about the automatic conveyer belt at the bottom of the channel that ferried you up to the top and deposited you back into the upper pool. It did sound pretty intriguing, but I wasn't ready yet to confront the future.

"It's also totally safe," Rob continued. "It's pool-drop." In the language of rivers, this meant that if you came out of your boat, you'd eventually reach a calm pool below the chaos where you could get to shore. "Plus, if you swim, you won't trap your foot under a rock, be driven into an undercut, or be sucked to the bottom of a whirlpool."

"Yeah, I get it," I interrupted, the words coming out louder than intended.

"There are a couple of small holes, but if you wind up swimming, they will release you pretty quickly. The worst that can happen," he continued, "is that you scrape your knees against the concrete at the bottom of the channel or you bang an elbow against the walls."

"That's all?" I said sarcastically. "Now I'm psyched."

Over the next two months, that flicker of intrigue had grown, and now I stood on the side of the concrete channel at the U.S. National Whitewater Center, wondering if I could even get back into a kayak without being stricken by paralyzing panic. I was now experiencing all the familiar signs. I could feel my heart beating in my chest and was having trouble getting a full breath. My limbs felt numb and lifeless. The eggs I'd eaten for breakfast refused to digest, and they kept coming up in the back of my throat in a dry heave. Ever since my scare on the Usumacinta, I'd felt shattered. I'd desperately wanted to rebuild, but when I thought about getting back into a kayak, it felt like a physical wall lowering down on me. And it didn't matter how many Tony Robbins motivational programs I listened to or how many times I told myself I could do it; I was bathed in a wash of fear that made me feel frozen, stuck in place.

As I pulled on my splash top, my nervous system felt overexposed, like a power line with a frayed wire, crackling and spitting electricity. The puzzling part was that I'd already survived much harder rapids than anything I would encounter here at the Whitewater Center, with much greater consequences. So why did I feel paralyzed? With all that training under my belt, I hadn't gotten better. Instead I had actually regressed. Maybe part of it was the realization of what I was doing. You start out in high spirits, totally clueless to all the dangers and pitfalls, and one day something happens, and those consequences become terrifyingly clear.

I had assumed that I would find a way to keep pushing forward, at first incrementally, perhaps, but then building until I was rising in a sweeping arc upward, all the way to a dramatic crescendo, but that had been dead wrong. That arc, if it ever existed in the first place, had been severed in the Usu. Maybe it wasn't always linear, I speculated. Maybe progress was more like a giant wave in a big river hole that rises upward and then crashes backward on itself before continuing its run downstream. If the arc was broken and there was no way forward, maybe I had to go backward.

As I finished suiting up, I had to pee again. It was my fourth time that morning, having to hurry around the corner of the gear shed to find the bathroom. My shrunken bladder seemed to be another symptom of my apprehension. I was waiting outside the door when it swung open, and Rob stepped out. "What a coincidence seeing you here, Big E," he said. Rob was frequenting the bathroom for an entirely different reason than fear. His prostatectomy caused incontinence that frequently sent him to the men's room.

"You and I are quite a pair," I said as I stepped inside and we traded places. Rob had somewhat recovered from his low point on the Usu, but he was a far cry from the Hammerhead. After his three androgen deprivation therapies that stripped his testosterone to zero, it had been slowly climbing back. He now had about as much as a typical woman. Sometimes he would unexpectedly collapse onto the nearest bench, face flushed and bathed in sweat, experiencing an overwhelming hot flash like those experienced in menopause. Yet, despite that, he was here, and it made me want to be stronger.

One of the center's kayak instructors, Casey Eichfeld, had agreed to be our second guide. Since he knew the channel better than anyone, he would be my lead caller, while Rob would paddle ahead, assuming the role of safety, in case I swam. Casey was on the national team, currently training for his second Olympics. I took a breath, feeling fortunate to have an Olympic paddler as a guide.

I needed to start by getting my combat roll back. After the Usu, I had lost it, or at least it had become totally unreliable. Sometimes I'd manage to get upright weakly, but other times, I'd get partway up, plop back over, immediately revert into panic mode, and pull my skirt. When that happened, Rob had told me, "You've got to keep trying. Sometimes, it takes three or four tries. You have a lot more oxygen than you think, but you have to get the intellectual part of your brain talking to the primitive part, and the intellectual part needs to rule."

I spent the morning warming up by paddling around the top pool. Seven giant pumps pulled the water from the bottom pool back to the top, and the water surged out through mesh screens. I paddled hard against the force of the jets, like paddling upstream against a powerful current. I practiced my roll and then worked with Casey on the various commands. Rob called it "getting calibrated." When Casey said, "Small right," or "Hard left," we had to be in sync. As Casey called directions, Rob paddled nearby, giving input. "That wasn't a small right. That was more like ninety degrees . . . All right, that's more like a small right."

After a couple of hours, there was no way to delay any longer.

"Ready to do this thing?" Casey called out.

"I guess so," I called back, and we floated from the calm pool into the channel. A few ripples rolled over my boat. The first rapid was called Entrance Exam. I went through the first wave. I was expecting a warm-up, but it smacked me hard, and I was instantly over. I managed a weak roll, but the wave had shoved me far to the right. "Eddy!" I yelled, flooding with trepidation. "I need to eddy out."

I bobbled sideways over a man-made rock, just inches beneath the surface, and flipped again. That was too much for my nervous system. The intellectual side of my brain didn't even make an appearance, but the primitive side screamed and reacted. I pulled my skirt, coming up sputtering with waves crashing over my head. I tried to take a breath but instead swallowed a huge gulp of chlorinated water. I wound up swimming through four more rapids, finally washing into a giant pool a third of the way down.

Rob was there beside me. "Grab my boat," he called, and he towed me to a small island between the channels. I sat on the edge of the pool for a good forty minutes with my face in my hands. I was shivering under my dry top despite the warm day. In my swim, water had hammered into my ears and down my throat, and I felt dizzy and sick. Palms pressed against my eyes, I was in the Usumacinta again, paddling for my life, the bottomless whirlpool behind me. But to my horror, I realized I was going backward, not forward. It was slowly drawing me in. Then I was yanked over and sucked out of my boat. I spun and tumbled in the monstrous swirl, fighting for air as the black water greedily sucked at my shoes.

Even though I knew I was safely on dry land, I couldn't escape the disorienting dreamscape, thrashing and toppling me over and over. Rob, now sitting next to me, brought me out of my vision.

"I know you don't want to hear this," he said, "but the best thing right now is to get back in your boat. We'll take a break, and we can chill out for a while, but you've got to get back in."

I wasn't really listening. Entrance Exam, the first rapid, was like a test you had to pass to earn the right to venture downriver to the real rapids below. I had failed the Entrance Exam, and I didn't belong here. All I was thinking was, *How do I let Rob down easy, tell him I'm quitting this sport, that it's not for me, even though he's already put so much time and effort into trying to coach me?* I just wanted to go home to my wife and kids. I missed them intensely and should have been at Arjun's soccer game rather than flailing and half drowning down a man-made river in North Carolina!

"What about this," he said. "To the left of the main channel, there's what is called 'the instructional channel.' We'll stay in that channel for a while, until you build back some confidence."

I forced open a sliver of light in my mind, knowing Rob had done his typical thing, throwing his foot out before the door could slam shut. He was offering me a way to move forward, even though it involved taking yet another step back. For the next two days, I stayed in the instructional channel. It only had three small waves—with easy drops into flat pools—before it flowed back into the main channel, right into the same pool where I'd wound up after my swim. I'd get down to that pool, pull over, and hike my boat up to the top, over and over again, trying to rebuild.

Later that afternoon, we sat on the side of the course drinking iced teas. I was spent.

"Tough day," Rob said.

"Yeah," I replied. "I'm honestly not sure if I'm bold enough for this sport."

"Boldness isn't everything," he responded. "There are lots of ways to face a challenge. Have I ever told you about the squirrel strategy?" he asked.

"No," I answered, now curious and ready for any story that didn't involve kayaking . . . and water. "But a squirrel's kind of puny. Better to be a lion."

"Not necessarily," he continued. "Behind my house, there's a family of squirrels, and my wife and I love watching them out our window in the morning as we drink coffee. It provides hours of entertainment. We also love to feed them, but it was getting boring laying out a bowl and watching them gorge themselves, so I got curious and decided to rig up a little experiment. It was a rope system, sort of like a swing set. We hung it from a sturdy tree branch, but instead of a swing seat, we attached a wooden plate with a screw protruding from the middle. On the screw, we wedged a cobb of corn. The plate swing dangled there about four feet off the ground. At first, the squirrels would stand underneath it and stare up longingly. Then they'd jump at it, but it was winter, and the snow made it too slippery for them to get enough traction. After that, they'd climb up the tree trunk to about the same level as the plate, trying to get some elevation. They'd dig in with their claws, push off, spin around in midair, and actually land on the plate. They were amazingly accurate, but there was one problem. They'd hit the plate at such velocity, they'd send it swinging across the yard and spinning out of control, with the squirrel hanging on for the ride of its life. The look on their faces was hilarious! I could practically see the little thought bubble appearing above their heads saying, 'This isn't going to work.' Then they'd inevitably fall off and slide across the snow.

"But over the course of a few weeks, they got the idea to climb the tree and maneuver along the high branch until they were directly over the hanging rope. But they would abruptly come to a stop, because they had no idea how to climb down a rope. After another week, one guy finally figured out how to grab the rope with his hind legs, his sharp little claws biting in, then use his front paws to slowly slide face-first down the rope to the food-filled

platform. He was fat and happy that day. The process wasn't quick. It was it-
erative, a willingness to use lots and lots of trial and error, to keep trying new
techniques until they figured it out. What's interesting is that squirrels aren't
super intelligent or strong or exceptionally talented, but they're notoriously
persistent. I'll take tenacity and persistence over genius and boldness any day.
You just keep throwing yourself at the problem until one day you succeed accidentally. My wife, Annette, is the ultimate squirrel," he continued. "She
actually calls it the Squirrel Strategy."

Rob's wife was impressive. In her day, she'd been one of the top rock
climbers in the country and had been on the cover of *Rock and Ice*.

"Because you've climbed Mount Everest and done a bunch of amazing
things, all of them blind, people assume you must be fearless, but if you have
the motivation and perseverance, and you choose not to give up, you don't
have to be a lion. You can be a squirrel."

"I think I see where you're going with this." I laughed. "What you're saying is that Annette and I aren't smart, strong, or talented."

"Exactly, Big E!" Rob smiled and slapped me on the back.

When I got back home, I decided to squirrel away at another obstacle that
weighed on me as much as my kayak training. Our fledgling No Barriers
organization was barely staying above water. Our first domestic summit in
Squaw Valley had filled up so fast, we had to shut off registration a month
before the event. It had been a huge success, and we'd received hundreds of
letters from participants. One exclaimed:

> To say the NO BARRIERS FESTIVAL *was powerfully informative*
> *would be a gross understatement. As a multiple-disabled person strug-*
> *gling to survive, I saw and heard things that left me incomprehensibly*
> *moved. And I thank you for putting it together.*

However, when we tried to replicate it the next year, we couldn't raise
enough funding. Our existing sponsors hadn't been interested in continuing, forcing us to cancel. It was baffling how we'd done so much right, yet

momentum had come to a dead halt. I think we had failed to clearly articulate how the No Barriers message was relevant to people's lives and especially beyond those with physical disabilities.

In my travels, I was constantly on the lookout for the right partners who could help us, and while speaking at a fund-raiser in Miami, I was introduced to Harry Horgan, the director of a wonderful organization that taught disadvantaged kids and disabled folks how to sail and do other water sports. We had held our past festivals in the mountains, but the ocean seemed like an equally powerful environment to express this No Barriers idea. Harry enthusiastically agreed to host the next summit out of their facility in Key Biscayne. However, despite all our good intentions, the problems had begun almost immediately; squabbles surfaced over who would do what and how much money each of us was responsible for raising. When the event was finally under way, torrential thunderstorms canceled some clinics, and technical troubles made our sound system nearly inaudible. Our innovation forum presented to an almost empty auditorium, and our overall attendance was lower than Squaw Valley by 150 people.

Recovering from that misstep, we held our next festival in Winter Park, Colorado. We now called the event the No Barriers Summit. It was a big improvement but was plagued by similar problems. Some of the events weren't well organized. Buses showed up late. Participants got lost trying to find where to go, and attendance still fell short of our goals.

Our first few summits were totally volunteer efforts, led by Jim Goldsmith and his wife and supported by Mark Wellman, Hugh Herr, and me. But if we were going to continue, it was becoming abundantly clear we needed someone putting in a full-time effort. We hired our first executive director and expanded the board with a deaf and blind salesman, a writer who was also a quadriplegic, and a professor with a spinal cord injury who had been a pioneer in electrical nerve stimulation that enabled him to stand up for brief periods of time. However, it still wasn't enough.

Our few mixed successes still felt unpredictable and shaky, like my recent combat roll. Our new team was devoted, but we had a confidence problem. We talked and talked about how we wanted to grow and where we wanted to be in five years, but we were having trouble selling an idea that only partially

Chad Jukes nears the summit of Lobuche, elevation 20,075 feet, as part of our inaugural 2010 Soldiers to the Summit expedition. Six years later, Chad reaches the summit of Mount Everest. *Courtesy of Didrik Johnck*

Blind veteran Steve Baskis ascends Lobuche. He says, "Blindness is like a deep, dark black abyss that I stare into. It's never-ending." *Courtesy of Didrik Johnck*

After descending Lobuche, we celebrate in the greatest way: by passing around different sweaty, unwashed prosthetic legs and drinking a few toasts out of them. *Courtesy of Didrik Johnck*

Matt Burgess (R) holds an ice axe with his S2S team. Even though the group poses happily in front of Cotopaxi, the smiles mask the volcanic mood of the expedition. *Courtesy of Didrik Johnck*

Plodding, picking, weaving, and wheezing, an exhausted Matt Burgess crests the ridge and sees the summit of Cotopaxi. *Courtesy of Didrik Johnck*

Rob and I emerge from the depths of the Gran Cañon de San José on my second training trip to the Usumacinta in southern Mexico. We camp that night on the beach, just above Whirlpool Rapid, where the year before, I'd come close to quitting kayaking forever. *Courtesy of Skyler Williams*

Rob about to perform a ritual sacrifice amidst the ancient Mayan ruins of Piedras Negras. *Courtesy of Skyler Williams*

I run one of the many travertine waterfalls on the Rio Chocolja, a tributary of the Usumacinta; it's momentarily frightening as I hit the edge and go airborne. *Courtesy of Rocky Contos*

Casey Eichfeld guides me as I punch through "Entrance Exam," the first rapid on the wilderness channel at the U.S. National Whitewater Center. On my first attempt, I fail the exam. *Courtesy of Sarah Anderson*

(Front to back) Me, Casey Eichfeld, and Rob Raker ride the conveyor belt at the U.S. National Whitewater Center that ferries you from the bottom of the channel and deposits you back into the upper pool for another run. *Courtesy of Skyler Williams*

Andy Holzer and I touch the cross that signifies the summit of the Red Tower. As Andy says, "No sighted people, only blinds." *Courtesy of Heinz Zak*

Lonnie Bedwell breaks the mold. A farmer from Indiana becomes a world-class kayaker. *Courtesy of James Q Martin*

Rob guiding me through Tombstone Rapid on the Shoshone section of the Colorado River. Narrow, rocky rivers are a nightmare for blind kayakers. *Courtesy of Skyler Williams*

The amazing Mandy Harvey performs "It's a Wonderful World" on stage at the No Barriers Summit. *Permission by No Barriers USA*

Captain Ryan Kelly in his Blackhawk helicopter, Baghdad, Iraq, 2005. *Permission by Ryan Kelly*

My family and I experience the famous thermal springs of Yellowstone that bubble up from below. On our way home, another geyser erupts in our lives as we learn about Arjun's birth mother. *Permission by Weihenmayer Family Collection*

Adrian Anantawan fulfills his dream to play his violin from a mountaintop. The sound starts softly, dipping and idling, then soaring up and piercing the thin mountain air. *Courtesy of Skyler Williams*

Upon our discovery of Arjun's mom, Kanchi writes, "For all these years, I have been wondering where he was, how he is. Now I know. Now I just wish to meet him again. He is my son, and he is yours too." *Courtesy of Rob Raker*

My team and I take Arjun kayaking down the Upper Colorado a week before I leave for the Grand Canyon. I emerge at the bottom of the rapids frazzled and breathing hard, while Arjun rides the waves with a dancer's grace and comes out smiling. *Courtesy of Michael Brown*

My team approaches Navajo
Bridge on the Grand Canyon,
signifying the beginning of
our No Barriers expedition.
Only 277 miles to go! *Courtesy
of James Q Martin*

I learn a lot
about rivers
and life while
paddling with
Harlan Taney.
*Courtesy of James
Q Martin*

I charge into
24 Mile Rapid.
Seconds later,
I'm upside down.
*Courtesy of James
Q Martin*

Baffled by the radios' inconsistencies, Steven Mace, Skyler Williams, and I painstakingly test different configurations. *Courtesy of James Q Martin*

Harlan and his sister, Marieke, on the lap of their father, Guerin Taney. Harlan says, "One minute he'd be throwing a refrigerator across the room, and the next, he'd be scooping you up in his arms and telling you how much he loved you." *Permission by Harlan Taney*

Horn Creek Rapid features the steepest drop in the Grand Canyon. Anticipating this rapid over breakfast, my eggs were about to turn into a vomit omelet. *Courtesy of James Q Martin*

After many days being drenched in silty water and sandblasted at beach camps, it's refreshing to jump into the clear, fresh water of Elves Chasm. *Courtesy of James Q Martin*

After making it through the inner gorge, Harlan and I celebrate. The acoustics are amazing in the Grand Canyon. *Courtesy of James Q Martin*

Raft team leader Randy Tucker surrounded by a festive throng, during our wild Grand Canyon dance party. *Courtesy of James Q Martin*

To celebrate my birthday, Timmy O'Neill and the team build a "Burning Erik," much like the famous "Burning Man" of the festival in Nevada's Black Rock desert. At the last Burning Man, the structure was 105 feet tall, and even though the Burning Erik is less than three feet, I still feel honored. (Note: We only burned the cardboard and wood that we brought down the river.) *Courtesy of Rob Raker*

Harlan talks me through "the line" on Lava Falls, the most feared rapid in the Grand Canyon. *Courtesy of James Q Martin*

Although I'm terrified going into the V-Wave, I silently repeat our familiar mantra: "Relax. Breathe. Be at peace with the river." *Courtesy of James Q Martin*

Going through the massive Kahuna waves backwards in Lava is not part of the plan. Moments later, that same wave snaps Harlan's carbon fiber paddle in half. *Courtesy of James Q Martin*

Wordlessly, we bushwhack through the tamarisk scrub. As Timmy says, "It's time for a little bit of Lava 2.0." *Courtesy of James Q Martin*

I give thanks to Harlan and the river. The open heart policy is revealed under a star bear sky. *Courtesy of Andy Maser*

Lonnie and I perform a blind paddle high-five as we drift the final few hundred yards to the take-out at Pearce Ferry, the end of our journey. *Courtesy of James Q Martin*

Marine staff sergeant Dan Sidles, a member of our first S2S expedition to Lobuche, later becomes a mentor in the program. "Home," he says, "that's where the real war begins." In the spring of 2016, Dan lost his battle with PTSD, and took his own life. *Courtesy of Didrik Johnck*

Turned back by a crevasse below the summit of Gannett Peak, the No Barriers Warriors team stops to share a few war stories, shed some tears, and throw their nightmares into the dark tomb. *Courtesy of Didrik Johnck*

existed. At a retreat, one of our board members said, "We're pulling off some pretty impressive events, but if anyone saw how we were making the sausage, with just one paid staff member and a few part-time volunteers, they'd run away in horror."

I knew we needed to continue to bring in the right people, those with the passion, expertise, and connections to carry our movement forward, but I hesitated, afraid that those people might see us for what we were today instead of what we aspired to be, and they'd run for the hills.

At our next retreat, I came straight to the point. "We've survived some summits, and for those who had attended, they'd been extraordinary, even life-changing, but we've only managed to limp forward. There's a big difference between surviving and actually building toward something bigger."

"We've had a good run, through five summits," a fellow director replied, "but we've hit the wall. Maybe it's time to think about closing up shop."

Over the next few months, I brought the headquarters to Golden where I could monitor it more closely, and I stressed over what to do. This thing I loved, that was just barely forming, was about to die. The truth of it was that there were hundreds of good ideas like No Barriers, and most of them had died invisible deaths behind the scenes. There were parallels with climbing expeditions; when I stood on top of mountains, these moments were exciting and dramatic, but they represented only the tiniest sliver of a bigger picture. For every hour climbing, there were a hundred hours spent toiling behind the computer, building the infrastructure, getting clear on goals and expectations, and networking and communicating with sponsors.

If No Barriers was going to become sustainable and grow into something significant, we would need to build up the internal organization, and that would rest on finding the right leader. I knew now I couldn't do this alone. I began interviewing dozens of candidates, but none felt right. What I needed was someone who didn't see this as a day job, but possessed the intensity and drive of a founder. That made me think of my old friend Dave Shurna, the founder and executive director of Global Explorers.

His organization had a mission of growing youth into global citizens through travel. Four years before, I'd helped him start his blind youth program, leading our first trip in the Grand Canyon and then other expeditions through the Peruvian Andes. Dave was on my radar, since he'd recently asked me to help Global Explorers make a fund-raising pitch to the outdoor retailer REI. At the end of the meeting, the executive had asked a blunt question: "I get hundreds of requests a year. What makes you different from all the other programs like NOLS and Outward Bound?" We didn't have a very good answer.

Dave and I met in the same coffee shop where we had conspired to start the blind youth program. Sitting with our lattes in hand, I came straight out with it.

"Dave, I respect you a lot. You're bold. You're a rare person who knows how to take something that barely exists and grow it into something real. I know this is a wild hair, but we should come together."

Instead of shutting me down immediately, Dave asked, "How do you see that working?" His voice was so even-keeled; I couldn't read whether he was intrigued or just being polite.

"You have the vision, the energy, the knowledge. You even have the staff and infrastructure. In some ways, you're more No Barriers than we are. But what you don't have is the mission. You frame your purpose around the benefits of travel, which is important, but not the most important. Traveling is only a means to an end. We travel and explore the globe so we can learn how to break through barriers in our lives, so we can come home and contribute something back. That's the glue that connects every person who lives and breathes, whether you have a disability or not. Global Explorers and No Barriers are doing similar things already; we're just using different words. We're both small. We're both struggling, but together, we could become exponentially better."

After my speech, I felt drained. I had just laid it out there, like pouring my entire latte onto the table, and now it was Dave's turn to respond. I wondered if I'd revealed too much—shown too much of my hand. I waited for him to disagree, or to say something noncommittal. Instead he said, "You know, I've kind of been thinking the same thing."

On my second trip out to the Whitewater Center, I graduated from the instructional channel and back into the main course, ending in the pool where I'd washed out on my first swim. In three days, I had ten runs, five successful rolls, and two swims.

After the center closed that evening, Rob and I strolled down the side of the channel. Each night, the center turned off the pumps, and all the water drained down to the bottom pool. As we walked, we stopped at each rapid, now so quiet and benign. Rob took my finger and pointed to the concrete features and rubber pylons that created the rapids. They were now totally exposed. Sunset, the first rapid after the middle pool, was created by a steep concrete ramp running into a concave boxy hole. Then came the devious M-Wave. At full flow, it was two lateral waves crashing together in a chaotic pile; if you saw it from above, upstream, it would look like a downriver-facing M. Two gates pinched the flow into a tight narrow tongue. After the gates, the water fanned out and rebounded off underwater structures and came back onto itself. Immediately afterward, Shut Down made a fierce river-wide hole, consisting of another sharp drop-off. The line-up ended with Biscuits and Gravy, formed by a series of underwater structures that twisted the channel left and right into two steep waves coming from different directions. They were a one-two knockout blow before you dropped into the calm bottom pool.

As Rob described the bottom of this man-made channel, it struck me what a rare opportunity we had to study the features that created so much energy and turbulence on the surface. On wild rivers, those boulders, drop-offs, and narrow pinches between rocks were covered by rushing water, but now revealed and decoded, they felt a little less menacing.

The next morning, the head of the kayak school talked me into swimming the channel. We put on our PFDs, and he swam in front of me, looking back and yelling, "Swim right . . . more right! Get your feet up! Here it comes!" As I hit each rapid, I quickly got the knack of holding my breath as it sucked me down and held me under for a few seconds before finally releasing me on the other side. Afterward, we got into a tandem kayak with me in front, and he steered me through the entire course, further bolstering my confidence.

Back home again, the No Barriers / Global Explorers merger was happening surprisingly fast. There were piles and piles of things to be completed, and Dave threw himself into the process with ferocity. He laid out an aggressive

plan that would take us step by step to become one organization within eighteen months. It would consist of a trial period in which Dave would be putting
together the foundation: budgets and insurance, staffing plans and fund-
raising plans, all new branding, assessments of each side's strengths and weak-
nesses, and layers upon layers of legal paperwork. Dave insisted on a separation
policy, to enable us to divorce equitably in case it didn't work out.

"We're like fiancés in love," I joked. "Hope we don't need an annulment."

A friend of my father put up some seed money to keep us afloat during
the formation of the merger. Everything was moving forward. I was blown
away when Dave boldly made the decision to give up the name Global Explorers and become No Barriers. In the give-and-take, he only invited three
No Barriers board members to join the merged organization. It stung to have
to tell three directors who had been there almost from the beginning that
they couldn't go forward with us.

Tom Lillig, from Dave's team, ran an advertising agency, and he was
tasked with helping us to develop our new branding. He conducted interviews with both groups and carefully examined the two organizations. Tom
met with us and presented his team's ideas. "I like the current tagline of No
Barriers," he said, then read it aloud: "'*What's in your way*?' I really like that
question it asks," he continued. "It acknowledges that there are real barriers
in front of us and that there are ways through them. But the problem is that
questions are passive. We need a proclamation, something that states, at our
core, what we believe in. Another problem is that it overlooks the second part
of the equation."

"What do you mean?" Dave asked.

"Erik, I remember you referring to an internal light that exists in people.
Well, I think that's what's missing—the second half of the equation. Whether
you call it a light, or a soul, or the human spirit, it's all predicated on the
belief that inside us there's something that exists, a real thing that we can
tap into, that we can grow. And it can grow so strong it can transcend those
very real barriers in our way. So we've tried to fill in that second half. So here
it goes . . ." He paused and then read it aloud: "What's within you is stronger
than what's in your way."

That night, I shared the quote with Ellie in one of our regular hot tub sessions. Like me, she loved it. Then I broached a topic I'd been sweating over for a month, ever since the beginning of the merger. "How hard are you supposed to believe in something?" I asked.

"Depends on what it is," she said. "How much did Sabriye believe? How much did Hugh believe? How much did Kyle believe?"

That answered my question loud and clear, and the next day, I excitedly shared with Dave what I wanted to do. "We're going to need some serious money to really jump-start this thing. I want to raise a million dollars for No Barriers. I don't have anywhere near that kind of money, but I'll donate all my speaking fees, and I'll reach out to all my contacts and any groups I've spoken to before to let them know what we are trying to achieve. I don't know how long it will take, but I pledge not to stop until I reach my goal."

On my third trip to the Whitewater Center, I was finally getting into a rhythm. After Entrance Exam, I'd cut hard right into an eddy and regroup. Then we'd charge out, making the delicate turn downriver. If I didn't turn enough, I'd blast into a narrow eddy on the other side and slam into the wall. Turn too much and I'd crash off another wall and be bounced sideways into a succession of powerful, topsy-turvy waves. In the big pool, I'd eddy out again and take another rest. The biggest and most difficult rapids I would face all loomed below, and finally, I could no longer postpone the inevitable.

"Ready to do this thing?" Casey asked. It was the exact same question he'd asked before I took my disastrous first run at the Whitewater Center. I pulled out into the channel and headed down. Casey had told me about a hose that shot a plume of cold water into the middle of the channel. "If it hits you, you'll know you're lined up right."

I felt the spray hit the top of my helmet just before I entered the first series of waves. Then I crashed into Sunset, which punched me hard, and I went over but managed to roll up immediately. Next up was M-Wave. Casey said that we needed to hit it on the left and use the force of the rapid to bump us slightly to the right and into the main flow. It was a turbulent storm of white water, and I entered at the wrong angle. The force drove me hard to the left into a crazy swirling eddy. It happened so fast; Casey missed it entirely, shot

past, and was gone. I spun around and around, getting disoriented and slamming off the jetty below me. I almost flipped but managed to recover. Having no voice commands, I paddled as hard as I could toward the roar of
M-Wave, which I figured was upriver. The eddy fence grabbed my bow, spun
me around, and slammed me sideways into the next rapid, aptly named
Shut Down, which flipped me with what felt like a violent shove. My helmet
cracked hard against the shallow concrete bottom. I was trapped in a hole. I
pushed my paddle up near the surface, and the recirculating hole shot me
upright, but I was instantly over again. I rolled and flipped several more times
in quick succession. On my fourth rotation, I felt my veneer of confidence
wash away. I pulled my spray skirt and swam.

That evening, Rob and I sat on the edge of the channel, feeling the sun
sink lower in the sky. I noticed how quiet it was when then pumps had been
shut off for the night.

"You're improving a lot," he said, "but I still sense a hesitation in you.
Think about it like skiing. They tell you to lean down the hill, but that seems
so counterintuitive, like the last thing you want to do. But skiers know that if
you commit and lean down the mountain, your skis will come around into a
beautiful turn. Paddling's the same. If you paddle like you're expecting to flip
all the time, it makes you timid. You'll feel it in your paddle strokes, in the
way you lean, in the way you turn. It's a funny thing, because the more defensive you are, the worse you'll paddle and the more you'll flip. But if you
paddle aggressively, you'll charge through those waves."

The next morning, I walked out of the changing room and knew something was up. Rob and the head kayak instructor were conspiring in the
corner.

"Big E, check out all these boats," Rob started.

He walked me around the storage room and, in typical Rob fashion, had
me touch all the different boats sitting on the racks. There were boats of every
size and shape, some with sharp noses like the fin of a shark, and some with
fat, stubby bows. Some were long and skinny. Others were giant tanks. Some
had smooth, round surfaces, and others had sharp angles.

"In all your training, you've only tried one boat," he said.

He was right. I'd bought a boat early on, and I'd grown used to it, bringing it faithfully to the center each trip.

"The Whitewater Center is the perfect place to experiment," he continued, "to try a lot of boats and test them out. You know the course at this point, so now you can change small variables and come away with what works best for you."

Rob was pushing as always, and I pushed back. I hadn't even made it down the full course without swimming, and that was with the boat I knew.

"No. I think I'm good," I replied.

Rob continued deliberating on the upside of trying new boats, but while he talked about the different choices, all I could think about was the downside. Sure. In theory, a new boat might work better, but that was all speculation. What if it didn't work better? What if it were worse? I didn't really like my current boat, but I was a person of systems and repetition. My pre-kayak ritual looked the same every time. I adjusted my seat to exactly the right tightness, snug enough to allow my knees to bury into the knee braces and my feet to press against the bulkhead, but not tight enough to hold me in if I needed to swim. I'd ratchet my seat to the perfect position. I'd count the plastic ridges on each side to determine whether both sides were even. It had to be eighteen clicks of the ratchet on each side, eighteen ridges on the plastic tabs that I could touch and count. I knew the rest of the boat too, even for all its flaws. I knew the flatter bottom made it tippy. It had a bow that sliced into the rapids in a grabby way that often flipped me, even in smaller rapids. I knew all the ways it fell short, and that knowledge had been earned the hard way, through a thousand hours of flipping, swimming, crashing into rocks and gasping for air, and countless mornings spent with my heart exploding out of my chest, trying to choke back the dread that burned in my throat and threatened to send my breakfast spewing back out. It wasn't just a boat. It represented everything I had been working for, everything I had gained up to this point. Now, Rob was trying to open yet another door and shove me through it. Behind me was what I knew, but through the door was just more darkness and fear. The intellectual side of my brain told me I couldn't be seriously injured at the Whitewater Center. The worst thing was a swim, resulting in bloody knees and elbows; but if it didn't work, if it led to disaster, that door might close, this time for good, and snap the fragile hope I was clinging to.

As usual, Rob was relentless. As I kept arguing against it, I knew I was being worn down. If I dug in any more, it would be bordering on obstinacy. Finally, when I was convinced I was outplayed, I succumbed. I started with a boat similar to mine and began adding new variables each run. "I think you may like this one," Rob said as I slid into a boat a bit shorter than mine with a fat bow. As I paddled, I found myself riding smoothly through the rapids. The bow had so much volume; I'd bust through the waves and quickly resurface on the other side. Even when I got sideways, the round surface was more forgiving and kept me upright long enough to throw a hard brace. I was feeling more confident as I paddled through rapids that had previously felt violent and explosive. Now I bobbed through them like a cork. I had my first complete run that afternoon—no flips, no swims.

As I headed home to Colorado, allegations were all over the news that Greg Mortenson of the Central Asia Institute was flying around on private planes and using his charitable organization to sell his book and keep it on the Best Seller List. There were even accusations that parts of his book had been fabricated. It was all blowing open. Greg was a climber who had turned to building schools for girls in Afghanistan. He had good intentions and was raising millions through his reputation and celebrity, but somewhere along the way, it seemed that the line between his personal life and his organization got blurred. His organization was in serious jeopardy of collapsing. Dave sent me the article as if to say, "We can't have this happening to us."

"I'm not Greg Mortenson," I insisted, "and we're not the Central Asia Institute." But Dave's reservations settled in, and the topic entered almost every conversation.

"This won't be the Erik Weihenmayer Foundation," he warned me, and I was a little affronted.

"I never intended to wrap No Barriers around my finger," I assured him. "The whole reason for this merger is to build something that doesn't die when you and I die."

As we dove into a sea of details, I began noticing Dave's reservations. Soon, small, manageable situations began blowing out of proportion, and there seemed to be an invisible barrier between us. If an outsider had asked Dave or me about our vision for the future, our answers would have looked remarkably the same, but you wouldn't know it from our conversations. The final straw came on a committee meeting as we planned the upcoming Summit in Telluride. The committee was made up of two directors and two staff members. I said, "It would be exciting to have the attendees get together for a breakfast and do a No Barriers activity together. I think that would be unifying for our new community to understand the No Barriers message."

"Erik," one of the staff members responded, "we've got a Summit to plan here, and every time you throw out a new idea, it distracts us from our real job."

I was caught off guard. Our former No Barriers culture had been a stark contrast to this new one. We had prided ourselves on being direct and honest. We thrived on dreaming about the future and generating ideas how to get there, yet that process had just been abruptly shut down. My assessment was that our new culture suffered a fatal flaw. They lacked metacognition, the ability of knowing what you didn't know.

It was a lesson I'd learned while training for my first of the Seven Summits, Denali, in Alaska. Until that point, I'd been primarily a rock climber, knowing almost nothing about big glaciated mountains. I'd committed to attempting Denali in fifteen months. It was a steep learning curve, not just going from A to B, but A to Z, in just over a year. Not wasting time, I reached out to every mountain expert I knew, or had ever known, and asked them to take us under their wing. I couldn't afford to bluff my way through, and it was a vulnerable feeling to know so little, but in that short window, I came away knowing everything from rope travel to self-arrests to hauling injured climbers out of crevasses. It was a process that could have taken ten years, but by the time we left for Denali, I was ready.

I knew if you possessed metacognition, it meant the fast track to growth, but it required being comfortable with the fact that you didn't have a clue. If you lacked it, then ideas and questions became threats, and you were doomed to blunder forward, unwilling to accept help and repeating the same mistakes.

On the surface, it appeared as defensiveness, even arrogance, but I knew it derived from fear. While the No Barriers staff was planning youth activities, an area well within their expertise, everything went smoothly. Yet now that they were being pulled in directions they didn't fully understand, cracks were beginning to appear.

When I expressed my opinion to Dave, the conversation degraded into barking at each other. I told Dave that he wasn't listening, and Dave lectured me about the difference between board and staff roles. He accused me of trying to exert too much influence on the organization. Without discussion, he made a decision to dismiss the summit planning committee. Now I was fuming. In confidence, one of Dave's directors told me that his board had met to weigh the merits of a possible merger. Dave had told them the organization was in a difficult place. Growth was stagnant, and although the youth programs brought in revenue, the organization was just squeaking by month to month. He told the board he was going to resign. There was a possibility Global Explorers would fold.

"I've invested everything," Dave said, his voice cracking, "and I'm watching my life's dream fall apart." I had proactively chosen Dave and his organization, but now I wondered whether he'd chosen us, in turn, out of belief or desperation. As it all devolved, I got a note from Dave explaining that we'd had too many disagreements and that the final merger decision would be postponed for twelve more months, past the original deadline: "Culture is paramount to the long-term success of any organization. We cannot in good faith approve a merger outright until we determine if we can fix organizational culture issues."

I felt all our work, all the momentum slipping away. Dave served as the intermediary between his Global Explorers team and mine, No Barriers. Ultimately, both entities would need to vote unanimously to sign on the dotted line. Back and forth the accusations went, and suspicions grew. It reminded me of our Tibet team and the sub-factions that had arisen and almost torn us apart from the inside out.

"No one is communicating," I complained to Dave. "Maybe I'm oversimplifying this," I said, "but why don't we just get our two sides together and talk this thing out? Maybe we can get to the source of our barriers. We've got to become one team—not Dave's team, not Erik's team. We've come too far to turn back." But Dave was unwilling to bring the factions together.

On my subsequent trips to the kayak center, my heavy anxiety about flipping began to lift. I noticed my energy level rising and my focus sharpening. In the middle of the action, I felt my awareness expanding. I started to hear the rapids and comprehend their shapes, to lean in against the waves that tried to shove me back, to anticipate the jarring currents and fight against them. I was rarely flipping these days, but once I came into M-Wave a little crooked, flipped, and was upside down in the heart of the two crashing waves. As my helmet slammed the concrete bottom, I almost reached for the tab on my spray skirt, but I could feel time slowing down. *Hang on*, I told myself. *Hold on a few seconds longer.*

I lifted my paddle toward the roiling surface and popped up, riding and dropping through the energy beneath my boat. Casey began teaching me skills like a "boof." In Shut Down, Casey would yell, "Boof!" and I'd reach my paddle over the trough, grab the backside of the wave, and launch myself up and over. He taught me to charge upstream into a crashing wave, and by leaning just right, surf it left and then back right. I hated the fact that I wasn't able to hear Casey's commands in the rapids, so we again started experimenting with different radio systems, different headsets, different microphones. I also began to perfect my ferries, an essential river skill, in which I charged out of the eddy, broke through the eddy line, and—at precisely the right upriver angle—used the current to surge across the channel. It was a science to lean in the right direction while the forces of the river grabbed your boat and tried to flip you. At the end of a long day, we busted through Biscuits and Gravy into the bottom pool. Casey gave me a high five.

"You're crushing it," he said, "but you know what the coolest part is? You've got a smile on your face."

At No Barriers, we had finally scheduled an in-person board retreat, and as it approached, I was increasingly disheartened. Dave wanted to bring in an outside consultant who could facilitate us through our troubles. I suggested Paul Stoltz and his partner, Jeff. Dr. Stoltz had coauthored my second book, *The Adversity Advantage*, and he was an expert on organizational culture.

As our meeting came to order, I said, "I know it looks uncertain ahead, and we've had some growing pains, but this idea is bigger than us. We ask our youth and vets to trust us and believe in the future. We ask our donors to do the same, but when it comes right down to it, we don't trust it ourselves."

George Heinricks, the CEO of a high-tech company, piped in, "We are like two people getting married and now we've gotten cold feet and are constantly delaying the wedding. In fact, it's turning into the longest engagement in history."

"There's an elephant in the room here," our facilitator, Paul, added. "If you don't confront it, then everything else ahead is kind of meaningless. I have a sobering reality to share with you today," he continued. "Most mergers fail. Our colleagues at Harvard tell us 80 percent of organizations that set out to achieve a successful merger fall short or fail outright. And culture change is like rehab: The more you try and fail, the lower your chances. By definition, you have to become statistical outliers, the weird ones who beat the odds and succeed. So I ask you not to see this as an exercise in culture change. This is your defining moment, the first real substantive step in your No Barriers quest."

The room was dead silent. "I just don't think we're ready," a director finally stated. "The branding work has barely begun. Our bylaws aren't finished, and we have reams of legal paperwork to complete."

"We also have two very different cultures, and it's going to be a lot of work to truly integrate them," another added.

"Is that the real source of the pain?" Paul asked quietly. "Is there anything else?"

Julie, from Dave's team, spoke up. "From my perspective, we have a good little organization here," she said. "We serve youth, and we know what we're doing and why we exist. I remember when I led one of my first youth trips. It was to Costa Rica. We camped out in the jungle and spent most of the night lying on our backs looking up at the night sky and noticing all the constellations. One of the girls on the trip was from the inner city of Chicago. She was a first-generation American. She told me it was the first time in her life she'd seen the stars." Her voice broke as she continued on, "A few years ago, she graduated from college, the first in her family. So I know we're here to talk about the future of No Barriers, but we're throwing everything into something that's not even real, and all I keep thinking about is what we may be losing."

I didn't blame her. In fact, my heart ached with all she was feeling and trying to understand. She was being asked to leave something she had known, had given birth to, something she had cherished and believed in. It didn't matter in the slightest that it couldn't last, that it probably would have died. None of that mattered, because it represented the sum total of her life thus far. She had known her purpose and could see it as brightly as the stars in the night sky. Now we were moving ahead toward something, but no matter how well we tried to articulate it, nobody could say for certain where it would lead. There was something fundamentally human, I acknowledged, about letting go and trying to embrace something you cannot see. Hugh Herr called this "believing without seeing; having faith in a future that has not yet occurred."

"If we move forward," I said, "lots of things will be in flux, but youth will always be a part of No Barriers. If we do this thing well, we'll give many more kids a chance to see those stars, I promise."

That seemed to break open the floodgates. Everyone began talking at once. In the midst of the excitement, Tom Lillig got up and said, "I'll be right back," and he sprinted out the door. Ten minutes later he reemerged panting and covered in sweat. He held a bottle of champagne and a stack of plastic glasses in his hands. He popped the cork, and it sailed across the room. A couple of minutes later, we signed the papers and became No Barriers. Everyone raised their plastic glasses, and we toasted to the future. But I thought, partly, we were toasting to ourselves and that we had just broken through a barrier of our own.

As I headed out of the boardroom and toward the bathroom, I noticed that Julie had stepped out ahead of me and had joined another woman in the hallway. They were standing close together whispering. Their voices were so close, I thought they were actually holding each other, and I could hear that they were crying softly. I hurried by, puzzled why they were tucked away in the hallway having a somber moment while the rest of the board celebrated. Then it hit me, like crashing into the M-Wave. I knew I had just stolen upon a private moment as they mourned their loss. Something about the scene made me think about my old boat, now tucked away in my crawl space. It had been a good boat, and I had known every inch of it. Eighteen clicks of the ratchet got my seat just right. There were so many things that were unknown, who could blame me for clinging on to that feeling of safety and comfort a little too long? That boat had served me well, but it could only take me so far. Passing by the women as they were hugging, crying, and saying good-bye to Global Explorers, I knew exactly how they felt.

19

THE OTHER BLIND GUY

By the summer of 2012, I felt like I was making an inkling of progress. I'd gotten back on Clear Creek, near my house, and on sections of the Colorado River like Radium and Shoshone. I was even planning a big training trip down the Rio Marañón at the headwaters of the Amazon. I'd heard that some of the canyon walls there are nearly ten thousand feet high on both sides. It's no wonder it was dubbed the Grand Canyon of South America.

In early September I'd just come off a training trip with my team on Westwater Canyon of the Colorado. We'd kayaked eighteen miles in a day, farther than I'd ever paddled, and through some fierce rapids like Skull, named for a sharp dagger-spine of rock in the middle that's best to avoid. I'd slipped between a crazy eddy fence and the Skull rock, clipping the sharp surface with my right elbow. Lower down, I had blasted through some punchy holes and was starting to feel solid. Our radios were working for now, and my directions and reactions were getting in sync with the commands. As we drove out of the expansive desert, we got back into cell coverage. My friend Steve Mace pulled out his phone and checked Facebook.

"Erik. You're not going to believe this," he said. "But some other blind guy just kayaked the Grand Canyon—at least that's what this press release says. His name is Lonnie Bedwell, and he's a farmer from Indiana and a retired navy veteran."

First I thought it was a joke, but then when he didn't laugh, my smile went limp, replaced by flat-out shock. I couldn't believe it. From the beginning, as I had learned to kayak, slamming into rocks, flipping my boat, and swimming through rapids, I'd end each day with an ongoing pronouncement: "At least I learned something today . . . I learned exactly why there aren't any other blind kayakers in the world." But even though it was a joke, I had built a life around being the first, a trailblazer, and had gotten used to it. In fact, when Rob had once said, "There are seven billion people on earth, and you're the only blind whitewater kayaker," I had to admit, my ego had swelled. As we drove, my defense mechanisms kicked into gear: Maybe he could actually see, at least a little bit. He's faking it. Maybe he'd gotten in a raft for part of the descent. Maybe he had skipped some of the big ones like Crystal and Lava. There had to be an explanation other than a blind farmer from Indiana had just scooped me.

On our last trip to the Whitewater Center, Rob had used the squirrel strategy to talk me into going down the Grand Canyon on a scouting mission. "Grand Canyon rapids are orders of magnitude bigger than anything you've experienced so far," he said. "You could probably just go and do it, but that's a very big leap."

He was right about a recon trip. It was a really good idea. I'd told him many times, and my goal wasn't just to survive the Grand Canyon. You don't learn much from barely surviving, from squeaking through by the skin of your teeth. I wanted to earn the right to be there, to take everything the river could throw at me, and thrive in that frenzied environment.

He continued, "So why not go down the canyon and kayak a few of the biggies? Then you'll have more confidence and you'll know whether this is realistic or not. It'll still be a leap, but it's the most incremental leap you can take to move to the next level. It's what a squirrel would do," he finished.

So for eleven days, we'd gone down the canyon in a giant thirty-seven-foot J-rig, two giant inflatable tubes connected by a welded metal frame. Rob said it looked like a pack of hot dogs. The boat had a thirty-horsepower motor, just enough power to thrust its snout in the right direction as it blasted through rapids. The river guides had drawn out a map for Rob with the rapids I might like to try. The boat would motor us through the flat sections, and just as the roar came into range, we'd slither into our kayaks and seal launch off the side tubes, dropping into the white water. I can't say I was excelling, but I was pleasantly surprised that I survived some of the giants.

One of the big tests was Granite. No two rapids are made alike. Each has its own distinct character. Some are like riding massive ocean swells so steep they crest, collapse, and crash over you. Some rapids present a massive hole that must be avoided at all costs, and others are a one-two punch and then you're through. But Granite was known for being violent, like going into the ring with Mike Tyson. There was no gentle bobbing through splashy waves with a "Yee-haw!" at the bottom. On the river map the guides had sketched for Rob, he wrote, "Granite: Erik will flip at least twice and will emerge upside down."

When Rob read me those notes, I felt sick. It turns out they weren't exaggerating. I paddled into Granite and it was like riding the back of a *Tyrannosaurus rex*, mad and foaming with rage. The smooth tongue was deceptive as it led me downward and abruptly spilled me over a huge drop, right into a maelstrom. A succession of lateral waves immediately blasted over me from both sides, striking me like fists. The massive waves crashed against the right wall and smashed back at me. I was punched from waves coming from the left. Then from the right again, and then more lefts. As I furiously hurled my body back and forth, bracing my paddle against the laterals, I was simultaneously diving into deep, gaping holes that, like the mouth of the *T. rex*, grabbed and tried to chew off the bow of my boat.

When I emerged on the other side upright, sucking in air and collapsing my body over the front of my kayak, I was as surprised as I had ever been. When I'd summited Mount Everest, although I knew it was a huge endeavor, I was convinced it was repeatable. *Someday*, I thought, *another blind person will stand up here. It's within the realm of possibility.* But below Granite, still shaking with adrenaline, I laughed—and it came out as a snort, with snot and river water spewing from my nose. There wasn't a chance in hell any other blind person would ever subject themselves to the insanity of Granite. My goal to be the first blind kayaker down the Grand Canyon was totally safe.

I couldn't get over how completely wrong I had been. Part of me wanted to be happy for this Lonnie guy. It wasn't all about being first, I thought. This was a sign that blind people were coming on strong, breaking through barriers, surpassing expectations, even my own accomplishments. It was a good thing for the world, I told myself, but close up, it still stung. I had already received a lot of media attention surrounding my kayaking—in *Outside*, *Men's Journal*, even *The New York Times*. I had garnered some new kayaking sponsors. I felt deflated and a little embarrassed. All the endless hours of training and bleeding may have been for nothing.

As rare as blind kayakers and blind climbers are, I'd actually experienced a similar situation before, a story that would have been perfect for an episode of *Ripley's Believe It or Not!* Right after our second No Barriers Summit in Cortina, Italy, I'd stayed after the event to climb a few days in the Dolomites with my climbing partner, Mike O'Donnell, one of my Mount Everest teammates. The famous Tre Cime towers were colossal, jaw-dropping vertical spires, with dozens of choices for routes depending on their difficulty and the temperature. For hot days, there were routes in the shade, and for cooler days, routes in the sun. It was a chilly day in July, so on the spot, we picked a south-facing route called the Yellow Edge—Spigolo Giallo in Italian—and by 8:00 A.M. were several pitches up. Suddenly, I heard the whir of a helicopter just behind me, too close to the face, and it made me twitch. I cursed under my breath as I yelled to an Italian team to our left, "Do you know what the helicopter is doing? Is there a rescue?"

They called back in heavily accented English, "They are filming the blind man."

That's impossible, I thought. *Nobody even knows I'm here.* We'd just picked the route this morning.

Puzzled, I kept climbing and tried to focus on the challenging climb in front of me. At each belay station, Mike and I discussed possible explanations for the helicopter, but neither of us had a clue. An hour later, Mike was pulling in my rope above me. "There's a nice ledge up here," he called down. When I pulled over the top, Mike said something almost assuredly never heard before high up on a rock face: "You're not going to believe this, but there's another blind guy on this ledge."

"Come on!" was all I could say.

"I'm dead serious," Mike went on. "A blind Austrian is making a documentary."

"I guess that explains the helicopter," I added.

"There are also a couple of camera guys hanging from ropes, and a couple of other climbing guides," he continued. "Looks like a pretty big production."

I traversed along the ledge and heard a group of climbers talking heatedly in German. Then one of them was pushed forward, and a voice rang out, sounding very serious, a little like Arnold Schwarzenegger in *The Terminator*: "Who is ziss blint mahn? Vot iss hiss name?"

I imagined his situation, organizing a complicated and, most likely, expensive film shoot, involving months of training for an audacious undertaking. The mood is supposed to be one of awe: Look at this amazing blind man climbing a giant Dolomite tower. On game day, the helicopters are swarming. The cameras are all in position. "It's impossible . . ." "It's unheard of . . ." and then *another* blind guy pops casually onto your ledge. "Hey, everyone. Funny meeting you here."

You'd surely think it was a grand plan—to sabotage it all on purpose. A random meeting of two blind climbers on the side of a rock face was impossible. No wonder, I realized, he was speaking to me in the third person.

"My name is Erik," I replied.

Now, at least talking directly to me, he asked, "How hard do you climb?"

"Maybe 5.11," I answered, starting to feel I was under interrogation.

"Do you lead climb?" he asked.

"Sometimes," I answered.

"What is your training regimen?" the third degree continued.

I thought for a minute, then blurted out, "Strudel!" and patted my belly.

I heard his climbing guides huddling and repeating the word *strudel* like they were trying to decipher this new cutting-edge training diet from America. Then one said louder, "Ah! *Apfelstrudel*." And they all broke into laughter. That seemed to break the tension, but he had one last question to close out his cross-examination.

"What is the highest thing you've have ever climbed?"

"Mount Everest," I said.

"Ah, *yah*!" he said, now animated, his voice becoming lighter. "You are the Mount Everest Erik." Then he finally stepped forward, and he found my hand and shook it vigorously. "My name is Andy Holzer. Good to meet you, Everest Erik."

For the rest of the day, we climbed right behind Andy and his party. I found we both climbed about the same level and at equal speed. In the late afternoon, Mike and I topped out and met Andy on the tiny summit, the size of three dining room tables stacked end to end. Andy and I sat together, eating our snacks.

"Andy," I said, "I hear it's a long rappel down with a lot of loose rocks. What do you know about it?"

He conferred in German with his team and then said in a sly voice, "Erik, I have a surprise for you . . . I'd like you to be a guest in my helicopter."

The next few minutes were a blur as the small helicopter rose up from the valley, hovered for a moment, and then gently lowered the back of its skids onto the edge of the rock. The wind buffeted the helicopter up and down as the pilot tried to hold his position. Two of Andy's guides grabbed my arms and led me toward the chopper. I reached out and found the rope ladder with my hands, climbed it, and fell into the cabin that was tipped downward at a forty-five-degree angle. More people and gear piled in behind me, and we squeezed in as the back door slammed shut. Without warning, we dropped out of the sky, my stomach rising and trying to escape from my mouth. It seemed as though we were in free fall for a dizzying minute, and I was getting extremely nervous, but it finally leveled out on a cushion of soft air, and we gently touched down. I exited into an alpine meadow outside a Rifugio. Andy's wife, who had been following the activity through the radio, stepped forward and greeted me with an enthusiastic hug. She handed me and Andy steins of beer, and we did what two blind guys always do when they meet halfway up a rock face: We raised our glasses and tried to clink them together. We got it right on the third try, and his team, along with Mike, all cheered.

"Erik," Andy said, "we are like blind brothers."

"Like brothas from anotha motha," I replied. That one was lost on him.

Then I continued, "Andy, I'd like to make another toast—to climbing with you again someday. Just one request: You have to bring the helicopter."

A few months later Andy called me with another surprise. He wanted me to return to the Dolomites so that we could climb another difficult face together. But "this time" he added, "no sighted people. Only blinds."

How could I turn down such a request? So the next spring I was back in the Dolomites, this time on the Austrian side of the border in an area near where Andy lived in Linz. Andy had a route picked out, the Red Tower, five rope lengths and one of his favorites. He'd climbed it many times. The day before our solo climb, we ascended it with a sighted friend, so I could memorize the way as it traversed right and left, over rock roofs, up a wide chimney, over a ridge, and down into a narrow gully that led to the top plateau. I memorized the tricky moves: where to place the metal gear in the pockets and cracks to prevent a fall and the best places to stop to set up an anchor and belay the other up.

On our big day, we stood gearing up at the base of the climb, readying for our ascent. Andy said, "Erik, give me your hand. Best of luck for the next hours ahead," and I squeezed his palm in friendship. We'd come a long way since our first meeting. In the vernacular of climbing, Andy and I "swung leads," meaning we took turns leading up the face with the rope trailing, until we found a good spot to stop and bring the other up. Each of us had to feel our way upward, every couple of meters finding small fissures to jam in the metal protection. Because I was Andy's guest, he gave me the hardest section to lead, a steep face with a big overhanging roof to surmount. Under the roof I paused for a long time, not wanting to go any farther without placing some gear. My hands scanned all around the rock, desperately trying to remember where the crack had been. Finally, I yelled down, "Andy, I can't find anywhere to place a piece here!"

Turns out, Andy was blessed with a photographic memory. He yelled back, "I've given you about twelve feet of rope, so I think you are under the roof now. If you reach your left hand up one foot and three feet to the left, I think you will find an old piton hammered into the rock. It is a good one."

I scanned my palm along the smooth stone, and there it was, right where he said it would be. Finding the piton and clipping in gave me the confidence to climb up over the roof. Above, I got to a ledge and belayed Andy up. He took the next lead, up a strange chimney that got wider and wider. Ultimately he had to tiptoe out left onto a blank face and find pitons that were pounded into tiny thin seams in a sea of rock. Thank God he took that section, I thought. I could have never found those pitons. Andy let me take the last lead. I popped over the ridge and found the correct gulley system to top us out.

From there, the adventure wasn't over. We still had to traverse across a wide, flat plateau and over a gaping rock crevasse to gain another higher buttress. Somewhere on that second formation was a two-meter-high metal cross, wired down and bolted to the rock that marked the true summit. The other challenge was that the only way to rappel off the summit was the same way we had climbed up. One specific gulley was the only way down. Choose the wrong one, and we'd rappel into space and quickly run out of rope. So we placed some gear in a groove between two large boulders and made an anchor just above the gulley. We clipped our rope to it and trailed it behind us as we traversed the flat plateau. I told Andy, "We're like Hansel and Gretel from the Grimms' Fairy Tales, trailing our rope behind us like bread crumbs to find our way home." From then on, I became Hansel and Andy became Gretel as we called back and forth, looking for the way across the crevasse. In one precise spot a giant boulder had been lodged in the crevasse, creating a natural bridge. You had to find this boulder bridge, or the crevasse was too wide to cross: If you missed it, you'd drop hundreds of feet to the valley floor. I had brought a trekking pole and used it to feel over the lip of the crevasse, while Andy held a pile of small rocks in his hand and strategically threw them over the edge, trying to pinpoint the strike against the rock bridge. "Hansel, I think it's over to the left," Andy said.

"No, Gretel, I think it's to the right," I countered, feeling something solid as I probed my pole outward.

We scrambled over the wedged boulder and gained the final buttress. Andy crabbed his way to the cross, clicking with his tongue and sending echoes against the metal frame. When I arrived seconds later, Andy gave me a big hug.

"Congratulations, my friend. We have reached a summit together, two blinds."

Then he took my finger and pointed it over the edge. "Somewhere down there is my house and my wife. She is waving up at us. Do you see her, Erik?" He laughed.

"Yes. I can hear her too," I replied. "Yodel-ay-hee-hoo," I called out over the valley. "I can also smell dinner cooking. I think she's making Wiener schnitzel. I'm starving."

The night before, Andy and I had listened to the documentary filmed when we had first met. He had translated as the German voice-over announced Andy Holzer, famous blind climber, attacking the infamous Spigolo Giallo. Then, suddenly, I appear on the ledge, and the voice-over adds quizzically, "Now, a second blind climber joins Holzer. He is American Everest climber Erik Weihenmayer."

"I was a little angry when I met you that day," Andy admitted. "I thought, *Who is this other blind man here to ruin my outing?* Then I thought we would be trying to best each other, you and I, but that was not the case."

He was right. It would have been natural for our relationship to be competitive, but for some reason, it had never felt that way. In fact, Andy had pegged it after stepping out of the helicopter together, like "two blind brothers."

Rather than seeing him as a threat, I had felt deep kinship with Andy: how he'd been born blind in a small Austrian village, and how his family would not let him be left behind; how they were afraid but had made the courageous decision to allow him to go into the mountains for the very first time. Not climbers themselves, they had helped him pack his rucksack and had stood on the porch to see him off as a neighbor had led him toward his first rock face. I loved comparing notes on our techniques, both developed in isolation. Andy had a curious scurrying style of movement with his hands dropped low on holds and pushing his body upward, while I reached high and scanned my hands methodically until I'd found just the right series of holds to connect the dots. I loved that we could both find the bridge over the crevasse, me with a trekking pole and Andy with a handful of rocks. And most of all, I loved that two total strangers had grown up in remarkably different places on the globe, yet with parallel lives that had brought them to the mountains one day, at the exact same time and the exact same place. And now we were friends, standing together as equals, touching the very same metal cross high above his house. I had been to peaks all around the world, to the summits of much harder mountains and much higher mountains. The same went for Andy. But reaching the top together ranked as one of the proudest and most satisfying moments of my life. It was hard to explain, but I understood that my life was richer for having met Andy.

So now driving east on I-70 toward home, I thought about all the massive preparation it had taken to get ready for this kayaking project: multiple trips to the Green River, the Usumacinta in Mexico, the U.S. National Whitewater Center, and hundreds of hours training on my local rivers. It had taken everything I had to keep going. And now, just as it was feeling within reach, some other blind man had popped onto my ledge. *Who is this other blind kayaker here to ruin my outing?* I asked silently, and in my head, I sounded a little like Arnold Schwarzenegger. But an idea was beginning to brew, and as it got stronger, I could feel energy and motivation returning to my body. *When I get home*, I thought, *maybe I'll give this guy, this Lonnie Bedwell from Indiana, a call.*

20

THE BLINDEST MAN IN THE WORLD

Back at home, I called Lonnie Bedwell to congratulate him on his successful trip and asked him if he'd like to meet that spring at the U.S. National Whitewater Center. Lonnie was game and agreed right away. When Rob and I arrived, Lonnie and his kayaking partner were waiting in front of the gear room. I heard Lonnie's country accent, with the little hint of a joke always present in his crackly voice. We'd been together just a couple of minutes when he asked, "Erik, what's the scariest thing you can do to a blind person?"

"Put them in a kayak in the middle of white water?" I immediately answered.

"No. That's second." He laughed. "The scariest thing is when someone puts a plunger in the toilet without telling you," he answered, bursting into his raspy guffaw.

Over the next few days, Lonnie and I took runs down the channel, and I noticed how different our kayaking styles were. Lonnie wasn't a high-tech guy. He told me he didn't have a cell phone. He didn't use radios for kayaking, but instead preferred one guide right in front of him yelling at the top of his lungs, "On me! On me!" He had another kayaker just behind him yelling micro-commands like "Small left! Small right!" If Lonnie was off-line, his front guide borrowed military language to yell, "Gun sights on me!" Lonnie told me his front guide gave him more confidence to go out into the rapids, to have a sound to track.

Rob said our general paddling styles were very different as well. While I was methodical, measured, even cautious sometimes, Lonnie's style was frenzied. He took three paddle strokes for every one of mine, and he hardly ever hesitated, hunched forward like a water strider skittering over the surface. Both techniques seemed to work equally as well, but they also seemed to reflect our starkly different personalities.

"We should make a movie together!" I shouted over to Lonnie as we bobbed and circled around in an eddy. "We'll call it *The Redneck and the Gentleman*."

"I like the sound of that," he said, "but won't your family be a little upset that you're calling yourself a redneck?" and he broke into his signature cackle of a laugh.

Despite our differences, Lonnie and I shared one major attribute that connected our lives like glue. "I don't know about you," Lonnie said, "but I can't even describe it sometimes. They're telling you what to do, but trying to get through, just with that sound and trying to read the river by feel, I get so turned around, I hardly know which way is up or down."

I didn't have to stretch to know what he was saying. Kayaking blind was like riding an avalanche of moving water that shifted violently from second to second, tossing you in every direction. Trying to survive in that tumultuous environment guided only by the faint sound of a voice, by the roar of the river, and by what I could feel under my boat, it felt like sensory overload. It was the art of embracing chaos—and hands down the scariest thing I'd ever done.

On our next run, we stopped again in the same eddy, laughing over Lonnie's last epic battle with Shut Down. He'd gotten sideways and was caught in the fierce hole. He rolled up over and over, each time the unforgiving current knocking him over again and refusing to release him. Rob told me that when he emerged, he consistently had a big grin on his face. Another boat ultimately tried to come in and bump him out, but it must have jarred him, and he finally pulled his skirt and swam.

"I swam at Shut Down on my last visit," I said. "I came in too slow and got window-shaded and flipped so hard, I cracked my helmet against the concrete channel bottom. I swam out of my boat a lot sooner than you did. Oh yeah, and unlike you, I wasn't smiling."

"Yeah. That was one sweet ride," Lonnie said. "I was having more fun than a possum in a slop bucket—that is, until that other boat smacked me. I told my guide to send me right into the middle of that hole."

"Uh," I responded. "Why would you ever do that?"

"So I could figure out how to get out of it," he explained like he was talking to a simpleton.

Unlike me, who'd embraced the squirrel strategy, Lonnie seemed fearless. He was a true lion. "You may be the most badass blind guy I know!" I shouted over to him as our boats swirled and collided in the eddy.

That was no exaggeration. His family owned a farm in Dugger, Indiana, and over our lunch break, he talked about chainsawing trees and mowing his own pasture on the property, with no sighted assistance. "I'm out there with my mower most every day," he said, "mowing around my pond."

"How can you tell where you are in relation to the pond?" I asked.

"Oh, it's easy to tell," he replied, "when you hit the water. Mowing's nothing. After that, I started trying to figure out how to drive nails with my hammer. Hitting the nail wasn't a problem, but it was most often the nail at the end of my thumb. Once I figured that out, it led into building houses. I've helped build about thirty now: everything from framing to sheeting to wiring. I tell people, 'I'm your man—if you don't care if your lights turn on.' My favorite, though, is roofing."

"A blind guy kayaking is one thing," Rob piped in, "but a blind guy on a roof?"

"Yeah, people always question that," Lonnie replied. "They ask, 'What are you doing on that roof?' and I answer, 'I'm on a roof? How in blazes did I get up here?'"

Lonnie told us how he laid down the tarpaper and nailed the shingles by feel. "I only had one little mishap," he admitted. "There was a boy who was supposed to give me a shout when I was near the edge. One day I was walking up there, and he said, 'Left, left,' and I stepped right off the side. Broke my pelvis in two places. Turns out, he was a little distracted by two cute gals passing by." With that, Lonnie cracked up.

"Lonnie," I said, "you're one crazy dude. I think we're going to learn a lot from each other."

Similar to the way I felt with Andy Holzer, I was surprised I didn't feel more competitive around Lonnie. Pre-Lonnie, I had been the only blind kayaker, and being first had fed my sense of importance, my pride and ego, but now, I had to admit, there was another feeling washing over me, and it felt good. Of course, it was fun to compare our different approaches as well as the experiences that united us, but there was something even deeper. I'd read about an old tortoise who lived on the Galapagos Islands in a pen all by himself. He was the last of his species. Appropriately, they'd named him Lonesome George. As empathetic as Rob and my other guides were, they could never totally relate to what it was like to kayak blind, to the shock of being knocked over by a wave that you had no clue was coming, no time even to take a breath, or the uncertainty of rolling up again and not knowing what direction you were facing, and whether you were about to be clobbered again. And when it came right down to it, there was just one blind guy, alone and scared, pinned upside down against a rock, being washing-machined in a hole fighting for a breath. During all my training, I had an inkling how that tortoise may have felt. But now, I had a partner to share experiences with, to flail and bleed with. It was comforting and made me feel a little bolder—like what we were trying to do wasn't so insane after all.

"We're like the Wright brothers," Lonnie said, "getting a little farther and a little higher each try." I imagined me and Lonnie, side by side in our old-fashioned biplane, taking off into the yellow-blue yonder, but in my mind, the two of us looked a little like tortoises.

After paddling together all day, we sat at a table on the side of the channel. I drank lemonade while Lonnie ordered a Crown and Coke. He'd stumbled upon kayaking in an improbable way. Lonnie had raised three daughters as a blind single dad on his farm. When they were grown, he started looking for other pursuits. "I was too busy raising my family for a long time," he said, "but now I had some time for myself."

In 2012, he was visiting a disabled veterans' sports clinic in Colorado when he heard about an introductory kayaking class they were giving in a swimming pool. It was run by an organization, Team River Runner, that took veterans paddling. Lonnie decided to check it out and got the chance to sit in a kayak and paddle around. He was intrigued, and a couple of months later, the head of Team River Runner, Joe Mornini, invited him out to a camp on the Yellowstone River in Montana, where he got to paddle for a week in moving water. After that, Mornini invited him on a rafting trip down the Grand Canyon, but Lonnie asked if he could try to kayak it instead. Mornini said that in order for that to happen, Lonnie would have to do at least a thousand rolls. So the next day, Lonnie borrowed an old kayak from a friend and dragged it down to his small pond. "At the end of the day," Lonnie said, "I went back to the house and called Joe and told him I'd just done a hundred rolls and by the end of the week, I'd probably get to a thousand. Joe was silent on the other end. He finally said, 'You may have gotten your roll down, but you need a lot more experience.' So I called a friend who invited me down here to the Whitewater Center. I also kayaked four or five different natural rivers before I left for the Grand Canyon."

"I don't think I know how you lost your sight," Rob asked.

Lonnie took a breath and then said, "Well, I was quail hunting with Dick Cheney. Maybe you heard about it on the news?" Lonnie burst out laughing. Rob and I chuckled too.

"That's not so far from the truth," he went on. "My best friend shot me in the face with a twelve gauge." I stopped laughing, not sure if he was messing with us again.

"We were turkey hunting in thick bushes, and something moved above me. My friend just whirled around and shot me from nine paces away. I still have lead shot pellets in my face that you can feel under my skin."

Lonnie took my hand, and he had me feel a bead that I could roll around just under his eye.

"Now, I'm not saying I don't have bad days," he went on, "but I practice what I used to preach to my daughters when I tucked them in at night. 'When you wake up in the morning,' I'd say, 'when your feet hit the floor, if you decide right then it's going to be a good day, 99 percent of the time, it will be.'

And on the rare occasion sometimes when there might be something come up to change that, I would take them back to their bedroom and ask, 'Which side of the bed did you get out on?' I'd make them tell me, and I'd say, 'Now get back in bed and get out again on the other side.' It'd always make them laugh. That's the mind-set I try to live by."

"But what if your bed's pushed up against the wall?" I asked, pleased with myself.

"That's why I wear cowboy boots. There's a reason why they call them shit kickers," he answered. "You just kick yourself a little hole in that wall and you crawl on through."

"I like this guy," Rob said, laughing and slapping Lonnie on the shoulder.

"Lonnie," I said, changing topics to something I'd been wanting to bring up all night, "I don't know about you, but people often tell me how 'inspirational' I am."

"Oh yeah. I get that all the time," Lonnie interjected.

"And I know they mean it as a compliment, but sometimes that word can divide us. It says, 'You're that inspirational blind guy, and you exist over there, yet I'm just a normal person, and I exist over here.' As you know, in a little more than a year, I have plans to kayak the Grand Canyon. If one blind guy paddles it alone, people can easily write it off as some kind of anomaly, but if two blind guys paddled it together, then the story gets bigger, and it becomes more about what's possible for everyone. It says that all of us can push forward and be that inspiration. So what I'm getting at is, will you join me on my expedition?"

I heard the wooden legs of Lonnie's chair scrape over the concrete patio as it slid back, and then I felt Lonnie's wiry arms around me. "Partner," he said. "I'd be honored."

On both of our previous Grand Canyon trips, we had ended the descent at 225 miles, Diamond Creek, where most tourists stopped. But that was more than fifty miles shy of the official end of the canyon. A total of 277 miles marked the terminus, where the Grand Wash Bluffs gave way to the desert landscape of Lake Mead. So our upcoming trip would be a first blind descent of the entire Grand Canyon. And even better, it would be a double-blind descent.

Rob pointed his camera at Lonnie and asked, "Anything you want to say on this momentous occasion?"

"I do," Lonnie responded. "There are barriers in our way, but you can step through a wall that you think you're imprisoned behind to a world that you no longer thought existed. It's there. No matter what your struggle is in life, you've just got to get up, and step, and rise above it, and live. When we get knocked down, what stops us from getting up again is three things: fear, pity, and pride. It's easy to stay down, but it's hard to give up those foolish things and just live."

That night, we came up with the idea of making this journey our No Barriers pledge, a way to engage others along the way. I had met so many good people through all the No Barriers programs who were fighting through all kinds of challenges and trying to find purpose. Many just needed a kick start to lose weight, to stop smoking, to start that dream business, or to give up the demons of the past. So before we set out, we'd ask the No Barriers community to make a pledge of their own to break through a barrier in their lives and to live by our credo, "What's Within You Is Stronger Than What's In Your Way." We hoped to bring a million people aboard.

As a parting gift, we gave Lonnie a life vest from one of our sponsors. I heard later his suitcase had been too full so he'd worn it onto the plane. I envisioned Lonnie sitting peacefully in his seat with his mustache, clad in denim overalls, cowboy boots, and bulky life vest—completely oblivious to the stares.

"The lady next to me asked me why I was wearing a life vest," he wrote me. "I told her I was scared of flying—in particular, of a water landing."

Back home again, I traded one blind guy for another. I had three days planned with an acquaintance of mine, Daniel Kish. He and his team had led a clinic at a past No Barriers Summit teaching a technique Daniel called FlashSonar. Daniel was a pioneer within the visually impaired community and had been getting a ton of attention lately. Some were now calling him "the real-life Batman." I was a big believer in bringing on the right systems and tools. They'd helped me take my kayaking to a new level, but they'd also been instrumental in everyday life. Learning to use a long white cane and to read Braille had made the difference in expanding my parameters as a blind teenager. Lately, I'd begun using a talking GPS device to run with my new guide dog, Uri, on the network of trails crisscrossing the mesa behind my house. I used a computer with a Braille display and keyboard, screen-reading software on my PC, and a talking iPhone. But FlashSonar was a tool that wasn't fully understood, even among educators for the blind, and I was fascinated by it. The technique was based essentially on what bats do, using the feedback from sound vibrations to navigate their environment. Most blind people did it to some degree, at least subconsciously, or "passively," as Daniel put it. When I was learning mobility skills at the Carroll Center for the Blind in Massachusetts, the teacher had us walk down a hallway past an open door and notice how the sound changed from a boxy, confined chamber to a more open-flowing sensation. I'd used the technique ever since to squeeze information from the landscape. While hiking on a trail in the mountains, I could orient myself by hearing the slope running upward on one side and the expanse dropping away on the other. I could hear the rock walls, and more than once, it had saved me from a collision with a tree or a boulder. In my neighborhood, I used it to hear parked cars or the sides of buildings.

Daniel, however, was the guru, and he had taken echolocation to a whole new level. I'd heard online videos of Daniel riding a single bike through L.A. and pointing out features along the way, like statues and gargoyles in front of buildings. One video that had gone viral seemed almost like fiction; it was one of Daniel's blind students playing a game of Ping-Pong with his sighted brother. Recently, Daniel and his blind posse had taken up mountain biking on trails, and another of his protégés had ridden his bike successfully through a complex obstacle course for a reality TV show.

So I had invited Daniel out to Golden for a few days; I wanted to up my bat skills. Walking around in front of my house, Daniel taught me how to make sharp clicks with my tongue and listen to how the sound echoed off objects to figure out their size, shape, density, and distance. We kicked off with a simple exercise of Daniel holding up plastic plates to my left or right and me trying to identify which side they were on. Then we walked around the neighborhood investigating different sounds like mailboxes, houses, trees, and bushes. As we navigated, Daniel would ask questions to get the images more clearly defined in my brain: "Describe how that sounds. How does it sound different from the tree you just heard?"

"It somehow sounds softer than the tree, and not as tall. Maybe it's a shrub?" Then I'd reach out to feel it and confirm with my hands.

We then tested my skills in the park by trying to identify trash cans, water fountains, picnic benches, and rocks. By the end of the second day, I was finding metal poles in a pavilion and even locating thin metal signposts. It all took immense concentration, reminding me of my exploration with the Brain-Port, but I was blown away by how quickly the shape and texture of objects began solidifying in my brain.

To get home again from the park, I always walked the same way: Cross the road and follow the bike path for a half mile, eventually intersect with another road, take a left, and go up the hill to my front door. This was the most straightforward route, but I also knew of a shortcut that my kids often used. I'd never tried it, since it required me to head left off the bike path at an obscure spot, cut across some high grass, cross a gully with a small creek, cross an old railroad track, and find a set of stairs hidden in the shrubs that led to my back fence. I mentioned to Daniel that it would be cool to find the way to my backyard, and that's all it took before his mind was whirling.

"Let's give it a try," he said.

"But I've walked the bike path fifty times," I said, "and I can't find any distinguishing clues that would tell me where to turn. I even had one of my kids yell at me from the back porch as I walked back and forth, but nothing: no bend in the path, no uphill or downhill, no fence post, no crack in the pavement."

"Let's reverse-engineer it," he answered. So we walked home the normal, longer way, came out my backyard, and managed to make our way over the rough terrain to the bike path. When we hit the pavement, he said, "Just to start, we'll leave a stick here as a bread crumb."

Then we walked to the park and turned around toward home again. As we went along the bike path, Daniel had me point out observations about my surroundings. I could hear horses stomping and rustling behind a fence to the right and a wind chime jangling on a back porch far to the left. "Not reliable enough," Daniel said. But as we got closer toward the stick, perhaps three hundred yards away, Daniel had us stop. "What do you notice?" he asked.

It was a short bridge that crossed an offshoot of the creek. The pavement rose up just the tiniest bit, and I could hear water trickling below. "I feel the bridge," I said, "but we're still a long way away from the turn," I answered.

But as we walked another minute, Daniel had us stop again, and then he asked, "What do you hear now?"

I could hear what I guessed to be a clump of tall trees to the left that blocked the open sound of the sky behind them. We continued forward. "What about now?" he asked.

"It sounds open again, like we've passed the trees and there's just prairie grass again."

Still farther ahead, there was another longer clump of trees, and then another open stretch. Several clumps later, I heard the sound open up again, and my foot crunched on the stick. "There's your shortcut," Daniel said. "Cross the bridge, count four clumps. Turn left. Pass Go and collect $200."

We crossed over the creek, intersected my back fence, made a deduction to traverse left, and a couple of minutes later, we located the stairs into the gate. When I stepped into my backyard, I was a little floored. Already that year, I'd climbed some formidable mountains and kayaked raging white water, but I don't think anyone would have ever believed me if I'd told them that my most meaningful breakthrough was finding my own back door with Daniel. *Sometimes, the barriers closer to home were the most profound*, I thought as I leaned on my back fence listening to the gulch we'd just crossed. But I didn't know the half of it.

When my kids got out of school that spring, we decided to fulfill a typical rite of passage for every red-blooded middle-class American family: We rented a giant RV and headed to the Grand Tetons and Yellowstone National Park. We kayaked and swam in freezing Jackson Lake, with ice and snow running down the slopes and into the water. We hiked some spectacular peaks and rock climbed. We rode our bikes, Ellie captaining the tandem, past herds of bison, pronghorn, elk, bighorn sheep, and even a grizzly basking in the sun across a river. As we rode, I told jokes to the kids like, "What did the buffalo say to his son before he left for school?"

" 'Bye, son.' "

And the kids groaned.

Each night, we'd come into a different campground. Other tourists were constantly smiling and giving her the thumbs-up when they'd see Ellie behind the wheel. I was really proud of her, having never driven a thirty-six-foot monstrosity before. She was pretty nervous, especially when reversing. Backing up into our campsite, the kids would scramble to the back and stand next to the windows, Emma on the left and Arjun on the right, shouting frenzied directions. "Keep going," Arjun said.

"No. Stop," Emma said, correcting. "Don't you see that tree?"

"What tree?"

"The one right there in front of your face."

"Right, more right."

"You mean left."

"I meant the other left."

"Stop! Stop!" The RV bounced over the wooden barrier, and a tree branch thudded the back panel.

Somehow we survived those first few tries and, within a few days, were becoming seasoned pros—with a few exceptions like when we pulled out in the morning with our side awning still up or with our door still flapping open. At night, Arjun was in charge of starting the fire. He loved positioning the kindling, crisscrossing the sticks, crumpling the paper, and positioning it all just right. Ellie would grill the burgers and hot dogs; Emma was our resident expert on s'mores. She had impeccable timing, each one coming out golden brown; Arjun, of course, liked to set his aflame and then blow out the small bonfire.

I was in charge of dreaming up the campfire stories that would weave and ramble late into the night. One of my favorites was about a little boy nicknamed Scaredy-Cat Jones, who was petrified of everything, including bugs, snakes, heights, water, strangers, loud noises, and especially the dark. He'd pee in his bed, wake up with frequent nightmares, and never wanted to leave his house, but he inevitably would be drawn into adventures, and with knees knocking, teeth chattering, and plenty of whimpering, he'd be forced to confront his deepest terrors. He'd constantly find himself rappelling into pitch-black caverns chasing a neighbor's beloved lost dog, or being pursued by gangsters, crawling on his belly through caves, fighting through flapping vampire bats with needle teeth and giant squirming caterpillars, and squeezing through claustrophobic chambers so tight, he had to exhale. Once he had to shred all his clothes, including socks and underwear, to make a rope to swing across a bottomless pit with the whispering voices of demons calling up at him. In midflight, the homemade rope snapped, and he found himself flying through space and plastered against the vertical rock wall on the other side. With toes and elbows bleeding, and with shaking limbs, he inched up the crumbling face toward safety. At the end, he'd always bring the dog home, foil the crooks, and save the day. In appreciation, the town would always hold a parade, picking him up on their shoulders. "Scaredy-Cat Jones!" they'd shout. "The bravest kid in the world!"

Another story was about two friends, both outcasts, nicknamed String Bean and Butter Bean. String Bean was rail-thin and had a gangly, awkward gait, while Butter Bean was short and plump with a raspy chain saw voice. They both had flunked out of knight training, being so weak and ineffectual they could hardly hold up their heavy armor and weapons. But when the knights' ship was sunk by a sea serpent and they were all drowned, the two were forced to step up and come to the aid of their village. Along the way, the gargantuan monsters would inflict terrible punishment. The two heroes lay bloodied and broken, arms crushed by falling boulders, nearly drowned by slithering tentacles, hideously burned by dragon flames. However, they'd always emerge, saved at the last moment by a magic wizard building a set of golden arms that enabled String Bean to wield a mighty battle-axe, or a mermaid's potion retrieved from the depths of the lake that allowed Butter Bean to breathe underwater. Or they'd discover the healing waters from a mystical spring that not only healed the burns, but made their skin impermeable to the searing flames. Afterward in the RV, lying in our bed, Ellie said, "I love your stories, but nobody seems to get through them without being pulverized or maimed."

On our last day, we went on a guided tour of the park. Present-day Yellowstone is a vast basin of tranquil forests, meadows, and lakes, but it all sits inside the crater of an ancient supervolcano. One of its many catastrophic eruptions left a hole the size of Rhode Island that was slowly filled back in with lava and ash. The park guides told us the skin of the earth was still thin inside the caldera, which accounted for the hundreds of geysers, hot mud flows, and hydrothermal pools. The highlight of the tour was visiting one of the thermal springs that boiled up from below. This one was unique because you could lie down nearby with your ear pressed to the ground and feel the energy building from far below. The underground chamber would begin to tick and pop, then the ground would begin to tremble, then rumble, getting louder and more intense. "Here it comes!" one of us would yell excitedly, and thirty seconds later, a fountain of scalding-hot water would shoot up into the air. It had gone up so high that by the time it reached us, it was just a cool mist, refreshing on a hot day. We lay there for hours, completely absorbed and trying to predict when the next eruption would happen.

As we left the park the next day, I was feeling satisfied and happy. The trip had provided the final stitches in knitting our new family together. As we neared the front gate, the end of our vacation was signified by the chimes of our smartphones sounding as loads of e-mails began coming through. One of those e-mails would change our lives.

It read:

Dear Ellen and Erik:

I am the director of a program that has been working in Nepal for several years in child rights projects. Most recently we have learned that your son Arjun has a mother in Nepal that would like to meet him. She has been looking for him for six years now. Kanchi, the mother, is happy to see that Arjun is with a nice family and doing fine. It is only Kanchi's wish for him to know that he has another mother in Nepal and if possible for them to meet there one day.

That night in our hotel room, Ellie read me the note, and we both sat in shocked silence for a long time. We didn't know if it was real or a hoax. "This isn't rational," Ellie said, "but what if she wants him back?"

Ellie had just voiced our deepest lurking fear—that we could lose our child. Worst of all was the fact we'd thought we were doing something good. We had plucked a grain of sand from the universe, but that speck already had a mother. Sitting on the bed, I recalled our time in Kathmandu. "It was so murky," I said, "so hard to assess what was right and what was wrong, who was honest and who was corrupt. You just didn't know whom to trust. We followed their rules. We crossed our t's, and still, we got burned."

I remembered visiting a Nepali orphanage outside of town. It was ten times nicer than the Helpless Children Protection Home. In fact, it was the cleanest facility I'd ever seen in Nepal. The kids had open fields to run in and real playground equipment. They laughed and seemed happy. The director seemed sincere, charismatic even. He spoke elegant English. Later, however, I learned it was one of the most corrupt organizations in Nepal, illegally exporting children to India for slave labor and prostitution. As part of our records, there had been a police report stating that Arjun was found starving in the street. It appeared that was all made up. There was even an article and picture published in a local newspaper asking if anyone claimed this child, but it was rigged as well. The newspaper was an obscure one, and the majority of Nepalese were illiterate anyway.

"I refuse to feel bad," I said angrily. I couldn't help but think, if we hadn't taken him home, he'd be selling chewing gum on the street right now, maybe drugs, or worse. "The life he has is a thousand times better. He hit the lottery. And how were we supposed to know?"

"The dreams, the inconsolable wailing," Ellie said. "There were clues. We should have known."

She was right. We were culpable. Our passion and desire had made us hyperfocused on bringing Arjun home at any cost. We had leaped through all the flaming hoops like two circus lions, charging through the system, oblivious to the clouds of corruption. I had just finished a couple of weeks with two remarkable blind friends who didn't seem blind at all. One not only kayaked white water, but chainsawed trees and roofed houses as well as a sighted person. The other could navigate a mountain bike by seeing with his ears. I knew now that I was the only truly blind person among them. I had totally failed to see this coming. *Erik Weihenmayer,* I thought, *the blindest blind man in the world.*

Over the months, we learned that Arjun's mother was from a small village a couple of hours east of Kathmandu. Her husband had left her, and she and

Arjun had moved to the city for work. But she had fallen into selling drugs on the street, and soon she and Arjun had been rounded up and put in prison. Arjun's murky half dreams of a jail cell were real. Even worse, we learned that the orphanage director, Sabitri, was most likely part of the duplicitous scheme. She had shown up one day, pronouncing that the Helpless Children Protection Home would care for Arjun while Kanchi finished her sentence, and then immediately proceeded with an international adoption. She had even had the gall to allow Arjun to visit his mother before we arrived to complete the final paperwork. At just four years old, Arjun had said good-bye and sworn to his mother that he would always take care of her, and then Sabitri had whisked him away. He had never seen her again.

There was more than enough turbulence at home, so it was hard to contemplate facing more of it as I left for another training trip to the Whitewater Center. In the Denver airport, Rob was ahead of me on the escalator. At the top, he turned around and broke into laughter. "Big E," he said, "there's this goofy-looking blind guy right behind you." What he was referring to was a motivational poster with my picture on it. It read CLIMBED EVEREST BLIND. VISION. PASS IT ON.

Rob made me stand there as he snapped photos. Although I was proud of that poster, sometimes, I thought, catchy sayings like that made it look too easy. I thought of Rob's description when he went from a still photographer to a videographer. Photos were two-dimensional. They only captured a slice of reality, just the final moment of victory. As I stood there awkwardly, a guy rushed over and said excitedly, "Dude, that's you? Wow." Then he shook my hand and said, "Barriers are only in the mind. Anything is possible!"

Although I was flattered, secretly, I wanted to yell, "Anyone who says anything is possible hasn't lived long enough or reached far enough!" That statement seemed to defy everything I knew—everything I understood about shoving up against massive barriers that tried to knock you flat. After the guy had left, I turned to Rob and said, "If anything were possible, Lonnie would be racing NASCAR."

After three days of training, I had to fly to Chicago to speak at a No Barriers fund-raiser, and I was traveling alone. I'd done that hundreds of times and felt totally comfortable. In O'Hare, my guide dog, Uri, and I weaved through the terminal, throngs of people all around us, beeping cars, noise, and chaos everywhere. I was feeling tired and wanted a cup of coffee. Eventually, I smelled the aroma and wandered around trying to find the right shop. I finally found it by bumping into the guy at the end of the line. "Oh, excuse me," I said. He mumbled something awkwardly in response. I careened into the condiment cart, almost knocking it over. With my coffee finally in hand, now I had to find the baggage claim carousel. I asked several people directions. A few answered. I found the escalator and then heard the doors open, and I lurched onto the train into a sea of bodies. Someone stepped on Uri's foot. He yelped in pain. Doors opening, we followed the noisy crowd. "This is baggage claim carousel number 10," a nice voice said. Then with my knees leaning on the rail, I bent forward touching each of the hundreds of bags circling around: soft cases, hard cases, bags of every shape and texture, allowing my fingers to trail across each one as they sped by. Then finding a shape like my suitcase, I snatched it up from the pile, probing and investigating the contents. After a few misses, I finally snatched one up and felt Uri's dog bowl bulging inside.

Now, with my bag and suit jacket over my shoulder, I found the door and proceeded outside for a cab. Someone walking in front of me must have seen a taxi and started sprinting. Uri lunged forward to follow but failed to look up at the metal pole protruding diagonally into space. My recent FlashSonar training didn't kick in either, as my forehead slammed into the beam. It knocked me down, and I lay on my back on the sidewalk in a puddle of oily water. My suit jacket went flying, along with my coffee. So did all the stuff in my bag; there must have been a zipper open. The vision inside my brain pitched, and I closed my eyes tightly, trying to get everything to settle, but the world continued to sway and spin. Up and around the world leaned, like a Tilt-A-Whirl at an amusement park. Then everything flipped over for a moment. I squeezed my eyes shut a few more times, and the sensation finally went away.

As blood poured down my face and into my eye, I thought about the motivational poster Rob had spotted on the wall and wished it were that easy. No, I thought, barriers were not imagined or just perceived. They were real things, with real substance, as real as a square iron bar across a tender forehead, and they hurt a lot. In fact, right at that moment, they felt much more substantial than anything on the river or in the mountains. The cruelest part was trying to push forward, trying to navigate, fighting through one challenge after another, trying to learn these complex languages of the heart and mind, trying to build something important. You think you're plodding forward, ascending higher, making some progress, and *wham*—you're lying flat on your back with blood running into your eye. Everything you counted on, everything you thought was real, turned out to be a lie. And some barriers were even worse than an iron bar, because they weren't solid or predictable. They were as elusive as the whirlpools on the Usu. They rose up from perfectly calm water, from seemingly nowhere, and even from behind. They sucked you down and flipped you, holding you there. But what you didn't know was that it wasn't just the whirlpool flipping you. It was the whole world flipping upside down. It was everything you thought you understood, everything you believed you could hang on to. And how were you ever supposed to fight that?

21

EDDIED OUT

Rob and I had just finished a training session paddling Clear Creek. We were sitting on the back of his tailgate taking off wet gear when he said, "E, I've been thinking about the Grand Canyon trip approaching. You know, I'm off the androgen deprivation therapy now, and feeling okay, but my PSA is still rising pretty fast. People with my kind of cancer, well, it's incurable, my prognosis is not good, and it's unknown how long I'll be around. I'd bought some property on the east side of the Sierras for when Annette and I retire; that's probably not happening anymore. We're looking to buy a new house, a one-level, without stairs, so I'll be able to stay there as long as I possibly can."

Rob was contemplating thoughts so overwhelming, they didn't seem real. My brain didn't even know how to process them, but in his typical style, he was confronting the future clearly, with different scenarios drawn out to their logical conclusions, plan A, B, and C. "By next year," he continued, "by the time of our trip, I just don't know what my situation will be. So I've been thinking, you should reach out to some other kayakers. What about that guy you mentioned from your first Grand Canyon trip with the blind kids?"

Rob was referring to Harlan Taney, the young kayak safety guide, described by his sister as "half-human, half-dolphin."

"You said he was pretty awesome, and he knows the Grand Canyon better than anyone, so let's test him out," Rob said.

Rob was right. When I'd met Harlan, he could describe all 165 rapids down there with his eyes closed, and he knew all the best lines through, which changed in the myriad of different water levels.

"Where should we test him?" I asked, fearing I was stepping into something I might regret.

"Well, that brings us to the second idea I've been pondering. We need a river we can train on this winter, and I think we should go back to the Usumacinta." My gut lurched a little, and my face must have twitched, because Rob jumped in, "I know you got in a little over your head, but you're a way different paddler from what you were a year ago. It's a big Grand Canyon–style river, and you already know it and what to expect."

"I think that's the problem," I replied. "Do you really think it will be different?"

"One hundred percent!" he answered.

So once again, in March of 2013, I sat in my kayak on the fertile banks of the Usumacinta with the buzzing whine of insects swarming around my head and the growl of howler monkeys above. I thought about the "open-heart policy" shown to me by Matt Burgess. I slowed my breathing, forced the air into my lungs, and slid in for another whirl. Before the trip, I'd called Harlan and said something silly like, "Hey, I'm not sure if you remember me, but we met on a No Barriers trip five years ago."

Harlan laughed on the other end and replied, "Yeah. I remember." After listening to a description of the project and asking a few questions, he immediately agreed to join us. In fact, I got a strange impression—like he'd suspected I'd be calling someday. So now on the Usu, Rob guided me through the flat water, coaching Harlan on our technique and systematically handing over the guiding reins. Harlan was observant and a quick study; by the end of the day, we were getting calibrated. That night, sitting together at dinner, since Harlan was the newbie, we tried to coax some stories out of him. Rob had recently read a magazine article on him and said, "Harlan, tell us about your recent speed attempt on the Grand Canyon. Sounded pretty epic."

Harlan seemed a bit reluctant at first, but soon he had warmed up and was rolling on a wild tale. "I've always been infatuated by water," he started, "how it flows, by its energy and power. When I was just starting out as a Grand Canyon guide, I used to look out at the water from the beach as it rushed by and think, *We've stopped for the night, but the river never stops. It just keeps moving.*"

As he spoke, I got a sense he was reliving that scene in his mind, seeing the moon's reflection off the rippling water. "I didn't care so much about breaking records," he said. "I was more interested in experiencing the Grand Canyon the way the river saw it, to ride the flow, almost like current. Fourteen years after that seed was planted, I felt ready, and it all came together: the goal of kayaking the entire length, 277 miles nonstop and alone. I launched at midnight, right on the peak of a forty-five thousand cfs flood stage."

Harlan had paddled through the night, everything going smoothly, on pace to crush the speed record that had been set way back in 1983. However, just below Grapevine Rapid at mile eighty-two, a giant boil slammed him into the canyon wall and trapped him there, stuck between the boil and the rock. It flipped him and pounded his boat for a long time. After several roll attempts, he pulled his skirt and wound up swimming three miles downriver before he could retrieve his boat and kick to shore. "I drained about three gallons of water out of each pant leg in my dry suit," he said. "I was so pumped full of adrenaline, I got back in and paddled down to Phantom Ranch where I had a food cache."

Refilling his water jug at the spigot, he noticed his hand was bright purple. "It kind of stopped working," Harlan said. "It was seizing up, and I couldn't rotate it or hold my paddle very well."

So, knowing he was only a third of the way, he made the painful decision to abort his attempt. He shouldered his one hundred–pound, eighteen-foot-long kayak and hiked 4,500 feet out of the canyon.

I thought back to Rob and Rocky's horrific, near-death tales, recited on our first trip down here, and envisioned the Mayan crocodile and jaguar gods of the underworld, drawing out hauntingly dark memories of adversity and suffering, and trying to rekindle my fears. But they must have begun losing some of their power over me, because I managed to force myself back into my kayak the next morning and retrace our journey of the previous year, past

Piedras Negras, past the cascading waterfalls where we'd jumped off the cliff, past the camp where RPGs had ripped through the night, and past the Rio Chocolja, where we had dropped over the succession of travertine waterfalls. This time, I kayaked through the inner gorge, the same roiling canyon where the Gypsies had swum and where Gypsy John had almost lost his life. I paddled through Whirlpool Rapid, where I'd had my own meltdown and thought my river journey was over.

On our last night, we sat around the campfire, eating long silvery fish caught with spearguns made by the locals. Harlan seemed quiet and peaceful most of the time, happy to listen to the river stories, laugh at the jokes, and strum the guitar he'd picked up in a local market. But besides the recounting of his speed run, I realized, after our first GC trip and a week of him guiding me, I still knew practically nothing about his life. That night, after the others had gone to bed, we stayed up talking, and I peppered him with questions. Harlan's childhood sounded pretty idyllic. He described growing up in Flagstaff, Arizona, before it became a yuppie tourist destination, full of coffee shops and yoga studios. His father, Guerin Taney, had made a living as a blacksmith, but his true passion was working with metal, fashioning eclectic pieces like a deer's head out of an old car bumper or an abstract design made with coat hangers and fire pokers, all fused and twisted together. "He was very talented," Harlan said, "but it always remained a hobby. He didn't have the business savvy to show his work or sell anything."

Harlan's family didn't own much. Their prized possessions were three old beater vehicles: a pickup truck, a Volkswagen Bug, and an old school bus. "Except," Harlan said, "we only had one engine between all of them. It actually hung from chains in our living room." His dad would switch the engine from one to the other, depending on the activities: in the truck if he was going to shoe horses or do some forging, in the Bug for a trip out to Lake Powell, or in the bus if they were heading up into the San Francisco Peaks. They'd spend a lot of weekends up in the mountains picking mushrooms, watching the aspens turn to gold, and shooting an old black powder rifle. Harlan said, back then, all the mountain roads were dirt, and there was not a soul around for miles.

His father believed in tough love. Guerin taught Harlan how to ride a horse at age five by putting him on the back of a goat. He would slap the goat on the rump and get him riled up as little Harlan went for a ride across the field, the goat bucking and kicking. When Harlan fell off, Guerin picked him up, brushed him off, and threw him back on again. He told Harlan, "Son, when you can ride a goat, you can ride a horse."

"I remember, about at that same time, he was forging metal," Harlan said, "and he pulled this big piece of red-hot metal out of the forge and set it down on the floor. He was pulling another piece out when I backed up, right into the first piece. It burned my calf, searing into my leg. As I yowled in pain, he just hoisted me up and dunked me in the quench tank, a fifty-gallon barrel of cold water. He said, 'You're fine,' and I stayed there in freezing waist-deep water for a long time, until he pulled me out. That was our family: 'Get up; keep going. That's what we do.'"

After passing the goat test, Harlan and his dad would saddle the horses, pack the saddlebags, and ride for days. Once, they trotted straight up old Route 66 and tied the reins to the hitching post outside his father's favorite saloon. Harlan would sit on a bar stool drinking root beers while his dad drank whiskey. Once, his father, a 250-pound bruiser, came to the defense of a lady in the bar. He took on three bikers, beat them senseless, and tossed them each out the door. Guerin wore a cowboy hat and a silver heart pendant on a thick chain around his neck: "Half-cowboy, half-hippie," Harlan said. "One minute he'd be so mad he'd be throwing a refrigerator across the room, and the next, he'd be scooping you up in his arms and telling you how much he loved you."

As Harlan talked about his father's wild life—driving cars off cliffs for fun, motorcycle accidents, drunken nights with police billy clubs cracked over his head—I couldn't help but think of my brother Mark. I knew firsthand that being near those kinds of people was like being in the front row of the most amazing fireworks show you've ever seen: Bombs exploded above in the most brilliant patterns and colors. You couldn't take your eyes away, yet you also knew if you got too close, there was a high chance you'd get burned. "He was a bighearted, large-living man," Harlan said, "but he didn't always take care of himself." He'd suffered from grand mal epileptic seizures, and Harlan remembered a few times when he convulsed on the floor, his tongue hanging out of the side of his mouth. "But he never did anything about them. He refused to get help."

"What about your mom?" I asked. "She must have been pretty strong to handle all that."

"My mom has been the greatest rock in my life," said Harlan. As he spoke, I noticed his quiet, even-keel voice drop just a touch deeper with emotion. "She's an amazingly talented, educated person. She speaks six languages fluently. She has two degrees and could have done anything. But she chose to be a parent above everything. She worked multiple jobs: cleaned houses, did landscaping, and worked her entire schedule around my sister and me. Our house was a shanty cobbled together with plywood; we would have been psyched to reach the poverty line, but we were a tight little team and took care of each other. She bought backpacks from climbers selling their secondhand junk and got us scholarships to climbing and skiing camps. I was the kid in the down jacket covered in duct tape with the feathers pouring out. But I was also the kid on the podium. My first climbing rope was frayed down almost to twine, and I learned how to make a webbing harness, because I couldn't afford a real one. My mom made sure I had a book on knots, and I'd disappear into the forest every weekend to build zip lines, the ropes running from tree to tree. My first kayak was from a garage sale. She never allowed us to miss out on anything, and she told us we could never be defeated—that there was a way around or through anything. Some people might look at that life and think we were just a bunch of dirtbag poor people, but I only have memories of pride. I honestly felt like I was sitting at the richest table in the world."

When Harlan was nine, his mom took him out of fourth grade for eighteen days on his first rafting trip down the Grand Canyon. "It was as poorly organized as a trip could be," Harlan said, but out of his 160 subsequent trips, it was still his most vivid. He said, "It was like my eyes were opened."

He spent hours on the wide beaches building driftwood forts and tossing sticks into the water, watching them drift away and wondering where they'd end up. But scouting the different rapids, that joy on the beach was replaced by terror. While scouting House Rock Rapid, he saw another trip's boat flipping end over end with all the people and gear tumbling out. A few nights later, his group had camped above Crystal Rapid. "We could hear its roar all night long, and I was scared as hell," he said.

"But Lava was the worst. I was almost puking." His mom, rowing the raft, had gotten sucked too far right and slammed against Cheese Grater Rock, a sharp black volcanic boulder halfway down. It was lucky their raft wasn't shredded. Their boat became wrapped around the house-size boulder. As water rushed over the edge and the raft sank lower, his mom hung on to Harlan's life jacket. "I was halfway in the water and felt myself being sucked away, but she was there, pulling me back into the boat, yanking me to safety. Six years after that, I started working in a raft company, patching boats, scrubbing life jackets, and knowing what I was going to do. When I was seventeen, I got my first paid trip down the Big Ditch."

Harlan's path seemed to defy reason. He'd confronted the fury of Lava at an impressionable age and had almost been lost. Most people would have run away from that adversity, burying it and trying to forget, but Harlan had only been drawn closer to the river. Although I didn't fully understand the implications, I was fascinated and resolved to try to model it.

On our last day of the Usu, Harlan guided me through the biggest rapid, San José. As we rode the shifting, bucking line through the minefield of boils and whirlpools, Harlan's voice had a calming effect. Through his commands, both his competence and confidence were loud and clear, but it was never bravado. Instead, it felt like a deeply learned appreciation of the river, a Zen-like acceptance. When we reached our take-out in Boca de Cerro, I'd paddled every mile.

"Rob, you were right," I said as we dragged our boats up the bank. "It felt like a different river this time."

"Of course," Rob replied, "the water level was lower this year, but it wasn't just the river that changed. I'm proud of you."

Throughout the trip, Rob had fallen back, allowing Harlan to do the majority of the guiding. But I knew he was always nearby, observing, analyzing, and deducing. I suspected, at some point soon, I'd be hearing his conclusion. It happened on the plane ride home, just as I was drifting off into sleep. I felt Rob nudging me with his elbow.

"Hey, E, you awake?" he asked.

"I am now," I said, yawning.

"Erik, in my opinion, guiding a blind person is rather challenging, and just because someone is a good boater doesn't mean they'll necessarily be a good guide. It's way too easy just to go into autopilot, but guiding you requires deep thinking about what it would be like paddling without sight and what is the most effective way of communicating, to constantly be asking yourself how it is working or not working. It's a problem solving process: execute, evaluate, modify if necessary, then repeat. I can tell you I've been assessing Harlan for the last week, and I want you to know, he's your man—no question."

Rob also recommended we add a few more guides to the team roster. "Even with Harlan and me," he said, "it's still not enough. You're putting in all this time and effort, so let's stack the odds. If something happened to Harlan or me, we should have other guides ready to step in, and it's good to have a wide talent pool anyway to share the responsibilities."

So back home again, we brought aboard three additional guides. Steven Mace was twenty-five years old and the son of my old climbing partner Charley Mace. He hadn't followed his dad into the mountains, but instead had established himself as an expert river man, both a rafting guide and formidable kayaker. We also enlisted Timmy O'Neill, who was not only a climbing legend, but had been paddling a kayak since he was nine years old with his father. He had a reputation of being a wild man who did stand-up comedy and made underground climbing films about "buildering," free-soloing the sides of buildings and even tall bridges throughout New York City. However, behind the popular image was a meticulous planner and brilliant strategist. It also made sense to recruit Skyler Williams, my right-hand man at my small speaking company in Golden. Skyler had started kayaking to be able to help with my learning process and had come along on some of the training trips, and he was such a strong athlete and quick learner that he was soon a vital part of our kayaking team.

At this point in my training, it came down to one crucial objective. We had to become a cohesive team that understood how to fluidly step in and out of different roles and respond seamlessly to the wide array of challenges we'd encounter on the Grand Canyon. The way to achieve this was to log a lot of river miles together. So we all began heading out to local paddling areas like Shoshone and the Upper Colorado. Both areas were long drives, almost three hours, west on I-70, over the Rockies. As we were driving one day, Timmy said, "Let's try the Eisenhower Tunnel test." The Eisenhower Tunnel is situated on the top of the Continental Divide at over eleven thousand feet, making it one of the highest highway tunnels in the world. It's almost two miles long. The test was to try to hold your breath all the way through, for at least two minutes—that is, if you broke the speed limit.

"You can't do it cold," he warned. About twenty minutes before the tunnel, he taught me how to do what he called "active breathing" by slowly pulling air into my lungs for twelve seconds, holding it for ten seconds and then letting it out again for another eight. "It may come in handy for you when you're sputtering in a hole." He made a loud burbling sound with his lips. "It's saved me a few times—once on a rapid on the Ottawa River, Phil's Hole, where I was de-paddled, de-boated, and almost de-lifed."

I paused my breathing exercise to laugh nervously.

Timmy said, "People say it's dangerous to do the Eisenhower test when you're driving, but I've never passed out once. At least I don't think I have."

When the tunnel arrived, we took a last breath and tried to hang on. Timmy made it the whole way, but I was at least thirty seconds shy. However, I found active breathing to be a great tool for calming my nervous system and loading my lungs with oxygen. I started practicing it each time as a pre-kayaking ritual.

On one training session, Steven Mace was learning to guide me. He gave me the perfect line to get around a massive hole. I squeaked by, hearing its ferocious churn to my right, but a couple of minutes later, I was beginning to worry why I hadn't heard him call any directions into my earpiece. Then, as I feared, my radio gave a long beep, indicating that the distance of the Bluetooth signal had reached its limit. I turned around, trying to listen through the deep rumble. I was now bouncing off rocks, doing 360s and just managing to lean the right way each time to absorb the blows. Hearing another big rapid below me, I pushed back the panic and paddled hard toward what I thought might be the edge of the river. I found myself in a shallow swirling eddy and clung to a rock with one hand, paddle in the other, as the current tried to spin me around and spit me out the bottom.

Finally, I heard a thread of sound in the air that began to assert itself above the river noise. It was a voice. Rob was furiously paddling toward me, screaming for me to hang on. When he pulled up beside me, panting hard, he told me what had happened: Steven had gotten me past the hole, but had failed to account for himself. His boat caught the edge of the hole, and he was yanked in, flipping end over end. He rolled up at least nine times but couldn't escape. Exhausted and out of air, he'd finally relinquished, pulling and swimming. The hole finally released him, but when he eventually made it to shore, he was half-drowned, beaten, and demoralized. His boat and paddle were somewhere downriver, and he noticed the hole had stripped him of his river booties.

When Rob found me in the eddy, I knew he was without a radio—it was still attached to Steven. The rapids below were big and loud, but hiking out of the canyon wasn't an option. "Remember plan B?" Rob asked, and we floated together for another twenty minutes as I tried to fortify my resolve. I realized then, thinking about what had just happened to Steven, that there were serious consequences for my guides, not just for me. When we finally began descending again, I could barely hear Rob. We entered a tumbling cauldron of white water, and I was knocked over, rolled up, and immediately knocked over again. Upside down and being dragged downriver, my head slammed against underwater boulders. When I rolled up, my knuckles were scraped and bloody, and I could feel my elbows bleeding beneath my paddling jacket. Then I was flipped a third time, and upside down in another hole, I fought to right myself. When Rob saw me, he had to resort to his old trick of purposely flipping as well so he didn't torpedo me. Somehow, we got through. "How about another run?" Rob suggested at the bottom of the canyon.

"No, thank you. Not today," I said with my head hanging and hands shaking.

Another day, Timmy was guiding and directed me around another large hole to my right, but the eddy line to my left grabbed my bow and spun me.

Before he could say anything, I slammed directly into the overhanging rock wall. It cracked my helmet as I flipped over instantly. When I rolled up again, my lips were split, and I could taste blood. But I had bigger worries: I was entering another rapid, and the waves were tossing me left and right. What had distracted my team was a family full of rafters who had spilled directly into the hole I'd just missed. Their raft had flipped, and they were all swimming for their lives. There were two young kids and even a couple of small dogs in the water all at once. Timmy pulled me over to the edge, and my team paddled out to pull the family to safety. When everyone was all collected on shore again, we flipped their raft upright. The little kids were bawling and clutching their parents. They feared the dogs were drowned. However, an hour later, we found both of them washed up downriver. They were miraculously alive.

The father, who we learned was named Donald, had been the one rowing. As he sat in glum silence, Timmy reached into their cooler, cracked a beer, took a long swig, glanced over at the crying children, and said, "Donald, well, the good news is, at least your dogs still love you."

Over the next year, we made several training trips to Peru. With warm water, hot sun, and massive snowmelt off the Andes, it was an ideal boating destination, with exotic-sounding rivers like the Marañón, the Apurímac, the Yanatile, and the Urubamba. We also headed north of the U.S. border to the Ottawa River, to the very place where Timmy had almost been "de-lifed." The purpose was to do a course called "Desensitization to Big Water." For a week, the guides repeatedly had us paddle into massive holes like Phil's, which upended you and held you down for about fifteen seconds before releasing you. It didn't matter how great a combat roll you had; you weren't coming back up with the force of Phil's holding you under. So the key was patience, to just relax and wait it out. Fifteen seconds didn't seem that long to hold your breath, but being throttled around and around, over and over, beneath ten tons of crashing water, it seemed like an eternity. With each underwater beat-down, I was getting plenty of chances to practice the Eisenhower Tunnel test.

Coming home from that trip, for the most part, I felt proud of myself. I'd begun to rebuild my skills and my confidence after being shattered on that initial trip down the Usumacinta. Physically, I was improving, making it through rapids that I would have pulled my skirt and swum through a year ago. Yet my progress wasn't like getting over the flu; symptoms still lingered at the edges. In moments of stress, like when I was entering a rapid, an almost paralyzing dread would surge up and engulf me. I was also still suffering those dreams of floating down the river blind, without a guide, being tossed at the river's mercy.

I thought about the different soldiers I'd worked with over the years who struggled with PTSD. I didn't want to be presumptuous and give my nightmares a name—no bullets were flying at me, and no IEDs were exploding—but it sometimes felt like I was responding in a similar way, like my brain was an old scratched vinyl record skipping at the same musical notes, playing over and over. It wasn't a song I liked either. No matter how hard I tried, I couldn't shut it off. I hoped my brain wasn't scratched, doomed to repeat an endless feedback loop.

There was one veteran I'd met on our last Soldiers to Summits expedition named Captain Ryan Kelly. As he guided me down the trail, I'd learned a lot about his life. He had served as a Black Hawk helicopter pilot and company commander in Iraq and had come home with PTSD. He lived in denial of the symptoms for seven years before finally giving in to pressure from his family and seeking help. Now retired, he had a master's degree in playwriting from Columbia University, and he wrote plays, all of them revolving around our nation's wars, and the characters were all struggling with the aftermath as they tried to heal.

I thought Ryan might have the insight to help me with my own challenges and especially with those reoccurring dreams. Ryan was kind enough to meet me at the public library. After catching up, I tried to broach the subject but hesitated. Then I went ahead and told him about my experience on the Usu. "This may sound weak," I said, "but I think something's wrong with me, maybe something wrong with my brain, like it got broken somehow."

"You're talking about PTSD?" he asked. I nodded, embarrassed. "When I came home from Iraq, I had those same perceptions," he said. "I was pretty messed up and didn't even know it. I wouldn't go see anybody about it because I thought I could deal with it. I hadn't been blown up. I came home with all my limbs. In my mind, I was a man, so I should be able to conquer anything I set my mind to, especially this imaginary problem. But after a lot of support from my family and after counseling, I know now, there's no such thing as a weak man or a brave man; there's just a man. That's all."

"But you served our country," I said. "With a ton of combat missions. I'm just trying to get back in my kayak."

"This isn't just a soldiers' disease," he continued. "In fact, that phrase clouds the issue. I think that everybody sooner or later will experience some degree of trauma, the process of being crushed and having to rebuild." He laughed ironically. "Hell, we're born into trauma. It's all blood, tears, and pain. Whether it be a fear of getting back in your kayak, or losing your house because you've gone bankrupt, or being in an abusive relationship and not having a clue how to get out, or being a doctor in an emergency room, or trying to help somebody and they don't want to help themselves; maybe you watch them dwindle away and die. They're gone, yet you have to live with it. That's trauma. That's part of being human."

"But when does trauma become PTSD?" I asked.

"The question becomes how it affects you," he answered, "how you process it, how you adapt or redirect, or change with it. And sometimes that trauma feels so overwhelming; you get stuck for a time, maybe forever. I don't know a lot about kayaking, but maybe it's like being stuck in an eddy and you want to get back into the current; the current is where you know you should be, but there's a barrier that you can't get through, no matter how hard you try, or how bad you want it. People tell you, 'Just think positive thoughts or put on a brave face,' but that doesn't get you through either. I believe all our experiences are recorded in our subconscious. Nothing ever gets left behind. And those experiences, negative or positive, are who we become. Sometimes those events are so overwhelming, they get embedded in our souls like a vibration that you feel—no matter what. The trauma becomes part of you. It melts into you."

"How did yours happen?" I asked.

"It wasn't just one thing," he replied. "My nemesis was constantly being under the gun, always preparing for the worst—sometimes waking up and not knowing if I'd be alive by the evening or just for the next ten minutes.

There's an underlying pressure that wears on you, that changes you over time. But even worse than that were all the decisions I had to make that involved the lives of others. Those were soul crushing. There was one night when I was sleeping. About 2:00 A.M., this sergeant rushes in and wakes me up. He's panicked. 'There are possible insurgents coming through the wire, on foot,' he said. We didn't know exactly how many there were. I'm thinking, the helicopters and living quarters would be the ideal target, so I'm yelling, 'Everybody, load your weapons! Get to your positions! Get your shit on! Wake the colonel!' I threw on my clothes and ran over to the TOC—the tactical operation center—and I was floored to find no one there. I didn't have any information except for what was coming in over the radio, and the information was coming at me very fast. I immediately activated our security plan. Part of that is you send roving guys out in Humvees with machine guns and then you put the checkpoint people out there to block the roads, like interior perimeters, to signal all vehicles and make them stop. The rule is, if they don't stop, you light them up. It was pandemonium, guys running around in their underwear with loaded guns. We're not infantry; a lot of us were pilots, so this was not a good situation. And I was the only officer in the TOC, so I was tracking all the radios. Then I get a call from one of my soldiers on a checkpoint, and he says, 'There's a bus coming toward us, and it's not slowing down. I'm flashing lights, and it's not slowing down. Permission to engage.'

"I said, 'Where is it coming from?'

"He yelled, 'From the PX area! Permission to engage! Permission to engage!'

"That was the moment," said Ryan, "maybe only a couple of seconds, but scenarios are flying through my head. If I give the order, it will kill everybody on that bus. Inside, it could be our own guys, or it could be the terrorists who'd breeched the wire, gotten ahold of that bus, and packed it full of explosives. This was the last checkpoint before our living quarters, an entire battalion housing 350 people. The guard is still yelling, 'It's speeding up! I'm flashing my Humvee headlights, I'm locked and loaded, permission to engage!'

"If we light them up and it's the enemy, I win—if it's a bunch of GIs, then I lose. The guy on the radio was actually a friend of mine, and at that point,

I remembered before deployment his daughter sitting on my lap and asking me to bring her daddy home. But I made the decision. I am going to gamble and sacrifice the lives of my men. I thought, *If I'm wrong, then you're going to die, and that's the way it's going to be.*

"I said, *'Do not engage!'* And you know who was on that bus? It was full of eighteen-year-old American GIs coming back from the PX. They were eating Doritos and drinking Dr Peppers, cranking tunes, absolutely clueless, and I almost killed them all."

"You made the right decision," I said, trying to reassure him.

"Yeah," he replied. "The emergency that'd started the whole thing turned out to be a bunch of dumbasses, civilian contractors who were sneaking back onto the base with a case of beer. But in the long run, it doesn't really matter, because when we got home, the guy at the guardhouse invited me over for a barbecue. His kids hugged me and said, 'Thank you for bringing my daddy home.' What was I supposed to say? 'I'd already made the decision to sacrifice your daddy—the fact that he's alive is just dumb luck'?"

I tried to comprehend how hard that split decision must have been and how it still weighed on him.

"Then, a couple of years later," Ryan went on, "my wife got pregnant, and she started to get this rash on her. It just appeared out of nowhere. We went to the doctor, and he immediately sent us to a cancer specialist, and that doctor said there's a 50 percent chance it's inflammatory breast cancer. This kind of cancer meant that unless she started chemo in the next week, it might be too late. And oh yeah, the chemo would abort the baby. My wife said, 'No, I am going to keep this child,' but I tried to talk her out of it. I said, 'You have to abort the baby because if you say no, neither one of you may live. I can't bear losing both of you.' Funny thing is, that after three more weeks of biopsies and more tests, we found out it was just a rash. Everything's cool, but it wasn't really, because I was this close to losing it all. When I think about that moment, it's so terrifying, I have to push it away, but it just keeps floating up again. And it always comes around, always back to the war."

"So it's not about a physical injury," I said, "not about something done to you. More like something you did, something you did to someone else, something you might have done differently."

"Yes," he said. "And sometimes it's about impossible scenarios with impossible decisions, in the face of impossible forces. It all rattles around and ties you up. And at the end of the day, you feel hope being ripped away, or potential or desire. All you're left with is regret, guilt, and a sense of helplessness. And when it comes right down to it, you begin to wonder if you're a bad person, like maybe you deserve it, and this is some kind of penance."

When Ryan stopped, we both sat quietly sipping our coffees as images played through my head: I saw my brother Mark in the ring boxing with Anita, and she was about to deliver the knockout blow. There was Rob in his kayak, barely able to move after his back injury on the Usu, trying to confront his future with a disease that had no easy or logical answers. But most clearly, I saw little Arjun, recently arrived in America, staring at a book on the solar system, convinced he had arrived on an entirely new planet. Everything he'd known, everything he'd hung on to, all left behind.

Sitting across from Ryan, I recalled Harlan's speed attempt, how he'd yearned to experience the Grand Canyon from the river's perspective. Like Harlan, like Ryan, I also wanted to be in the current, but the fear and uncertainty felt so palpable, I thought it might crush me. To have a chance to make it through a rapid, so many factors had to come together. A subtle paddle stroke, the timing of my reaction, or pure dumb luck all determined whether I'd be high-fiving at the bottom or smashing face-first into a rock, or swimming through the rapid and having to be rescued by one of my team. And most of that depended on me. Just one mistake would throw me into even more mayhem and danger. Then I'd have to respond in kind to those new threats.

It was a lot to carry, and I felt the weight. I didn't want to let down my guides, my team, my family, and myself. Often, I found myself questioning whether I had what it took to rise to those forces. If I had stopped after climbing Mount Everest, I could have always remained "Super Blind," the illusion of myself fixed and eternal. But I was starting over, and the past didn't matter. What if it had been a mistake, a fluke? What if I wasn't the person I thought I was, or hoped to be? That realization wouldn't just scratch the vinyl record of my mind, but would shatter it.

"But I believe there is a way to rebuild," Ryan began again, fortunately interrupting my thoughts. "If trauma is about powerlessness, about a loss of control, then maybe overcoming it is trying to prove that you're not insignificant, that you have an ability to impact your life, to be able to move forward or sideways, or even backward. People often say, be brave, but I don't really know what that means. Fear and courage—they're not a permanent state of being. They're just choices. If you choose fear, it leads you down a path until it owns you. But the opposite is also true. Every day, I try to practice small acts of courage. You decide to wear that shirt that you love but you know everyone else hates, or you have a Coke instead of a beer, or you push down your pride and decide to ask for help, or you decide to get back in your kayak one day—even if it's just in your garage. Those also lead you down a path, and soon it begins to build. Then when the moment comes that requires great courage, you're ready."

22

SMILE

In July 2013, my family and I went to the sixth No Barriers Summit in the historic mountain town of Telluride, Colorado. At the opening ceremony, I welcomed the five hundred people in the audience and then introduced a recent acquaintance who was one of the growing community of No Barriers ambassadors. Mandy Harvey was a professional singer who had released two albums and played to sold-out shows in clubs around the country, including two performances at the Kennedy Center in Washington, D.C. As she sang classics like "Over the Rainbow" and "Fly Me to the Moon," her voice was so pitch perfect and beautifully haunting that it was hypnotic. After her set, as she introduced herself to uproarious applause, some must have been wondering why she'd been performing sign language as she sang. It all made sense as she casually mentioned that she was deaf—not just hard of hearing, but profoundly, unequivocally deaf. The audience sat in amazed rapture. Many, I noticed, were sniffling and crying.

After Mandy, Adrian Anantawan, a world-class violinist, took the stage. He played Paganini's Caprice no. 24 in A Minor. Adrian was born missing his right arm just below the elbow, making him an unlikely candidate to become a concert violinist. He told the audience that when growing up, his family had never asked what would be the easiest instrument for a person with only one arm to learn. They'd ignored that question entirely, simply asking themselves, what instrument makes the most beautiful music? The answer had set the trajectory of Adrian's life. At ten years old, his parents took him to a prosthetist who rigged up a plaster cast that fit over his stump. Adding a piece of aluminum tubing that connected to the base of the bow enabled him to manipulate the bow back and forth across the strings.

"At first, the instrument fought against me," he admitted. "For the first ten years, I sounded like a dying cat! But everything I put into the instrument, it eventually gave back to me in the most profound ways." Adrian had performed all over the world, including in front of three American presidents.

Adrian said that it had been a dream of his to play his violin on a mountaintop. So early the next morning, we set out with a group of No Barriers youth from around the country, and several hours later, our team—including kids who were blind, amputees, and teens who had never before been in the mountains—stood on a high summit above the deep valley of Telluride. We gathered around Adrian and listened to him play. The sound started softly, dipping and idling, then soared up and pierced the thin mountain air. The deeper notes spread out and reverberated against the distant cliff faces. As I listened to his bow dancing over the strings, I immediately recognized the song and quietly sang the words:

> A—mazing Grace! How sweet the sound, that saved a wretch like me!
> I once was lost, but now am found, was blind, but now I see.

Later that afternoon, back in the auditorium, a friend of mine rolled onto the stage for a demonstration. Amanda Boxtel had been in a wheelchair for almost thirty years, but on this day, she stood up using a cutting-edge exoskeleton technology. As she walked across the stage, I listened to the electric whir and hum of the gears lifting and lowering her feet. Arjun, next to me, said, "Whoa, Dad, she looks like Iron Man."

I followed the sound as she carefully descended the set of stairs, walked in front of the crowd, pointed at a group of wheelchair users in the front row, and said to them, "Get ready to walk."

Afterward, Ellie took a photo of Amanda and me. As Amanda said, "Cheese," I listened to where her voice emanated from.

"You're about five foot seven." I laughed. "I never knew that." I gave her a big hug.

On the last day, we presented Hugh Herr with the inaugural No Barriers Lifetime Achievement Award for his work on prosthetics technology. His new BiOM ankle system, just released, was again revolutionizing the field of bionics, similar to the Rheo knee I'd held in my hands seven years ago at the Cortina No Barriers Summit. The new BiOM held sophisticated microprocessors and sensors in the joint that emulated the functions of lost muscles and tendons, enabling it to move in the same way as a biological ankle. He showed us how he could use an app on his iPhone to program the degree of flex and spring. Then he tapped his toes on the stage, just to show off a little. "I imagine a future when leg amputees will be able to run faster than people with biological limbs," he said. "A world where visually impaired people are no longer visually impaired. A future in which technology is so advanced and sophisticated that people with unusual minds and bodies will no longer be disabled. I think, in the twilight years of this century, we will have a world in which disability no longer exists."

Kyle Maynard closed out the summit with his harrowing account of climbing Mount Kilimanjaro. He described the intense pain in his elbows only three days into the expedition. On the fourth day, at twelve thousand feet, he went into his tent and cried. The summit remained over seven thousand feet above him, and his team figured it would take another fifteen days. Kyle had to reckon with the fact that he wasn't going to make it, that he'd provided false hope for all the people who'd believed in him, especially those military heroes lying in hospital beds somewhere who were following the climb. But what hurt the most was breaking his promise to a woman named Vicky. He'd met her randomly, learning that her son, Corey, a marine, had been killed in combat five months earlier. Corey left behind a wife and three daughters. It had been his dream to travel after his deployment and to climb Kilimanjaro someday. Vicky asked Kyle if he would carry Corey's ashes to the summit. On the spot, he agreed. Kyle was determined not to break that promise, but the grueling days and the intense pain were wearing him down. So he and his team made a bold decision: Instead of sticking to the standard route, they would save twelve miles by choosing a shorter, but much steeper and more dangerous route. It was his best chance.

Ten days after beginning, Kyle, exhausted and covered with dirt, crawled over the top, stopping near the sign that marked 19,341 feet. All day, he'd been carrying Corey's ashes on a lanyard around his neck. At a flat spot between two rocks, his team helped retrieve the lanyard, and while fighting back tears, Kyle spoke softly, "It's an honor to be able to bring you here, brother." Then he poured Corey's ashes onto the earth as he looked down into a sea of clouds, then forest, and farther, the African savanna, all the way to the Indian Ocean.

Kyle told us that, while crabbing slowly toward the summit, he'd get frustrated and discouraged each time he'd look up at the great distance he still had to go. He said he tended to do that in life way too much. So he began forcing himself to stop and look back at the vast terrain he'd already traveled. Our No Barriers movement had been similar; an idea had begun with three friends atop a desert tower more than ten years ago. Along the way, its future had felt so uncertain; it had almost fizzled and died. So now it was gratifying to sit in the audience and soak in what we'd built, a powerful force for change and transformation.

However, as inspiring as the summit was, it didn't reveal any immediate answers to the dilemma we faced about Arjun's recently discovered Nepali mother. The subject weighed heavily on us, and we consulted Arjun's therapist, whom he'd been seeing once a week since his arrival in the United States. Arjun was still at the age that talk therapy wasn't as effective as play therapy. So during his sessions, he was able to choose from a huge array of toys, objects, and figures and manipulate them in a giant sand tray. The idea behind it was to help Arjun resolve conflicts, remove obstacles, and gain acceptance.

In the beginning, for a long while, Arjun only involved inanimate objects like seashells, spools of thread, and driftwood. There were no living creatures in his imaginative play. When Arjun was having a rough week, when there was conflict around the house or at school, his made-up games would involve ambulances, fire trucks, and police cars. Pretend sirens blared; imaginary

fires blazed. His play seemed in crisis. So it was a breakthrough when, many
months later, he took a toy house off the shelf, buried it, and then, at the end
of the hour, uncovered it and placed it atop the sand. His therapist shared
with us that it might be a sign he was beginning to accept his new life with
us. It was an even bigger breakthrough when, many months later again, he
placed a family of dinosaurs in the house: a mother dinosaur, a father dinosaur, and two baby dinosaurs. It was impossible to tell, but I hoped the babies
were a boy and a girl. Those many months showed Ellie and me that the bonds
of a family didn't form instantaneously. Love, trust, and cohesiveness were
built one stitch at a time, and we feared this new revelation might just tear
that fragile knitting apart. Arjun's therapist agreed. "He is not psychologi-
cally prepared to deal with the magnitude of this information," she said.
"I say protect, protect, protect."

In the hot tub behind our house, we discussed what to do. Ellie and her
brother had been adopted themselves, so she had firsthand perspective.
"When I was growing up, I was curious about where I came from. I wanted
to meet someone who looked like me and had my blood running through
them. But now, I can understand why my parents did a closed adoption. Your
worst nightmare is that there might be a loophole, a weak spot in the system,
a reason why it didn't stick, a change of heart—something that will disrupt
your family, something that will take your child away. And I know how
unfair that feeling is because Arjun's mother was a victim. She didn't deserve
this."

"And what if she got sick and died?" I asked. "We would then be responsible for holding back an important piece of Arjun's life. We'll remove his
prerogative. At some point, he's got to confront this, to own his history."

"He may find out anyway," Ellie said.

We knew this was the age kids got curious and Googled their names. Recently, there had been an article written by an organization working to connect Nepali moms and their children and exposing the corruption. They'd
chosen to show a photo of Arjun and Kanchi—despite our request to keep
Arjun's photo off the Internet.

In the end, we both felt strongly that he just wasn't ready to know. "It's all too fragile right now," Ellie said. "Maybe when he's sixteen or so, when he's more mature, when he can handle this better."

Our biggest fear went even deeper, though. It came down to commitment. There were times, like on our Green River trip, when Arjun's doubts flared up and this new family hadn't felt real. The next time we sent him to his room for misbehaving, would he be thinking, *My real mother wouldn't have done that*? He already had a fantasy life that blurred with reality. When he was little, he'd imagined floating up from his foul-smelling bedroom in the orphanage, full of other farting boys, and flying over the city of Kathmandu like a superhero. It was a natural escape mechanism, but when his family, friends, or school weren't going well, could this become a Peter Pan fantasy to always hold on to as a plan B? Uncle Rob was a strong advocate of plan Bs, but in this instance, it could become a wedge, a way of rejecting his present circumstances. It would be natural to wonder if that other life might have been better.

I recalled those early hints that Arjun had memories of his mother. He had even spoken the words aloud: *jail*. They floated in his subconscious, emerging from time to time above the surface like a dream you can't quite remember. We had wondered why Arjun had wailed on the bed that night before flying away, not like the tears of a boy who skinned his knee, but as Ellie described, "a wail as deep in the heart as pain could go." Unbeknownst to us, a few months earlier, he'd been visiting his mother in jail, saying good-bye and pledging not to abandon her. He had no idea where he was going but knew what he was leaving. That half memory was a lot for a boy to carry, and there was no way for it not to cause a wound. But it was our job as parents to repair that injury, to help it heal and scar over. That would enable Arjun to move forward, to grow and develop into a healthy, happy young man who trusted his family and felt a deep bond with other human lives. Most importantly, he had to believe that, although bad things happened, the world was a good place that you could navigate with confidence.

However, what if it became more than a wound, but instead a break, like snapping a dry twig in half? What if that break was too wide to span? What if this became the reason why the journey ended, stuck in that no-man's-land between two worlds—loyalty to the past or loyalty to the new life? Training for the Grand Canyon had taught me that if you wavered, the fears and reservations would sink down and paralyze you. Commitment was the only way forward.

When Arjun had kicked the soccer ball with Uncle Rob behind the hotel on that very first meeting in Nepal, his spark and talent were obvious. It was further revealed when he came to America and learned English in three months and figured out how to ride a bike, with no training wheels, in three days. In that first spring, Arjun had joined a soccer club, and parents would frequently comment on his quick reflexes, exceptional coordination, and intuition for the game. But as the kids his age progressed through the years, they seemed to develop quickly, and some emerged as star players. Arjun appeared, however, to be falling behind. I didn't care whether he was a star, but I did want him to be proud of himself as he worked through a process and continued to grow and improve. I hated to see him go from such natural talent to coming in last during sprints, not following the coach's advice, and clearly holding back as the other kids gave their all. It seemed as if he didn't know how to tap into that spark, or like something else was blocking that spark from igniting. I thought of the race we'd had on that sand dune when Arjun had stopped before the finish line, and I wondered what would push him to reach inward and begin growing what he had inside. By the second half of the season, he wasn't playing very much, mostly riding the bench, and was a nonfactor during the games. At age ten, the club split into thirds, with Arjun chosen for the C-level. His team had a painful season, not winning a single game, and for the majority of the games, not scoring a single goal. Sometimes we'd make the mistake of trying to give him advice on the car ride home: "You're flat-footed out there . . . You're not trying to get open . . . You're letting your opponent beat you to the ball."

But the language gap was wide, and Arjun would often get angry. "You're saying I stink."

"Not at all," I'd step in. "I think you're awesome and just wonder why you hold back."

"Well, basically, you're saying I'm not any good."

Often it would degrade into an argument, and we noticed Arjun beginning to lose interest. He skipped a season, trying some other sports like wrestling and baseball, but the next fall, a friend from school asked him to play on a new soccer team, just formed. It was the best news, because the team was part of a recreational league. There'd be no pressure; the goal was just to play and have fun. But I admit it was a little hard from the sidelines as Ellie described the kids goofing off, giggling and poking each other as the coach tried to give feedback. Once during practice, Ellie gave me a play-by-play as Arjun and another boy moved the plastic cones in order to shorten the distance of their dribbling drill. The other kids high-fived them and made them out to be heroes.

During games, Arjun fell right in as the boys bunched together, hogged the ball, and refused to communicate with each other. It was like he worked hard to be a chameleon, to not stand out, to be at the level of the lowest common denominator. Most infuriating was when the team was losing by one goal with a few minutes to go. Instead of sprinting and rallying, they began walking and joking around, already defeated in their minds. Ellie and I weren't sure if this rec team was sending Arjun the right message.

Six months went by, and we debated what to do about his Nepali mom. It was on our minds constantly. As parents, our hearts were burdened with the knowledge of a mother who had lost her only son, but also as parents, we knew the fragility of Arjun's emotional state. Ultimately, we decided to do nothing. We found ourselves retreating and protecting our son. Protect, protect, protect! We had to keep him safe at all cost.

In December, Mandy Harvey was in town for a holiday concert. We'd stayed in touch since the summit. She drove out to Golden, and we walked along Clear Creek, where I'd spent hundreds of hours training. "I loved your performance at the summit," I said as the winter sun shone down on our faces.

"Yeah. It's ironic I'm even up there at all," she replied. "I had no intention of ever becoming a performer. I wanted to be a choir teacher. I'm super shy, and I get stage fright! My freshman year of high school, I was in a choir vocal competition. There was only my dad, four other people, and the competition judge, but even with that small audience, I started shaking, and then I started crying, and then I turned around and sang the rest of the song while they stared at my butt, because I couldn't look at them."

Mandy was born with a connective tissue disorder that affected her hearing. Her ear canals would frequently fill with fluid and were susceptible to infections, resulting in multiple surgeries. "When I was about four, I had an entire year when my eardrums didn't vibrate. I started lip reading because it compensated for what I wasn't sure I was hearing. When I was in eighth grade, I went on an airplane on a school trip. The change in air pressure perforated both eardrums, and it was six months before they recovered."

In high school, her hearing stabilized, and being from a musical family, Mandy joined an elite choir. They performed all over the world, including a concert at the Sydney Opera House.

As we walked and I listened to Mandy relate the string of events that sent her spiraling downward, I felt stunned. It seemed like a cosmic joke, like a bizarre scene I remembered from the opening credits of *Monty Python's Flying Circus*. A cartoon image of a guy innocently stands with flowers growing from out of his head. A brass band plays in the background as an oversized foot comes down from the sky and, for no reason at all, crushes him and his flowers. And to add to the joke, the squish is associated with a loud fart noise. As Mandy began Colorado State University as a music education major, the cosmic foot was about to drop.

Almost immediately, her residual hearing started declining again. She noticed she couldn't understand her professors and started moving closer and closer to the front of the room. One day she could no longer hear them at all. She was panicked, just faking it, trying to survive. As I listened to her story, I was viscerally feeling every word, remembering my own experience in middle school as the print in books got smaller and smaller and the whiteboard got farther and farther away.

As if losing her hearing were not enough, she tripped one day, and being particularly vulnerable to injuries due to her connective tissue disorder, she dislocated her knee, ripping all the ligaments around it. She had a surgery the third time to repair her ACL and was in a wheelchair for a month. Mandy now had to get to class by pushing herself on her chair down an icy path to catch what she termed "the short bus." She began missing a lot of class, sitting in her dorm room, depressed in the dark. "People would come up and say, 'That must be really hard.' I could barely understand them. I just wanted to escape. I was a shell of a person who they pitied. They talked to me, and I just sat there staring at them."

"All the things you're talking about, it's like I'm reliving my own story of going blind," I admitted. "You hate the fact that people are looking at you in a certain way. You feel like an egg that's been cracked and squished on the ground, and everyone's looking at the mess."

"Yeah," she agreed. "And sometimes they're just poking it, and you're like, 'Stop! You're not really seeing me. I used to be something else!' It doesn't make sense, but somehow it felt like it was my fault. I felt responsible. Somebody could say, 'You look beautiful today,' and I'd still cry because one way or another, they were only saying that because they had to. Inside, I was convinced I was broken. I was that disgusting egg."

That feeling of being responsible was compounded when Mandy decided to join a church for a little solace. One night the group surrounded her. They put their hands on her and began to pray for a miraculous cure. "I stopped going after that. It was like they were saying I was the cause, that if I only had more faith, I'd be healed. I got really confused then, like, what had I done? Or why had God forgotten about me? But my father said, 'God's not a genie, and he's not poking you with a stick just to put you through a trial.' Things just happen. This is a flawed world. He said, 'Maybe God's watching the whole thing and crying along with you.'"

In the second semester, her musical theory class was taking their first test. The teacher played a piano song, and the students had to score it by tallying out the rhythm and notes. The teacher was facing Mandy, and from her chair, she couldn't see over the back of the piano to know if his fingers were moving, and Mandy was too embarrassed to get up. After the test, she sat there with a blank paper as everyone began leaving. The teacher brought Mandy down to the dean, where they said, "I'm sorry, but this isn't going to work."

"They were just waiting for the shoe to drop," Mandy said, "and it dropped that day. I've never been so mad in my life. All I wanted to do was punch a kitten or smash a car. I'd been given a letter saying I was being released from that class." Her dream of becoming a choir teacher had died, and she had no idea what to do next.

Mandy was walking back from class that afternoon on the bike path. She was just out of the wheelchair. "A guy began waving in front of me," she said. "I didn't know what he was trying to say." Then it became clear as a bicyclist plowed into her back. "A month before, I'd gotten fitted for hearing aids. They only worked for a couple of weeks; my hearing was too far gone at that point. They were $3,000 apiece, and insurance didn't cover them. My parents paid for them out of pocket, even though they had just declared bankruptcy. My dad had taken the money out of his retirement fund. That day I happened to be wearing them when the bike hit me. One of them fell out, and I fell on top of it and crushed it." The fall also put her back in the wheelchair for another week and set her recovery back for months. "I just fell on the pavement, but it was like I'd fallen down a well," she said.

Soon after that, the faculty dropped Mandy from the music program. "It was more humiliation," she said, "but I was going to at least finish the semester. That was my 'fuck you.' I'm going to do it. I have to finish."

"What was it like at the end when you left that place?" I asked.

"When we started driving away, it was euphoria," she said. "I just wanted to go home and be done with this nightmare. But then after we left the city limits, it was a feeling of being crushed under a weight. I had let everyone down. Then I just got really quiet and I stopped talking to people. I shut down. I wasn't even mad. I was numb."

Mandy went home to live with her parents again. She spent a lot of time by herself in her room. "I barely got out of bed. I had so little energy, everything became a math problem: seventeen paces to the bathroom, eight paces from my bed to the door. I hadn't just lost the ability to hear music but simple things, like the ease of conversation, or the sound of a whisper, being able to hear people calling out from behind me, or the click of the door latch on my car when I push the remote. If I have kids in the future, I'll never hear them say, 'I love you.' I had to mourn the loss of the life I thought I'd have."

"I know," is all I said. "I remember." Then I asked, "When did you let it die?" wondering if she'd have a clue what I was asking.

She knew immediately and replied, "It took about a year, but I watched it die, laid it to rest, and I said, 'Good riddance.' Then I had to start over as a new person."

An amazing thing happened after that. Mandy's father, always a tremendous supporter, convinced her to begin singing again, just the two of them, like they had done together since Mandy was a young girl. There was no pressure either. The two of them decided to record a song, "Come Home" by OneRepublic, as a gift for her old voice coach, Cynthia Vaughn. Her father played the guitar while Mandy sang. "I was just going to hand Cynthia this little song that we recorded on a tiny fifteen-dollar digital recorder, and it was just going to be private between the two of us, a thank-you for all her help over the years." When she played the song, Cynthia began crying, and Mandy assumed it was because she sounded terrible.

"I know I sound horrible," Mandy said.

"No," Cynthia replied. "They're tears of joy." Mandy had somehow retained her near-perfect pitch.

I thought about my first meeting with Dr. Bach-y-Rita, who had proven the truth of neuroplasticity. He had shown the scientific world that it was the *brain* that saw, not the eyes. I wondered if he knew his theory applied to deaf singers too. It was the brain that heard, not the ears. Dr. Bach-y-Rita would have been proud of Mandy.

In 2008, Mandy's voice coach convinced her to sing at open mic night at a bistro in Fort Collins, Colorado. She still had doubts. "I thought I was going to suck," she said. But when they told her she was going on in two minutes, something powerful occurred.

"The thing that I had feared the most all of my life, all through my childhood, was losing my hearing. And that had already happened," Mandy said. "So I thought, *What's the worst that can happen here?*" With her hand on the piano so she could get the tempo through the vibrations, she stared at a spot on the wall above the audience and summoned up the courage to begin singing. The audience's applause told her that she could actually do this, and the folks at the bistro invited her back the very next week. Soon, Thursday nights were "Mandy Night." Sometimes she'd appear barefoot so she could really feel the vibrations through the instruments, the drums through her feet and the bass through her chest. "I couldn't hear myself sing, so I'd lost the ability to scare myself, to judge myself, which was the big factor behind my nerves. I had always wanted to be perfect. I always wanted to do things so well that I debilitated myself, stopping myself from performing the way I wanted to. I was trying to live up to a standard that was nonexistent. But I was now a new person, and that enabled me to stop worrying about how it came out. The crazy part was that the people who knew me both when I could hear and after I went deaf said I sang better after."

I'd bought four tickets to hear Mandy perform that night at a popular jazz club in Denver to a packed holiday concert. I sat with my family at a small table, Ellie and I drinking beers and the kids enjoying Shirley Temples. We'd prepared by listening to Mandy's CDs, and all of us had our favorites. We bet cherries from the kids' drinks which song she'd start with. Ellie won as Mandy started with "Rocking Around the Christmas Tree." Like the summit, the crowd cheered with love and admiration. Her following was cult-like, with Mandy's voice elevated by her fans and the rising energy in the room. The mood then shifted and became more subdued as she introduced her next song, "Smile," made famous by Nat King Cole. "I learned sign language back in college," she told the crowd, "as I was losing my hearing. It's pretty ironic that my sign name became *Smile*." She held her hand up to the crowd and made an *M* by tucking her thumb under three fingers, and then brought her hand up to her face and drew a grin. It was Mandy's signature slang— combining the sign for *M* with the sign for *smile*. "I always thought it was funny; anyone who had burrowed into my soul at that time would have seen that it was hell in there. So this song reminds me to keep smiling through it all."

Her version was stripped down and simple, with Mandy's voice at the center. Somehow it conveyed both strength and vulnerability, all at once.

Smile though your heart is aching, smile even though it's breaking.
When there are clouds in the sky, you'll get by.
If you smile through your fear and sorrow, smile and maybe tomorrow
You'll see the sun come shining through for you.
Light up your face with gladness, hide every trace of sadness.

Although a tear may be ever so near,
That's the time you must keep on trying,
Smile, what's the use of crying?
You'll find that life is still worthwhile
If you just smile.

Though I couldn't see them, I was pretty sure Emma, Arjun, and Ellie were smiling right along with Mandy. I know I was. Then Ellie whispered in my ear that Mandy's pianist had been giving her visual cues by looking up and nodding proudly when it was her beat to begin singing. It reminded me of how I relied on Rob and Harlan and my other guides to kayak a river, or how a kid depended on his family to grow into a strong, healthy adult. Arjun was no exception. He was leaning on Ellie and me to make the right decisions to support him, the way Mandy was lifted up by the audience, the way she rode atop the swell of belief coming from her band. As parents, it was our responsibility to keep Arjun safe, to build his trust, confidence, and happiness, to make sure the world never hurt him again. But maybe that was impossible. I'd been too wrapped up with how I thought life was supposed to be, rather than seeing it as an adventure. Mandy had surely watched her life radically change. She had been thrown down a deep well and had eventually found her way out by discovering an inner voice. I wondered what that voice was telling me now. Part of it was screaming that Arjun wasn't ready; our family wasn't ready. We needed to circle the wagons and fight this new circumstance that had dared to change our family so swiftly and completely.

My mind flashed back through the last six months of indecision, of pain and worry, all the way back to the No Barriers Summit in Telluride, and I found myself reliving that day on a peak with Adrian Anantawan, the concert violinist. Similar to Mandy, his story represented that inner voice, often so foreign and counterintuitive. But maybe when you got down to the very core, it sounded something like Mandy's songs, or like Adrian's violin soaring over the mountains, pure and simple, like sound transformed into joy. Then I knew what to do. Arjun had a Nepali mother. She existed. That was truth, and it was to be celebrated. It was a life reborn. I leaned into Ellie, pulled her in tight, and whispered, "He needs to know."

"You're talking about Arjun, aren't you?" she asked.

"Yeah," I said.

She squeezed my hand. "I've been thinking the same thing," she whispered back.

That week, we sent photos and a letter to Kanchi through the Nepali organization and then asked Kami Tenzing Sherpa to meet her. During their introduction, he filmed a video greeting that he subtitled in English, and we watched it on Ellie's computer.

"Namaste to Arjun's mommy and daddy," she began. "I am happy you have given Arjun a better education than I could have ever provided. I am also happy, because I always used to give him dal bhat, and now you are doing the same. He always said, 'Give me dal bhat, Mommy.' He's crazy about it." Kanchi was beginning to cry as she continued, "I am happy that I got to see his pictures. You are both very kind. You took my son under your care when he was a very small child and have raised him. You've given him more happiness than I ever could and motivated him to do better. You have done a great job in raising him, and I am very happy from the heart to know that. For all these years, I have been wondering where he was, how he is. Now I know. Now I just wish to meet him again. He is my son, and he is yours too."

Ellie and I both cried along with Kanchi, and we were pretty certain this was not a scam by the way she cried. But we'd been duped before, more than once, so we decided on a plan that would give us absolute proof. It was perfect timing, because coincidently, Uncle Rob was heading out soon on a trek through the Himalayas with his wife and friends. So we asked him to take a day and meet Kanchi. Ellie had found a DNA kit online and showed it to Rob. "Somehow," she said, "you're going to have to swab her cheek for a DNA sample."

"No problem," Rob said, smiling and eager for the challenge. Just as tricky, Ellie had to get a DNA sample from Arjun and send the two samples off to a company to see if they were a match.

Ellie and I sat on Arjun's bed one night and reminded him that Ellie was also adopted—just like he was. "Are you ever sad?" she asked. "Do you ever think about your Nepali family?"

Arjun nodded.

"I know about that curiosity," she admitted. "I want to give you permission to ask yourself, 'What the heck happened?' That curiosity is natural. It's all such a mystery."

"Would it be okay," I stepped in, "when Uncle Rob goes to Nepal, if he were to ask around? Maybe ask some questions?"

Again, Arjun nodded.

Two weeks later, at the end of his trek, Rob and Kami arranged a meeting with Kanchi at the headquarters of the organization that had connected us. Rob introduced himself and explained that Arjun called him "Uncle Rob." He explained how he'd been a part of Arjun's life from the beginning. He flipped through various photos of Arjun: at the Telluride Summit, at camp, kayaking, and rock climbing. He showed a video of Arjun playing his new saxophone. Kanchi smiled, and Rob mentioned that Arjun had that same smile. "He's very smart," Rob bragged. "He's in a special accelerated math class."

As Kanchi listened, her eyes began to tear up. "I cry too much," she said. She revealed, "When he was little, he told me that when he grew up, he'd protect me and take care of me, but now I am alone. I worry Arjun will forget about me."

Rob assured her that Ellie and I had nothing but empathy for her situation and hoped this meeting would be a step in reestablishing a relationship. Then it was time for Rob to get her DNA. He showed her how to rinse her mouth and swab her cheek. As he demonstrated with the Q-tip jammed in his mouth, he made goofy faces, and by the end of the meeting, everybody was giggling and taking photos. "We'll make this a DNA party," Rob said cheerfully. "I'm so glad to be able to hold your hands and go back and tell the Weihenmayers that we were able to meet."

Then he asked Kanchi for any parting words for Arjun. "Always be honest. Study hard. I give my blessings, and I am waiting," she said.

When Rob reported back, "Mission accomplished," Ellie implemented the next step in the scheme. But how could she trick Arjun into a cheek swab without having to explain what it was for? Luckily, Ellie had done her research; earwax was an ideal source of DNA. Looking at Arjun's ears, she exclaimed,

"Gosh! You gotta clean those things!" She helped him use a Q-tip to clean them, and afterward, she stealthily plucked the dirty Q-tips out of the garbage and put them into a plastic bag.

When the results came back, they were a match, no question. So that night, Ellie and I asked for a family meeting. We sat on the couch in the living room, and, before I lost my nerve, I came straight out with it. "Arjun," I said, "you know how Uncle Rob was in Nepal? Well, we found your Nepali mom. I want you to know, it doesn't change anything. We will always be your family. This will always be your home. Emma will always be your sister, and we'll always be your parents, but now you have two mothers, a second mom who loves you." We put our arms around him and said, "You never have to worry or wonder. When you're ready, only when you're ready, you can meet her. She's there, and she's waiting."

We then showed the kids a picture of Kanchi. She wore a striped dress with a pretty purple-and-blue scarf draped around her neck. Her face was round, and her long black hair was pulled back. Like the first picture Ellie saw of Arjun, Kanchi wasn't smiling. She looked stoic, perhaps defiant; her face wore the burden she'd been carrying.

Arjun didn't have any questions. He must have been utterly overwhelmed. We gave him the picture, but he buried it away under his bed. Every week or so, Ellie would check in to see if he had any questions, or if he wanted to talk more, but each time, he hardly said a word.

On the fourth week, however, Ellie had an idea. "How would you feel," she asked, "about making a little video, so Kanchi could see your house and learn a bit about your life?" He mulled it over for a few minutes, and to my surprise, he agreed.

When they filmed the video, I was away on a river trip, but on my return, I listened to it again and again. It contained no soaring speeches or emotional revelations. It was just an eleven-year-old kid giving a tour to a new acquaintance. But something within it was very brave, and I got a sense there was more of this kind of courage to be revealed.

"Namaste," he begins. "This is my house. We live in Golden, Colorado, next to the mountains." Arjun points to a toy plane. "This is a LEGO set that I made," he says, "and I think it's pretty cool because I made it without instructions." Next, he points to a half dozen awards. "These are some of my medals I got; this one's from wrestling. Right now I'm in soccer. In the winter, I do indoor soccer and wrestling. They're pretty fun, and I know some kids on the teams."

He holds up a picture. "I drew this in fourth grade with watercolors. They're aspen trees. We get to travel a lot. We went to Croatia this year. I have stuff from Hong Kong, and I also have some stuff from Hawaii." He points to a shark poster, displaying all the different classifications. He walks outside to his backyard. "This is one of our chickens. We named her Little Red Hen." The chicken begins clucking as he places it in its pen. Then he walks across the yard and lets our two dogs out of the side yard gate. "Sit." Instead of sitting, Uri lies down at Arjun's feet, and he lies down next to him, stroking his back. "He's a guide dog, and he helps my dad go through the airport." Then Ellie joins Arjun. She pets Uri and adds, "Arjun's job is to brush and walk the dogs."

Lastly, Arjun grabs his soccer ball and begins juggling. He gets to six before the ball escapes and hits the driveway. He tries again and gets to fifteen.

Arjun then does a trick move with the ball rolling up the back of his ankle. He kicks it up over his head with his heel.

The video ends with Ellie and Arjun kicking the ball back and forth. Then they sit on our front yard swing together. Waving good-bye, Arjun says, "Thank you." Then, with a smile, he speaks the Nepalese translation: "*Dhanyabad.*"

In August, just before leaving for the Grand Canyon, I planned a father-son adventure for Arjun and me. As I'd been upping my kayaking skills, Arjun had been joining me on Bear Creek Lake and Clear Creek. He was such a natural; he had a solid roll at age nine and a "hand roll," a roll without a paddle, at age ten. So I thought it was the right time for his first kayaking trip down a big river.

We headed to the Upper Colorado with the team. Arjun loved being one of the boys, squeezed into the backseat of Skyler's truck, trading insults, burping, noogies from Steven, and the chance for us to break out all the jokes that hadn't worked on each other in years:

"AJ, did you see that apomi out the window?"

"No. What's apomi?"

"Nothing. What's up with you, homey?" This was followed by another round of noogies.

Through the rapids, his paddling technique and balance actually surpassed mine. I'd emerge from the bottom breathing hard and frazzled, while Arjun would ride the waves with a ballet dancer's grace and come out smiling. "Dad," he'd say, "that wasn't so hard."

The day proceeded with splash fights and chases, purposely trying to flip each other. Steven finally got Arjun with a classic river joke: "Hey, I think you have a rip in your dry top." Steven pointed to Arjun's armpit area, and when Arjun lifted his arm to check, Steven pushed his elbow, sending him over. Arjun came up sputtering, and he was officially initiated. Although he was utterly exhausted by the end, he paddled all fifteen miles. At the end of the day, we sat relaxing together at the edge of the river, and I thought it was the moment to break away from the "bro"-atmosphere.

"AJ," I said, "you know I'm off in about a week. I want you to be a good boy while I'm away."

Arjun sat still, not that comfortable with direct statements or overt emotion, but nevertheless, I put my arm around him and rubbed his back. Recently, we had produced a bunch of No Barriers flags, and we told people to bring them out and hold them high at significant moments. I thought this qualified, so I pulled one from the zipper pocket of my dry top and handed it to Arjun. "I want you to have this," I said. "You deserve it."

"Why you crying, Dad?" Arjun asked.

"They're not tears," I said, wiping them away with the back of my hand. "My face is just wet from river water."

"If you say so," he replied.

"You've been through more than most boys your age," I forged on. "I want you to know I'm proud of you, and I think you're very brave." Then I tussled his hair, gave him a tight hug, and got up quickly before more tears could flow.

23

THE WEIGHT OF WATER

It seemed almost unreal, like a dream I'd wake up from as soon as I entered the bracingly cold water of the Colorado River. But on September 7, 2014—eight years after first descending the canyon with Harlan Taney, and four years after committing to this adventure while standing atop a mountain with Kyle Maynard—we were finally here in the smoldering furnace of Lees Ferry, our put-in on the Grand Canyon.

I believed I was as ready as I'd ever be, though some doubts still lingered. We all helped unload and organize piles of equipment we'd need for three weeks on the river, from Paco pads and folding chairs to giant ceramic water filters and three burner stoves. The meat and vegetables had all been frozen solid, and even though the air temperature would most likely top one hundred degrees in the lower canyon, perishables would last the whole trip in superinsulated coolers that were submerged at the bottom of the rafts. At an average of forty-eight degrees, the river water was a natural refrigerator. We also carted out the portable toilets that river people affectionately called "groovers," for the grooves they formed on your butt cheeks. The Grand Canyon was a pristine ecosystem. There were strict regulations about packing out all garbage and human waste. From past trips, I'd gotten used to muddling along narrow, weaving, bouldery trails, through tangles of prickly plants, and past wild visitors like scorpions and rattlers to find the groover, always tucked away in a discreet location at one end of camp.

Once everything had been unloaded, Rob led me through the maze of gear to cool off, and we stood ankle deep in the icy water, splashing our faces and soaking our caps and bandannas. For a year, I'd been memorizing the river's fabled rapids and their different mileage points, and now their names chanted like a chorus in my head: Hance, Sockdolager, Horn Creek, Granite, Hermit, Crystal, Deubendorff, Upset, and of course, Lava Falls. Even though it was 179 miles from where I stood, the thought of Lava terrified me. Most people agreed that this four hundred–yard stretch of raging chaos was the biggest, baddest rapid in the Grand Canyon. In 1869, John Wesley Powell's team had the good sense to portage their gear around it, even though it took three hours of backbreaking work. Then they'd lowered the boats on ropes through the maelstrom. In the modern age, Lava was responsible for more wooden boats splintering, more rubber rafts folding like tacos, and more kayakers swimming for their lives than any other of the 165 rapids.

I remembered Harlan's story of his first Grand Canyon expedition, twenty-five years before, when he'd been pitched out of the raft and his mom had clutched his life jacket, desperately clinging to him, right there on the big black Cheese Grater Rock. The very thought of it flip-flopped my stomach and made me want to run for the groover. But there were plenty of rapids between Lees Ferry and Lava Falls that could easily hammer me, plenty of whirlpools, boils, holes, and fierce eddy lines. So I told myself not to think too far ahead, just to focus on each day, on every single paddle stroke.

Rob's hand on my shoulder pulled me out of my thoughts. "You cold, Big E?" he asked. It was eighty-five degrees already, at 10:00 A.M. "You're shivering a little," he said.

"I guess I'm a little nervous," I admitted.

Rob patted me on the back. "Big E, we got this," he said. "The good thing about this canyon is that it warms you up. The rapids get progressively harder each day until Lava when you've been paddling already for two weeks. We're gonna be fine."

Our team of kayakers numbered ten and reflected the history of my progression as a boater. In the midst of his cancer fight, thankfully, Rob was there. Not only would he guide me himself, he would be in charge of creating the plan of attack for each rapid, placing the various team members in the right positions. Rob had been the force behind this entire process, even when I thought the door might be closing, and I owed him everything.

Next, there was Rocky Contos, who'd organized so many training trips in Mexico and South America; Steven Mace, who had faithfully come down to Golden almost every day of the previous summer to help me train; and Skyler Williams, who had been instrumental in organizing all the gear and sponsorships. Thanks to Sky and my father, Ed, Nature Valley was helping to pay for the expedition and had provided enough granola, nuts, and energy bars to feed an army.

The multifaceted Timmy O'Neill had also signed on. Before I left, Ellie had described a photo on Timmy's website: Timmy is buried in the sand, only his head visible, a mint julep sitting in front of him with a straw leading to his mouth. However, behind his sometimes outlandish first impression, he was a mentor and a philosopher, and he had become a trusted friend.

Lonnie had organized two guides who would trade off leading and following. Seth Dahl was a Montanan who'd served seven years in the 163rd Infantry; and Chris Drew was an accomplished paddler who worked as a kayak instructor and raft guide. Even though Lonnie and I each had our own guides, Rob emphasized that ultimately we were all one unified team, with interchangeable parts who would work together to ensure success and safety for all.

My main guide down the river would, of course, be Harlan. How lucky I had been to meet him on that first Grand Canyon trip. His knowledge of "the Big Ditch" was unrivaled. He'd obtained all the permits from the National Park Service and organized raft support. The staff at No Barriers believed it was important to capture the story of the first double-blind descent of the canyon, so Harlan had spent a week customizing a thirty-seven-foot inflatable motorized raft with twelve solar panels that charged an array of batteries with fourteen thousand watts of storage capacity; it was enough to not only power my vital radio communications, but the four video cameras and four laptop computers to organize and edit the video footage. He'd also created a mobile, lightweight boom as effective as a Hollywood crane—but portable and wireless—that could withstand the rigors of weather and water. To direct the film for No Barriers, I'd invited Michael Brown, who'd made the documentary on our Mount Everest ascent and a film on our first No Barriers S2S expedition in Nepal with the military veteran team. He was well versed in how to capture beautiful stories in rugged environments.

Arizona Raft Adventures—or AzRA for short—organized all our river logistics. Their large, motorized rafts would carry the tons of gear and food so we could concentrate exclusively on safely kayaking the river. AzRA was the same company that had taken me and the blind teenagers down the Grand Canyon with Harlan and Marieke years before, so it was all coming full circle. Since that first trip, the owner, Fred Thevenin, had been a huge supporter and had gone out of his way to make sure we had everything we needed.

When all was ready and the three support boats loaded, we eased into the river under what Harlan described as a "clear crystalline sky." There had been many months of preparation and buildup, so it felt good to finally be on the water. A soft breeze blew against my face. Later in the day, that wind could rage, a result of rising heat that forced the air up the canyon. Often it blew so fiercely, it canceled out the effects of the water current so you had to fight your way downriver. However, for now, the sun and breeze felt perfect. I did a practice roll, and when I came up, I took a deep breath and listened to the muffled sound of the river funneling skyward, filling the canyon and reverberating off the sheer rock walls to either side. I could already sense the majesty of this place, as well as its menace.

As we passed under the Navajo Bridge, just a few miles below the put-in, Rob paddled up to me excitedly reporting that he had seen a California condor right overhead. They'd been unknowingly decimated by lead poisoning, reduced to just one remaining bird in the wild by 1987; but with reintroduction efforts, they were slowly making a comeback.

"It's a good omen!" Rob said excitedly. "Although I don't really believe in omens," he then corrected himself.

Approaching Badger Creek Rapid, I could hear tourists hooting and hollering from the cliffs five hundred feet above us, wishing us a bon voyage. By now I was concentrating more on the rising murmur of water ahead, and I felt the zing of acceleration under my boat as our team took its positions. Timmy, Steve, and Skyler went through first and then eddied out below the rapid, ready to rescue any swimmers or retrieve any boats or paddles. I went second with Harlan just behind me calling commands in my headset. Rob slipped in behind Harlan, scanning the rapid and keeping an eye on me, ready to swoop in and assume commands should Harlan flip or have any problems of his own. "Easy forward," Harlan called over the radio. "Small left. Now easy right." I bounced over giant wave swells. "Now charge!" Harlan yelled, and a wave hit me unexpectedly from the side. I braced hard and felt myself tipping. *Do not flip and swim in your first rapid*, I scolded myself. I recovered and managed to stay upright. Sitting in the eddy below Badger, Harlan and Rob eased up to me, and Rob slapped me on the back.

"Nice job, Big E. One rapid down, just 164 to go." Then he let out a big honking laugh that echoed off the canyon walls.

Lonnie's team came through next, with Seth in front and Chris behind, and Lonnie between them. Seth was hollering loud, "On me! On me!" and kept shouting all the way through. Rocky was the last to pull into the eddy. He was serving as sweep, or as we had begun to call it, the "Hail Mary." If all else failed, he'd be the guy to help any stragglers who'd gotten into trouble and had somehow been left behind.

As we paddled out of the eddy and back into the current, the sound of Badger Creek faded slowly behind us, replaced by hoots of encouragement and paddle high fives. Timmy glided up beside Rob and said, "We're under way, Papa Duck. And excellent orchestration of our first rapid, I might add."

"Papa Duck?" Rob repeated quizzically.

"Yeah," said Timmy. "You're E's original guide, the man who's most responsible for us all being here. You're the proud daddy who watches over his baby ducklings and makes sure they're safe." Then he patted Rob on the back, leaned in, and said more quietly, "And you are the elder statesman of the team."

We all chuckled, but as I thought about it, the name was perfect. Rob was paternal, not in an overbearing way, but like a good sheepdog watchs over his flock, attentive and aware. His role had changed from being my lead guide to now being one of the secondary guides, supporting Harlan. This had actually been Rob's decision. He'd known that Harlan's experience and unparalleled knowledge of the Grand Canyon made him the best choice to guide me. It was a typical Rob Raker maneuver, absolutely devoid of ego, and I respected him even more for it. Though he had stepped back, I knew he would always be nearby, always right behind or on the periphery, watching every move to make sure his team was safe and the trip would go smoothly. Timmy was right. He was our Papa Duck.

Now on flat water, our flotilla spread out over the wide river. Rob paddled off to see if he could spot more condors or bighorn sheep on the cliffs. The muscles in my arms were already feeling the effect of what would dominate much of the next three weeks: paddling flat water downstream into variable headwinds. Harlan had warned us: "When people envision the Grand Canyon, they only think about white water, but between those rapids, there's a lot of flat water, 91 percent to be exact. So there'll be plenty of time to chat and chill between the carnage."

It was three miles until the next rapid, Soap Creek, so Harlan and I settled into a steady rhythm, rolling underwater every few minutes to stave off the heat. Then I heard a quick splash. Harlan chuckled and said, "E, check this out. Hold out your hands." I lay my paddle across my boat and put my palms up, and he plopped a large, slimy, wriggling trout into my hands. He'd seen it swimming in the clear water and literally plucked it out of the river. I smiled in disbelief before dropping it back. Harlan had such an intimate relationship with this place. I remembered how on our first trip down here, his sister had described him surfing and flipping in the play waves, how he was virtually one with his kayak, and he and his kayak were one with the river. On the Usu, he'd told me that, during one busy year guiding biologists and private trips, he'd spent over one hundred days down here. He knew every bend, every side canyon, every tributary, every beach, bench, and riffle. I was awed by that kind of deep connection and knowledge. I remembered then his tale of his first trip through the canyon at nine years old, and something struck me.

"Hey," I said, trying to keep my boat straight in the swirls, "when you came down here that first time with your mom, how come your dad didn't join you? You told me those great stories about riding horses and camping out together. Was he working or something?"

Harlan was quiet for a moment. I'd noticed that about him; he never just spouted out a response, but instead seemed to first carefully consider the question.

"He might have taken me if he'd been around," Harlan said finally. "But he died two years before, when I was seven. It was tough on me and my sister, but we got through."

After that, I let it rest, the only sound the blurps of our paddle blades cleaving the water in unison.

In the late afternoon, after several more rapids, we reached the Supai Ledges, just as an impressive September squall began pattering raindrops on the flat rock shelves. The patter turned into a full-on deluge, and everyone scurried to set up tents, and some of the boys bivouacked in caves between the overhanging ledges of rocks. As sheeting rains cascaded down the canyon walls, it felt like something of a celebration. After a successful first day on the river, most of us stripped down and stood beneath the superheated water-falls pouring off the cliffs, showering in the warm wash, laughing. The rain came down so hard, I could hear chunks of earth falling from the walls across the river and splashing violently into the water.

After dinner I hustled to my tent, which was on a flat shelf of rock right next to the river. It was still raining, and I wanted to get dry, stretch out my tight lower back, and ponder what lay ahead. Soon, I heard soft footsteps and then a head poking into my tent door. "Hey, Erik." It was Harlan.

"Come get out of the rain," I said.

"Proud first day," he said, sitting on a sleeping pad next to me.

"We have a couple of pretty big rapids tomorrow, don't we?" I asked.

"House Rock and the Roaring Twenties are a little spicy," he answered, "but we'll be fine. We'll definitely need to be on our game, though."

Spicy was guide-speak for *exciting*.

Harlan was quiet for a long time. The sound of pummeling rain on the nylon tent became rhythmic, almost percussive. "When you asked me today about why my mom took me down here, it got me thinking back on that time," he said. The rain came down harder, and Harlan zipped the tent most of the way shut.

"I was the one who found him," he said. It came out quiet and measured, but it felt to me like something he'd wanted to say for a while.

Now I was the quiet one, waiting for a time before I asked, "What happened?"

"Remember on the Usumacinta I told you what a wild man he was? He didn't take care of himself. Ox-strong, but hefty too. And there was his untreated epilepsy. Well, anyway, one evening when I was seven, I heard the shower running upstairs and I went up there—maybe because the shower had been running too long. I knocked on the door, and no answer. All I could hear was that shower running and running and what sounded like water splashing against the floor. So I pushed the door open and walked in, and there was my dad, lying in the bathtub. One of his arms was flung outside the tub, with the showerhead just spraying down on his face. His face was blue, which, even at seven, I knew wasn't right."

I didn't know what to say. So I just waited, and he continued talking over the sound of the rain and the river.

"Water was cascading all over his face, pouring into his open mouth. Water running onto the floor. I was frozen, unable to move. I was fixated on the water. Finally, I thought, maybe I could wake him up. I went over and pulled on his arm and tried to move him, but he was 250 pounds lying in the bathtub. I couldn't budge him. Later, I wandered around in this blurry daze as the paramedics came and they loaded my dad on a backboard and then rushed him to the hospital. I sat there in the waiting room. I felt numb and helpless to do anything. Then the doctors came out and shook their heads and told us, 'He's gone.'"

I thought of young Harlan standing there looking at his father's face, too frozen to act. And what was there to do anyway, I wondered, in the face of such massive forces weighing down on him?

"How could you know, or understand, anything of what had happened?" I asked. Then, only in my head, I added, *Or how your life would change as a result of that day?*

"I don't think I had a way to process those words, or what I'd just witnessed," Harlan replied. "We were left destitute, utterly impoverished. We had to put buckets on the floor to catch rain from the leaky roof. For a long time after that, I felt sort of paralyzed, an overwhelming dread of more loss. I gained a ton of weight—eventually tipping about 260 in high school. After his death, my mom and sister told me I went real quiet. I hardly spoke a single word for two years."

I'd felt that same powerlessness after the death of my mother when I was a teenager, and a plaguing fear that my future would be a succession of loss and pain. The rain was letting up, just a soft tapping on the tent now.

"Rain's died down," Harlan said, unzipping the fly and peering out. "I got some gear to organize, but I wanted you to know I wasn't avoiding your question this afternoon."

After he left, I lay there thinking about him for a long time. I had always thought of Harlan as indestructible, superhuman, and it made me realize how hard it was to truly know a person, to see through that impenetrable armor, all the way to the child, shattered, speechless, and carrying the weight of that water on his soul. Harlan was my lifeline, and the irony wasn't lost on me. He was the one responsible for calling precise, split-second commands; I totally relied on his voice, yet after his father's death, he had been forced to claw his way out of a deep well of despair just to find his own voice again. And now, his voice was taking me down the river.

I awoke to morning sun drying the tent and the rock shelves we'd camped on. As we launched our kayaks, the river smelled of earth, and the water felt textured, thick with silt. That silt was already covering my face, in my mouth and eyes, in my underwear and clothing. "The Colorado River has the highest percentage of silt to water of any other river in the world," Harlan said, "and after it rains, it turns to sludge." Rob confirmed that the water had gone from clear, where we'd started near the Glen Canyon Dam, to "chocolate milk."

Shortly, we came to House Rock Rapid, the first considerable rapid of the canyon. It was rated about a 7 on the Grand Canyon 1–10 scale. "Stay right, stay right," Harlan warned me as we drew near. But his voice was garbled and choppy over the radios, cutting in and out. *Great*, I thought, feeling frustration and fear expanding inside me. *The first big rapid, and the radios are already failing!* "Large hole on left! Hard right!" I barely made out the words through my earpiece.

The force of the water and lack of clear communication had put me on the defensive. I tensed up and leaned back, my head cocked awkwardly to the side as I strained to hear. The movement became violent, abrupt, tossing me up and down. Amid the tumult, the paint-shaker motion, and the boomeranging barrage of river noise, I recovered and did what Rob and Harlan had taught me. I paddled hard.

"Charge!" I finally heard Harlan say, muffled and distant. I slammed into a cold wall of water. A powerful lateral wave lurched me sideways as the world tossed and turned in dizzying confusion. "Brace left! Brace left!" Harlan squawked, and I righted myself, half hearing "Charge!" I dug in, air, spray, and sound engulfing me. "You're good, you're good," Harlan's voice crackled as I bounced through the last set of tail waves and eddied out, slumping in relief.

The next ten miles were through the Roaring Twenties, a bunch of big rapids in quick succession. A third of the way through, we stopped at one of the giant waves to try to surf it, one of Harlan's favorite hobbies. We all waited in the eddy, and when it was my turn, Harlan tried to get me angled just right, and then gave a "charge" command to get me paddling hard across the hole, leaning hard and bracing upriver and desperately trying to stay upright. For a moment, I rode the wave laterally, back and forth, before being flipped and flushed out the bottom. Neither Lonnie nor I had the technique down, but Steven, Rob, and Timmy could stay on the wave for thirty seconds or more, while Harlan managed to stay in the longest, doing spins and cartwheels. I gave up after a few tries, happy to float in the eddy, listening to the yips and critiques of the team, but Lonnie was persistent. He must have charged that hole a dozen times, each time getting flipped, spit out the bottom, and eagerly awaiting another try. Our styles were definitely different: I was methodical and conservative, while Lonnie had more of a "yee-haw" attitude, attacking the big rapids like a rodeo cowboy riding a bull.

"Lonnie hit that play wave like the lawn dart that he is," said Timmy. "He's got a sharp point, and he launches in hard and headfirst, ready to impale anything in his way!"

We all laughed, and "LonDart" became his official river name.

Throughout the rest of the Roaring Twenties, the radios were driving me crazy and increasing my stress level exponentially. Sometimes they worked and sometimes they didn't, and the unpredictability was the most disconcerting aspect. In Rapid 24.5, a set of powerful waves sent me and my kayak airborne. When I landed in the storm of water, Harlan yelled, and it came out as "Brrrr rttt!" and it took me a second to process that he was saying, "Brace right!" but when I leaned right, it was too late. A crashing wave pounded me from the left. I went under, finally rolling back up at the bottom of the rapid. By the end of the Roaring Twenties, that mental tension had translated into physical exhaustion. My upper body was tight, my reactions delayed and imprecise.

When we got to camp, I was quiet and on edge. "A rapid has enough wild cards," I said to Skyler dejectedly. "I don't need another one." In the midst of big, loud chaos, it was so comforting to have a voice in my ear. It gave me confidence. Without that tether to another human being, I felt alone, like that sea of water would engulf me and overpower me. The team gathered on the rocky bank and began troubleshooting, reading through the manual, testing the on and off switches, carefully examining the "manpacks" to see if water had gotten inside or whether one of the seals had been compromised.

Skyler, who'd been part of the search for a radio solution for a couple of years, was frustrated. "It's kind of voodoo," he said. "Sometimes they work; sometimes they don't."

Rob, a scientist to the core, took charge and brought a systematic approach. We had two complete units, with extra headsets, and all the components seemed to be affected, but we sequentially went through each configuration, manpack A with headset A, B, and C, then manpack B, with headset A, B, and C, and so on. Rob suggested we keep a log of the best pairings, and Skyler carefully jotted it all down in his notebook. Surprisingly, some arrangements did work better than others, but none were all that great.

"There's also the possibility," Rob added, "that it might be a Bluetooth-related issue. Some kind of interference."

Skyler thought the chances of that were slim to none, but he bit his lip and made the rounds to the whole team, including the AzRA guides, making sure they dug into their dry bags to confirm their cell phones were turned off, as well as making sure the film crew had all their computers shut down. At the end of all the problem-solving work, we still had no clear solution, and it was jeopardizing the trip.

Thankfully, the next two days were light on rapids, with long stretches of flat water. Harlan and the other guides could rest their voices, and Steven cleverly attached his iPod to a couple of waterproof speakers, which he slung over his back. Lonnie and I fell in behind him, paddling in rhythm to our favorite high-energy tunes like "Up on Cripple Creek" by The Band, and "Proud Mary," a.k.a. "Rolling on the River" by CCR. Music sounded clear and sharp with the beats reverberating crisply off the canyon walls. Since following a constant sound was way more efficient than responding and readjusting to voice commands, it made the miles go pretty quickly, except for the occasional times Lonnie and I would unexpectedly collide, paddles clanking or Lonnie's boat spearing mine in LonDart fashion.

At midday, we stopped at Redwall Cavern, a stunning three hundred–foot-deep natural alcove in the limestone where we had also stopped on our first Leading the Way trip, with the blind kids running barefoot relays across the sand. I walked around inside with Lonnie, trying to teach him some of the FlashSonar techniques I had learned from Daniel Kish. Lonnie was a quick study at most things he attempted. On the beach the day before, he'd actually won a game of horseshoes, ending it with a ringer! I clicked my tongue and clapped my hands, showing Lonnie how the sound changed as we neared the back wall of the alcove. Then we reversed and listened to the echo grow more expansive as the ceiling got higher, until the sound opened up entirely at the mouth. It was cool inside, and we hung out there for an hour before we entered the scorching sun again.

At the end of the day, I was pretty fatigued, not only from the burning heat that, in my dry top, made me feel I was stewing in my own personal sauna, but from concentrating so hard on following Harlan's commands, which were increasingly difficult to decipher through the radios. His voice had begun sounding so distant, it was like he was calling down to me from the moon. I shouted over to Skyler, "Sky, can you snag me the sat phone?" We'd planned to use it only for emergencies, but I figured failing radios after only a few days of paddling qualified. *Houston, we have a problem*, I thought. We managed to scramble up to an open place on the ledges where we got a decent sat signal, and I called the radio communications company in the U.K. Derek, the owner, luckily answered and readily agreed to express-air two more units. However, a lot of logistical parts would need to come together. Derek would have to build and test the units and overnight ship them from Europe. They'd need to clear customs in Phoenix and be driven to Flagstaff. Then Marieke, Harlan's sister, would have to drive them to the South Rim, where one of Harlan's friends would hike them down to Phantom Ranch at the bottom of the canyon. We'd be to Phantom in less than a week, and if there was one mishap in the chain, I'd have no working radios for the biggies: Horn Creek, Granite, Crystal, Upset, and most important, Lava Falls.

That night, the crew hung out pretty late after dinner, having a few beers and telling river stories. As usual, Timmy provided the entertainment by dragging out two giant dry bags, which clanged and jingled. He reached inside and began handing out musical instruments: old guitars, drums, triangles, cowbells, tambourines, and percussive shakers. Everyone took an instrument and began jamming in a circle, with Timmy whimsically leading and improvising lyrics, usually about someone on the trip like Papa Duck or Lonnie the LonDart. Then he'd call out a name and that person would have to sing a verse impromptu. Rob laughed as Lonnie came out of his tent, having changed into his overalls and cowboy boots. He grabbed the only two ladies on the trip, rafting guides Katie and Kelly, and began country swing dancing with both of them.

I went to bed as the party was still cranking and fell into a half sleep, but I awoke again to the sound of soft drumbeats, jangling bells, murmuring, and giggling, all moving around my tent. I could hear Timmy at the front of the line, orchestrating his troops. Steven was behind him, and the entire team in succession, their instruments and chanting growing louder and louder. By the time I was fully awake, I began processing what they were singing. It had the soft tone of a lullaby, but the words weren't from any children's song I'd ever heard.

Erik, Erik of the river, peeing in his kayak when he tips . . .
Erik, Erik of the river, farting underwater when he flips . . .

Then I heard them unzipping my tent door and sticking their heads in as they sang in my face.

Erik, Erik of the river, first one to the groover every morn . . .
Erik, Erik of the river, hoping he won't poop himself at Horn.

They kept going, getting softer and softer, like they were trying to lull me back to sleep. I smiled. "You guys are insane," I said.

"It's a 'be well' lullaby," said Timmy in a mischievous whisper. "It's a mythical folk tale, a scatological love ballad about a man's journey down the river as he conquers his fears and emerges victorious."

And with that, Timmy zipped up the door, and I heard the fading sound of strumming, tambourines jangling, and their voices:

Erik, Erik of the river, he's got a bomber roll . . .
Erik, Erik of the river, don't go in that munching hole.
Erik, Erik of the river.

When I woke up again and rolled over, I could hear that most people had turned in, but Harlan and Timmy were still up, talking in hushed voices. As I lay awake listening, Timmy said, "It's pretty wild guiding him. It's like playing two video games simultaneously. I imagine the bow of his boat as the avatar on the screen and I'm trying to see ahead, past the exploding waves, navigating him through the minefield of rocks, holes, and hydraulics. And sometimes the Erik avatar spins or surges when you don't anticipate it, and your best trajectory goes out the window. Now you're on a new line through more unexpected chaos, and you say to yourself, 'Okay, get ready for a wild ride!' What makes the game so challenging, and brilliant, is that while operating the Erik avatar, I'm also trying to maneuver the Timmy avatar, so I'm not getting hammered myself. It's like virtual reality, but the consequences aren't so virtual."

Harlan said, "Yeah. I know. I feel such intense responsibility. Especially in the bigger rapids, the ones coming up. It's just chaos, waves crashing from all directions, and there's always that potential that the river takes me down, or washes me in one direction and him in another, or I flip upside down. That is a very stark reality, and I think about it constantly. I mean, we are just these little beings and this river is very, very powerful. It doesn't matter how good you are, or how many trips you've done through the canyon: the river is the boss."

After, I was up a long time, seeing the video game of Timmy's creatively disturbed mind with the little Erik icon being steered crazily through the hazards. As I drifted off into a fitful sleep, the cartoon Erik icon was being sucked into a dark abyss, which belched loudly as it swallowed. An upbeat voice said, "Thanks for playing," and a little tune played, which sounded strangely like "Erik of the River."

After another day of paddling mostly flat water, we made it into camp with enough time to spend the late afternoon heading up the steep switch-back trail to the cliff-side Nankoweap Granaries, hundreds of feet above the river. Small hollowed-out rooms were carved into the sheer wall where ancient Pueblo peoples, ancestors of the current-day Hopi, stored seeds and grain to protect their food source from critters and rot. As Harlan and I sat on the rocks in front of the ruins, I said, "They must have been an industrious people to carve out a life in this arid desert."

"They were deeply connected to the river and this canyon," he replied. Then he took my hand and pointed upstream. "They also had salt mines a few miles from here," he said. "Some of the walls are still white as chalk. It was a rite of manhood for Hopi boys to take a pilgrimage from high up on the mesa down to the salt mines. They're sacred grounds."

As Harlan talked, I could hear the reverence in his voice, like Andy Parkin, from the second No Barriers Summit, talking about his sculpture, or Adrian Anantawan describing his violin, or Rob describing his discovery of a peacock flounder under the sand. "Like I said, I used to spend almost a third of the year down here," Harlan mused, "one eighteen-day trip after another. That gave me a chance to build a relationship with this place. I'd come back to town, scratched and bruised with big, giant bloody flaps of skin hanging off my heels. Sometimes I would wake up in my house, in the middle of the night, sweating and confused, because I didn't know where the stars were or what was upstream or what was downstream. I couldn't hear the sound of the river; I couldn't see the canyon walls because I was enclosed by the four walls of my room."

I could hear Lonnie and the team below, hoofing it back down the trail. Early evening winds began picking up, descending from the canyon rim. It felt so peaceful up here, I was in no hurry to leave. "This is my home," Harlan continued, "and I want to share it with you."

I had to admit, it was quite an impressive home. I could hear the huge canyon wall across the river and the open expanse of the sky above. Somewhere above I could hear the cry of a red-tailed hawk, and far below, I could hear the ever-present churn of the river as it pressed on toward the sea.

"I'm still afraid," I said, waving my hand in the direction of the river below. "I've tried to fight it, but sometimes I think the fear is winning . . . and the real big rapids are all still ahead."

Harlan paused, and I could tell he was also surveying the river, both upstream and down. "In kayaking, you're interacting with something that is bigger than you," he said, "something that is moving randomly in different directions. No matter how good you get, you can't always predict it. And once you're headed into the rapid, there's no STOP button. It's not like other sports where you can throw on the brakes and regroup. Once you've made the decision to go, you have to be okay with it and accept what happens. That's daunting, but I think it's also beautiful. The river does what it does."

"But how do you ever master that mind game?" I asked.

"I think it's a balance between control and letting go," he answered. "Try to control it completely, and the river crushes you. Give in completely, and the river will also crush you. It's ultimately about harnessing its energy and riding it for a moment."

"I think my mind gets in the way," I admitted.

"Physically, you have all the skills dialed," he said. "What you have to work on is calming yourself, being at peace, and accepting your decisions. And most importantly, not letting your mind screw up what your body is doing already."

What Harlan was telling me to do seemed strikingly similar to what Mandy Harvey had told me as we walked along Clear Creek in Golden. When she could still hear, she would get so nervous before a performance she would actually go backstage and vomit; but after she went deaf and could no longer hear her own voice, ironically, she found a way to let go of her expectations of the results and just go for it. "If I think about it too much," she'd told me, "my brain tries to hypermanage all the stuff I have no control over, like not being able to hear the piano or the sax. If I think about it over and over, I psych myself out to the point where I can't remember where the note is, and then I can't find it for the life of me. When I perform, I have to *not think*, just shut my brain up." And as she learned to bypass the brain, her voice had gotten stronger.

It was time to head back to dinner. As I stood up, brushed off my pants, and began probing my trekking poles for the jumble of descending rocks, I knew tomorrow began the Inner Gorge, and the radios were becoming a lesson in frustration. A wave of nerves passed through my body, but then I focused on my breathing and the soft rush of the river, letting it fill my consciousness. With each exhalation, I felt some of that weight lifting. *Maybe*, I thought, *I'll try it LonDart style.*

Waking on the seventh day, we had a series of four challenging rapids to navigate in succession, all rated about 8s: Hance, then Sockdolager, Grapevine, and Zoroaster. On the way across the beach to breakfast, I could hear Lonnie on the ground doing his morning ritual of fifty sit-ups, crunches, and push-ups, a military habit he'd stuck with. As I choked down some breakfast, feeling nauseous, our filmmaker, Michael Brown, asked me, "What are you thinking this morning?"

"I'm actually trying not to think," I answered. After consulting Harlan, he felt comfortable guiding me without radios. He'd try to stay right behind me and yell extra loudly. "If we get separated for any reason," he said, "don't panic. Relax. Breathe. Be at peace with the river. You're here, in this moment. Nothing else matters."

A mile out of camp, we came to Hance, a long, left bend in the river with the right side dubbed "the Land of the Giants," a series of big boulders to avoid.

"We'll work from the tongue of smooth water starting out on the right," Harlan said, "then skirt left, avoiding the big, potentially problematic holes created by those rocks."

Somehow I was able to follow Mandy's and Harlan's advice and to execute Harlan's directions, angling my boat against the crashing laterals coming off the boulders. I was actually surprised when Harlan yelled, "We're good! We're through it! Now we're just riding the squirrely water at the bottom!"

Sockdolager was up next, named by Major Powell. It was the phrase used at the time to describe a knockout blow in a boxing match. He was referring to the two massive sequential waves, about twenty feet from trough to crest. Harlan steered me in and lined me up straight against them. "Charge! Charge!" he yelled, and I rode up the first that felt almost vertical, and then down, digging with everything I had, exploding through the next that crashed over my head. I disappeared for a moment in the wall of water and then emerged on the other side into the bright sun. I think I was actually smiling.

After Grapevine and Zoroaster, we arrived at Cremation Camp, about a mile above the famous Phantom Ranch. Long, steep trails from both the North and South Rims of the canyon accessed Phantom, so we were joined now by throngs of hikers, some camping among the cottonwood trees along Bright Angel Creek. Somehow word had gotten out about the two blind kayakers coming down the river, and Lonnie and I posed for photos with several families. From the ranch bar/restaurant, Timmy helped me write a postcard home.

> Dear Ellie, Emma, Arjun—
> At Phantom Ranch mile 88 and day 7. It's 100 degrees outside, so stopped at the canteen for an ice-cold Arnold Palmer. Even though no working radios, made it through some big rapids today. Plenty more on the way! Lonnie and all kayak guides are crushing it. Miss you. Love you. Can't wait to "see" you. Love El Dad.
> Transcribed by Timmy 9/13/2014

Outside the window of the bar, I could hear nearly continuous mule trains carrying supplies up and down the canyon. It was comforting to know those hoofbeats were the link to my family. They'd be carrying my postcard almost five thousand feet up the Bright Angel Trail, and it would arrive back in Colorado in a few days.

That night, we settled into Cremation Camp, and after dinner, we began hearing clanking around the kitchen area. There wasn't enough wind to knock pots and pans over, so Timmy investigated, shining his light against the rocks. "Ringtail cats!" he exclaimed. "Two of 'em."

"Actually," Rob interjected, "the term *ringtail cat* is a misnomer. They're from the same kingdom, phylum, class, and order, but are from different families. Felines are in the Felidae family. Ringtails are part of the Procyonidae family."

"Thanks for the appropriately placed factoids," Timmy replied a little testily.

Harlan got up, chucked a rock over in their general direction, and shooed them away from the kitchen. I could hear them scrambling up onto the sheer rock wall right behind the camp. "Ringtails are beautiful, but pesky little critters," he said. He described them: long, striped tails and big, round ears. "They're nocturnal, and they get into all kinds of stuff if you leave it out. They'll chew a hole through a dry bag to get to free food!"

"Reminds me of the coons and possums back home on the farm," Lonnie added.

Then Harlan asked, "So, Lonnie, how does a farm boy from Indiana wind up kayaking down the Grand Canyon, anyway?"

Lonnie cleared his throat and said, "Well, it started with meeting the folks from Team River Runner and learning to roll in my little pond, but really, the truth of it is, it all started with my daughter Bug and me mowing the lawn."

Everyone smiled, ready for a signature Lonnie joke, but he was serious when he went on, "About three months after I lost my eyesight, after the accident, I was setting around my house doing nothin' feelin' sorry for myself, and I got up and decided to go outside. I had no mobility training, but I found a broomstick and used it to walk out through the yard, toward my barn. But before I got there, I ran into a tussle of weeds, about up to my chest. So I turned around and went back up to the house. My youngest daughter was standing there. Her name's Taylor, but I call her Bug. She was five years old at the time.

"She looked up at me, and she said, 'Daddy, what's wrong?' I said, 'Nothing, Bug.' Now, I couldn't see her, but I'm convinced she put her one hand on her hip and pointed her little finger at me. She said, 'Yeah, there is, Daddy. Tell me what's wrong!' I was getting called out by a five-year-old. I said, 'Well, Bug, if you got to know, I'm just a little frustrated. I can't get into my barn without walking through all those dern weeds, and I can't see to mow them.' She looked at me, and she said, 'Daddy, I'll help you.' I said, 'All right, girl, if you got the guts, take my finger, lead me to the garage.' "

I imagined this feisty little mini-Lonnie leading him through the grass, just as happy as a possum in a slop bucket.

"Bug led me around to the garage. I had my truck parked outside, but she led me around it and lifted up the big door into the garage where I stored my riding lawn mower. I said, 'Take me to the mower.' She took me over there. I got on it, put her on my lap, fired it up, out the door we went. Then she yelled, 'Stop!' I said, 'What?' She said, 'The truck.' I said, 'Where is it?' She said, 'Right there.' I said, 'Right where?' "

Lonnie had me now. I was leaning forward on my folding chair in anticipation. "I said, 'Point at it.' She pointed at it, and I felt her little arm. I turned the wheel, backed up, turned it the other way, and took off. Then I heard, 'Stop, the tree! Stop, the fuel tank!' 'Okay, Bug. If we got to go left or right, you start turning the wheel that direction. I'll feel it, and I'll help you.' She drove me right out to the barn. I had her get off the lawn mower, go back up to the house, and watch."

I was cringing, just waiting for him to collide into the side of the barn, or worse.

"I got my hand on the side of the barn, squared it up, and mowed a lap. Then I took that broomstick, held it against the barn and mowed a second lap. I held it all the way out and mowed the third lap. I shut the lawn mower off, and I went back up to the house. I could hear Bug just squealing, 'You did it, Daddy, you did it! I knew you could do it!' I picked her up and give her a big hug."

Timmy lifted his beer and said, "Toast to the LonDart. May he always charge on his mower the same way he charges the rapids. Women, small children, and livestock be damned."

"Timmy, I can assure you, I've never hit one cow," Lonnie corrected. "Maybe a squirrel or two." He chuckled at his joke and then resumed, "But about two minutes later, my dad pulled up into the driveway. He said, 'Who mowed around the barn?' I said, 'Tell him, Bug.' She told him, and he got mad, I mean furious. He said, 'I told you, if you ever need anything done around here, you let me know and I'll do it.' I said, 'No, Dad. You realize what just happened here?'

"He said, 'You mowed around your barn?' I said, 'No. Much more than that.'"

Lonnie's voice got softer, almost a whisper, and there was a deep pride in it. "I said, 'Do you see that little girl standing right there? To that little girl right there, and to her two sisters, my name is still Daddy. To that little girl right there and her two sisters, I'm still the man. To that little girl and her two sisters, I still can.'"

Everyone was quiet, soaking it all in. Then Lonnie asked, "Now, when I look into the mirror, you know what I see?"

Steven answered, "You see pride for everything you've overcome?"

"No," Lonnie replied. "I'm blind. I don't see nothin' in there."

Everyone laughed and groaned. He chuckled and then went on, "When we get up every day and we look in the mirror, we have to see worth. We have to see value. We have to see we're needed, we're loved, and we can make a difference. And when I look in the mirror now, I say, 'Yeedog, you're getting better looking all the time!'"

Lonnie guffawed and then said, "That day I got shot in the face, well, I thought the world had come to an end, but thanks to a child, I took a step, and the world was still there."

Harlan began strumming his guitar, and everyone sat listening to the river and the chords on the wind. Finally, Lonnie said, "Well, Harlan, how's a redneck hippie cowboy from Flagstaff end up spending most his life on this river, runnin' through this big canyon?"

Harlan did his typical pause as he thought and then said, "Well, listening to your story of mowing your lawn, I probably had one of those moments myself. It was on the river, when I was nineteen. I had just finished EMT school and was going down Cataract Canyon, a stretch of the Colorado several hundred miles upriver from here. There was a big spring flood, and the water level rose unexpectedly. It was raging, about fifty-five thousand cfs, four times bigger than the flow we're on now. We had four or five boats, and I was rowing one of them. We got in over our heads. We'd already had two rafts flip and two kayakers swim. Finally, we were able to get a few boats to shore and then spent half the day retrieving rafts that were stuck in eddies and others that were pinned on rocks. When we headed down again, two more people were thrown out of their boats and had to be rescued. There was one section of rapids so huge, we decided it was too dangerous to take passengers, but there was one woman on the trip named Jane. She was sixty, and she was a fireball. She was adamant about running this stretch. It was a private trip, so it was her decision, even though we tried to talk her out of it. She chose to ride with the trip leader, Greg. They were right in front of me, and I saw their boat get vertical at the top of a massive wave. It looked like Greg was torn out of his boat. I couldn't see Jane and figured she was down in the bottom of the boat. I went vertical too, catching the left side of the wave, and thought for sure I was going to corkscrew over, but somehow the front of my boat dropped. and I was still upright.

"I was rowing downstream, and Greg was swimming in the eddy with his boat and yelling, 'Jane's downstream! Jane's downstream!' I was pulling on the oars as hard as I could, and a quarter mile farther, saw Jane head-down, bobbing on the shoreline, up against the rocks. When I could eddy out below, I leaped from the boat while my friend James tied it off. I ran up the rocky shoreline until I came up over a large boulder. There she was, still facedown, water surging all around her and washing her up against the rocks and mud. I didn't want to see her face, but I had no choice. I jumped into the water and log-rolled her over onto her back, pulling her up onto a semi-flat rock."

Harlan took a swig of what I could smell was whiskey, then passed it on.

"I saw just what I had feared the most. The skin of her face was blue-gray, and there was sediment packed into her nostrils. Her eyes were glazed over and milky, staring right past me into another world. James arrived, and we went to work, checking her airway, her breathing, her pulse. I came up with nothing. She was dead. James handed me his knife, and I cut her shirt off. He started doing the breathing, and I launched into the compressions. I had never performed CPR on a person for real before, and I felt helpless. I guess I half expected, or hoped, that like in the movies she'd cough and spew out water and blink and come to, but we went for ten to fifteen minutes, and nothing. James said, 'Harlan, I think she's dead.' I thought so too, but I wasn't going to stop. She had a bowel movement then and was having 'agonal breathing,' which I knew from my recent training were her last, dying death gasps."

By now, all of us sitting there listening to Harlan's story had pretty much stopped breathing too.

"We kept working on her. We swapped positions, James on compression and me on breathing. After another fifteen minutes, I felt a pulse. James checked, but he didn't feel anything. I doubted myself then, thinking I was imagining it, or feeling my own pulse. I grabbed Jane's wrist again, and like a drumbeat, her heart was going. I kept rescue breathing for her, and her breaths grew shallow, sporadic, and gurgled. We turned her over on her side, and she heaved a bit and some frothy sputum dribbled out of her mouth. Her breathing began to improve, and after some more rescue breathing, it became regular enough that I let her do it on her own. From that point, all I could do was talk to her, and I never shut up. 'Come on, Jane, I'm here for you. Fight. I'm not giving up, so don't you dare either!'

"We carried her down on a backboard, got her on a raft, and then rode her downstream. She had a pulse, but it wasn't stable. It turned out that someone in our group had managed to kayak downstream and get a commercial trip to use their two-way radio to contact a passing airplane that then contacted a medical helicopter. At dusk, the medevac landed nearby, and the paramedics took over and got an IV going. We loaded her up into the bird, and off they went. All I could see were the lights flashing as they ascended out of the canyon.

"Then I just slumped onto the beach, life jacket still on, covered in her poop and pee and her vomit. Everything I'd just learned in EMT school said she was probably still going to die. The next morning, as we floated the thirty-two miles out, I was still numb from everything that had happened, but when we passed underneath the bridge two miles from our take-out, I saw a car parked up there. They were yelling down to us, 'Jane's okay! Jane's fine!'"

The whiskey was getting passed around faster now, and even I, usually not much for the stuff, took a big gulp. "What enabled her to live," Harlan said, "was the CPR from me and James of course, and the paramedics, but it was also something more. The Colorado River is extremely cold. That cold enabled her to survive way longer than any human is supposed to."

"Yes," Rob confirmed. "It's a documented phenomenon. It's called the 'mammalian diving reflex,' and it's not very well understood. Being immersed in cold water somehow slows down the heart, stops the breathing, and redistributes the blood flow toward the organs that need most of the oxygen—the heart, lungs, and brain."

"But also," Harlan continued, "it was the warm desert that helped raise her body temperature back to normal, at just the right rate: not too fast, not too slow. So the river and the canyon played a part as well. It was the river that took her, but it was also the river that saved her."

As Harlan spoke slowly and deliberately, I had a strong impression that he wasn't just talking about Jane. Seven-year-old Harlan had gazed upon his father, the water pouring over his face, and he had been powerless to do anything, unable to come to terms with what had happened. But twelve years later, Harlan had stared down at another bluish face, yet this time, he'd brought a woman back from the dead. It was as though the river had allowed him to earn some of that power back.

"I knew it didn't change the past," Harlan said, "but it changed something in me. I remember sitting in my boat, looking out into the river. The way the shadows from the canyon walls were casting out into the waves, it looked like the waves and the shadows were dancing. I thought about my life, and the lives of everyone around me, and I knew we were all in the hands of the river. Sitting above a rapid, no one ever really knows what the outcome will be. I think that's where my respect comes from; the fact that one person will pass through safely, and another may be asked to join with the river forever. But a big part of my life has been floating through these canyons and experiencing all the river is willing to reveal, if you are willing to give up yourself for a short while and listen."

24

FLOW

Since Rob's cancer diagnosis, he'd been learning how dairy and animal fats could accelerate the spread of prostate cancer, and he'd been trying to eliminate them. But he also knew that, unlike sparse mountain provisions, a river trip was full of temptation: chicken alfredo, steak fajitas with sour cream and shredded cheese, bread doused with garlic butter, and carrot cake and berry crumble. So Rob had made it his No Barriers pledge to restrict his diet to fruit, veggies, and fish during the entire trip. However, various team members had already been catching him break his vow, sneaking chunks of salami and cheddar. At breakfast, I was right behind him. He had just loaded a pile of bacon on his plate when Steven Mace—burly, bearded, and barrel-chested—cut in front of me, leaned into Rob, and said, "Hey, Rob, I have something for you."

Rob's eyes must have been preoccupied by the display of food on the table, because he asked, "What's that?"

"It's a river rock, and I want you to keep it in your pocket at all times. It'll be a reminder of your pledge. When you're feeling weak and about to break, grab it and hold it. Squeeze it tight, and it will help summon up your inner strength, your inner resolve."

"Cool," I said, "like the challenge coins they give out in the military."

"Or in AA," Timmy added.

"Yeah," Steven said, "your Grand Canyon challenge rock."

"Thanks, Steven. That's thoughtful," Rob said, sliding it into his pocket. "I'll start it at lunch." Then he reached for the bacon on his plate, but before Rob's hand landed on a piece, Steven snatched the entire pile off the plate and stuffed it into his mouth. Then he squeezed Rob's shoulder firmly and, between the smacking and chewing, managed to say, "Rob, you stay strong now."

I didn't laugh long, because Harlan sat down next to me and said, "It's a big day ahead, E. We've got Horn Creek, Granite, and Hermit, all rated 9s and all within a five-mile stretch." As I listened, I was barely managing to choke down my breakfast, leaving the bacon on my plate half-eaten. "We're just gonna take them one at a time. Horn Creek is up first, just a couple of miles downriver. It's got the steepest drop in the Grand Canyon. At this water level, these two big rocks jut out side by side. Some people say they look like horns, but, with the water pouring over them, I think they look more like big glassy domes or camels' humps; they are some of the most beautiful water features in the river. We'll shoot the gauntlet between them and take a few sizeable hits. We want to avoid what's below, if possible: a labyrinth of big waves, rocks, and holes. So we're going to be making a hard cut to the left; I'll call it out, guiding us away from those powerful, tricky hydraulics. But if we can't make the left move, we'll pivot and then just take those big crashers head-on."

"Sounds like a plan," I said, unable to take another bite. My eggs rumbled in my belly and were about to turn into a vomit omelet.

Once on the water, we passed under the Kaibab Bridge, leading to Phantom Ranch, and pulled over. There was news to celebrate. The Neptune Blue-Wave radios from the U.K. had arrived. Harlan's mom had found a courier to drive them from Phoenix halfway to Flagstaff, where Marieke, Harlan's sister, met the driver on the side of the road. Marieke then relayed them to a good friend of Harlan's who drove to the South Rim and hiked them down the steep, nine-mile Bright Angel Trail and hand delivered them to us, just in time. Skyler opened the box to check that everything was there. I just hoped they worked. I was going to need them.

Sooner than expected, I heard the distant rush of Horn Creek ahead. "We're gonna angle in from right center," Harlan said, "and split the horns."

I could hear him fairly clearly in my earpiece, which helped me with my ritual of trying to stay calm. I floated tentatively down a perfectly smooth tongue, like riding a moving sidewalk that you knew was leading you into a category-five hurricane. Then the bow of my boat dipped, and I dropped off the edge of the earth, accelerating into the storm. I paddled harder, leaning forward and squaring off against the big hits. As I continued to find myself upright, I felt some confidence rising. When Harlan gave the word, I edged left, leaning downriver and bracing my paddle against the surging waves. Then water exploded on top of me, and it hurled me over. Upside down, I waited for it to release me, and when I felt its energy subsiding, I rolled up, bracing for more action. Instead, I was surprised to hear the cheers of the team and Harlan. I was through it, through Horn, a rapid with a reputation so fearsome it had made it into the lyrics of Timmy's song, "Erik of the River."

There wasn't much time to celebrate, because the next thing I knew, we were entering the thunder of Granite. It had a strong pull to the wall on river right, with waves coming fast from both directions. I managed to remain upright, staying loose and reacting to the punches striking me from either side. Yet as I bucked and bounced, Harlan's voice went silent for several seconds. *No radios!* my brain screamed, but then I heard something faint, almost like static: "Blrglrgshshsh." Harlan, I realized, was upside down. I sensed I was pointing in the right direction, so just kept charging. Then there was a louder sound, a gasping breath, and Harlan's voice resumed: "Small left . . . charge!"

As I paddled into the tail waves that led me out of Granite, I thought, *Even Harlan can get rocked by this river.*

Up next was Hermit, which Harlan noted had the biggest waves in the canyon. "Think of it as a big, fun wave train," he said. But that "fun" included about a dozen waves in succession, some of them over twenty feet tall. As I dipped down into the troughs, I tried to keep my kayak pointed straight. Then I felt myself rushing up a wall of water so steep I was certain I would flip over backward. "Hang on!" Harlan yelled. "Lean forward!"

I pressed my torso against the hull of my kayak and managed not to tip. My kayak caught air off of the lip of that three-story wave, and I straightened up for the big drop into the next one. At the bottom eddy, Lonnie and I compared notes. We'd both flipped once, but then Skyler mentioned he'd gone over three times. "Blind guys rule! Sighted people drool!" I shouted to Lonnie, reaching out and finding his hand for a fist bump. We both pumped our fists in the air and cheered to Skyler's amused chagrin.

At camp, I was stripping off my wet gear and draping it to dry in the sun when I heard Rob and one of the raft guides in a debate on the best layering system to keep you warm and dry in the cold river water. I noticed it was getting pretty intense. "Hydro skins and wet suits are pretty much the same thing," the guide insisted. "And I never wear either of them under a dry top. They just hold in the moisture and make you feel cold and clammy."

"Actually," said Rob, "that's not exactly correct. Hydro skins are often constructed of materials like nylon, Lycra, and polyurethane, while wet suits are comprised of a blend of neoprene and butyl rubber. And lining the layers of a wet suit are a thin film of heat-reflecting metal oxide, such as titanium, copper, silver, even aluminum . . ."

At this point I could hear the guide exhale impatiently, and I pictured him wiping his brow in frustration. As I listened, I thought back to the image of Mr. Whoopee in the Tennessee Tuxedo cartoons. Rob had little interest in placating for the sake of avoiding friction. His focus lay in a dogged adherence to truth and accuracy, and that had saved my butt a dozen times, on and off the river. However, no matter the situation, Rob saw no STOP signs. I could hear the guide grumbling as he walked away. Timmy quickly took the opportunity to chime in, "That was an illuminating discourse on the chemical properties of hydro skins and wet suits." Then he asked, "Have you ever been diagnosed with Factsberger's syndrome?"

"No," Rob said. "Do you care to elucidate?"

"Well," said Timmy, launching into one of his legendary riffs, "it's a pretty serious condition wherein the patient—in this case, you—cannot refrain from disabusing someone of any utterance not factual, or deemed to be incorrect. It's the ruthless, unyielding pursuit of the facts at all cost. I'm not a doctor, but I'm pretty sure you are exhibiting a number of the classic symptoms."

I sat there giggling to myself at the term *Factsberger's*. From my teaching days, I knew it was a politically incorrect play on Asperger's syndrome, a form of autism, in which people have trouble interpreting social cues and emotions in others.

"And what would be the symptoms of this mysterious disease?" Rob asked, amused.

"Well," Timmy began, "if you had your own cologne line, it would be called Relentlessly Raker. If you were experiencing bad breath, you wouldn't use Altoids. You'd use Factoids! If you owned a restaurant, you'd call it Snacks and Facts. And if the periodic table were based on you, it would begin with *data* at the very top, followed by *actually, confrontation, debate,* and, last but not least, of course, *bacon.*"

"That explains it quite well," Rob replied, "but I would simply like to clarify that the biggest difference between hydro skins and wet suits is in the varying composites. Wet suits are designed using a sponge rubber technology, with nitrogen gas trapped within the cellular structure—"

"This is when I respectfully disengage from further discussion," Timmy said, and I could hear him slowly backing away.

When everyone was gone, Rob sidled up next to me. "I wasn't actually finished," he said. A pile of kayaks and dry bags were behind me. Rocks and bushes blocked me from the sides. Rob stood between me and the only escape trail. There was nowhere for this blind man to run. As he went on, further explaining the difference between closed-cell versus open-cell foam rubber and the importance of the specific thickness in millimeters, I realized that sometimes, you just couldn't escape the facts.

Heading out of camp, we immediately encountered a six-mile stretch called the Gems: six rapids, spaced one per mile—Agate, Sapphire, Turquoise, Emerald, Ruby, Serpentine. Although they were giant, they retained a feeling of friendliness. There were no monster holes or complex navigation to twist my gut. I just had to point 'er straight and ride the bucking river serpent.

After the excitement, Harlan had us pull over to a spot he'd discovered on one of his previous trips. He told us that the heavy thunderstorms early in the expedition might just awaken something special. We hiked along the beach, through some tamarisk bushes, and came to an alcove with a giant bedrock pothole that had been filled in with rainwater.

"Shhhhh," Harlan instructed. "Sit down and await the surprise." Within seconds, on cue, a cacophony of croaks emanated from the pond, as if Harlan, the conductor, had just waved his baton. We laughed hard, and then someone stupidly chucked a rock in the pond, probably thinking the frogs would respond by croaking again. Instead, they went totally silent, and I feared that had ended our encounter. Then Timmy let out his own frog song: "Err err err err, err err err err. BREEDEET." He simultaneously screeched and rolled out a clear click in the back of his throat. It was a near-perfect impression, and the frogs all belched right back at him, like they had a new leader.

Lonnie whispered, "Timmy, I'd be careful. I think they're in love with you."

"That's right," Harlan said. "That's their mating call, and looks like Timmy's got a few hundred admirers over there."

"Frog legs, and frog love," Timmy said in a husky baritone. "My two favorite things. I'm going to live here forever and be the Frog King—with my sexy, slimy harem."

As he continued to croak, and his groupies continued to call back in rapture, I began losing track of who was who. The analogy of the chorus was totally accurate. For a blind person, this was a symphonic masterpiece of nature, and we sat back enjoying the show for over an hour.

I heard wings flapping, and Harlan said, "A couple of mallards just landed over there."

Rob had been bouldering on the steep wall behind the pond, trying to get a better look at the frogs, and now he returned. "They're actually common mergansers," he corrected.

Timmy could not contain himself. "Factsberger's never sleeps, my friends," he announced. He then croaked, and his minions responded in kind.

Just before camp that evening, we reached a beautiful side canyon called Elves Chasm that Harlan wanted us to experience. We hiked up a damp, lush creek bed with several small waterfalls created by boulders that choked the channel. Several shelves up, we came to a deep pool with a tall waterfall pouring down. We all took turns swimming over and letting the clear freshwater pour over our heads, washing the sand out of our hair and faces. Behind the waterfall was an actual chasm, cool and damp from the water spray. We scrambled inside, and tucked ten feet back was a climb through a small, body-wide window that popped you into the sun again. From there, we carefully walked out on ledges to stand fifteen feet above the pool. As Lonnie and I hovered, toes curled over the lip, Timmy would shout directions, playing on our kayak commands: "Small left, gun sites on me. Now charge!" And then we'd leap into the air, plunging toward the pool.

Afterward, Lonnie and I sat in the back of the cave behind the waterfall. I tapped the rock ceiling right above my head and said, "It's kind of claustrophobic in here. Anything like the inside of a submarine?"

"Sure is," he agreed. "I was stationed on those attack subs for five years of my military career. Talk about confined spaces—on one of those deployments, the sub was diving, and I was cleaning the frame bay; that's like the ribs of the sub, underneath the main sump. Well, our tactical situation required us to dive quickly. Problem is that submarines compress with the water pressure. In other words, as the sub descends, the chamber gets smaller, and I mean mighty small. I was in a bad place, between one of those metal ribs and the sump, about to turn into Flatbread Lonnie. So I quickly rolled into the frame bay between the ribs, a spot with just enough room where I wasn't going to get squashed. I was stuck there, lying on my back."

"How long?" I dared to ask.

"Quite some time," he said, laughing at the recollection. "I suspect, fifteen or sixteen hours."

I shuddered, thinking that being flipped upside down in a kayak was nothing compared to being practically compressed to death in a submarine. "Some of the guys brought me some blankets," he said, "and reached in to hand me a pee bottle and some food. I told them that pancakes would fit the occasion." He guffawed again. "I just had to wait long enough for us to surface again and for the hull space to expand."

"How'd you get through it?" I asked. "Did you meditate or something?"

"Every now and then, one of the crew would holler down at me to see that I was okay, but other than that, I didn't meditate; I didn't count sheep. I just lay there sort of daydreaming. It was great training how to stay calm in tight spaces and not panic—like, upside down and out of air in a big ole keeper hole!" He cackled.

The story was vintage Lonnie. While most people would have been so rattled, they would have found their sanity slipping away, Lonnie was eating pancakes and cracking jokes with the crew. I didn't think that mind-set was anything he had learned. I suspected, when it came right down to it, he was just hardwired that way. He was a blind man who worked as a roofer, drove a mower, and ran a chain saw. Earlier on the trip, he'd told me more details about the day he got shot in the face. While his friend ran for help, Lonnie lay on the ground totally blind. He could feel blood running down his throat and beginning to clot there and knew that he might very well pass out due to the blood loss. If he did, that blood would coagulate in his throat and choke him. So he'd clawed around, eventually finding a tree limb lying in the dirt. He snapped a branch off and shoved it down his throat, the only way to clear his airway. Turns out, he lay there for hours and did wind up passing out. His clear presence of mind had saved his life. Whether being squeezed in the hull of a submarine or being blinded by shotgun pellets, Lonnie just took action and did what needed to be done, and that ability had made him ideally suited for kayaking. In fact, Lonnie's new trick was to go ahead of his guides through some of the more moderate rapids, without commands. He called it "blind freestyle."

I, on the other hand, was more methodical, pensive, and cautious. It took me six years to achieve what Lonnie had done in two. His guiding technique reflected that attitude; it was less precise than my system, but it achieved at a high level by charging straight ahead into the meat, reacting instinctively to the chaos that confronted him, flipping multiple times, and inevitably rolling up again at the bottom with a big "Yee-haw!"

I had to admit, I was a little jealous. Like it or not, I just didn't have Lonnie "the LonDart" boldness inside me. However, I still wanted to understand the nature of fear, how to stop it from paralyzing me, turning my belly sour with its chemical by-product, weighing me down, like struggling through an atmosphere with a massive gravity.

I often thought about all I had to lose by making a dumb or reckless mistake. I loved my family, my life; I loved growing the No Barriers movement; I loved waking up, stepping outside my front door, and feeling the cool fresh Colorado morning air combined with that touch of warm sun as it climbed higher in the sky. The thought of leaving it all behind continually consumed me. Most importantly, I remembered that day five years ago at the take-out on the Gates of Lodore when I had turned Arjun's small face toward mine and promised him that we would always be there for him. I couldn't break that promise.

That afternoon, we laid over at Dune Camp, around mile 120, a tiny spit of sand so sun scorched you had to wear booties so you didn't burn your feet. The arrival of the new radios had brought such promise, but now, to my intense frustration, they were also beginning to degrade. Harlan's voice was scratchy and distant—just like the previous sets. Skyler and Steven tinkered with them, trying out different headsets with different manpacks, but they were stumped. Sky was starting to call the radio situation his nemesis. The wind was picking up as Timmy dragged out the instruments, and as he started thumping on the bongos, it hit for real: hot, powerful gusts that kicked up sand.

"Boys, I don't think there's going to be any music tonight," Harlan said, "unless someone brought wind chimes. It's time to lash stuff down, put your dry bags in your tents, and dive in. It's about to blow."

We all scrambled to grab gear that was laid out to dry on boats, hanging over tamarisk branches, and strewn over rocks. Within minutes, everyone was in their tents, zipping up doors and windows and settling in for a hot wind scouring. Without ventilation, the tent was an oven. The wind howled so hard down the canyon that the tent kept lifting up and tugging at the stakes holding it down. I had endured plenty of hours in the mountains, waiting out bad weather, yet never had the storm been inside my tent; somehow, the sand had found its way inside, swirling around in mini-cyclones. I felt grit peppering me all night long, getting into my eyes, ears, and nostrils. I finally put a T-shirt over my face, but it didn't seem to help much. I could feel sand in my teeth and in my throat. I lay there most of the night, sweating on top of my sleeping bag and listening to the tent rattling and the wind roaring and whining outside.

When I awoke the next morning and crawled outside, Timmy and Harlan started chuckling. "You might want to douse yourself off in the river," Harlan said. "You're looking a little crusty."

"More like the Abominable Sandman," Timmy added.

I ran my hand over my face and arms. I was caked with sand from head to toe, and my hair felt stiff like straw.

"Hey!" said Harlan, now animated. "I have an idea I want to test." Apparently he was still looking at me, because he chuckled one more time before he walked over, grabbed the radios that were lying on a tarp, and brought them over to the giant ceramic water filter. He filtered a couple of gallons of river water and filled a big bucket. "This water is super clear now," he pronounced as he submerged one of the radio sets and let it soak for several seconds.

Rob peered into the bucket and remarked, "That's amazing," and he described the clean filtered water turning to the color of café au lait. "The comm systems are waterproof," Rob said, "but looks like silt and sand have been completely clogging the membranes and getting into the microphones too." Rob high-fived Harlan and said, "Nice job, Harlan. You should be an engineer."

After thoroughly soaking and drying all the other systems, the sound quality on the radios seemed to bounce back. They weren't as good as new, but they were good enough to get me through. For extra protection, Skyler took little latex finger cots from the medical kit, covered the foam microphones, and sealed around the edges with tiny, tightly coiled rubber bands.

At breakfast, I chuckled when I heard Steven's voice yelling, "Raker, where's your rock?" And I knew Rob must have been caught reaching for some sausage.

"I think it's in my tent," Rob stammered.

Steven sprinted ten feet across the sand and found a rock pile. He swiped one up and replied, "Well, here's another one. Don't lose it. Oh, and I'll take that sausage patty there," and he snatched it off Rob's plate.

The next few days were spectacular as we dropped down into the deepest and oldest part of the canyon. As I ran my hands over the ancient schist layer, almost two billion years old, jutting straight up from the river, Harlan said, "Welcome to the basement of the Grand Canyon." Some of the schist was smooth as marble through weathering and erosion; other sections were fluted and corrugated, and still others were scalloped and rippled from many millennia of being scoured by waves. We also entered Granite Narrows, the tightest section of the canyon at just seventy-five feet across. The walls rose here a mile above us.

Still in the narrows, we passed a feature called Helicopter Eddy. It was a super turbulent, violently recirculating eddy formed by a cutout in the rock wall river left. Harlan said emphatically that we wanted to avoid it. It had a toilet bowl effect and could shove you up against the canyon wall and pin you there, and if you were able to dislodge yourself from the wall, the eddy fence was huge and roiling, making it extremely difficult to get back into the river. However, just above it, Lonnie's guide, Chris, got slammed in the face by a wave that dislodged his contact lenses and rendered him temporarily blind. In that split second, Lonnie unintentionally paddled over the eddy fence and found himself spinning and smacking into the wall. I could hear his guides yelling from below, unable to help. It was impossible to paddle upriver. But Lonnie yelled back, "I'm good!" as he bounced off the wall and he braced hard, surfing the eddy fence for a moment. Then, luckily, the eddy spit him out the bottom, and he shot out upright, hooting and laughing.

"That was pure frickin' joy," he said. "More fun than a tornado in a trailer park! The most fun I've had since I went blind."

I just shook my head.

Just before reaching camp, we pulled into a little side creek that drained out of Matkatamiba Canyon, one of the highlights of the entire journey. We pulled our kayaks up onto a small gravel beach and took a hike that entered a narrowing and twisting slot canyon. Soon the limestone walls were so close I could spread my arms and easily touch both sides. Lonnie and I scrambled together up the smooth, tight groove, which shrunk even more. In places, the bottom was barely a shoe's width wide, and we had to climb above the tiny stream. To make it easier, I showed Lonnie a climbing technique called "stem-ming," in which you spread both legs wide and press your feet against the rocks. The oppositional force keeps you from sliding down. Lonnie caught on to stemming quickly, and we moved upward, splaying our hands and feet. Soon, we arrived at a massive amphitheater that flattened out into a natural rock patio. The entire place was a blind man's dream, with curves, grooves, and striations to touch and acoustics that seemed perfectly suited to Tarzan yells. The walls were also excellent for bouldering, with distinct extruding holds, deep indentations, and tiny shelves. Rob and I showed Lonnie some bouldering techniques, and I climbed twenty feet up the sidewall, coaxing

Lonnie upward behind me. As we ascended, I loudly slapped the good hand-holds and coached him how to place his toes in the pockets and to stand up, trusting his feet and balance. Getting back down was even more challenging, and I climbed below him, guiding his feet into the right positions. Lonnie said that, with his girls out of the house, he wanted to try all kinds of adventure sports, from ice climbing to tandem mountain biking, but especially rock climbing. I promised him that when we were back home, I'd have him out to Colorado to cut his teeth in the big mountains.

Back on the ground, I said, "I hope this is just the start of many adventures together," and I squeezed his callused hand.

"Thank you, brother," he replied. "I can't tell you what an honor it is to be here with you. It means the world to me!"

That night at Matkat Hotel Camp, most of the team had gone to bed early, but Lonnie, Timmy, Harlan, and I stayed up late trading stories.

"Upset's got me pretty nervous," I said. "I think we hit it tomorrow." Upset was one of the top-five rapids with many adversity stories to its name. I'd been fretting over it for the last few days.

"On one of my trips down here," Timmy said, "I went through Upset and got the bright idea of trying to punch the big center hole. I was instantly flipped and subbed."

"Subbed" was kayaker talk for being sucked way down and usually held there.

"I felt my boat being pulled down," Timmy went on, "and I was getting pummeled. It seemed like an eternity, but it was probably just ten seconds or so. Then I bobbed to the surface, but before I could roll up, I sensed my boat going down deep again for another beating. I thought seriously about pulling my skirt and swimming, but then I remembered all those drives through the Eisenhower Tunnel. Remember those, E? I kept saying to myself, 'Eisenhower Tunnel . . . Eisenhower Tunnel . . . Eisenhower Tunnel.' And just when I thought I couldn't hold on a second longer, it released me. I emerged on the other side and rolled up. I was probably under there for twenty-five seconds."

"I know that hole intimately," Lonnie said excitedly. "On my first trip here with Team River Runner, my guide said, 'Lonnie, whatever you do, don't get squirrely and drop into the big hole in the center.' So what do I do? Get squirrely and drop right into the big hole center. Took my first swim right there in Upset. Boys, I was plenty upset in Upset!" We all laughed at his joke, corny or not. "But tomorrow's a new day!" he exclaimed. "And you know what I like to say: 'Don't bleed before you're cut.'"

"I don't know how you do it," I said to Lonnie. "I guess the fear is still there for me. The consequences feel so real, and I haven't figured out how to block it out. I wake up in the morning, and there it is."

"That fear and anxiety only gets in the way," Harlan said, "clouding your movements and reactions. Then, the next thing you know, you're surrounded by massive chaos, and it overwhelms you. Instead, I think of it as surrendering everything to the river and channeling your energy into perfect focus, just reacting and becoming a part of what the water is doing."

I thought about how to achieve that state. For some people, I thought, it just came naturally. For others, it wasn't so easy. Then Timmy got up to help Lonnie find his tent, and it was just Harlan and me.

"In those first years I guided down here," Harlan said quietly, "after everybody would go to sleep, I would sit on the back of my boat and watch the river cruising by in the moonlight. I know this must sound crazy, but I'd watch the current, and I'd feel an almost uncontrollable impulse to dive in, to disappear, and to see where it took me. After that experience, it was like I'd formed a relationship with the river. Every trip I've paddled since, the last thing I do is to put my hand in the water, and I get that same yearning, the feeling of the current moving through my fingers, moving downstream. It's like a little conversation. I say, 'I'll come back someday, but for now, I've got some more life to live.' This is the place where I'll return someday, and that feels okay, like the river will take care of me."

As I retreated to my tent, I was conflicted. I kept mulling over what Harlan had said, and I couldn't figure out whether the river was an ominous demon or whether it was an entity I could trust, one that was inviting me forward. When did you fight the river with everything you had, and when could you trust it and ride the flow? It seemed like a paradox.

With no answers coming, I tried to relax with some music on my iPhone. On my playlist, I was happy to hear Mandy Harvey singing for me. It was her latest, with the same lilting, soothing feel of her previous work. I'd forgotten

I'd downloaded it. As a result of her experience at the No Barriers Summit, Mandy had taken another courageous step and had begun writing original songs. The outcome was "Try," and I listened to the words:

> I don't feel the way I used to
> the sky is gray much more than it is blue
> but I know one day I'll get through
> and I'll take my place again
> If I would try
> If I would try
> I don't love the way I need to
> you need more and I know
> that much is true
> so I'll fight for our break through
> and I'll breathe in you again
> So I will try
> So I will try
> There is no one for me to blame
> 'cause I know the only thing in my way
> Is me . . . so I will try, so I will try . . .

As I listened to her high, angelic voice, I was astounded. It was impressive enough to sing standards and jazz classics you'd heard in a past life with working ears, but it was another world entirely to compose and perform music as a deaf musician. The irony was that they were songs she would never actually hear. It seemed preposterous, like a boat that purposely gives up its mooring, floating on an ocean with no rudder or anchor or any tools to navigate, yet it still expects to sail toward its destination. That bold act moved beyond logic, into the realm of faith, like giving in to the unknowable, like kayaking a river you would never see, or like plucking up a child, one speck of sand from an endless beach. No matter how hard you tried, you could never truly see the canyon unfolding before you or the impact you made within it. The journey was incomprehensible.

And Harlan had known this too. "We are all in the hands of the river," he had said. Sitting high up at Nankoweap in the first week of the expedition, Harlan had admitted that, although the goal was to ride the energy of the river, it could only be done for a moment. He was right. It was all temporary. The river, I knew, would take us all back in the end. Perhaps, his confrontation with death and rebirth had enabled him to come to terms with this inevitability, or like Mandy, to give in to the unknowable. That acceptance had made the river go from something perilous to a guiding force, and in the process, it had washed away his fears.

When we reached Upset the next day, Harlan had everyone land and hop out to scout. Upset was already significant, but at this water level, thirteen thousand cfs, he said it got even trickier and more dangerous. He pulled me aside and spoke in a clear, measured voice. "Okay, it's pretty spicy, but there's a perfect line to snake it cleanly, although it'll feel counterintuitive. The setup is everything. You enter left, and you keep pushing left into these lateral waves. They're actually crashing off of the left cliff wall. Your brain is telling you don't go over there, but you have to go left. That big hole Lonnie and Timmy were talking about is to your right, and it is violent; it's a place you don't want to be. You want to hit the lateral perfectly on the left, catch the current, and sneak by the big hole on your right. Bam. Done. You got this, E!"

I nodded, but in reality I just kept thinking about that "violent" hole that had subbed Timmy and where Lonnie had swum, the place where you didn't want to be.

We got back in our boats. The safety guides paddled into position, and mercifully, as Harlan said, "Check, check," the radios were working. "E, don't let your mind get in the way here," I heard Harlan's soothing voice. "Your mind can be the barrier between you and the river, between thinking it and just feeling it and being there with it. If your mind gets in the way, then you're defeating the purpose of what this experience is about."

I let his words wash over me, nodding, slowing my breathing, pushing the fear to the outside edges of my awareness.

"I want you to try something," he went on. "Forget that I'm here, that I'm giving you commands to follow. Think of my voice as a line of communication to the water, as a conduit to the river. Allow yourself to feel the intricacies of the rapid. Envision the tongue, like a runway, as we drop in. Imagine the waves, the canyon light glimmering off them, foam and spray igniting in flashes of color and light. Feel the power of the big, green, beautiful waves. Try to truly be here, not fighting against it, not surviving it, but connected to this place. I'll be right behind you to share everything that we're doing."

"Okay," I said, listening hard to the deep rumble below and trying to feel the surface of the water through the bottom of my boat. I sat up, exhaled, and tried to pull some of the river's energy into my lungs. Then we were paddling toward Upset.

"Be clear, calm, in the moment," he said.

I focused on each paddle stroke, each riffle of the water, and the space between each breath. Time seemed to slow down just a bit as I dropped in, turning left and left and left against the massive waves surging off the canyon wall and collapsing over me. I busted through the cold wall of water and heard Harlan yell, "Hold that line!" I felt myself riding on a narrow seam, just between a swirling upheaval to my left, like bombs exploding on a battlefield, and the bottomless hole churning to my right, like a guttural roar coming up from the depths of the river. I rode the chaos, water, spray, and air all merging together, and it didn't feel as threatening, because I felt like I was a part of it. There was no kayaker, no boat, no paddle, just pure awareness, reacting without conscious thought. Then everything grew calm around me, and I knew the river had allowed me to pass through. I felt gratitude and joy flooding through my body, like current through the canyon.

Then Rob and Harlan paddled over and flanked me, both leaning in, the three of us hugging tightly. No one said a word for a long time. Then Harlan laughed, but not like hearing the punch line of a joke. Instead, it seemed to come from a long way away and carry with it the resonance of deep emotion. "E, I have to admit, most of the time, you and me look like a junk show out there. We're slingshotting by each other; one of us is often backward or sideways, but today, we were in perfect sync. Today, we found the flow!"

That evening at Tuckup Camp, the blazing sun finally passed behind the canyon rim, and the air grew soft and still. I sat on the sand, alone, at the river's edge, reflecting on my experience at Upset. It felt like six years of kayaking culminating in one brief but perfect moment, and I wanted to remember, to bask in it for a little longer. Harlan had said the river was too big to fight against. My ongoing dreams had been of the river swallowing me, pulling me down into darkness, into nothingness. Climbing mountains hadn't really prepared me either, I thought. Climbing was more about bringing yourself forth, asserting your will over an extreme, inhospitable environment. Yet trying to apply that learning to rivers had failed. Perhaps, the secrets of a river were not revealed by trying to exert the ego over it, but rather by letting go and allowing the river to consume you, all the way down to the core, by simply giving in to the unknowable and writing music you would never hear. By surrendering, it allowed the river to erode everything and wash away the crust, until there was nothing left but that inner light, the same one I had felt many years ago within Terry Fox. Unencumbered, that light was free to flow out and fuse with the landscape, with the energy of the unstoppable river. Maybe this was as close as we could ever get to understanding, just a brief mortal flash of that light connecting with something bigger, something mysterious and infinite.

25

LAVA

That evening, I asked Rob what made Lava Falls so formidable. In a river renowned for its powerful rapids, Lava definitely got the most attention and respect. It was the king of the canyon.

"Rapids form in three distinct ways," he replied. "First, there's a narrowing of the river channel. Next, there's an elevation drop, in this case about thirty feet from top to bottom. Both of these increase the velocity and turbulence of the current. And third, there's an uneven riverbed where boulders, shelves, drop-offs, and solidified bodies of magma all obstruct the water underneath the surface. Lava Falls is an example of all three factors coming together in a perfect storm. It's rated ten out of ten at all water levels."

"In March of 1995," Harlan added, "there was a massive debris flow, like a flash flood on steroids. A monumental rainstorm sent soil and rock, all the way up to boulders the size of SUVs, cascading down Prospect Canyon, left of Lava. That event constricted the river by about 50 percent."

"What was it like before that debris flow?" I asked.

"It was always big," Harlan said, "and it's different from the rapids upriver, because of the volcanism. Over the last 750,000 years, give or take, about a dozen huge lava flows poured down into the Colorado River. Others upwelled from beneath the surface. The magma cooled and formed these sediment-filled lava dams. Near where Lava Falls is today, there was a massive one, a thousand feet tall. They say it plugged the river and backed it all the way up to Lees Ferry—mile one. The lava dam was so enormous, they think it may have taken over twenty years to fill in the lake behind it."

Over the last few weeks, I'd been listening to a book written by Major Powell, who first ventured, as he put it, "down the Great Unknown." Lava had made a striking impression on him.

"What a conflict of water and fire there must have been here!" he wrote. "Just imagine a river of molten rock, running down into a river of melted snow. What a seething and boiling of the waters: what clouds of steam rolled into the heavens!"

"But even that colossal wall of hardened lava was eventually carved away by the river," said Harlan. "It kept pushing and pushing until it eroded the lava and broke its way through. Nothing stops the river in the end."

Then Rob interrupted, "Enough talk about Lava. Big E, we have some celebrating to do."

I had turned forty-six years old that day, and the team had planned a night of revelry. At dinner, Rob was quietly heading back to his folding chair with a steak on his plate when Steven yelled over, "Raker, where's your *rock*?"

Rob mumbled something about having lost it again.

"That's the third 'challenge rock' you've lost," said Steven. "If I didn't know you better, I'd think you were losing them on purpose!" With that, he jumped up, blocking Rob's way. I imagined Rob's eyes darting left and right, desperately grasping at escape routes. Then Steven said more gently, "I guess we can make an exception, just this one night, in honor of E's birthday, but tomorrow, don't forget your rock at breakfast."

I didn't have to see to know that Steven's acquiescence had planted a relieved smile on Rob's face.

For dessert, one of the guides baked a chocolate cake in the dutch oven, and everyone sang "Happy Birthday" as I blew out the candles. The team had thought of everything. Then Rob led Lonnie and me over to a flat area on the beach where he'd created what he called a "tactile art gallery," comprised of objects he'd been collecting along the river.

"Cool," Timmy chimed in. "It's the Grand Canyon Natural Art Museum for the Blind. We gotta take this on the road."

Rob excitedly pronounced that the challenge was for Lonnie and me to examine each exhibit and try to identify it. "I've assembled a unique collection of pieces for your Brailling pleasure."

I chuckled. Rob was referring to an ongoing team joke, of course, started by Timmy. When the guides set up the lunch table on the beach with all the fixings for sandwiches, Lonnie and I would line up with the team, our hands probing over the table. From a sighted perspective, I could understand how our fingers might have looked like little wriggling snakes as they explored the bread, cheese, ham, pickles, and onions. Once, my hand landed on the rim of an unknown jar, opened on the table. I did the natural thing, which was to lick my finger, discovering that it was mayonnaise, but after that, Timmy had begun calling it "Braille lunch."

"Since there's no mayonnaise in this museum," Timmy said, "you can Braille to your heart's content."

I dropped to my knees to explore the first object. It was placed artfully on a large, flat pedestal of rock. The item was made of wood, thin and curvy, and widening toward one end into a round dish. I traced my finger around the circular hollow where the dish had been perfectly carved by the elements. "Maybe some kind of horn, like a saxophone?" I said. Then Lonnie, who was kneeling right behind me, confirmed my guess. He picked up the driftwood sax and began blowing into it, doing an impression of Clarence Clemons of the E Street Band playing "Born to Run." Each piece was so beautiful; if I hadn't had an audience, I could have touched them forever. It was hard to believe these chunks of wood had been shaped through years of being tumbled and scoured by water, sand, and wind until they became hard, almost like they'd been petrified, and as burnished as porcelain. One of them was channeled by dozens of tiny worms boring their way through. Another felt like a head complete with eyes, nose, and a squiggly mouth. Protruding from the top were knots of tangled roots, like dreadlocks. Resting on a flat rock sat a judge's gavel, or maybe, I thought, a glossy peace pipe. Everyone passed it around, pretending to take puffs.

At the end of the line, I was bursting with appreciation. I'd never received a birthday gift quite like it. I imagined Rob, over the last week, stealthily pulling off the river on various deserted beaches; combing the nooks and crannies, his bushy eyebrows lifting and his face lighting up as he discovered new specimens. Then he'd carefully place them in his cockpit until it resembled a jungle of crisscrossing designs. Later, slipping away from camp, he'd exhaustively sort and pair the objects into the most unique treasures and then display them in the most fluid and logical order, and finally when finished, he'd step back and gaze down on his stunning creation—all for the Brailling pleasure of two blind friends. I pulled my attention from the peace pipe in my hands and said, "I can't believe you've been assembling this—all for us. I had no idea."

"You're blind," he said matter-of-factly. "It wasn't actually that hard to get away with!" And then he let out his biggest honk of a laugh and slapped me on the back.

When the others had drifted away, Rob and I sat in the sand with our feet in the chilly water and our backs against a steep hillock of sand. "I've been meaning to tell you something, Big E," Rob said. My heart jumped, remembering our talk in the hot tub that wild and stormy day in Moab after Castleton Tower, when he'd first told me about his cancer diagnosis. I braced myself for more bad news.

"I don't talk about this much," he said, "but the last few years have been hard ones. When I heard those words—*Stage IV*—it sounded like a death sentence. I've been a scientist all my adult life, and I pride myself on being a problem solver, being able to always find a solution. But I'm faced now with an overwhelming situation. There's no clear way forward. But I look at you, the way you deal with your own setbacks, whether it's the death of your mom and your brother, or going blind, or the challenges in your family. Instead of getting beaten down or mired in depression, you've done the absolute opposite. It's like there's a storm in front of you, and you turn into it, instead of away from it."

"A big part of why I'm able to do these things," I said, "is because of you and the team." I waved my hand toward the camp.

"I know how appreciative you are," he replied, "and you know I've enjoyed helping you learn to kayak. I kind of thrive on it. But I've gotten just as much in return. I try every day to adopt that approach: not to let the darkness seep in. I say to myself, 'Okay, this is the situation. This is your choice.' I can either be pissed off and bitter and let circumstances drag me down, or I can say, 'Okay, I have less time than I may have thought. Let's see how much fun, how much excitement, how much joy we can pack in right to the end!'"

"We've definitely packed a lot in," I said, smiling, reflecting on all the experiences. There had been many exotic trips to remote rivers as Rob was teaching me how to kayak, but even more memorable was going to Nepal to meet Arjun as a little boy, and finally bringing him home. We had summited Losar together, the stunning vertical ice climb; and more recently, Rob had returned to Nepal to collect DNA samples from Kanchi, proving beyond a shadow of a doubt that she was indeed Arjun's biological mother.

"I've been your guide on a lot of adventures," he resumed, "but you're guiding me as well." He paused, clasped my hand, and cleared his throat. "Thank you, Big E."

I didn't know what to say, but fortunately, I didn't have to, because Rob continued, "And there are some others who want to thank you as well." As if on cue, Skyler came over, sat down, and laid three letters in my hands. "They're from your fam," he said. "They've been stashed away in my dry box."

I missed my family deeply and wished they were here with me. School was in session, and it simply wasn't practical for the kids to miss three weeks of classes, but I still felt pretty guilty for leaving them for weeks on end. *Someday*, I thought, *I'll bring them back here, to this magical place.* So it was a bit of solace to have birthday wishes from them.

"We'll go by age," Sky said. "Arjun first."

Dear Dad,

Thank you for teaching me to kayak. Taking up kayaking has helped me in so many ways. It has helped my un-comfortableness of the water. The kayak seems safer now than when I started. It has helped me get used to bobbing up and down. I like the waves splashing against me. It has helped me get stronger in my triceps. Most of all, it's fun. I like watching people surf and go down the river fast. Happy Birthday, Dad!

Love, Arjun

Next was Emma's:

Dear Dad,

You have overcome challenges a "regular" person wouldn't have even thought of accomplishing, and I thank you for that. I thank you for being an explorer, a traveler, a pioneer, a daredevil and a hero. I thank you for pushing me to overcome my greatest fears, whether it be riding down the big slide at the swimming pool when I was five years old, or swimming into sea caves, or rappelling down that huge waterfall (even though I split open my foot). I have you to thank for most things in my life, and I hope you have a wonderful birthday!

Love, Emma

And finally he read Ellie's:

Erik,

You celebrate your birthday on the river today. What a fun way to mark such an important day. We've been on rivers during birthdays in the past, and they usually involve wearing yard sale dress-up costumes while joining in on some kind of crazy river challenge like sliding off an upside down raft, bouncing off the edge and into the water with poodle skirts flying. I'm happy for you and anticipate great fun today.

The other day, a neighbor said how tough it must be for me and the kids with you heading off on another long expedition. 'What a shame,' she said, 'to be left at home taking care of everything while Erik is away for so long. What sacrifices we wives make for our guys.' It made me think about all the adventures we've had together. Without mountaineering, we'd never have been married on the side of Kilimanjaro. Without mountaineering, I'd likely never have gone to Nepal, and Arjun would never have come into our lives.

Then, we have the five glorious family river trips we've taken over the years as you were learning this new passion. Our first was The Green River's Gates of Lodore, and it ended with a huge July 4th celebration of sparklers and slapping Paco Pads on the surface of the water, sounding even better than fireworks with the rifle crack through the canyon. Our next river trip on the San Juan found us loving the warm, bending and winding water, allowing us to ditch the boats and simply swim for miles. Through Desolation Canyon, we learned river terms such as 'spin-to-win' (when trying to avoid a river obstacle), 'hangovers' (half in, half out of the boat), and 'high-siding' (when lodged on a rock, everyone in the boat piling to the down-river side of the boat so not to flip). Two more trips sealed our love for rivers: The Apurímac River in Peru, where we toasted our bread on the sun-warmed kayaks after all the food was submerged in water, and the River of No Return on the Salmon.

We've watched our children grow up on these rivers, and it's been an opportunity to get closer as a family. Except that time our inflatable "Duckie" folded and Emma sailed over my head; I think that sealed her desire to never Duckie with me again. Arjun got air in one rapid, hands and legs reaching skyward. I shot through a class IV rapid with a friend where we lost our Duckie, thought we were swimming, and looked down to see the Duckie rise up from the river depths and position itself perfectly under our bodies for the rest of the rapid. Shooting stars at night, moon rising on ancient walls, hoot owls laughing.

Nope. That neighbor was dead wrong. All of these experiences are because of you. I think you picked your passions rather well, and we know there will be more family adventures ahead.

We're home raising a toast to you today, and we're so proud of your progress.

Love, Ellie

Ellie's note was prescient because that night, Timmy organized a contest that would display both individual flair as well as all the crazy, eclectic costumes that river guides always brought along on trips. Each participant would dance up a runway between a row of chairs in rhythm to a pounding techno beat, and three lucky rangers from the National Park Service, who were camping nearby, would judge the top performances. Katie gave me a play-by-play as everyone set their headlamps on to flashing-strobe mode to add to the dance club mood.

First came Harlan, in snakeskin-patterned Lycra hot pants, break-dancing with a backflip as a crescendo; then Skyler, in a purple miniskirt and skimpy halter top, dubstepping down the aisle, Papa Duck sauntering through, wearing a leopard vest and Gilligan-style sailor's hat, and Timmy, not to be outdone, clad in a shimmery pair of fuchsia tights and a fire engine red crop top with his hairy belly button showing. Kelly proudly sashayed through in a robin egg blue top with golden fringe hanging to her navel, zebra-striped tights, and furry white knee-high boots. I donned a pink helmet sporting pointy opera-style Viking horns, with a bumblebee tube top and a yellow tutu. On my behind, it read: MIDNIGHT STINGER. And finally came Steven, who wound up winning, in pastel blue tie-dyed tights, a leather pirate's jacket with furry cuffs, a salmon-colored feather boa tied as a necktie, and a resplendent pink flamingo hat whose legs served as a chin strap. He strutted around carrying a boom box the size of a car battery on his shoulder and gyrating to the tribal beat like a Chippendale dancer.

After the cross-dressing dance party, Timmy yelled out, "Now, for my gift, I implore everyone to face the fire pit! It's time for 'the Burning Erik Ceremony'!"

Timmy had recently been to the famous Burning Man festival, an annual gathering in Nevada's Black Rock Desert that creates a temporary, makeshift city. In a matter of days, the barren desert transforms into a metropolis of free-loving people from around the world who come to commune, express themselves, and dance under a giant wooden structure called the Burning Man. "At the end of the festival," Timmy announced, "the Burning Man is set aflame to signify renewal and rebirth."

The Burning Erik was human shaped, made from empty cardboard boxes that had held our expedition's food stores. He had a wooden block of a head, with tendrils of hair fashioned of thinly shredded cardboard. He stood with his legs splayed wide and his arms held aloft, in exaltation. At Timmy's last Burning Man, the structure was 105 feet tall, and even though the Burning Erik was less than three feet, I still felt honored. Then, with a little fanfare and some introductory words by Timmy, the Burning Erik was set ablaze. Soon all the instruments were out. The drumming and strumming began, the jangling of shaking tambourines chiming in. Everyone stood in a close semicircle surrounding the fire pit, watching and feeling the intense flames as Burning Erik dissolved, transforming into heat and smoke that rose into the night.

After most had gone to bed, Timmy, Steven, and I, as well as some of the river guides—Kelly, Katie, and Jay—lay on our backs on the deck of a raft as Timmy described the shape of the sky, bursting with stars, against the dark canyon walls.

"It's a Star Bear sky," he said dreamily.

"Care to explain that one?" I said.

"As I'm gazing up, E, I'm seeing a skyline of interconnecting cliffs, thousands of feet above us. They encapsulate the entire horizon. They perfectly align to form the shape of a massive ursine constellation, and he's all made of sky, with a billion stars as a backdrop."

I tried to imagine what he was seeing as he took my finger and pointed out its features. The image was starting to come together. "It's a cookie cut-out Star Bear," he said, "standing upright with paws paddling, head thrown back toward the cosmos."

"I think I see it," I said. "Its hind legs are upstream, and its nose is pointing down the canyon."

"Yeah," Timmy said. "The sky is supposed to be the negative space, but in this case, it's positive. The sky is providing the shape of that Star Bear. It's a paradoxical recognition that what isn't there still defines what is present. It's like two dudes, both without sight, instructing those who can see and giving meaning to all that's known."

"Timmy, I'm gonna need some time to interpret that," Kelly said, laughing, "but I do believe it's dancing up there."

"Let's go dance with it," Katie murmured.

"I think he can see us," I added. "He's looking down on us. We're like little specks of sand. He's pointing the way down the river, saying, 'Follow me. Follow me.'"

"No," Timmy corrected, "he's really asking, 'Why are you wearing a bumblebee tutu and zebra-striped tights? What are you thinking? You freak shows should retreat while you still can! Turn around now. You're insane.'"

Rising the next morning, I tried to force down some breakfast on a queasy stomach. My nerves were so raw by now, I was referring to breakfast as "bagels and bile" and "dry heaves and toast." The day started with a long warm-up to Lava, a fourteen-mile flat-water paddle that gave me plenty of time to contemplate what lay ahead. I tried to conjure up everything that Harlan had been telling me since we first launched, to keep my mind free from clutter and distractions, from doubt and fear, to be at peace with my decisions, and to channel the energy of the river. I tried to remove all the negative thoughts that enveloped my consciousness like silty water invading a clear stream.

About a half mile above Lava Falls, Harlan pointed out Vulcan's Anvil, a fifty-foot plug of basalt, rising straight up out of the middle of the river. "It's the cone of an extinct volcano," he said, "the last remnant of that thousand-foot dam."

One day the river will erode it all and take it downstream too, I thought.

Harlan told me that the Hualapai and Paiute tribes believed their ancestors met at the top of the anvil to solve disputes. It was a sacred place for them, a center of energy and power.

"In the afternoon light," Rob said, "it looks jet black." I had Rob direct me over to it, and I paddled a symbolic circle around it. As I raised my open palm toward the rock, I could feel its heat, even from a few feet away.

With Lava now booming below us, we pulled over and went ashore to scout, scrambling over the time-hardened lava rocks, river right. Six years of training and 179 miles through the canyon had led me here. In a way I couldn't believe it. The hour had arrived. We stood on an overlook above the rapid, and Harlan took my hand and pointed it across the river to Prospect Canyon, the source of the big boulders that had come down and constricted this section so dramatically. Below us, it sounded catastrophic, like a constant thunderclap, like a place where the earth was angry, roiling and erupting with a million tons of water instead of magma.

"Sounds big." I forced the words out of my diaphragm.

"It's definitely big," said Harlan, "but it's just another rapid. Don't go into this any differently than the others, like Upset. Remember what that felt like."

Lonnie was next to me and started talking in an exuberant chatter. "I remember Lava Falls when I had my eyesight, seeing it on *Wide World of Sports*. This raft went in there, hit the Ledge Hole, and flipped. I'll never forget the image of that big ole raft vertical, then upside down, all the rigging tearing out, coolers coming out, people flying out, and that rubber boat doing end-over-end flips."

I tried to picture the Ledge Hole, Lava's most infamous and awe-inspiring feature, a wide rock pour-over producing a wave twelve feet tall and, on the other side, a massive pileup of white water. It was known as the place on the Grand Canyon where you didn't want to be. "The thrill of victory and the agony of defeat," I managed to reply, and then I sank down on a rock.

"When I came through here my last time," Lonnie jumped back in, "I remember standing right here, where we are now, listening to that roar and feeling the vibration through my feet. You feel that? And I'm thinking, 'Okay, I'm gonna do this.' I dropped in, missed the Ledge Hole on the left, got a little squirrely on the right, flipped and rolled back up, and I'm digging with my paddle like a boll weevil through a tater patch, but I got flipped again, and my spray skirt imploded. I coulda swore it took my legs off. Ripped me right out of my kayak so violently, they told me my boat went flying in the air doing flips, twenty feet in the air. I finally popped up, paddle still in my hands, and one of my guides came and rescued me."

By the time Lonnie had finished recounting his run, I felt dizzy and listless. I thought I was going to puke. I tried to fight the nausea with the proactive breathing exercises Timmy had taught me, but I couldn't seem to breathe it away. I wasn't sure if it was Lonnie's story, the temperature that had topped one hundred degrees, the fourteen-mile paddle that morning, the exhaustion of the last two weeks, or all the pressure and buildup to this moment; maybe it was all of it, but I felt the veneer of confidence slipping away and the debris pouring in, constricting the current of my mind, strangling the flow. I could feel the weight of it all, like those obstructions lurking deep below Lava yet profoundly affecting what I would experience on the surface.

Harlan began describing the line, and I needed to maintain my composure. I listened to him as best I could, given the images of tumbling rafts and kayaks spinning through the air. He took my hand again, pointing it along the line. "We're gonna ease in center river right, just to the left of a strong eddy line. There are some really weird, powerful boils that are coming off the shore. They'll try to surf you to the left. Fight the spin and stay loose and relaxed. We'll have the Ledge Hole on our left and some big pour-overs to our right. We'll punch through two pretty sizeable surging waves and try to line up for the V-Wave. There are two of them crashing together. The right side's no good. It's a muncher, and behind it is the corner pocket—not a good place to wind up. So we'll charge it angling slightly left to punch through the left side of the V. It's a good hit, so if you get knocked over, you have enough time to roll up before the next features. If you stay upright, then we'll keep angling out into the river, so we avoid my old friend the Cheese Grater Rock. Then we'll straighten out and hit the Big Kahuna waves. There's a series of them, but two big ones. Then you just ride out the tail waves, and we're done."

Through my paddling booties, I could feel the burning lava rock scalding the bottom of my feet. Late afternoon wind whipped up the canyon. My lips were cracked, my throat parched, my tongue chalky.

"Ready to do this, E?" Harlan asked.

"I think so," I replied. I'd never been so terrified in my life.

I scrambled down the boulders and climbed into my kayak. Although I'd given up the practice of cranking the ratchets in my cockpit eighteen precise times, I still had a careful pre-paddling ritual that took several minutes and served as meditation. First, I pulled the ropes that tightened my backrest and the bulkhead under my feet. I made sure no folds on my dry top would get hooked over anything that would prevent me from wet exiting if I needed to. I pulled on my neoprene skirt, snapping it over my cockpit from back to front. I slid on my helmet, maneuvered the microphone in front of my lips, and wiggled the earpiece so it was flush against my ear. I buckled the chin strap, making sure there were no twists, wrapped the cord of my comm system around the shoulder strap of my PFD: two loops and tuck the system into the chest pocket. Lastly, I held my paddle out, rolling it in my hands; it was easy to grab it backward, so I carefully felt the paddle blades, noting the feathering and angle. We turned on the radios. They beeped to indicate they were working. Harlan was fairly clear: "Check, check," I heard. "Small left, small right, testing, testing."

We pushed into the river. I was floating out, away from anything solid, anything I could hang on to. It was happening. Lava's terrible bellow grew louder, beginning to cancel all other sound except Harlan's voice. "We're here, right now, in this moment; nothing else matters. Be clear and calm and concise."

But unlike Upset Rapid where my actions had felt crisp and fluid, and my surroundings had slowed, now it was my body moving slowly with the canyon racing by. My movements felt labored, my muscles stiff and tense. I felt the power of the current beneath my hull as it hurled me toward Lava's tongue. I wanted to put on the brakes and pull over, to rethink what I was doing, but there was no time.

"We're about a hundred yards above now," Harlan said. "Small left. Hold that line." I tried to execute his command, but my response time felt seconds behind, and my paddle strokes felt mushy, like I was disconnected from the water. "Small left again. Hold that line. Right there. Nice calm strokes; good thoughtful strokes. Hold that line."

I silently repeated our familiar mantra: "Relax. Breathe. Be at peace with the river."

His voice became louder, more urgent. "Approaching those boils . . . fight the spin, fight the spin." I was struck simultaneously from the right-side boils and the surging main left channel, but as I dug in with my paddle blade, fighting those invisible hands grabbing my bow, I reverted to a bad habit I thought I'd broken two years ago. I felt my upper body lean the wrong way, and I was instantly upside down, with no idea which direction my boat was pointing. My mind swirled like the current above and below me, like a blind man's version of a fun house, bombarded by mirrors, no sense of space or direction. I'd accepted the fact that I'd probably flip somewhere in Lava, but I would have never imagined being upside-down heading into it. How could this even be happening? It would have been comical if it weren't so insanely scary. I managed to get my paddle to the surface, snap my hips, and roll back up to the growl of the river. I heard Harlan yelling, "Hard left!" then instantly "Hard right!" and I tried to respond, but my reactions and movements were imprecise. My speed increased as I jostled and pitched over the entry waves and plunged down a slope into what had to be the V-Wave, then felt a collision like hitting a solid wall. My boat was thrown up and backward as I flipped again. My kayak spun above me as I managed to roll up once more, now hyperventilating.

Harlan's words came fast and loud now: "Left! You're good! You're good!" But I wasn't good. I could feel the current tugging me backward toward a deafening roar, like giant breakers pounding a beach. I was pointing backward going into the Kahuna waves. "Hard right!" Harlan yelled. "Charge! Charge!" But I couldn't get around in time. An enormous wave broke over me from behind, hitting me in the back of the helmet, knocking my body forward, and yanking my kayak down and under. My arms felt paralyzed as I was buried in an avalanche of water. Then I was over again, tumbling and gyroscoping under all that weight, the opposing currents violently grabbing at my paddle blades, trying to rip it from my hands. Somehow I rolled up in the midst of the storm, but there was no direction from Harlan. Then another wave hammered me from my left, and I fought to brace. I took a gasp of half air and foam as I went under again.

The howling roar became an underwater gurgle of exploding bubbles. Waves pounded my boat from above, bashing me down harder as each of my roll attempts got weaker. At last I was out of air, and I desperately reached for my grab loop and yanked, popping my spray skirt and launching myself out of my boat. I clawed for the surface, for air, inhaling water as more waves slammed down and spun and shook me. My head finally popped above the surface, and I gasped for breath. I could hear voices again—Rob's? Timmy's?— but not Harlan's as I felt a boat next to me and held on to it, trying to catch hold of something; it tipped a little, like the beginning of an Eskimo roll. I realized then I was feeling a smooth hull, the bottom of a boat. It was Harlan. He'd flipped too! I let go, and Timmy was beside me, hauling me toward an eddy.

Then I could hear Harlan again, his voice breathless and quavering, explaining that a big wave had snapped his carbon fiber paddle in half, the severed, jagged edge spearing him in the face. That's why he'd flipped. But I was hardly listening as Timmy deposited me on shore and I pulled myself up onto the slippery rocks at the river's edge, thankful to be out of that terrifying maelstrom.

I could hear my team's voices and their boats clacking into one another as they hovered in the eddy. Rob said, "You're done, buddy. No more big rapids." With shaking hands, I took off my helmet. Water and silt streamed down my face as I tried to process what had just happened.

"No worries, Erik," Harlan said. "You remember that old kayaking adage, right? We're all just between swims."

As I sat there, I tried to keep my face from reacting, trying to hide the shock and devastation. Lonnie ran Lava clean, just flipping once. The team whooped and hooted for his success, especially since he'd swum last year. I cheered for him too, but not with as much enthusiasm as I should have. I felt bitter, like I'd let my team and myself down. It felt as if I had dishonored the journey I was on.

We pulled off and camped at Tequila Beach just a half mile below, beside the rapid called Son of Lava. One kayaking tradition is called the Booty Beer. When a kayaker swims and has to be rescued, they have to chug a full beer out of someone's stinky paddling booty. I went along with the ritual, the boot tipped up to my lips as I guzzled warm, foamy beer, river water, and sweat, but I didn't taste it. Everything was numb. The boys tried to cheer me up, and Harlan said, "Look at it this way. Right now, you are as far from Lava Falls as you could possibly be. You are through it. Lava is behind you."

He was right in a way. Swimming through one rapid didn't make the entire trip a failure. In the overall scheme of things, it didn't really matter that I swam. I was through it. I was safe. I was alive. Part of me was glad it was over. It was a bitter relief. Now I could get on with it, move downriver, and never have to think about it again, but if that was the case, why did I feel a plaguing regret and a vague sense of possibilities unfulfilled? Years ago in Tibet, we'd failed to summit Lhakpa Ri and had gone on to find a "blind summit" that was just as good. But how were you supposed to know when to let go and when to hang on? When to let the river take you downstream toward something new and when to double back? I turned in early that night, exhausted, defeated, and confused.

Son of Lava rumbled outside my tent door. I listened carefully for a long time to its ebb and flow as waves built and curled and crashed down again; currents swirled, clashed, and mingled, and the water relentlessly churned and pounded over rocks. Everything, I thought, had a subtext, a language hidden beneath. I tried to understand what the river was saying, but was I wise enough to decipher it? I had believed, perhaps naïvely, that if you committed to something, if you trained hard enough, if you believed strongly enough, the barriers would open up before you like floodgates and you'd be treated to a glorious and well-earned storybook ending. Even through all the struggle and anxiety, the bleeding and shortfalls, I had secretly and stubbornly clung to this premise. Yet it hadn't ended that way, far from it. I had dreamed I would emerge changed in some way, strengthened by the journey. I'd wanted to flourish in the river, like Harlan; it had become a part of his mind and soul. Yet I still felt separated, like I was navigating in an alien landscape. I had swum through Lava, blind, frantic, bathed in fear, and emerging on the other end like a drowned rat. What did you learn from that, except that life was to be endured, to be survived? "Don't let that be the culmination!" I spoke aloud to my empty tent.

I recalled the Star Bear that Timmy had spied above us two nights before: paws reaching skyward and its snout pointing down-canyon, as if to say, "Trust me. Trust the river." But it had all been false, just empty sky with no substance, no meaning at all. I laughed bitterly. *Screwed by the Star Bear*, I thought, my face pressed into my sleeping bag. Maybe all these ideas, like belief, like faith, like will, they were just illusions, as void as an endless sky. They were human constructs to tempt us toward false hope, false understanding. And they were nothing in the face of such immeasurable power: the thrust of the mountains spewing magma and raining down boulders; the violence of rivers to bore through thousand-foot-high lava dams.

As I continued to toss and turn, the river seemed so loud, I could barely hear the group still reveling outside. Their voices were muted, droning into the night. The river, I thought, represented those massive forces bigger than me, bigger than all of us: that crushing diagnosis that radically altered the course of your life, the catastrophic event that changed the course of history, the adversity that knocked you down and defied you to get up again. Blindness was one of them. There was absolutely nothing I could have done in the face of it. Death was another. But misery, depression, disillusionment, alienation, fear: They were all second cousins. They rushed forward, splintering, pulverizing, disintegrating everything in their path, and we pretended we could somehow affect that unyielding trajectory. Even Harlan, who had achieved a level of mastery I still had trouble imagining, had been spit out the bottom of Lava, upside down, his paddle snapped in half and his nose almost broken. No. Humans were not the driving force, I thought. We were more like rocks in the river or the canyon walls, being scoured and eroded by circumstances and time. And I was powerless in the face of that energy.

But as those ideas and doubts flooded through my brain, there were persistent examples, a number of outliers, people who seemed to run counter to the theory. Rob was one of them. I remembered him on the Usumacinta, beaten down by the effects of cancer, his spine fractured, yet paddling furiously toward a drowning teammate and saving his life. His cancer had been a kind of challenge he'd never confronted before, yet, despite that, he bravely went forward to live fully and confront the uncertainty that lay ahead. There were other examples too. My old friend Mark Wellman had broken his back yet had climbed El Capitan. He'd performed a kind of alchemy, turning lead into gold. Then there was Hugh Herr and Andy Parkin, who'd both been shattered, having to rebuild themselves, and, in the process, had been renewed. Kyle Maynard had pioneered what seemed impossible and, with a great team around him, crabbed his way to the top of Kilimanjaro. Mandy Harvey had done something preposterous by learning to let go and write and sing music she would never hear.

It occurred to me that all these friends had something in common: Their actions were counterintuitive, defying the reality of what they saw and felt. They grew rather than diminished. They went in unlikely directions, instead of accepting safety and stagnation. And Terry Fox was always at the top of my list. Despite all the evidence pointing toward futility, he had chosen to run thousands of miles across a continent. He would never live to witness the results of his heroic act, yet he'd done it anyway, and that choice had made all the difference. Ryan Kelly had also made choices, and the weight of them had almost destroyed him, but he'd learned that courage wasn't a state of being. As he described it, courage wasn't a noun; it was a verb; it was a choice that you made every minute of every day, and he'd committed to choosing courage over fear.

If my life had anything in common with a rapid, it made sense that there was a map, one that was even harder to read than the one on a river. These people had illuminated parts of that map, had lit up the path like contrails in the sky, like bioluminescence in dark water. It was a map I desperately yearned to build and follow. And the choices I made would either paralyze me, send me spiraling into a whirlpool, or propel me forward, admittedly in crazy and unexpected ways.

It was staggeringly difficult, however, not to see the overpowering evidence of the world, and use it as validation to protect yourself, and to shut down. It took such relentless trust in your team, in what lay ahead, to stay open to the possibilities that existed like a blank canvas, or like the infinite sky that gave promise to those features that could be touched, heard and seen. I could still hear Harlan in my ear, just like that Star Bear, reminding me to have faith that the journey down the river was a good one.

Matt Burgess had almost allowed those prison bars to slam down and end his journey. He had been on the verge of leaving the No Barriers program and retreating back into the familiar darkness, but he'd known somehow that the mind and the heart were the windows to that internal light. As I'd told Ellie and the kids after returning home from that expedition, "Even though he'd wanted to close his heart, he'd done the opposite and opened it more. Sometimes you gotta just trust and give it a whirl."

Without much sleep, I crawled out of my tent. I heard soft voices and found Harlan and Rob already awake. They were next to the kayaks, talking quietly. I approached, swinging my trekking pole in front of me, and realized Timmy, Skyler, and Steven were there too. I pulled Harlan aside and said falteringly, "What do you say we . . . maybe . . . try it again."

"You know," he replied, "I've been thinking the same thing. In fact, I was hoping you'd say that." It was unanimous. Everyone agreed and began quietly suiting up. Lava Falls was one of the few major rapids on the Grand Canyon that you could actually portage around upstream and run again. So even though it felt backward, Harlan, Rob, Timmy, Steven, Skyler, and I began carrying our boats toward the top of Lava, wordlessly bushwhacking through the thick tamarisk scrub. This time, although the rapid was just as loud as it had been the day before, it sounded less menacing, and I felt calm.

Just below Lava, the navigable terrain ended, and we had to cross the river to reach the top of the rapid. As I paddled across the squirrely water below the tail waves, I flipped over in the clash of the eddy line and struggled to roll up again. I got up on my second try, and as soon as my head rose above water, I could hear the crash of Lava above. Again, I felt that panic shoot through my body like lightning.

"I'm having second thoughts," I said, "maybe I should rethink this." But the team ignored me and kept paddling. I knew that was their way of spurring me on. Soon we were across to the other side. Everyone grabbed their boats and kept trudging along the shoreline upstream. I followed. We finally dropped the boats at the put-in, and Timmy lightened the mood by enthusiastically proclaiming, "It's time to get a little bit of Lava 2.0!"

Then everyone was quiet again. I climbed into my boat and sat for a couple of minutes, listening to Lava below me. It was still cranking. Maybe it was impossible to fight those forces, I thought, to go toe-to-toe with them. They were just too big and powerful. There were moments to paddle against the flow, to reposition, but as Harlan had been repeating, there were also moments to ride the current, to harness the energy of the river and move with it. On Upset, I'd felt that synchronicity, and I'd assumed that once you experienced it, you would carry it permanently. Yet it dawned on me that such connection wasn't acquired once and then owned forever. That flow, that fusion of water and landscape and light—it was something that you had to constantly strive for. It was about struggling and flailing to find it once, and then again and again and again. And it would always be waiting.

I slid off the rocks, my boat slapping the water, and I was racing again toward the throat of Lava. Harlan's voice was just as it had been at Upset Rapid—a kind of melding with my thoughts. I committed to feeling and reacting instead of thinking, letting my body move with the current. As I headed down the tongue, beneath the butterflies, beneath the anticipation, I felt gratitude for whatever the river would take from me, or whatever it would give.

EPILOGUE

In June of 2016, we held our eighth No Barriers Summit at Copper Mountain, Colorado. As I stood on the stage about to speak at the closing ceremony, I could hear the murmur of the audience in front of me, a thousand people of diverse backgrounds and circumstances: people with physical disabilities, as well as those who struggled with obesity, brain injuries, and PTSD. There were those who'd survived cancer, strokes, addiction, and physical and emotional trauma. Surprisingly, lots of ordinary families had also joined our community, as well as CEOs and corporate leaders, who had taken the No Barriers principles and were applying them to their teams and organizations. Lastly, there were everyday people who just felt lost, or suffered from fear, anxiety, and self-doubt.

I could feel the energy under the Colorado sky as I began to speak: "It was while climbing a desert tower years ago with Mark Wellman and Hugh Herr," I started, "that I first asked myself, is there something that unites our experience? Whether you're blind, missing legs, or unable to walk—like the three of us—or whether you're a veteran who comes home feeling alienated and depressed, or a parent struggling to lead her family, or a kid whose barrier is that he's never been more than a mile from his house, or a teen in the suburbs who has no idea how to impact her world, or someone trying to grow a new idea into something magnificent. What is the glue that binds all of us together, every human who lives and breathes? Are there tools, ideas ... is there a mind-set, a light inside that we can all access—to equip us for that journey?

"The answer has led us all here, to this movement that we are building. And what is the fundamental message of this movement? I wish it were as simple as a motivational slogan like, 'If you believe it, you can achieve it,' but life is not a storybook, and its lessons can seem shifting and contradictory. Our paths can lead us toward suffering, yet sometimes, toward the beginnings of change."

The wind picked up and blew down from the mountain slopes and through the village. I could hear the No Barriers flags, hung from the stage, fluttering in the breeze.

"When I first started paddling into whitewater rapids, they appeared to me as utter chaos, but I found that if you pay close attention, and listen very carefully, you can discover a hidden map. Kayakers call this the line. It's hard to read and decipher. It's even harder to navigate. But if you manage to follow it, or even to get close, you can find a way through. That map, that line, that discovery, is what we call 'No Barriers.'"

After the closing ceremony, I said good-bye to hundreds of friends, and when it all quieted down, I sat on a bench, facing the Rocky Mountains. I could feel the morning sun on my back. I said a quick prayer for my brother Mark. "I hope you're proud of what I've tried to build," I said. "For you."

Then my mind scrolled through the last week of the Grand Canyon expedition. After a lot of internal angst, I'd decided to try Lava Falls again. My second run wasn't dramatically different from my first. I paddled just beside the right eddy line and hit the same boils, braced as I'd done before. I felt myself going over. This time, though, I consciously willed myself to lean and lift the edge of my kayak. I bobbled for a precarious second and then shot by into the entry waves. Again, the V-Wave knocked me backward. I flipped but stuck my roll, angling farther out into the river to line up against the next test. My entry into the Big Kahuna waves was far from ideal. I didn't quite get around and got slammed sideways. I rolled up, enveloped by collapsing water and foam, and was knocked over again. But this time I stayed calm, closed my eyes, and surrendered to the chaos as the roiling forces flipped and spun me around. "Eisenhower Tunnel," I repeated several times as I felt my oxygen waning. Then the water stilled around me. My roll came easily, and I felt myself bobbing down the bottom of the Big Kahunas with Harlan's jubilant voice yelling, "You're through! You're through! You did it!"

That night, one of Lonnie's guides, Seth Dahl, presented me with a drawing he'd been working on at various camps. He described it to me as a dark river cutting through a deep canyon. "The boils," he said, "often the worst when least expected, represent the unpredictability and hardship of the expedition. The imposing walls, massive and confining, forced us to confront our greatest challenges and our greatest discoveries."

Penned across one of Seth's canyon walls was a poem, written by Katie Proctor, one of our AzRA guides. She read it aloud:

Some say seeing is believing.

But I've been a witness.

To truth being felt.

The unseen is understood when experienced.

The open-heart policy.

Paddle in hand.

Each stroke leaving a wake of inspiration behind like currents expanding
out to distant shores.

You will never know the magnitude of their impression.

The momentum of possibility.

You will not be eddied out in your quest for experiencing the fullness
of current.

Strange how having the courage to live from a place of nonsense can
lead to the living of your wildest dreams.

Through the journey, children will ask you about faith.

Just trust and ah . . . give it a whirl.

Heart thumping.

Waves crashing.

Soul smiling.

Barriers dissolved under a Star Bear sky.

. . .

On September 27, 277 miles after putting in at Lees Ferry, our team rounded the final river bend, and I could hear the canyon walls shrinking and widening as the Grand Wash Bluffs gave way to the Nevada desert above Lake Mead. My mind swirled with conflicting emotions and memories from the river as our paddle strokes cleaved the smooth water. Harlan called out his final commands to me, "Small right. Hold that line," and I heard his voice crack a little. I thought he might be crying. Then my boat touched the shore, and, as I climbed out onto the sandy beach, I heard soft, smiling voices.

"Hi, Dad."

"Arjun? Emma?" That's when I began crying too as I reached out and swept them up in my arms. Ellie then stepped forward and joined the embrace, her warm voice whispering congratulations in my ear. As an extra surprise, a fourth familiar voice came forward, gravelly and accented. "Kami Tenzing Sherpa?" I asked incredulously. "Uncle Kami? All the way from Nepal?"

Then we were all hugging and swaying together. That's when I understood the source of Harlan's tears. He'd been bearing a lot during that last stretch as he saw my family waiting silently and expectantly on the beach. He'd also been carrying a burden throughout the entire project. He'd taken on the daunting responsibility of guiding me down a river that had once nearly taken his life, and he'd delivered me safely into the arms of my family, from his home, and now back to mine.

On the last night of our expedition, as I celebrated with my family at Pierce Ferry, I asked Ellie, "Where's Harlan?"

Ellie put her hand on my shoulder. "He's down at the river," she said reverently. "He's standing waist deep, and he's letting the water run through his fingers."

I remembered Harlan's ritual, his pact: "I'll come back someday, but for now, I've got some more life to live."

"It looks like he's having a conversation," Ellie said.

"I think he is," I replied.

Since the completion of the Grand Canyon expedition, the team had been charging forward in characteristic style. **Lonnie "the LonDart" Bedwell** outdid his accomplishment on the Grand Canyon by heading to Zambia with Timmy O'Neill and famous kayaker Eric Jackson. Together they paddled a twenty-five-mile section of the Zambezi River with rapids even bigger and fiercer than those of the Grand Canyon. When I asked him if he was scared of the crocs, he answered, "I wasn't too worried. If one came at me, I was told to paddle straight at it, and they usually duck. Then, of course, you turn around and paddle like hell!"

Lonnie still hunts with the man who accidentally shot him, and he recently organized a turkey hunt in Indiana for blind and visually impaired veterans. "Hunting blind," he says. "Why not?"

But topping all of his accomplishments, he finally took a leap and bought a cell phone. Although last time I called him, I got this voice message: "Hey, you've reached Lonnie. Thanks for calling. I'll call you back as soon as I can see to find the phone."

For **Steven Mace**, our expedition became a launching point. He distinguished himself as such a valuable hard worker, he was subsequently hired as a guide for Arizona Raft Adventures and now works in the Big Ditch.

When I asked **Timmy O'Neill** what he was going to do after the Grand Canyon, he said, "Continue to live a life of chaos, rebellion, mystery, and love." For his fortieth birthday, he BASE jumped off El Capitan and Half Dome in one day, and he continues to push the boundaries of climbing and slacklining. In honor of his brother Sean who was paralyzed, he helped found Paradox Sports, with a mission of promoting adaptive mountain sports. Most recently he's been volunteering with the Himalayan Cataract Project in developing countries like Ethiopia, assisting in eye surgeries to cure preventable blindness.

While poring over river maps of Peru, **Rocky Contos** made a remarkable discovery. The Apurímac in Peru had been established as the most distant source of the Amazon, but after careful examination, he determined that the nearby Rio Mantaro was actually eighty kilometers longer. Not wanting to miss out, Rocky scrambled to put together a plan and headed for South America. After hiking for two days to the headwaters of the Rio Mantaro, Rocky spent the next two months kayaking and traveling by boat, becoming the first person ever to complete the entire descent of the Amazon from its most distant source to the sea.

Rob Raker was diagnosed with Stage IV prostate cancer in 2010, but he has outlived the initial prognosis and is still going strong. In February 2016, Rob was accepted into a clinical trial at the NIH, a treatment involving a genetically tailored vaccine that could help his immune system fight the cancer. Since February 2016, his PSA has stopped increasing.

Just before Rob's sixty-first birthday, his dear friend Steve Edwards died of cancer. Steve was a fitness legend who helped develop P90X and was known for creating grueling birthday challenges. To honor Steve's life, Rob devised one of his own:

In 61 hours over the next 6.1 days I will attempt to:

Photograph 61 different species of birds,
Ski downhill 61,000 vertical feet,
Bike and hike 61 miles,
Run 6.1 miles,
Do 61 push-ups each of the six days,
Do 61 sit-ups each of the six days,
Rock climb 610 vertical feet at 5.10 or higher difficulty,
And try to have fun doing it all.

Harlan Taney spends as much time as possible in the Grand Canyon. Based out of Flagstaff, Arizona, his company, 4 Corner Film Logistics, has worked with the BBC on a reenactment of the Powell Expedition, a production on the condors of the Vermilion Cliffs, and projects to save the Grand Canyon from proposed mega-development. "It's a wild and sacred place," said Harlan, "one of the Natural Wonders of the World, and I intend to keep it that way." Recently, while working on a conservation film in the canyon, Harlan had a revelation. "The Grand Canyon," he said, "is only one of countless threatened environments around the world, and media content could be a powerful tool to preserve them all." As a result, he recently founded an organization to capture video footage of natural habitats that are endangered worldwide and archive them in an open-source database—all to create awareness for their protection. As Harlan excitedly told me the news, I remembered the story of his first trip down the Grand Canyon as a little boy, and I pictured other children tossing sticks into other sacred and wild rivers, watching them drift away, and having the chance to dream about where they go.

Besides my kayaking team, there were so many others whose lives had intersected with mine over the last fifteen years. It was quite a list. **Sabriye Tenberken** and **Paul Kronenberg**, from our Tibet expedition, expanded their Dream Factory by moving to Kerala, India, where they created Kanthari, a training center to help visionaries learn the skills to start their own social change projects throughout the developing world. A kanthari is a small but spicy chili that grows wild in every backyard of Kerala. Sabriye said that a kanthari is also a symbol of a new kind of leader, from the margins of society, who has the guts to challenge the status quo, who has fire in the belly, and innovative ideas to make a difference. Since its founding in 2009, they have trained one hundred forty-one participants from thirty-eight countries, resulting in more than eighty-five social projects that reach thousands of beneficiaries.

The Tibetan students were faring well too. After graduating from Braille Without Borders, **Kyila** completed Kanthari leadership training and founded Kiki's Kindergarten in Lhasa, where blind and sighted children play together and learn skills that prepare them to attend elementary school. **Sonam Bhumtso** graduated from high school and was one of the first blind students in China to pass her gao-kao (university entrance exam). She now studies Tibetan medicine. **Gyenshen** leads the Braille printing press that produces all the textbooks and materials for Braille Without Borders. **Tenzin** and **Tashi** run their own medical massage clinic with ten masseurs. Tashi also teaches Chinese at Braille Without Borders. **Dachung** started a medical massage clinic and was so successful he opened two more. After selling all three, he learned to play the flute. He did that well too and was soon the leader of a professional orchestra of blind Tibetans performing traditional Tibetan music.

Mark Wellman now works with veterans and disability organizations, traveling the country with his portable twenty-four-foot climbing wall, conducting adaptive climbing seminars. "Some of the participants," Mark said, "may not be able to dress themselves, or feed themselves, but if they can move just one finger, we can get them out of their chair and up on the wall. They can climb." And some of the results are profound. "I had one guy last year," Mark said, "who was born with spina bifida. He was obese and had to use a power wheelchair. He wouldn't even look me in the eye. We got him up on the wall, and a year later, he shows up again. But this time, he's lost a hundred pounds. He's using a hand-crank chair. He's looking me straight in the eye and smiling, and the best part—he's got a mohawk."

For **Kyle Maynard**, making history on Kilimanjaro wasn't quite enough. On February 21, 2016, Kyle crawled to the summit of Aconcagua, at 22,841 feet the highest point in South America.

Mandy Harvey admits she's still "afraid of nearly everything." Despite that, in 2016, she released her first full album of original songs, entitled *This Time,* and in the summer of 2017, she made it all the way to the finals of *America's Got Talent,* a primetime show seen by fifteen million viewers. "What's the point of having gifts," she says, "if you don't share them and use them to love others?"

Ryan Kelly, who helped me understand the nature of post-traumatic stress, is a playwright and novelist. All his works have centered around our nation's wars, but, now back from Iraq for ten years, he says he's finally ready for a new kind of book, this time a comedy. He describes it as "a story of hope."

At fifteen, **Emma** continues to volunteer at a rescue organization for stray dogs and cats. She's now fostered and found homes for seventy dogs. Her last, whom she named Duncan, was cracked in the head with a mallet soon after birth by his owner and thrown in a trash can. Somehow he lived. When Emma received the dog, he had a dent in his skull and stared straight ahead. Duncan had to be guided to his food and water dish. Yet with love and care, one week later, his tail was wagging, and he was running and barking in the backyard. Emma said, "Hey, Dad, Duncan is a No Barriers dog."

Ellie continues to be my greatest ally. Not only has she tolerated me over the years as I've delivered flowers with the petals all disintegrated after an unexpected downpour, washed dishes with syrup instead of dish soap (the bottles feel remarkably similar), or gone to dinner with one black shoe and one brown, she also pilots our tandem bike, guides me on skis, and, this summer, will once again be behind the wheel of a thirty-six-foot RV on another Weihenmayer family adventure. As a No Barriers pledge, Ellie started swimming again after a thirty-year hiatus and came away with a blue ribbon at the Colorado Masters Championship. Through our family's Reach Foundation, Ellie administers several scholarships for children throughout Nepal. Recently, she read me a note from one of our girls, Apsara:

> Dear Respected Family,
>   My school is very beautiful. There are big trees. There is a big playground. I study in grade 3, and I got distinction. I am toppest girl.
>   Thank you.

Ellie has also been instrumental in bringing animals to the No Barriers Summits, like Molly the pony, who had her leg chewed off by a dog after Hurricane Katrina and was fitted with a prosthetic leg. The bottom of her hoof is in the shape of a smile, so with every step, Molly leaves a trail of joy. "We should all try to do the same," Ellie says.

After playing in a recreational soccer league for a season, **Arjun** made a bold decision to pursue a spot on the A team again. At the tryouts he made several textbook crosses that resulted in goals. Ellie said the three coaches were observing and scribbling notes in their booklets. A few days later, Arjun was invited on to the A team, where he excels. This winter, in his indoor league, he scored a hat trick! As far as Arjun's Nepali mom, **Kanchi**, last year, we set her up with fuel, wax, and wicks to start her own candle business. Because of Kathmandu's frequent power outages, candles are in high demand. She makes about fifty pounds of candles a day, and when she sells it all, she makes much more than she did working construction. When Arjun turns sixteen, we plan to visit her in Nepal.

Recently, I was in Boston for a speaking event and visited **Hugh Herr** at MIT. He was excited to give me a tour of his new endeavor, the Center for Extreme Bionics, one of the most advanced research centers in the world. Hugh and his team are building bionic prosthetic ankles, knees, and hips, as well as exoskeletons that expand human performance and surpass what nature intended. The tour included equipment so sophisticated, it was hard to fully understand: treadmills surrounded by multiple cameras, computers, and pressure-monitoring devices able to record and map the human walking gait, and wheel-shaped devices that measured tissue properties in biological limbs to make socket molds and prosthetics much more comfortable than ever before.

After the Boston Marathon bombing in April 2015, Hugh took on a project to help a professional ballroom dancer, Adrianne Haslet-Davis, who'd lost a leg in the terrorist attack. Hugh and his team spent over two hundred days studying dancers with biological limbs, recording how they moved on the dance floor and the forces that they applied with their legs. Then the team programmed that intelligence into the computers within a bionic limb. One year later, Adrianne showed off her new prosthetic on the TED stage by dancing for the first time since her injury. She received a standing ovation. Inspired by this, No Barriers joined Hugh in a partnership to build specialized prosthetics to help other survivors run, bike, swim, and even dance again.

Most impressive of all, Hugh told me that he'd been working on "neural implants," a way of connecting bionic prostheses with the human biological nervous system, which will allow the user's brain and nerves to simultaneously coordinate knee and ankle joint movement. "In six months," Hugh said, "I'm scheduled to undergo surgery to become the first human test subject."

Finally, Hugh showed me some shelves, right next to the treadmill, that held numerous prototypes of prosthetic devices that had failed. "What happened to this one?" I asked, holding a metallic knee joint in my hand.

"I guess I had a brain lapse that day," Hugh said, chuckling. "You have to understand, most things in the lab wind up not working. So you deal with failure most of the time."

Hugh called it his "Shelf of Shame" and then laughed again. "Although I guess we shouldn't be ashamed of our scars," he said. How rare and lucky he was, I thought, to have a physical trail of his mistakes, ideas that hadn't turned out as he'd expected, yet had still shown the way.

I thought about his philosophy that it's important to reach and explore, "and if the world turns out to be different than you expected, to view that as adventure, not failure." Kayaking had validated that concept for me. Heading into every rapid, I'd desperately tried to stay on the line, knowing it was the clearest and cleanest way through. However, sticking the perfect line was a rare occurrence, and more often, the forces of the river had thrown me into wild and unexpected places. Perhaps that map, I thought, wasn't all about staying on course, but equally about falling off the line. It was in that turbulence where the greatest discoveries seemed to be made.

Seeming to corroborate that argument, a couple of years after our No Barriers Cotopaxi trip, I got an unexpected e-mail from **Matt Burgess**. At first, I was just relieved it wasn't from his lawyer. He wrote, "Erik, when I reached the top of Cotopaxi, it was one of the proudest moments of my life. I look at that moment in a picture hanging on my wall every day." Matt went on to describe his dog, Brinks, whom he'd trained as a service dog. Matt suffered from sleep apnea and used a CPAP machine, but sometimes he ripped it off in his sleep and stopped breathing. When that happened, Brinks would lick his face and wake him up. But Matt noted that many veterans and special-needs children couldn't afford the training service dogs required. So, inspired by Brinks's love and dedication, he made a decision to found his own organization. Freedom Fidos would select dogs from local shelters and train them free of charge, and he had already successfully placed twenty-three dogs, with a waiting list of over a hundred. He was now raising the funding to build a first-class facility to increase his impact. Matt told me his dogs had been responsible for stopping suicides, empowering veterans to get off psychotropic drugs, and contributing to hundreds of lost pounds.

Matt wrote:

Cotopaxi was a huge catalyst that put me on this journey. It propelled me to have the confidence to start Freedom Fidos. The mountain is a metaphor of life and it can teach us so much. So many times now, there are mornings I wake up feeling totally unprepared, totally unqualified, but I can reach out to the past, to something I did on that trip and grab on to it. So much of who I am today and what I believe about myself is because of those experiences. Some days now, I feel crushed, but no matter the snow or rain or ice, I can keep putting one foot ahead of the other, or as Charley says, "little by little, we go far." On the climb, about 75% of the time I wanted to quit. And there were times I broke down and wept. But while standing on top of Cotopaxi, seeing for miles around, feeling exhausted, sick, hungry, and flooded with emotions-what I will never forget was feeling that light. Now my greatest prayer is to live within its glow, and help others live there too.

The impact of No Barriers continues to grow exponentially. In 2017, we'll provide transformative experiences for nearly 5,000 diverse youth, more than 3,000 individuals at our Summits and events, and almost 300 warriors with disabilities. Our annual operating budget has nearly tripled since 2012 to $6 million per year. We have expanded to thirty full-time employees, more than fifty seasonal expedition leaders and a board of thirty visionaries. Most importantly, we are changing lives in ways Mark, Hugh, and I only dreamed of. After our recent Summit, a participant wrote, "Last weekend was BEYOND amazing and life changing! I didn't say this to anyone, but I've really been struggling to find a purpose in my life. Outwardly, I look very positive, but I had given myself a deadline: Find a reason to keep living, or I'll end it . . . Last weekend made me realize I have potential, and purpose, and I finally feel excited about life again—truly FEEL it, and not just putting on the outward mask for others. Words are inadequate to express my gratitude for giving me the opportunity to participate. I hope to be involved in every No Barriers for the rest of my life, and I'd LOVE to become more actively involved in putting it on and helping others gain the same experience!"

Yet, we haven't been able to save everyone. Marine staff sergeant Dan Sidles was a member of our first No Barriers expedition who reached the summit of Lobuche, and was a mentor on the second trip to Cotopaxi in Ecuador. Dan had been instrumental in helping Matt Burgess stick it out and not quit the program. While in Iraq, Dan was wounded twice and received a Purple Heart, but he'd told us the real war began when he got home. In the spring of 2016, Dan Sidles lost his battle with PTSD and took his own life. I attended his memorial on a windy yet brilliantly sunny day in the mountains above Winter Park, Colorado. The honor guard marched, and two buglers played taps. A soldier in full dress uniform laid the American flag over his urn. The ceremony ended with a group of bagpipers playing "Amazing Grace." It was the second time in three years I'd heard this song. The first was listening to Adrian Anantawan play his violin on a mountaintop above Telluride. It was a moment full of hope and possibilities. But this time, it was to say good-bye to Dan. The commander in charge read a passage from *The Grand Army Songster and Service Book*:

The march of our comrade is over and he lieth down in the house appointed for all the living. This grave reminds us of the frailty of human life and the tenure by which we hold our own. In such an hour as ye think not, the final summons may come which no one disobeys. It seems fitting that we should leave our comrade to rest under the arching sky, as he did when he pitched his tent or laid down in days gone by, weary and footsore by the roadside, or on the field of battle. Our departed comrades no longer hear the sound of waves or float upon the bosom of the deep, no longer sail beneath peaceful skies, nor are driven before the angry storm. May each of us, when our voyage and battles of life are over, find a welcome in that region of the blessed where there is no more storm-tossed sea, nor scorching battlefield.

As I went through the line to pay my respects, I reached out to touch the urn containing Dan's ashes. *Your struggle is finally over*, I thought. *Rest in peace.*

As for me, that September, I helped lead our next No Barriers Warriors expedition culminating in an ascent of Gannett Peak in Wyoming. After all the training, we headed out on the long trail through the Wind River Range. Countless times, my guide would stop on the side of the trail and, in a quiet, humble voice, describe the huge expanses of forest, alpine meadows with herds of elk, and surrounding skylines of granite ridges—with the wind scouring the grasses and rocking the trees.

Arriving at camp each night, covered in soft pine needles and surrounded by ponderosa pines, we'd play games that the team called the Gannett Olympics. They'd consist of shot-putting boulders, throwing branches like javelins, and flipping fallen tree trunks. One evening as the sun set, we played a game of charades. Going blind so young, I'd never learned and was reluctant to join in, but a few soldiers patiently taught me the signals, how to pull my ear to say, *Sounds like,* and how to bring my thumb and forefinger together to say, *Shorter word*. I sat back in amusement as these veterans, often so stoic, came out of their shells to dance crazily on a pile of rocks trying to act out an '80s TV show.

In the midst of the fun, the weight of the expedition was never far away. At each camp, our No Barriers flags encircled boulders and hung from ropes. Some soldiers had inscribed their flags with the names of friends, now deceased, with whom they were honoring this climb. Like Tibetan prayer flags, which send messages to the heavens, the flags flapped in the wind, sending tributes to the fallen. One night, a soldier awoke screaming, and it was a long time before many got back to sleep. I sat up too, pondering all the nightmares that sent the mind spiraling into an endless loop of pain and futility.

A few days later, I sat on the side of the trail, leaning against a tuft of grass, with Sergeant Paul Smith, a teammate who had been guiding me all day. Paul had a tough start to life. When he was a young teenager, his mother was raped and killed, and his father, completely overwhelmed, sent him off to military school. After graduating, Paul signed up for the army, serving his country faithfully in Iraq as part of the First Cavalry Division. But while he was traveling in a Humvee through Baghdad, an IED exploded, piercing him with shrapnel and burning him over 50 percent of his body. "There isn't a place on me," he said, "that isn't pitted with burns and scars. But the physical stuff is secondary. As a kid, I'd watched old John Wayne movies with the First Cavalry coming to the rescue. They're known as 'First Team'—one of the most decorated divisions in the entire army. I said to myself, 'That's what I'm gonna do. That's who I'm gonna be.' And now I was being airlifted away. I wasn't ready to go."

The guilt of that day, the feelings of letting down his team, of leaving them behind, of not being able to fight anymore, sent Paul spiraling downward. "It was straight-up shame," he told me. As a result, Paul's family fell apart. Paul was involved in numerous car accidents and a suicide attempt. He abused drugs and alcohol. One of the anniversaries of his injury he spent in jail. "I've wasted a lot of time beating myself up," he said. "But I feel like I've just woken up from a dream, and I know now, I need a life of purpose."

The next day, the guides climbed from our high camp toward the top on a scouting mission. When they returned that afternoon, they reported grim news. It had been an unusually warm summer, and the route to the top, normally snow, had melted away. In its place stood a wide-open crevasse, and beyond, a steep, twenty-meter section of hard, gray glacial ice, crumbling and desiccated. Everyone had been prepped repeatedly that nature was fickle. Conditions changed, and there was value in the journey itself. But despite that, their heads hung low as they absorbed what this meant. A teammate banged rocks together, the auditory manifestation of the internal anguish everyone was feeling. My heart broke with the knowledge of how hard each had worked just to be here. Some had given up alcohol; others painkillers. One veteran had lost sixty-five pounds, and another had used the program to work through an ugly divorce.

The guides all left the circle and asked the team to figure out what to do. Some were adamant. "If we can't summit, then let's get the hell out of here!" But others weren't ready to give up. An hour later, when the debate was finished, they'd made their decision. They'd climb Gannett as high as they could to celebrate their high point and conclude this experience with honor.

After climbing through the predawn and early morning, the team arrived at the crevasse. They gathered up and stared silently down into its depths. Their eyes rose up the wall that was blocking their way. "I'm tired of getting close yet falling short in my life," Paul said. "I'm going to summit something . . . I promise." A few war stories were shared around the circle. A lot of tears were shed.

"I'm not going to be defined by the war anymore," one soldier said.

Then another picked up a rock and threw it into the crevasse. It clattered on its way downward. "That rock represents my nightmares," he said, "and I'm putting them behind me."

Next, others began doing the same, picking up stones and chunks of ice and throwing their nightmares into the dark tomb.

"As much as I wish there was a way around this thing," Charley said to the climbers huddling together, "this is as high as we can safely go today. This barrier is real, and it's not going away. It's not going anywhere. But we can. So take a good look around. Be content. Be proud of how far we've come together as a team. Let's continue to honor the past, but now it's time to turn around and focus on what's out there." He gestured toward the terrain far below.

As the group picked up their packs and got ready to leave, one turned back toward the face and called out a name: "Sergeant Glenn Harris—Third Ranger

Battalion." Then others began calling out, and the names of their fallen comrades echoed off the glacier and rang out over the mountains like a twenty-one-gun salute.

"Sergeant First Class Sammy Hairston—Second Airborne."

"Private First Class Joseph Guerra."

As Paul Smith carefully descended, he turned back and yelled a name as well. "Second Lieutenant James Goins, tank commander, Alpha Company—First Cavalry Division."

On the way up, Paul had been forced to focus on his feet, checking every step, but now he paused for a moment to stare out at the Wind River Range and take in the view. He could see the sharp ridges and peaks below, capped with snow, thrusting out in different directions like shooting stars. He was so high, he could see over the ridges to the foothills far beyond that unfurled onto the Wyoming grasslands, and for the first time in a very long time, Paul could see his future. He took a last glance at the expansive amber prairie sweeping all the way to the horizon, swiped the tears rolling down his face, and headed down.

NO BARRIERS PLEDGES

Hello, I'm Joyce. I just turned sixty-seven this spring. My husband passed away ten years ago, and the last decade was an enormous struggle with grief and battling weight gain. I lost confidence and motivation. As time has passed, I am finally more at peace and want to move forward. My No Barriers pledge is to reclaim my life and the years I have left. I've always thought of myself as active and adventurous, and so as a start, I plan to hike across Scotland, a country that I love and a journey that I have always wanted to take.

Hi, I'm Amber. I'm a housewife and mother to four small children. I am lucky to have the luxury to be able to stay at home with my children while my husband works seven days a week to provide for the family. I am probably not your typical No Barriers person. I have no physical problems or challenges. But I am longing for meaning, adventure, and a team of friends. I often struggle with fear, but seeing all of the amazing people who are a part of No Barriers has inspired me. My No Barriers pledge is to be courageous and to teach my kids to be kind and brave as they grow up.

My name is Daisy, and I was tipping the scale at almost 250 pounds. In addition to knee and back issues, my doctor kept warning me about diabetes and other ailments associated with weight. I started taking care of what I was eating and trying to be active every day. Now almost four months later I have gone down to 216 pounds and have lost many inches. My oldest child will be getting married next year in December, and as the mother of the bride, I want to look and feel great for all the pictures. But most importantly, I want to stay healthy for my kids. So my No Barriers pledge is to get down to 175 pounds!

My name is David, and as a youth, I was constantly in and out of trouble. When I turned eighteen, I found a new life in the U.S. Army and served fourteen years as an infantryman. After getting out, I spent the next twenty years fighting with drug addiction and alcohol abuse. The good news is that this summer is three years of sobriety. My No Barriers pledge is to use my struggle to help other veterans who face depression, anxiety, and addiction by raising and then donating therapy dogs and running support groups.

To pledge, go to www.touchthetop.com

THE PLEDGE OF NO BARRIERS

I pledge to view my life as a relentless quest to become my very best self,
To always view the barriers in my life as opportunities to learn,
To find ways to build teams, serve those in need, and do good in the world,
To push the boundaries of what is possible,
And prove that what's within me is stronger than what's in my way.

ACKNOWLEDGMENTS

Erik: I just returned from a climb of Crestone Needle, an eighteen-hour summit day with a treacherous descent. For hours upon hours, I faced the rock, down-climbing with vast space behind me. My friends took turns, just below me, spotting me and giving me constant directions, saying where to grab and where to place my feet. When I reflect on their patience and dedication, it gives me chills to realize how fortunate I am to have such extraordinary teams in my life. Without these people, the course of my life would have been dramatically different. So I'd like to honor my great teams over the years, those allies who have rallied around the dreams of a blind man.

First, thanks to my Mount Everest team who defied the naysayers to help me make history in 2001, and especially our team leader, Pasquale. You challenged me not to make Everest the "greatest thing I ever do."

To Uncle Rob, aka "Papa Duck," I'm deeply grateful. You started me on my Grand Canyon journey and taught me so much about kayaking and friendship. Rob was also instrumental during the entire writing process. His archived photography, excellent memory, and acute attention to detail were indispensable throughout.

Harlan, thanks for keeping your eyes on me and helping me to navigate through the storm. You opened your heart, home, and family to us and brought such depth and passion to the project—it's been inspiring to get to know you.

Many thanks to my entire No Barriers Grand Canyon team for helping me to prepare and build the confidence to take on the challenge.

Skyler and my Touch the Top team, you make things happen behind the scenes and never get enough credit. I want you to know you rock.

To Dave and the staff at No Barriers, you bring our movement to life and are the alchemy behind the mission.

Thanks to Gail for championing this project, and to Laurie for believing in me twice now.

Love and appreciation to my dad, Ed, for recounting some wonderful family stories. I can still remember the roar of your A-4 Skyhawk swooping over our house in Hightstown and rattling the windows. Semper Fi.

A big bear hug to my bro, Eddi, for reminding us about his insane four-wheeling adventures with Mark, the hot peppers, and "Down in Orlando . . . !" We love you, Mark.

My deepest gratitude goes to my wife, Ellie, who read every page of the manuscript with care, diligence, and love. You sat awake many nights giving critical feedback that guided the book and its themes. You're the real writer of the family, and I couldn't have done this without you.

Thank you to Buddy Levy, my coauthor. We met in 2003 at an adventure race in Greenland when he was covering the event as a journalist. For several days, Buddy was embedded with my team, and he made the grueling miles go a little faster with his thought-provoking questions and sense of humor that lifted our exhaustion and made us belly-laugh along the trail.

Buddy: I watched in amazement as Erik paddled through iceberg-filled fjords, bushwhacked over bouldery terrain, rode a tandem mountain bike at frightening speeds, and summited numerous peaks. I already knew that he'd summited Mount Everest and was impressed by his mountaineering résumé, but tromping through Greenland with him, I came to know his humor, his determination, and his vision for obliterating barriers. I stayed in contact with Erik over the next decade, writing a number of magazine articles about him, going skiing with him, and getting to know his family. In 2013, I went to my first No Barriers Summit, and there experienced first-hand the unique assemblage of people connected by a shared philosophy, which is the No Barrier's motto: "What's Within You Is Stronger Than What's In Your Way."

I was fortunate to be invited on Erik's historic "kayaking blind" journey down the Grand Canyon in September 2014. At camp one late afternoon, we began discussing the idea of coauthoring a book about his life since descending from the summit of Mount Everest. Without really knowing exactly how we'd pull it off, we embarked on a very ambitious project together. There were moments near our final deadline when it felt like I'd been in a tiny tent on a mountainside with Erik for an entire year. It was a slog, and we worked long, hard, sometimes hair-pulling hours together. In the end, I have become as impressed by Erik's intellectual capacities, his vision and his philosophies about life, as I have been by his athletic accomplishments. He is a transformative person, and it's been an honor to be involved at such an intimate level with his story, his family, and his team. So thanks to Erik for entrusting me to help tell this remarkable story and for taking me along on this incredible journey.

Thanks especially to the Weihenmayer family for always making me feel at home on my visits, and making me feel like a part of the family.

My dear friend John Larkin has been a first reader on all of my books and he gave his honest, attentive, and sage wisdom on every page of the No Barriers book. Muchas gracias, Juan!

Also, cheers to my dear Free Range Writers, who are always with me.

Finally, to my wife, Camie, and my children, Logan and Hunter—your ceaseless support buoys me when I'm flailing in rough waters. You allow me to do what I most love: write stories.